SILANUS THE CHRISTIAN

SILANUS

THE CHRISTIAN

BY

EDWIN A. ABBOTT

AUTHOR OF "PHILOCHRISTUS" AND "ONESIMUS"

"The love of Christ constraineth us."
2 COR. v. 14.

WIPF & STOCK · Eugene, Oregon

Wipf and Stock Publishers
199 W 8th Ave, Suite 3
Eugene, OR 97401

Silanus the Christian
By Abbott, Edwin A.
ISBN 13: 978-1-60608-261-4
Publication date 3/8/2011
Previously published by Adam and Charles Black, 1906

TO THE MEMORY

OF

EPICTETUS

NOT A CHRISTIAN
BUT AN AWAKENER OF ASPIRATIONS
THAT COULD NOT BE SATISFIED
EXCEPT IN CHRIST

PREFACE

MANY years have elapsed since the author was constrained (not by *a priori* considerations but by historical and critical evidence) to disbelieve in the miraculous element of the Bible. Yet he retained the belief of his childhood and youth—rooted more firmly than before—in the eternal unity of the Father the Son and the Holy Spirit, in the supernatural but non-miraculous incarnation of the Son as Jesus Christ, and in Christ's supernatural but non-miraculous resurrection after He had offered Himself up as a sacrifice for the sins of the world.

The belief is commonly supposed to be rendered impossible by the disbelief. This book is written to shew that there is no such impossibility.

The vast majority of the worshippers of Christ base their worship to a very large extent—as the author did in his early youth under the cloud of Paley's *Evidences*—on their acceptance of His miracles as historical facts. In the author's opinion this basis is already demonstrably unsafe, and may be at any moment, by some new demonstration, absolutely destroyed.

Nevertheless such worshippers, if their worship is really genuine—that is to say, if it includes love, trust, and awe, carried to their highest limits, and not merely that kind of awe which is inspired by "mighty works"—will do well to avoid this book. If doubt has not attacked them, why should they go to meet it? In pulling up falsehood by the roots there is always a danger of uprooting or loosening a truth that grows beside it. Historical error, if honest, is better (and less misleading) than spiritual darkness. For example, it is much better (and less misleading) to remain in the old-fashioned belief that a good and wise God created the world in six days than to adopt a new belief that a bad or unwise or careless God—or a chance, or a force, or a power—evolved it in sixty times six sextillions of centuries.

To such genuine worshippers of Christ, then, as long as they feel safe and sincere in their convictions, this book is not addressed. They are (in the author's view) substantially right, and had better remain as they are.

But there may be some, calling themselves worshippers of Christ, who cannot honestly say that they love Him. They trust His power, they bow before Him as divine; but they have no affection at all for Him, as man, or as God. What St Paul described as the "constraining" love of Christ has never touched them. And yet they fancy they worship! To them this book may be of use in suggesting the divinity and loveableness of Christ's human nature; and any harm the book might do them can hardly be conceived as equal to the harm of remaining in their present position. One may learn Christ by rote, as one may learn Euclid by rote, so as to be almost ruined for really knowing either. For such learners the best course may be to go back and begin again.

It is, however, to a third class of readers that the author mainly addresses himself. Having in view the experiences of his own early manhood, he regards with a strong fellow feeling those who desire to worship Christ and to be loyal and faithful to Him, if only they can at the same time be loyal and faithful to truth, and who doubt the compatibility of the double allegiance.

These, many of them, cannot even conceive how they can worship Christ at the right hand of God, or the Son in the bosom of the Father in heaven, unless they first believe in

Him as miraculously manifested on earth. Not being able to accept Him as miraculous, they reject Him as a Saviour. To them this book specially appeals, endeavouring to shew, in a general and popular way—on psychological, historical, and critical grounds—how the rejection of the claim made by most Christians that their Lord is miraculous, may be compatible with a frank and full acceptance of the conclusion that He is, in the highest sense, divine.

Detailed proofs this volume does not offer. These will be given in a separate volume of "Notes," shortly to be published. This will be of a technical nature, forming Part VII of the series called Diatessarica. The present work merely aims at suggesting such conceptions of history, literature, worship, human nature, and divine Being, as point to a foreordained conformation of man to God, to be fulfilled in the Lord Jesus Christ, of which the fulfilment may be traced in the Christian writings and the Christian churches of the first and second centuries.

It also attempts, in a manner not perhaps very usual, to meet many objections brought against Christianity by those who assert that its records are inadequate, inaccurate, and contradictory. Instead of denying these defects, the author admits and emphasizes them as being inseparable from earthen vessels containing a spiritual treasure, and as (in some cases) indirectly testifying to the divinity of the Person whom the best efforts of the best and most inspired of the evangelists inadequately, though honestly, portray. Specimens of these defects are freely given, shewing the modifications, amplifications, and (in some case) misinterpretations or corruptions, to which Christian tradition was inevitably exposed in passing from the east to the west during a period of about one hundred and thirty years, dating from the Crucifixion.

These objects the author has endeavoured to attain by sketching an autobiography of an imaginary character, by name Quintus Junius Silanus, who in the second year of Hadrian

(A.D. 118) becomes a hearer of Epictetus and a Christian convert, and commits his experiences to paper forty-five years afterwards in the second year of Marcus Aurelius Antoninus and Lucius Verus (A.D. 163).

EDWIN A. ABBOTT.

Wellside, Well Walk,
Hampstead.
28 *Aug.* 1906.

SUMMARY

Quintus Junius Silanus, born 90 A.D., goes from Rome at the suggestion of his old friend *Marcus Æmilius Scaurus*, to attend the lectures of Epictetus in Nicopolis about 118 A.D.

Scaurus (like Silanus, an imaginary character) born about 50 A.D., is a disabled soldier, and has been for many years a student of miscellaneous Greek literature, including Christian writings. In reply to a letter from Silanus, extolling his new teacher, Scaurus expresses his belief that Epictetus has passed through a stage of infection with "the Christian superstition," from which he has borrowed some parts of the superstructure while rejecting its foundation.

Silanus, in order to defend his teacher Epictetus from what he considers an unjust imputation, procures the epistles of Paul. His interest in these leads him to the "scriptures" from which Paul quotes. Thence he is led on to speculate about the nature of the "gospel" preached by Paul, and about the character and utterances of the "Christ" from whom that "gospel" originated. The epistles convey to him a sense of spiritual strength and "constraining love." He determines to procure the Christian gospels.

During all this time he is occasionally corresponding with Scaurus and attending the lectures of Epictetus, which satisfy him less and less. Contrasted with the spiritual strength in the epistles of Paul the lectures seem to contain only spiritual effervescence. And there is an utter absence of "constraining love."

When the three Synoptic gospels reach Silanus from Rome, he receives at the same time a destructive criticism on them from Scaurus. Much of this criticism he is enabled to meet with the aid of the Pauline epistles. But enough remains to shake his faith in their historical accuracy. Nor does he find in them the same presence that he found in the epistles, of "constraining love." The result is, that he is thrown back from Christ.

At this crisis he meets Clemens, an Athenian, who lends him a gospel that has recently appeared, the gospel of John. Clemens frankly admits his doubts about its authorship, and about its complete accuracy, but commends it as conveying the infinite spiritual revelation inherent in Christ less inadequately than it is conveyed by the Synoptists.

12 SUMMARY

A somewhat similar view is expressed by Scaurus, though with a large admixture of hostile criticism. He has recently received the fourth gospel, and it forms the subject of his last letter. While rejecting much of it as unhistorical, he expresses great admiration for it, and for what he deems its fundamental principle, namely, that Jesus cannot be understood save through a "disciple whom Jesus loved."

While speculating on what might have happened if he himself had come under the influence of a "disciple whom Jesus loved," Scaurus is struck down by paralysis. Silanus sets sail for Italy in the hope of finding his friend still living. At the moment when he is losing sight of the hills above Nicopolis where Clemens is praying for him, Silanus receives an apprehension of Christ's "constraining love" and becomes a Christian.

No attempt has been made to give the impression of an archaic or Latin style. Hence "Christus" and "Paulus" are mostly avoided except in a few instances where they are mentioned for the first time by persons speaking from a non-Christian point of view. Similar apparent inconsistencies will be found in the use of "He" and "he," denoting Christ. The use varies, partly according to the speaker, partly according to the speaker's mood. It varies also in quotations from scripture according to the extent to which the Revised Version is followed.

The utterances assigned to Epictetus are taken from the records of his sayings by Arrian or others. Some of these have been freely translated, paraphrased, and transposed; but none of them are imaginary. When Silanus says that his friend Arrian "never heard Epictetus say" this or that, the meaning is that the expression does not occur in Epictetus's extant works, so far as can be judged from Schenkl's admirable Index.

The words assigned to Arrian, Silanus's friend, when speaking in his own person, are entirely imaginary; but the statements made about Arrian's birth-place and official career are based on history.

Any words assigned by Scaurus to his "friend" Pliny, Plutarch, or Josephus, or by Silanus to "the young Irenæus," or Justin, may be taken to be historical. The references will be given in the volume of Notes.

Scaurus and Silanus occasionally describe themselves as "finding marginal notes" indicating variations in their MSS. of the gospels. In all such cases the imaginary "marginal notes" are based on actual various readings or interpolations which will be given in the volume of Notes. Most of these are of an early date, and may be based on much earlier originals; and care has been taken to exclude any that are of late origin. But the reader must bear in mind that we have no MSS. of the gospels, and therefore no "marginal notes," of so early a date as 118 A.D.

CONTENTS

CHAPTER		PAGE
I	The first lecture	15
II	Epictetus on the Gods	25
III	Arrian on the oath of the Christians	33
IV	Scaurus on Epictetus and Paul	41
V	Epictetus alludes to Jews	54
VI	Paul on the Love of Christ	65
VII	David and Moses	77
VIII	Epictetus on Sin	85
IX	Arrian's departure	91
X	Epictetus on Death	97
XI	Isaiah on Death	102
XII	Isaiah on Providence	109
XIII	Epictetus on Providence	117
XIV	Paul's conversion	125
XV	Epictetus's gospel	136
XVI	Paul's gospel	143
XVII	Epictetus confesses failure	151
XVIII	Paul's only record of words of Christ	160
XIX	How Scaurus studied the three gospels	172
XX	Scaurus on Forgiveness	183
XXI	Scaurus on the Cross	193
XXII	Scaurus on Mark	201
XXIII	Scaurus on some of the miracles	211
XXIV	Scaurus on Christ's Birth	220
XXV	Scaurus on Christ's Discourses	234

CHAPTER		PAGE
XXVI	Scaurus on Christ's Resurrection (I)	248
XXVII	Scaurus on Christ's Resurrection (II)	257
XXVIII	The last lecture	267
XXIX	Silanus meets Clemens	280
XXX	Silanus converses with Clemens	291
XXXI	Clemens on the fourth gospel	302
XXXII	Clemens lends Silanus the fourth gospel	312
XXXIII	Scaurus on the fourth gospel	322
XXXIV	The last words of Scaurus	333
XXXV	Clemens on the Sacrifice of Christ	347
XXXVI	Silanus becomes a Christian	360

CHAPTER I

THE FIRST LECTURE

"*I forbid you to go into the senate-house.*" "*As long as I am a senator, go I must.*" Two voices were speaking from one person—the first, pompous, coarse, despotic; the second, refined, dry, austere. There was nothing that approached stage-acting—only a suggestion of one man swelling out with authority, and of another straightening up his back in resistance. These were the first words that I heard from Epictetus, as I crept late into the lecture-room, tired with a long journey over-night into Nicopolis.

I need not have feared to attract attention. All eyes were fixed on the lecturer as I stole into a place near the door, next my friend Arrian, who was absorbed in his notes. What was it all about? In answer to my look of inquiry Arrian pushed me his last sheet with the names "Vespasian" and "Helvidius Priscus" scrawled large upon it. Then I knew what it meant. It was a story now nearly forty years old—which I had often heard from my father's old friend, Æmilius Scaurus—illustrating the duty of obeying the voice of the conscience rather than the voice of a king. Epictetus, after his manner, was throwing it into the form of a dialogue:—

"*Vespasian.* I forbid you to go into the senate-house.

"*Priscus.* As long as I am a senator, go I must.

"*Vespasian.* Go, then, but be silent.

"*Priscus.* Do not ask my opinion, and I will be silent.

"*Vespasian.* But I am bound to ask it.

"*Priscus.* And I am bound to answer, and to answer what I think right.

"*Vespasian.* Then I shall kill you.

"*Priscus.* Did I ever say that I could not be killed? It is yours to kill; mine, to die fearless."

I give his words almost as fully as Arrian took them down. But his tone and spirit are past man's power to put on paper. He flashed from Emperor to Senator like the zig-zag of lightning with a straight down flash at the end. This was always his way. He would play a thousand parts, seeming, superficially, a very Proteus; but they were all types of two characters, the philosopher and the worldling, the follower of the Logos and the follower of the flesh. Moreover, he was always in earnest, in hot earnest. On the surface he would jest like Menander or jibe like Aristophanes; but at bottom he was a tragedian. At one moment he would point to his halting leg and flout himself as a lame old grey-beard with a body of clay. In the next, he was "a son of Zeus," or "God's own son," or "carrying about God." Never at rest, he might deceive a stranger into supposing that he was occasionally rippling and sparkling with real mirth like a sea in sunlight. But it was never so. It was a sea of molten metal and there was always a Vesuvius down below.

I suspect that he never knew mirth or genial laughter even as a child. He was born a slave, his master being Epaphroditus, a freedman of Nero's and his favourite, afterwards killed by Domitian. I have heard—but not from Arrian—that this master caused his lameness. He was twisting his leg one day to see how much he could bear. The boy—for he was no more—said with a smile, "If you go on, you will break it," and then, "Did not I tell you, you would break it?" True or false, this story gives the boy as I knew the man. You might break his leg but never his will. I do not know whether Epaphroditus, out of remorse, had him taught philosophy; but taught he was, under one of the best men of the day, and he acquired such fame that he was banished from Rome under Domitian, with other philosophers of note—whether at or before the time when Domitian put Epaphroditus to death I cannot say. In one of his lectures he described how he was summoned before the Prefect of the City with the other philosophers: "Come," said the Prefect, "come, Epictetus, shave off your beard." "If I am a philosopher," he replied, "I am not going to shave it off." "Then I shall take your head off." "If it is for your advantage, take it off."

But now to return to my first lecture. Among our audience were several men of position and one at least of senatorial rank. Some of them seemed a little scandalized at the Teacher's dialogue. It was not likely that the Emperor would take offence, for in the second year of Hadrian we were not in a Neronian or Domitian atmosphere; moreover, our Teacher was known to be on good terms with the new Emperor. But perhaps their official sense of propriety was shocked; and, in the first sentence of what follows, Epictetus may have been expressing their thoughts: "'*So you, philosophers, teach people to despise the throne!*' Heaven forbid! Which of us teaches anyone to lay claim to anything over which kings have authority? Take my body, take my goods, take my reputation! Take my friends and relations! 'Yes,' says the ruler, 'but I must also be ruler over your convictions.' Indeed, and who gave you this authority?"

Epictetus went on to say that if indeed his pupils were of the true philosophic stamp, holding themselves detached from the things of the body and with their minds fixed on the freedom of the soul, he would have no need to spur them to boldness, but rather to draw them back from over-hasty rushing to the grave; for, said he, they would come flocking about him, begging and praying to be allowed to teach the tyrant that they were free, by finding freedom at once in self-inflicted death: "Here on earth, Master, these robbers and thieves, these courts of justice and kings, have the upper hand. These creatures fancy that they have some sort of authority over us, simply because they have a hold on our paltry flesh and its possessions! Suffer us, Master, to shew them that they have authority over nothing!" If, said he, a pupil of this high spirit were brought before the tribunal of one of the rulers of the earth, he would come back scoffing at such "authority" as a mere scarecrow: "Why all these preparations, to meet no enemy at all? The pomp of his authority, his solemn anteroom, his gentlemen of the chamber, his yeomen of the guard—did they all come to no more than this! These things were nothing, and I was preparing to meet something great!"

On the scholar of the unpractical and cowardly type, anxiously preparing "what to say" in his defence before the magistrate's tribunal, he poured hot scorn. Had not the fellow, he asked, been practising "what to say"—all his life through? "What else," said he, "have you been practising? Syllogisms and convertible propositions!" Then came the reply, in a whine, "Yes, but he has authority to kill me!" To which the Teacher answered, "Then speak the truth, you pitiful creature. Cease your imposture and give up all claim to be a philosopher. In the lords of the earth recognise your own lords and masters. As long as you give them this grip on you, through your flesh, so long must you be at the beck and call of every one that is stronger than you are. Socrates and Diogenes had practised 'what to say' by the practice of their lives. But as for you—get you back to your own proper business, and never again budge from it! Back to your own snug corner, and sit there at your leisure, spinning your syllogisms:

'In thee is not the stuff that makes a man
A people's leader.'"

Thence he passed to the objection that a judicial condemnation might bring disgrace on a man's good name. "The authorities, you say, have condemned you as guilty of impiety and profanity. What harm is there in that for you? This creature, with authority to condemn you—does he himself know even the meaning of piety or impiety? If a man in authority calls day night or bass treble, do men that know take notice of him? Unless the judge knows what the truth is, his 'authority to judge' is no authority. No man has authority over our convictions, our inmost thoughts, our will. Hence when Zeno the philosopher went into the presence of Antigonus the king, it was the king that was anxious, not the philosopher. The king wished to gain the philosopher's good opinion, but the philosopher cared for nothing that the king could give. When,

therefore, you go to the palace of a great ruler, remember that
you are in effect going to the shop of a shoemaker or a grocer
—on a great scale of course, but still a grocer. He cannot sell
you anything real or lasting, though he may sell his groceries
at a great price."

At the bottom of all this doctrine about true and false
authority, there was, as I afterwards understood, a belief that
God had bestowed on all men, if they would but accept and
use it, authority over their own wills, so that we might conform
our wills to His, as children do with a Father, and might find
pleasure, and indeed our only pleasure, in doing this—accepting
all bodily pain and evil as not evil but good because it comes
from His will, which must be also our will and must be honoured
and obeyed. "When," said he, "the ruler says to anyone, 'I
will fetter your leg,' the man that is in the habit of honouring
his leg cries, 'Don't, for pity's sake!' But the man that
honours his will says, ' If it appears advisable to you, fetter it '."

"*Tyrant.* Won't you bend?
"*Cynic.* I will not bend.
"*Tyrant.* I will show you that I am lord.
"*Cynic.* You! impossible! I have been freed by Zeus.
Do you really imagine that He would allow His own son
to be made a slave? But of my corpse you *are* lord. Take
it."

In this particular lecture Epictetus also gave us a glimpse
of a wider and more divine authority imparted by God to a
few special natures, akin to Himself, whereby, as God is supreme
King over men His children, so a chosen few may become sub-
ordinate kings over men their brethren. Like Plato, he seemed
to look forward to a time when rulers would become philosophers,
or else philosophers kings. Nero and Sardanapalus, Agamemnon and Alexander, all came under his lash—all kings and rulers
of the old *régime*. Not that he denied Agamemnon a superiority
to Nero, or the right to call himself "shepherd of the people" if
he pleased. "Sheep, indeed," he exclaimed, "to submit to be
ruled over by you!" and "Shepherd, indeed, for you weep like
the shepherds, when a wolf has snatched away a sheep!"

From these old-fashioned rulers he passed to a new and

nobler ideal of kingship: "Those kings and tyrants received from their armed guards the power of rebuking and punishing wrongdoing, though they might be rascals themselves. But on the Cynic"—that was the term he used—"this power is bestowed by the conscience." Then he explained to us what he meant by "conscience"—the consciousness of a life of wise, watchful, and unwearied toil for man, with the co-operation of God. "And how," he asked, "could such a man fail to be bold and speak the truth with boldness, speaking, as he does, to his own brethren, to his own children and kinsfolk? So inspired, he is no meddler or busybody. Supervising and inspecting the affairs of mankind, he is not busying himself with other men's matters, but with his own. Else, call a general, too, a busybody, when he is busy inspecting his own soldiers!"

This was, to me, quite a new view of the character of a Cynic. But Epictetus insisted on it with reiteration. The Cynic, he said, was Warrior and Physician in one. As a warrior, he was like Hercules, wandering over the world with his club and destroying noxious beasts and monsters. As a physician, he was like Socrates or Diogenes, going about and doing good to those afflicted with sickness of mind, diagnosing each disease, prescribing diet, cautery, or other remedy. In both these capacities the Cynic received from God authority over men, and men recognised it in him, because they perceived him to be their benefactor and deliverer.

There are, said Epictetus, in each man two characters—the character of the Beast and the character of the Man. By Beast he meant wild or savage beast, as distinct from tame beast, which he preferred to call "sheep." "Sheep" meant the cowardly, passive-greedy passions within us. "The Beast" meant the savage, aggressive-greedy nature, not only stirring us up to external war against our neighbours, but also waging war to the death against our inward better nature, against the "Man." The mark or stamp of the Beast he connected with Nero. "Cast it away," he said. The opposite mark or stamp he connected with the recently deceased Emperor, Trajan. If we acted like a beast, he warned us that we should become like a beast, and then, according to his customary phrase, "*You will have*

lost the Man." And was this, asked he, nothing to lose? Over and over again he repeated it: *"You have thrown away the Man."* It was in this light—as a type of the Man—that he regarded Hercules, the first of the Cynics, the Son of God, going on the errands of the Father to destroy the Beast in its various shapes, typifying an armed Missionary, but armed for spiritual not for fleshly warfare, destroying the Beast that would fain dominate the world. But it was for Diogenes that he reserved his chief admiration, placing him (I think) even above Socrates, or at all events praising him more warmly—partly, perhaps, out of fellow-feeling, because Diogenes, too, like himself, had known what it was to be a slave. Never shall I forget the passage in this lecture in which he described Alexander surprising the great Cynic asleep, and waking him up with a line of Homer:—
"To sleep all night suits not a Councillor,"
—to which Diogenes replied at once in the following line, claiming for himself the heavy burden (entrusted to him by Zeus) of caring like a king for all the nations of the earth:—
" Who holds, in trust, the world's vast orb of cares."
Diogenes, according to our Teacher, was much more than an Æsculapius of souls; he was a sovereign with "the sceptre and the kingdom of the Cynic." Some have represented Epictetus as claiming this authority for himself. But in the lecture that I heard, it was not so. Though what he said might have been mistaken as a claim for himself, it was really a claim for "the Cynic," as follows. First he put the question, "How is it possible for one destitute, naked, homeless, hearthless, squalid, with not one slave to attend him, or a country to call his own, to lead a life of equable happiness?" To which he replied, "Behold, God hath sent unto you the man to demonstrate in act this possibility. *'Look on me, and see that I am without country, home, possessions, slaves; no bed but the ground, no wife, no children—no palace to make a king or governor out of me— only the earth, and the sky, and one threadbare cloak! And yet what do I want? Am I not fearless? Am I not free? When saw ye me failing to find any good thing that I desired, or falling into any evil that I would fain have avoided? What fault found I ever with God or man? When did I ever accuse*

anyone? Did anyone ever see me with a gloomy face? How do I confront the great persons before whom you, worldlings, bow abashed and dismayed? Do not I treat them as cringing slaves? Who, that sees me, does not feel that he sees in me his natural Lord and Master?'"

I confess that up to this point I had myself supposed that he was speaking of himself, standing erect as ruler of the world. But in the next instant he had dropped, as it were, from the pillar upon which he had been setting up the King, and now, like a man at the pedestal pointing up to the statue on the top, he exclaimed, "Behold, these are the genuine Cynic's utterances: this is his stamp and image: this is his aim!"

He passed on to answer the question, What if the Cynic missed his aim, or, at least, missed it so far as exerting the royal authority over others? What if death cut his purpose short? In that case, he said, the will, the purpose, the one essential good, had at all events remained in its purity; and how could man die better than in such actions? "If, while I am thus employed, death should overtake me, it will suffice me if I can lift up my hands to God and say, 'The helps that I received from thee, to the intent that I might understand and follow thy ordering of the universe, these I have not neglected. I have not disgraced thee, so far as in me lay. See how I have used these faculties which thou hast given me! Have I ever found fault with thee? ever been ill-pleased with anything that has happened or ever wished it to happen otherwise? Thou didst beget me, and I thank thee for all thou gavest me. I have used to the full the gifts that were of thy giving and I am satisfied. Receive them back again and dispose them in such region as may please thee. Thine were they all, and thou hast given them unto me.'" Then, turning to us, he said, "Are you not content to take your exit after this fashion? Than such a life, what can be better, or more full of grace and beauty? Than such an end, what can be more full of blessing?"

There was much more, which I cannot recall. I was no longer in a mood to note and remember exact words and phrases, and I despair of making my readers understand why. Able philosophers and lecturers I had heard before, but none like this man. Some of those had moved me to esteem and gained my favourable judgement. But this man did more than "move" me. He whirled me away into an upper region of spiritual possibility, at once glad and sad—sad at what I was, glad at what I might be. Alcibiades says in the Symposium of Plato that whereas the orator Pericles had only moved his outer self to admiration, the teaching of Socrates caught hold of his very soul, "whirling it away into a Corybantic dance." I quoted these words to Arrian as we left the lecture-room together, and he replied that they were just to the point. "Epictetus," he said, "is by birth a Phrygian. And, like the Phrygian priests of Cybele, with their cymbals and their dances, he has just this power of whirling away his hearers into any region he pleases and making them feel at any moment what he wishes them to feel. But," added he thoughtfully, "it did not last with Alcibiades. Will it last with us?"

I argued—or perhaps I should say protested—at considerable length, that it would last. Arrian walked on for a while without answering. Presently he said, "This is your first lecture. It is not so with me. I, as you know, have heard Epictetus for several months, and I admire him as much as you do, perhaps more. I am sure he is doing me good. But I do not aim at being his ideal Cynic. '*In me is not the stuff*'—I admit his censure—that makes a man into a King, bearing all the cares of all mankind upon his shoulders. My ambition is, some day, to become (as you are by birth) a Roman citizen"—he was not one then, nor was he Flavius Arrianus, but I have called him by the name by which he became known in the world—"and to do good work in the service of the Empire, as an officer of the State and yet an honest man. For that purpose I want to keep myself in order—at all events to some reasonable extent. Epictetus is helping me to do this, by making me ashamed of the foul life of the Beast, and by making me aspire to what he calls 'the Man.' That I feel day by day, and for that I am thankful.

"But if you ask me about the reality of this 'authority,' which our Teacher claims for his Cynic, then, in all honesty, I must confess to doubts. Socrates, certainly, has moved the minds of civilised mankind. But then he had, as you know, a 'daemonic something' in him, a divine voice of some kind. And he believed in the immortality of the soul—a point on which you have not yet heard what Epictetus has to say. As to Diogenes, though I have always faithfully recorded in my notes what our Teacher says about him, yet I do not feel that the philosopher of the tub had the same heaven-sent authority as Socrates, or as Epictetus himself. And, indeed, did you not yourself hear to-day that God gives us authority over nothing but our own hearts and wills? How, then, can the Cynic claim this authority over others, except as an accident? But I forget. Perhaps Epictetus did not mention to-day his usual doctrine about 'good' and 'evil,' about 'peace of mind' and about the 'rule' of our neighbours as being 'no evil' to us. It reappears in almost every lecture. Wait till you have heard this.

"Again, as to the origin of this authority, the Teacher tells us that it is given by God—or by Gods, for he uses both expressions. But by what God or Gods? Is not this a matter of great importance? Wait till you have heard him on this point. Now I must hasten back to my rooms to commit my notes to writing while fresh in my memory. We meet in the lecture-room to-morrow. Meantime, believe me, I most heartily sympathize with you in your admiration of one whom I account the best of all living philosophers. I have all your conviction of his sincerity. Assuredly, whencesoever he derives it, he has in him a marvellous power for good. The Gods grant that it may last!"

CHAPTER II

EPICTETUS ON THE GODS

ARRIAN was right in thinking that the next lecture would be on the Gods. I had come to Nicopolis at the end of one of the lecture-courses, and had heard its conclusion—the perfecting of the Cynic. The new course began by describing the purpose of God in making man.

But at the outset the subject was, not God, but the Logos—that word so untranslateable into our Latin, including as it does suggestions of our Word, Discourse, Reason, Logic, Understanding, Purpose, Proportion, and Harmony. Starting from this, Epictetus first said that the only faculty that could, as it were, behold itself, and theorize about itself, was the faculty of the Logos, which is also the faculty with which we regard, and, so to speak, mentally handle, all phenomena. From the Logos, or Word, he passed to God, as the Giver of this faculty: "It was therefore right and meet that this highest and best of all gifts should be the only one that the Gods have placed at our disposal. All the rest they have not placed at our disposal. Can it be that the Gods did not wish to place them in our power? For my part, I think that, if they had been able, they would have entrusted us also with the rest. But they were absolutely unable. For, being on earth, and bound up with such a body as this"—and here he made his usual gesture of self-contempt, mocking at his own lame figure—" how was it possible that we should not be prevented by these external fetters from receiving those other gifts? But what says Zeus?" —with that, the halting mortal, turning suddenly round, had

become the Olympian Father addressing a child six years old:
"*Epictetus, if it had been practicable, I would have made your dear little body quite free, and your pretty little possessions quite free too, and quite at your disposal. But as it is, don't shut your eyes to the truth. This little body is not your very own. It is only a neat arrangement in clay.*"

After a pause, the Epictetian Zeus continued as follows, falling from "I" to "we." Some of our fellow-scholars declared to Arrian after lecture that Epictetus could not have meant this change, and they slightly altered the words in their notes. I prefer to give the difficult words of Zeus as Arrian took them down and as I heard them : "*But, since I was not able to do this,* WE *gave you a portion of* OURSELVES, *this power*"—and here Epictetus made believe to put a little box into the child's hand, adding that it contained a power of pursuing or avoiding, of liking or disliking—"*Take care of this, and put in it all that belongs to you. As long as you do this, you will never be hindered or hampered, never cry, never scold, and never flatter.*"

The change from I to WE was certainly curious; and some said that "we gave," *edōkamen*, ought to be regarded as two words, *edōka men*, "I gave on the one hand." But "on the one hand" made no sense. Nor could they themselves deny that Epictetus made Zeus say, first, "*I* was not able," and then, "a part of *ourselves*." I think the explanation may be this. Epictetus had many ways of looking at the Divine Nature. Sometimes he regarded it as One, sometimes as Many. When he thought of God as supporting and controlling the harmonious Cosmos, or Universe, then God was One—the Monarch or General to whom we all owed loyal obedience. Often, however, "Gods" were spoken of, as in the expression "Father of Gods and men," and elsewhere. Once he reproached himself (a lower or imaginary self) for repining against the Cosmos because he was lame, almost as if the Cosmos itself were Providence or God: "Wretched creature ! For the sake of one paltry leg, to impeach the Cosmos!" But he went on to call the Cosmos "the Whole of Things." And then he called on each man to sacrifice some part of himself (a lame man, for example, sacrificing his lame leg) to the Universe: " What ! Will you not make a present of it (*i.e.* the leg) to the Whole of Things? Let go this leg of yours! Yield it up gladly to Him that gave it! What! Will you sulk and fret against the ordinances of Zeus, which He—in concert with the Fates present at your birth and spinning the thread for you—decreed and ordained ? "

I remember, too, how once, while professing to represent the doctrines of the philosophers in two sections, he spoke, in the first section, of "Him," but in the second, of "Them," thus: " The philosophers say that we must in the first place learn this, the existence of *God*, and that *He* provides for the Universe, and that nothing—whether deed or purpose or thought—can lie hidden from *Him*. In the next place [we must learn] of what nature *They* (*i.e.* the Gods) are. For, of whatever nature *They* may be found to be, he that would fain please *Them* and obey [Them] must needs endeavour (to the best of his ability) to be made like unto *Them*."

What did he mean by "THEM"? And why did he use THEM directly after HIM? I believe he did it deliberately. For in the very next sentence he expressed God in a neuter adjective, "If THE DIVINE [BEING] is trustworthy, man also must needs be trustworthy." He seemed to me to pass from masculine singular to masculine plural and from that to neuter singular, as much as to say, "Take notice. I use HIM, THEM, and IT in three consecutive sentences, and all about God, to shew you that God is not any one of these, but all."

Similarly, after condemning the attempt of philosophers to please the rulers of the earth, he said, " I know whom I must needs please, and submit to, and obey—God and *those next to Him*." But then he continued in the singular (" *He* made me at one with myself" and so on). And I think I may safely say that I never heard him allow his ideal philosopher or Cynic to address God in the plural with " ye " or " you." It was always " thou," as in the utterance I quoted above—" Thine were they all and thou gavest them to me."

Well, then, whom did he mean by "those next to" God? I think he referred to certain guardian angels—" daemons " he called them, and so will I, spelling it thus, so as to distinguish it from "demon" meaning "devil"—one of whom (he said) was allotted by God to each human being. This, according to Epictetus, did not exclude the general inspection of mankind by God Himself: "To each He has assigned a Guardian, the Daemon of each mortal, to be his guard and keeper, sleepless and undeceivable. Therefore, whenever you shut your doors and make darkness in the house, remember never to say that you are alone. For you are not alone. God is in the house, and your Daemon is in the house. And what need have these of light to see what you are doing?"

This guardian Daemon, or daemonic Guardian, was said by some of our fellow-scholars to be the portion of the divine Logos within us, in virtue of which our Teacher distinguished men from beasts. Notably did he once make this distinction—in answer to some imaginary questioner, who was supposed to class man with irrational animals because he is subject to animal necessities. "Cattle," replied Epictetus, "are works of God, but not preeminent, and certainly not parts of God; but thou"—turning to the supposed opponent—"art a fragment broken off from God; thou hast in thyself a part of Him. Why then ignore thy noble birth? Why dost thou not recognise whence thou hast come? Wilt thou not remember, in the moment of eating, what a Being thou art—thou that eatest—what a Being it is that thou feedest? Wilt thou not recognise what it is that employs thy senses and thy faculties? Knowest thou not that thou art feeding God, yea, taking God with thee to the gymnasium? God, God dost thou carry about, thou miserable creature, and thou knowest it not!"

We were rather startled at this. In what sense could a miserable creature "carry about God"? Epictetus proceeded, "Dost thou fancy that I am speaking of a god of gold or silver, an outside thing? It is within thyself that thou carriest Him. And thou perceivest not that thou art defiling Him with impure purposes and filthy actions! Before the face of a mere statue of the God thou wouldst not dare to do any of the deeds thou art daily doing. Yet in the presence of the God Himself, within thee, looking at all thy acts, listening to all thy words and thoughts, thou art not ashamed to continue thinking the same bad thoughts and doing the same bad deeds—blind to thine own nature and banned by God's wrath!"

From this it appeared that the Daemon in each man was good and veritably God, and turned men towards God and goodness; but that some did not perceive the presence and were deaf to the voice. These were "miserable wretches" and "banned by God's wrath." Thus in some sense, the same God seemed to be the cause of virtue in some but of vice in others. This accorded with a saying of Epictetus on another occasion that God "ordained that there should be summer and winter, fruitfulness and fruitlessness, *virtue and vice.*" Then the question arose, To how many did the Logos of God bring virtue and to how many did it result in vice? And again, Did it bring virtue to as many as the Logos of God, or God, desired? Or was He unable to fulfil His desire, as in the case of that imaginary opponent, for example, so that the Supreme would have to say to him, as to Epictetus, "If I could have, I would have. But now, make no mistake. I could not bring virtue unto thee." I was disposed to think that Epictetus would have laid the blame on the opponent, who, he would have said, might have obeyed the Logos in himself, if he had chosen to do so. According to our Teacher's doctrine, God would say to this man nothing more cruel, or less just, than He says to all, "I could not force virtue on thee, nor on any man. If I forced virtue on thee, virtue would cease to be virtue and God would cease to be God." But still the uneasy feeling came to me—not indeed at the time of this lecture (or at least not to any great extent) but afterwards—that the God of Epictetus was hampered by what Epictetus called "the clay," which He "would have liked" to make immortal, if He "had been able." What if each man's "clay" was different? Who made the clay? What if God controlled nothing more than the shaping of the clay, and this, too, only in conjunction with the Fates? What if the Fates alone were responsible for the making of the clay? In that case, must not the Fates be regarded as higher Beings, even above the Maker of the Cosmos—higher in some sense, but bad Beings or weak Beings, spoiling the Maker's work by supplying Him with bad material so that He could not do what He would have liked to have done?

Epictetus, I subsequently found, would never see difficulties of this kind. He represented the Supreme as a great stage manager, allotting to all their appropriate parts: "Thou art the sun; go on thy rounds, minister to all things. Thou art a heifer; when the lion appears, play thy part, or suffer for it. Thou art a bull; fight as champion of the herd. Thou canst lead the host against Ilium; be thou Agamemnon. Thou canst cope with Hector; be thou Achilles." He did not add, "Thou canst spit venom and slander against the good and great; be thou Thersites." But I did not think of that at the time.

For the moment, I was carried away by the fervour of the speaker. "He," I said, "has been a slave, the slave of Nero's freedman; he has seen things at their worst; and yet he believes that virtue, freedom, and peace, are placed by God in the power of all that will obey the Logos, His gift, within their hearts!" So I believed it, or persuaded myself that I believed it. Epictetus insisted, in the strongest terms, that the divine Providence extends to all. "God," he said, "does not neglect a single one, even of the least of His creatures." Stimulating us to *be* good instead of *talking* about being good, he exclaimed, " How grand it is for each of you to be able to say, *The very thing that people are solemnly arguing about in the schools as an impossible ideal, that very thing I am accomplishing. They are, in effect, expatiating on my virtues, investigating me, and singing my praises. Zeus has been pleased that I should receive from my own self a demonstration of the truth of this ideal, while He Himself tests and tries me to see whether I am a worthy soldier of His army, and a worthy citizen of His city. At the same time it has been His pleasure to bring me forward that I may testify concerning the things that lie outside the will, and that I may cry aloud to the world, 'Behold, O men, that your fears are idle! Vain, all vain, are your greedy and covetous desires. Seek not the Good in the outside world! Seek it in yourselves! Else, ye will not find it.' Engaging me for such a mission, and for such a testimony as this, God now leads me hither, now sends me thither; exhibits me to mankind in poverty, in disease—ruler in* fact but no ruler in the eyes of men—banishes me to the rocks of Gyara, or drags me into prison or into bonds! And all this, not hating me. No, God forbid! Who can hate his own best and most faithful servant? No, nor neglecting me. How could He? For He does not neglect the meanest of His creatures. No, He is training and practising me, He is employing me as His witness to the rest of mankind. And I, being set down by Him for such high service as this—can I possibly find time to entertain anxieties about where I am, or with whom I am living, or what men say about me? How can I fail to be, with my whole might and my whole being, intent on God, and on His commandments and ordinances?"

I noted with pleasure here the words, "He does not neglect the meanest of His creatures." To the same effect elsewhere, speaking of Zeus, he said, "In very truth, the universal frame of things is badly managed unless Zeus takes care of all His own citizens, in order that they may be blessed like unto Himself." A little before this, he said about Hercules, "He left his children behind him without a groan or regret—not as though he were leaving them orphans, for he knew that no man is an orphan," because Zeus is "Father of men."

In all these passages describing the fatherhood of God and the sonship of man, Epictetus spoke of virtue as being, by itself, a sufficient reward, in respect of the ineffable peace that it brings through the consciousness of being united to God. But how long this union lasted, and whether its durability was proof against death—as Socrates taught—about this he had hitherto said nothing. The Cynic, he again and again insisted, was God's son; but he did not insist that the son was as immortal as the Father. Sometimes indeed he described the man of temperance and self-control as "banqueting at the table of the Gods." Still more, the man that had passed beyond temperance into contempt of earthly things—a rank to which Arrian and I did not aspire—such a Cynic as this he extolled as being not only fellow-guest with the Gods but also fellow-ruler. These expressions reminded me of what we used to learn by heart in Rome concerning the man described by Horace as "just and firm of purpose." The poet likened him to Hercules transported aloft to the fiery citadel of heaven, and to the Emperor Augustus drinking nectar at the table of the Gods. But this was said about Augustus while he was still alive; and the poem did not seem to me to prove that Horace believed in the immortality of the soul. However, what Epictetus said about that will appear hereafter. For the present, I must explain why the teaching of Epictetus concerning the Gods, although it carried me away for a time, caused me bewilderment in the end, and made me feel the need of something beyond.

CHAPTER III

ARRIAN ON THE OATH OF THE CHRISTIANS

UP to the time of my coming to Nicopolis, my faith in the Gods had been like that of most official and educated Romans. First I had a literary belief not only in Zeus but also in Apollo, Athene, Demeter, and the rest of the Gods and Goddesses of Homer, tempered by a philosophic feeling that some of the Homeric and other myths about them, and about the less beautiful divinities, were not true, or were true only as allegories. In the next place I had a Roman or official belief in the destiny of the empire, and a recognition that its unity was best maintained by tolerating the worships of any number of national Gods and Goddesses; provided they did not tend to sedition and conspiracy, nor to such vices as were in contravention of the laws. Lastly, I recognised as the belief of many philosophers —and was myself half inclined to believe—that One God, or Zeus, so controlled the whole of things that it would hardly be atheistic if I sometimes regarded even Apollo, and Athene, and others, as personifying God's attributes rather than as being Gods and Goddesses in themselves—although I myself, without scruple and in all willingness, should have offered them both worship and sacrifice. Personally, apart (I think) from the influences of childhood, I always shrank from definitely believing that the One God ever had been, or ever could be, "alone."

It was with these confused opinions or feelings that I became a pupil of Epictetus. And at first, whatever he asserted about God, or the Gods, he made me believe it—as long as he was speaking. When he said "God," or "Zeus," or "Father," or "HIM," or "THEM," or "Providence," or "The

Divine Being," or "The Nature of All Things," or whatever
else, he dragged me as it were to the new Name, and made me
follow as a captive and do it homage. But afterwards there
came a reaction. The limbs of my mind, so to speak, became
tired of being dragged. I longed for rest and found none. My
homage, too, was dissipated by distraction. When he repeated
as he often did—addressing each one of us individually, and
therefore (I assumed) me among the rest—"Thou carriest about
God," he seemed to say to me, "Look within thyself for Him
whom thou must worship." That was not helpful, it was the
reverse of helpful—at least, to me. I felt vaguely then (and
now as a Christian I know) that men have need not only to
look within, but also (and much more) to look up—up to the
Father in heaven with the aid of His Spirit on earth. It was
due to Epictetus that at this time I—however faintly—began
to feel this need.

Epictetus seemed to have no consistent view either of the
unity of God or of the possibility of plural Gods. In Rome, we
have three altars to the Goddess Febris, or Fever. Epictetus
once referred to Febris in the reply of a philosopher to a tyrant.
The latter says, "I have power to cut off your head"; the former
replies, "You are in the right. I quite forgot that I must pay
you homage as people do to Fever and Cholera, and erect an
altar to you, *as indeed in Rome there is an altar to Fever.*" It
was hardly possible to mistake the Master's mockery of this
worship. On the other hand, he was bitterly sarcastic against
those who denied the existence of Demeter, the Koré her
daughter, and Pluto the husband of the Koré. These deities
our Master regarded as representing bread. "O, the gratitude," he exclaimed, "O, the reverence of these creatures! Day
by day they eat bread; and yet they have the face to say ' We
do not know whether there is any such a being as Demeter, or
the Koré, or Pluto!'" It never seemed to occur to him that
the worshippers of Febris might retort on him, " Day by day
scores of people in Rome have the fever, and yet you have the
face to say to us Romans, 'I do not know whether there is any
such a being as Febris or Cholera!'"

I think he never spoke of Poseidon, Ares, or Aphrodite, and

hardly ever of Apollo. Even Athene he mentioned only thrice in Arrian's hearing (so he told me), twice speaking of her statue by Phidias, and once representing Zeus as bemoaning His solitude (according to some notion, which he ridiculed) after a universal conflagration of gods and men and things, "Miserable me! I have neither Hera, nor Athene, nor Apollo!" It was for Zeus alone, as God, that our Teacher reserved his devotion. And for Him he displayed a passionate enthusiasm, the absolute sincerity of which it never entered into my mind to question; nor do I question it now. Under this God he served as a soldier, or lived as a citizen. To this God he testified as a witness that others might believe and worship. In this view of human life—as being a testimony to God—his teaching was most convincing to me, even when I felt, as I always did, that something was wanting in any conception of God that regarded Him as ever being "alone."

Now I pass to another matter, not of great interest to me at the time, but of great importance to me in its results, because it led to my first knowledge—that could be called knowledge—of the followers of the Lord Jesus Christ. It arose from a passage in the lecture I described in my last chapter. Epictetus was speaking about "the whole frame of things" as being a kind of fluid, in which the thrill of one portion affects all the rest, and about God and the Guardian Dæmon as feeling our every motion and thought. He concluded by calling on us to take an oath—a military oath, or *sacramentum*, as we call it in Latin—such as soldiers take to the Emperor. "They," he said, "taking on themselves the life of service for pay, swear to prefer above all things the safety of Cæsar. You, who have been counted worthy of such vast gifts, will you not likewise swear, and, after taking your oath, abide by it? And what shall the oath be? Never to disobey, never to accuse, never to find fault with any of the gifts that have been given by Him; never to do reluctantly, never to suffer reluctantly, anything that may be necessary. This oath is like theirs—after a fashion. The soldiers of Cæsar swear not to prefer another to him; God's soldiers swear to prefer themselves to everything."

On me this came somewhat as bathos. But it was a frequent paradox with him; and of course, in one sense, it was not a paradox but common sense. What he meant by bidding us "prefer *ourselves*" was "prefer *virtue*," which he always described as each man's true "profit." Everyone, he said, must prefer his own "profit" to everything else, even to father, brothers, children, wife. Zeus Himself—so he taught—prefers His own "profit"—which consists in being Father of all. Take away this thin veil of apparent egotism, and the oath might be described as an oath to live and die for righteousness, for the Logos or Word of God within us, and, thus, for God Himself. But why, I thought, disguise loyalty under the mask of self-seeking? This notion of a military oath taken to God, and at the same time to oneself—and an oath, so to speak, of negative allegiance, not to do this or that—did not inspire me with the same enthusiasm as the more positive doctrine and the picture of the wandering Cynic going about the world and actively doing good and destroying evil.

Arrian, however, was taking down this passage about the military oath with even more than his usual earnestness and rapidity. "Did that impress you?" said I, as we left the lecture-room together. "On me it fell a little flat." He did not answer at once. Presently, as if rousing himself from a reverie, "Forgive me," he said, "I was thinking of something that occurred in our neighbourhood about fifteen years ago. You know I was born in Bithynia. Well, about that time, there was a great outbreak of that Jewish superstition of which you must often have heard in Rome, practised by the followers of Christus. They are suspected of all sorts of horrible crimes and abominations, as you know, I dare say, better than I do, being familiar with what the common people say about them in Rome. Moreover the new work just published by your Tacitus—a lover of truth if any man is—severely condemns them. I am bound to say our Governor did not think so badly of them as Tacitus does. Perhaps in Rome and in Nero's time they were more savage and vicious than among us in Bithynia recently. However, that matters little. The question was not about their private vices or virtues. Our Governor

Chapter 3] ON THE OATH OF THE CHRISTIANS 37

believed them guilty of treasonable conspiracy. So he determined to stop it.

"Stop it he did; or, at all events, to a very great extent. But the point of interest for me is, that when these fellows were had up before our Governor—it was Caius Plinius Cæcilius Secundus, an intimate friend of the Emperor Trajan—he found there was really no mischief at all to be apprehended from them. Secundus had heard something about a *sacramentum*, or military oath—and this is my point—which these people were in the habit of taking at their secret meetings. Naturally this convinced him at first that there must be something wrong. But, when he came to look into it, the whole thing came to no more than what I will now tell you. I am sure of my facts for I heard them from his secretary, who had a copy of his letter to the Emperor. It was to this effect, '*They affirm that the sum total of their crime or error is, that they were wont, on an appointed day, to meet together before daybreak and to sing an alternate chant to Christus, as to a God, and to bind themselves by an oath—not, as conspirators do, to commit some crime in common, but to avoid committing theft, robbery, adultery, fraud, breach of faith. This done, they break up. It is true they return to take food in common, but it is a mere harmless repast.*' After the Governor had gone carefully into the matter, putting a few women to the torture to get at the truth, he came to the conclusion that this so-called military oath, or *sacramentum*, had no harm whatever in it. The thing was merely a perverted superstition run wild. He very sensibly adopted the mild course of giving the poor deluded people a chance of denying their faith as they called it. The Emperor sanctioned his mildness. Most of them recanted. Things settled down, and promised to be very much as they were before. At least so the Governor thought. We, outside the palace, were not quite so sanguine. But anyhow, what struck me to-day was the similarity between the military oath of these Christians and the military oath prescribed by our great Teacher to his Cynics."

"But," said I, "does it not seem to you that our military oath ought to be a positive one, namely, that we Cynics will go anywhere and do anything that the General may command—and not a negative one, that we will abstain from grumbling against His orders?" Arrian replied, "As to that, I think our Master follows Socrates, who expressly says that he had indeed a daemon, or at all events a daemonic voice; but that it told him only what to avoid, not what to do." "Surely," replied I, "what Socrates said on his trial was, 'How could I be fairly described as introducing new daemons when saying that *a voice of God manifestly points out to me what I ought to do?*'" "I do not remember that," said my friend, "but we are near my rooms. Come in and let us look into Plato's Apologia."

So we went in, and Arrian took out of his book-case Plato's account of the Speech of Socrates before the jury that condemned him to death. "There, Silanus," said he, "you see I was right." And he pointed to these words, "There comes to me, as you have often heard me say, a divine and daemonic something, which indeed my prosecutor Meletus mentioned and burlesqued in his written indictment. This thing, in its commencement, dates back (I believe) from my boyhood, a kind of Voice that comes to me from time to time, and, whenever it comes, it always"—"Mark this," said Arrian—"*turns me back from doing that (whatever it may be) which I am purposing to do, but never moves me forward.*"

I seemed fairly and fully confuted. But suddenly it occurred to me to ask my friend to let me see Xenophon's version of the same speech. He brought it out. I was not long before I disinterred the very words that I have quoted above, "*a Voice of God that manifestly points out to me what I ought to do.*" And the context, too, indicated that the Voice—which he calls *daemonic*, or a *daemonion*—gave positive directions, recognised as such by his friends.

This very important difference between Plato and Xenophon in regard to the daemon of Socrates, as described by Socrates himself, interested Arrian not a little. "Come back," he said, "in the evening, when I shall have finished reducing my notes to writing, and let us put the two versions side by side and see how many passages we can find agreeing." So I came back after sunset, and we sat down and went carefully through them.

And, as far as I remember, we could not find these two great biographers of this great man agreeing in so much as a dozen consecutive words in their several records of his Apologia, his only public speech. Presently—Arrian having Xenophon in his hand and I Plato—I read out the well-known words of Socrates about Anytus and Meletus, his accusers, and about their power to kill him but not to hurt him. "What," said I, "is Xenophon's version of this?" "He omits it altogether," replied Arrian; "but I see, reading on, that he puts into the mouth of Socrates an entirely different saying about Anytus, after the condemnation. Let me see the Plato." Taking it from my hand, he observed, "Our Master, Epictetus, who is continually quoting these words of Plato's, never quotes them exactly. 'Anytus and Meletus may kill me but they cannot hurt me'—that is always his condensed version. But you see it is not Plato's, Plato's is much longer."

So the conversation strayed away in a literary direction. We talked a great deal—without much knowledge, at least on my part—about oral tradition. I remarked on the possibilities in it of astonishing divergences and distortions of doctrine—"unless," said I, as I rose up to go, "it happens, by good fortune, to be taken down at the time by an honest fellow like you, who loves his teacher, but loves the truth more, so that he just sets down what he hears, as he hears it." "I do my best," said Arrian; "but if it were not nearly midnight, I could shew you that even my best is not always good enough. I suspect that such sayings of our Master as become most current will be very variously reported a hundred years hence."

"Good-night," said I, and was opening the door to depart, when it flashed upon me that all this time, although we had been discussing Socrates, and assuming a resemblance between him and our Master, we had said nothing about that great doctrine in the profession of which Socrates breathed his last—prescribing a sacrifice to Æsculapius as though death were the beginning of a higher life—I mean the immortality of the soul. "I will not stay now," said I, "but we have not said a word about Epictetus's doctrine concerning the immortality of the soul; could you lend me some of your notes about it?" "He seldom speaks of it," replied my friend; "when he does, it is not always easy to distinguish between metaphor and not-metaphor. My notes, so far, do not quite satisfy me that I have done him justice. He is likely to touch on it in the next lecture or soon after. I should prefer you to hear for yourself what he says."

"One more question," said I. "Did our Master ever, in your hearing, refer to that last strange saying of Socrates, 'We owe a cock to Æsculapius'? Sometimes it seems to me the finest epigram in all Greek literature." "Never," replied Arrian. "He has never mentioned it either in my hearing, or in the hearing of those whom I have asked about it. And I have asked many."

Departing home I found myself almost at once forgetting our long literary discussion about oral tradition, in the larger and deeper question touched on in the last few minutes. Why should not Arrian have been able to " do justice " to Epictetus in this particular subject? Was it that our Teacher did not quite "do justice" to himself? Then I began to ask what Epictetus had meant precisely by such expressions as that men may become "fellow-banqueters" and even " fellow-rulers " with " the Gods." " If God Himself is immortal, how," said I, " can 'God's own son' fail to be immortal also?"

All through that night, even till near dawn, I was harassed with wild and wearying dreams. I travelled, wandering through wilderness after wilderness in quest of Socrates and nowhere finding him. Wherever I went I seemed to hear a strange monotonous cry that followed close behind me. Presently I heard a flapping of wings, and I knew that the sound was the crowing of the cock that was to be offered for Socrates to Æsculapius. Then it became a mocking, inarticulate, human voice striving to utter articulate speech. At last I heard distinctly, " If Zeus could have, he would have. If he could have, he would have. But he could not."

CHAPTER IV

SCAURUS ON EPICTETUS AND PAUL

THE cock was still crowing when I started out of my dream. It was not yet dawn but sleep was impossible. When Arrian called to accompany me to lecture, he found me in a fever and sent in a physician, by whose advice I stayed indoors for two or three days. During this enforced inaction, I resolved to write to my old friend Scaurus. Marcus Æmilius Scaurus—for that was his name in full—had been a friend of my father's, years before I was born; and his advice had been largely the cause of my coming to Nicopolis. Scaurus had seen service; but for many years past he had devoted himself wholly to literature, not as a rhetorician, nor as a lover of the poets, but as "a practical historian," so he called it. By this he meant to distinguish himself from what he called "ornamental historians." "History," he used to say, "contains truth in a well; and I like trying to draw it out."

For a man of nearly seventy, Scaurus was remarkably vigorous in mind and thought, with large stores of observation and learning, of a sort not common among Romans of good birth. His favourite motto was, "Quick to perceive, slow to believe." I used to think he erred on the side of believing too little, and his friends used to call him Miso-mythus or "Myth-hater." But over and over again, when I had ventured to discuss with him a matter of documentary evidence, I had found that his incredulity was justified; so that I had come to admit that there was some force in his protest, that he ought to be called, not "Myth-hater," but "Truth-lover."

In the year after my father's death, when I was wasting my time in Rome, and in danger of doing worse, Scaurus took me to task as befitted my father's dearest friend—a cousin also of my mother, who had died while I was still an infant. He had long desired me to enter the army, and I should have done so but for illness. Now that my health was almost restored, he returned to his previous advice, but suggested that, for the present, I might spend a month or two with advantage in attending the lectures of Epictetus, of whom he knew something while he was in Rome, and about whom he had heard a good deal since. When I demurred, and told him that I had heard a good many philosophers and did not care for them, he replied, "Epictetus you will not find a common philosopher." He pressed me and I yielded.

Since my coming to Nicopolis, I had written once to tell him of my arrival, and to thank him for advising me to come to so admirable a teacher. But I had been too much absorbed in the teaching to enter into detail. Now, having leisure, and knowing his great interest in such subjects, I wrote to him even more fully than I have done for my readers above, sending him all my lecture notes; and I asked him what he judged to be the secret of Epictetus, which made him so different from other philosophers. Nor did I omit to tell him of my talk with Arrian about the Christians and their *sacramentum*.

Many days elapsed, and I had been attending lectures again for a long time, before his letter in reply reached Nicopolis; but I will set it down here, as also a second letter from him on the same subject. In the first, Scaurus expressed his satisfaction at my meeting with Arrian (whom he knew and described as an extremely sensible and promising young man, likely to get on). He added a hope that I would take precisely Arrian's view of the advantage to be derived from philosophy. But a large part of his letter—much more than I could have wished—was occupied with our "wonderful discovery" (as he called it) that Plato and Xenophon disagreed in their versions of the Apologia of Socrates. On this he rallied us as mere babes in criticism, but, said he, not much more babyish than many professed critics, who cannot be made to understand that—outside

Chapter 4] ON EPICTETUS AND PAUL

poetry, and traditions learned by rote, and a few "aculeate sayings" (so he called them) of philosophers and great men—no two historians ever agree independently—he laid stress on "*independently*"—for twenty consecutive words, in recording a speech or dialogue. "I will not lay you a wager," said he, "for it would be cheating you. But I will make you an offer. If you and Arrian, between you, can find twenty identical consecutive words of Socrates in the whole of Xenophon's Memorabilia and Plato's Dialogues, I will give you five hundred sesterces apiece[1]. Your failure (for fail you will) ought to strike you as all the more remarkable because both Plato and Xenophon tell us that Socrates used to describe himself as '*always saying the same things about the same subjects.*' That one similar saying they have preserved. For the rest, these two great biographers, writing page upon page of Socratic talk, cannot agree exactly about '*the same things*' for a score of consecutive words!"

He added more, not of great interest to me, about the credulity of those who persuaded themselves that Xenophon's version must be spurious just because it differed from Plato's, whereas, said he, this very difference went to shew that it was genuine, and that Xenophon was tacitly correcting Plato. But concerning the secret of Epictetus he said very little—and that, merely in reference to the *sacramentum* of the Christians which I mentioned in my first letter. On this he remarked that Pliny, with whom he had been well acquainted, had never mentioned the matter to him. "But that," he said, "is not surprising. His measures to suppress the Christian superstition did not prove so successful as he had hoped. Moreover he disliked the whole business—having to deal with mendacious informers on one side, and fanatical fools or hysterical women on the other. And I, who knew a good deal more about the Christians than Pliny did, disliked the subject still more. My conviction is, however, that your excellent Epictetus—rationalist though he is now, and even less prone to belief than Socrates—has not been always unscathed by that same Christian infection (for that is the right name for it).

---

[1] In "Notes on Silanus," **2809***a*, the author repeats this offer.

"Partly, he sympathizes with the Christian hatred or contempt for 'the powers of this world' (to use their phrase) and partly with their allegiance to one God, whom he and they regard as casting down kings and setting up philosophers. But there is this gulf between them. The Christians think of their champion, Christus, as having devoted himself to death for their sake, and then as having been miraculously raised from the dead, and as, even now, present among them whenever they choose to meet together and 'sing hymns to him as to a God.' Epictetus absolutely disbelieves this. Hence, he is at a great disadvantage—I mean, of course, as a preacher, not as a philosopher. The Christians have their God, standing in the midst of their daily assemblies, before whom they can 'corybantize'—to repeat your expression—to their hearts' content. Your teacher has nothing—nay, worse than nothing, for he has a blank and feels it to be a blank.

"What does he do then? He fills the blank with a Hercules or a Diogenes or a Socrates, and he corybantizes before that. But it is a make-believe, though an honest one. I have said more than I intended. You know how I ramble on paper. And the habit is growing on me. Let no casual word of mine make you doubt that Epictetus is thoroughly honest. But honest men may be deceived. Be 'quick in perceiving, slow in believing.' Keep to Arrian's view of a useful and practical life in the world, the world as it is, not as it might be in Plato's Republic—which, by the way, would be a very dull place. Farewell."

This letter did not satisfy me at all. "Honest men," I repeated, "may be deceived." True, and Scaurus, though honest as the day, is no exception. To think that Epictetus, *our* Epictetus—for so Arrian and I used to call him—had been even for a time under the spell of such a superstition as this! I had always assumed—and my conversation with Arrian about what seemed exceptional experiences in Bithynia had done little to shake my assumption—that the Christians were a vile Jewish sect, morose, debased, given up to monstrous secret vices, hostile to the Empire, and hateful to Gods and men. What was the ground for connecting Epictetus with

Chapter 4]   ON EPICTETUS AND PAUL   45

them? Contempt for rulers? That was no new thing in philosophers. Many of them had despised kings, or affected to despise them, without any intention of rebelling against them. What though Epictetus suggested, in a hyperbolical or metaphorical way, a religious *sacramentum* for philosophers? This was quite different from that of the Christians as mentioned by Arrian. I could not help feeling that, for once, my old friend had "perceived" little and "believed" much.

Perhaps my reply shewed traces of this feeling. At all events, Scaurus wrote back, asking whether I had observed in him "a habit of basing conclusions on slight grounds." Then he continued "I told you that I knew a good deal about the Christians. I also know a great deal more about Epictetus than you suppose. When I was a young man, I attended the lectures of that most admirable of philosophers, Musonius Rufus. About the time when I left, Epictetus, then a slave, was brought to the classes by his master, Epaphroditus; and Rufus, whom I shall always regard with respect and affection, spoke to me about his new pupil in the highest terms. Afterwards he often told me how he tried to arm the poor boy with philosophy against what he would have to endure from such a master. Many a time have I thought that the young philosopher must have needed all his Stoic armour, going home from the lecture-room of Rufus to the palace of Nero's freedman.

"But I also remember seeing him long before that, when he came one morning as a mere child not twelve years old, along with Epaphroditus, to Nero's Palace. I was then about fourteen or fifteen. After we had left the Palace—my father and I—we came upon him again on that same evening, staring at some Christians, smeared with pitch and burning away like so many flaring torches, to light the Imperial Gardens—one of Nero's insane or bestial freaks! I have never been able to forget the sight, and I have often thought that he could never forget it. Somewhere about that time, one of the Christian ringleaders, Paulus by name, was put to death. As happens in such cases, his people began to collect every scrap of his writings that could be found. A little volume of them came

into my hands some twenty years ago. But long before that
date, all through the period when Epictetus was in Rufus's
classes, the Christian slaves in Rome had in their hands the
letters of this Paulus or Paul. One of them, the longest,
written to the Christians in Rome (a few years before Paul was
brought to the City as a prisoner) goes back as far as sixty years
ago. Some are still earlier. I saw the volume more than once in
Cæsar's Palace in the days of Vespasian. This Paul was one
of the most practical of men, and his letters are steeped in
practical experience. Epictetus, besides being a great devourer
of literature in general, devoured in particular everything that
bore on practical life. The odds are great that he would have
come across the book somewhere among his slave or freedman
friends.

"But I do not trust to such mere antecedent probabilities.
You must know that, ever since Epictetus set up as a philosopher, I have followed his career with interest. Recluse
though I am, I have many friends and correspondents. These,
from time to time, have furnished me with notes of his lectures.
Well, when I came to read Paul's letters, I was prepared to
find in them certain general similarities to Stoic doctrine;
for Paul was a man of Tarsus and might have picked up these
things at the University there. But I found a great deal more.
I found particularities, just of the sort that you find in your
lectures. Paul's actual experiences had been exactly those of
a vagrant Æsculapius or Hercules. Your friend idealizes the
wanderings of Hercules; Paul enacted them. Paul journeyed
from city to city, from continent to continent, everywhere
turning the world upside down—Jerusalem, Damascus, Antioch,
Ephesus, Colossæ, Philippi, Thessalonica, Corinth, Jerusalem
again—last of all, Rome. Everywhere the slaves, the poor, the
women, went after him. Everywhere he came into collision
with the rulers of the earth. If he did not proclaim a war
between them and his God, he at all events implied war.

"Now this is just what Epictetus would have liked to do.
Only he could not often get people to take him in the same
serious way, because he had not the same serious business in
hand. I verily believe he was not altogether displeased when

the Prefect of the City banished him with other philosophers of note under Domitian. I know certain philosophers who actually made money by being thus banished. It was an advertisement for their lectures. Don't imagine that *your* philosopher made, or wished to make, money. No. But he made influence—which he valued above money.

"However, the Emperors and Prefects after Domitian were not such fools. They knew the difference between a real revolution and a revolution on paper. A mere theoretical exaltation of the mind above the body, a mere scholastic laudation of kingship over the minds of men as superior to kingship over their bodies—these things kings tolerate; for they mean nothing but words. But a revolution in the name of a *person*—a person, too, supposed by fanatics to be living and present in all their secret meetings, 'wherever two or three are gathered together,' for that is their phrase—this may mean a great deal. A person, regarded in this way, may take hold of men's spirits. Missionaries pretending—or, still worse, believing—that they are speaking in the name of such a person, may lead crowds of silly folk into all sorts of sedition. They may refuse, for example, to adore the Emperor's image and to offer sacrifice to the Gods of the State; or they might even attempt to subvert the foundations of society by withholding taxes, or by encouraging or inculcating some wholesale manumission of slaves. This sort of thing means war, and Paul, fifty years ago, was actually waging this war. Epictetus longs to be waging it now. As he cannot, he takes pleasure in urging his pupils to it, painting an imaginary battle array in which he sees imaginary soldiers waging, or destined to wage, imaginary conflicts with imaginary enemies.

"Hence that picturesque contrast (in the lecture you transcribed for me) between the unmarried and the married Cynic—which, besides the similarity of thought, contains some curious similarities to the actual words of Paul. It ran thus, 'The condition of the times being such as it is, opposing forces, as it were, being drawn up in line of battle'—that was his expression. Well, what followed from this non-existent, hypothetical, imminent conflict? The Philosopher, it seems, must

be a soldier, '*undistracted*, wholly devoted to the ministry of
God, able to go about and visit men, not bound fast to private
personal duties, not *entangled* in conditions of life that he cannot
honourably transgress.' And then he describes at great length
a married Cynic dragged down from his royal throne by the
claims and encumbrances of a nursery. Now this same 'undis-
tractedness' (using the very word) of unmarried life Paul
himself has mentioned in a letter to the Corinthians, where he
says that 'owing to the pressing necessity' of the times, it was
good for a man to be unmarried, and that he wished them to
be 'free from anxiety.' He concludes 'But I speak this for
your own profit, not that I may cast a noose round you but
that you may with all seemliness attend on the Lord *undis-
tractedly*.' Again, he writes to one of his assistants or subalterns,
'Endure hardship with me as a good soldier of Christ Jesus.
No one engaged in a campaign is *entangled*'—your friend's
word again—'in the affairs of civil life.'

"I lay little stress on the similarity of word, but a great
deal on the similarity of thought. There is no such conflict as
Epictetus describes. There is no such 'line of battle'—not at
least for us, Romans, or for you, Cynics. But *there is for the
Christians*—arrayed as they are against the authorities of the
Empire. And that reminds me of your Epictetian antithesis
between 'the Beast' and 'the Man.' It is a little like a
Christian tradition about 'the Beast.' By 'the Beast' they
mean Nero. They have never forgotten his treatment of them
after the fire. For a long time after his death they had a
notion—I believe some of them have it still—that the Beast
may rise from the dead and persecute them again. They also
expect—I cannot do more than allude to their fantastic dreams—
a sort of 'Son of Man' to appear on the clouds taking vengeance
on the armies of the Beast. So, you see, they, too, recognise an
opposition between the Man and the Beast. Only, with the
Christians it is of a date much earlier than Epictetus. It goes
back to a Jewish tradition, which represents a sort of opposition
between the empires of Beasts and the empire of the Son of
Man, in a prophet named Daniel, some centuries ago.

"Epictetus, of course, does not believe in all this. But still he persuades himself that there is such a 'line of battle' in the air, and that he and his followers can take part in this aerial conflict by 'going about the world' as spiritually armed warriors, making themselves substantially miserable—or what the world would call such—while championing the cause of unsubstantial good against evil. All that you wrote to me about the missionary life and its hardships—its destitution, homelessness, nakedness, yes, even the extraordinary phrase you added from Arrian's notes about the cudgelled Cynic, how he 'must be cudgelled like a donkey, and, in the act of being cudgelled, must love his cudgellers as being the father of all and brother of all'—all this I could match, in a compressed form, from a passage in my little Pauline volume. Here it is: '*For I think that God has made a show of us Missionaries*'— Missionaries, or Apostles, that is their name for their wandering Æsculapii—'*like condemned criminals in the arena. We have been made a theatre-show to the universe, to angels and men......: —up to this very moment, hungering, thirsting, naked, buffeted, driven from place to place, toiling and labouring with our own hands. Reviled, we bless; persecuted, we endure. Men imprecate evil on us, we exhort them to their good. We have been made as the refuse of the universe, the offscouring of all, up to this very moment.*'

"Again, elsewhere, Paul brings in that same Epictetian contrast between the external misery and the internal joy of the Missionary: '*Never needlessly offending anyone in anything, lest the Service*'—which your philosopher calls 'the service of God'—'*be reproached, but in everything commending ourselves as the Servants of God, in much endurance, in tribulations, in necessities, in hardships, in scourgings, in prisons, in tumults, in toils, in watchings, in fastings.*' Now comes the contrast, indicating that all these things are superficial trifles, the petty pin-pricks inflicted by the spite of the contemptible world, but underneath lie the solid realities:—'*in purity, in knowledge, in longsuffering, in kindness and goodness, in the holy spirit, in love unfeigned, in the word of truth, in the power of God.*'

"This leads Paul to the thought of the armour of God, and the friends and enemies of God, the good and the evil, which this wandering Christian Hercules has to deal with: '*By the arms of righteousness, on the right hand and on the left; by glory and dishonour; by ill report and good report*—,' he means, I think, 'glory in the sight of God, dishonour in the sight of men,' and again, 'ill report on earth, good report in heaven.' And so he continues, '*as knaves and true*'—that is, 'knaves in appearance, in the world's false judgment, but true men in the sight of Him who judges truly.' It is a marvel of compression. And it is kept up in what follows:—'*misunderstood* [*i.e.* by men] *and well understood* [*i.e.* by God]; *dying, and behold we live; under the headsman's scourge, yet not beheaded; grieving, but always rejoicing; beggars, but making many rich; having nothing, yet having all things for ever!*'

"You will be tired of this. But your zeal for your new teacher brought it on you. You admire his 'fervour.' Then what do you think of this man's fervour? He could give points to Epictetus both for fervour and for compression. I admit that Paul has not your master's dramatic flash, irony, and epigrammatic twist. But, as for 'fervour,' here, I contend, is the original Falernian, which your friend Epictetus has watered down. Not that I blame him, either as regards style or in respect of morality. His humorous description of the nursery troubles of the married Stoic was very good—for his purpose, and for a lecture. But it would not have suited Paul. A lecturer must not be too brief. If Epictetus were to pack stuff in his lectures as Paul packs it in his epistles, your lesson would sometimes not last five minutes.

"But I am straying from the question, which is, whether Epictetus borrowed. Let me give you another instance. The Christians are permeated with two notions, the first is, that they have received an 'invitation,' 'summons,' or 'calling' (*Klēsis* they call it) to a heavenly Feast in a Kingdom of Heaven. The second is, that, if they are to attain to this Feast, they must pass through suffering and persecution, by 'witnessing' or 'testifying' to Christ, as being their King, in opposition to the Gods of the Romans. This 'witness,' or *martyria*, is so closely associated in their minds with the notion of persecution that 'martyrdom,' with them, has come to imply, almost always, death. Now, as far as I know, the Greeks do not anywhere use the word 'calling' in this sense. But look at what Epictetus says about a sham philosopher, who, having been 'called' by God to be a beggar, 'disgraces his *calling*': 'How then dost thou mount the stage now? It is in the character of a witness *called* by God, who says "Come thou, and bear witness to me."' Then the sham philosopher whines out, 'I am in a terrible strait, O Lord, and most unfortunate. None take thought for me; none give to me. All blame me. All speak evil of me.' To which Epictetus replies, 'Is this the witness thou wouldst bear, *bringing shame on the calling wherewith He hath called thee*, in that He honoured thee with so great an honour, and counted thee *worthy* to be promoted to the high task of such a witnessing?' Now this phrase, 'worthy of the calling,' is Pauline in thought, and Pauline in word. Here is an instance, from a letter to the Thessalonians, 'That our God would *count you worthy of the calling*.' And Paul writes to the Ephesians, 'That ye walk *worthily of the calling wherewith ye were called*.'

"Again, you yourself remarked to me on the strangeness and originality of Epictetus's expression about 'eating,' namely, that, in the very act of eating, or going to the gymnasium, or whatever else, the philosopher was to remember that he was 'feeding on God' and 'carrying about God,' and that he must not 'defile' the image of the God within him. Well, I admit it is strange, but I do not admit that it is original. I can match it in the first place with another passage from Epictetus himself, where he bids some of his uppish pupils, who wished to reform the world, first to reform themselves. 'In this way,' he said, 'when eating, help those who eat with you; when drinking, those who drink with you.' In the next place, I can match both out of the letter to the Corinthians, which says, 'Ye are *God's temple*,' and 'If anyone destroys *God's temple*, him will God destroy,' and again, 'Your body is *the temple of the Holy Spirit*, which ye have from God.' It adds that people cause shame to others and injury to themselves by greediness at the sacred meals they take in common; and lastly, says Paul, '*Whether therefore ye eat or drink, or whatsoever ye do, do all to*

4—2

the glory of God.' There are things like this, of course, in Seneca, but none, as far as I know, that come so near as Epictetus does to the language of Paul.

"I could quote more from Paul, and also from other sacred books of the Christians, to shew that Epictetus is indebted to them. But I have been already led on by the fascination—to me it is a fascination—of a merely literary discussion, to say more than enough, and a great deal more than I intended. Let me conclude with an extract from a letter I lately rummaged up from my dear old friend Pliny, whom I greatly miss. He was the former Governor of Bithynia about whom you wrote. It refers to a very fine fellow, Artemidorus by name, a military tribune, son-in-law of the excellent Musonius (Epictetus's teacher, whom I mentioned above). 'Among the whole multitude of those who in these days call themselves philosophers, you will hardly find one so sincere, genuine, and true, as Artemidorus. I say nothing about his bodily endurance of heat and cold and the most arduous toil, of his indifference to the pleasures of the table, of the strict control with which he keeps his eyes and his passions in order. These are great virtues, but only great in others. In him they are but trifles compared with his other merits.'

"So wrote Pliny. Well, for me at all events, 'to keep eyes and passions in order' is not 'a trifle.' Perhaps it is not 'a trifle' for you. I fully believe that Musonius's successor— for as such I regard Epictetus—in spite of some opinions in which I cannot quite follow him, will help you to attain this object. Give yourself wholly to that. I knew Artemidorus. So did your father. We both thought him the model of a soldier and a gentleman. Believe me, my dear Quintus, it would be one of the greatest comforts in my last moments if I could feel assured that—to some slight extent in consequence of advice from me—the son of my old friend Decimus Junius Silanus was following in the footsteps of one whom he so esteemed and admired. Farewell."

This was the end of the letter. But out of it dropped a paper containing a sealed note. On the paper were these words: "To convince you that I had not judged your philosopher unfairly, I transcribed a few passages from other Christian documents, containing words assigned by Christians to Christ himself, which seem to me to have influenced Epictetus. On second thoughts, I have come to think it was waste of my time. That it might not waste yours too, I was on the point of throwing the thing into the fire. But I decided to send it rather than let you suppose me to be a crotchety, suspicious, prejudiced old man, ungenerous towards one whom both you and I respect with all our hearts. I grant that I am slow to believe in new *facts*; but I need hardly assure you, my dearest Quintus, that I am not slow to believe in good *motives*—the motives of good men, tried, tested, and proved, by such severe trials as have befallen your admirable Master. Rather than suspect me thus, break the seal and read it at once. But I hope you will not want to read it. Discussions of this sort must not be allowed to distract your energies as they might do. Better burn it. Or keep it—till you are military tribune."

CHAPTER V

EPICTETUS ALLUDES TO JEWS

I DID not open the sealed note, though I was not convinced that Epictetus had been a borrower. Paulus the Christian had begun to interest me, because of Scaurus's quotations and remarks on his style. Indeed he interested me so much that I determined at once to procure a copy of his letters. But Christus himself—whom I call Christus here to distinguish the meaning with which I used the name then from that with which I began to use the name of "Christ" soon afterwards—Christus, I say, at that moment, did not interest me at all.

Moreover I was impressed by what Scaurus said about a military career. Though too young to remember much about the shameful days of Domitian, yet I had heard my father describe the anguish he used to feel, when letters from the Emperor to the Senate came announcing a glorious victory (duly honoured with a triumph) after which would come a private letter from Scaurus informing him that the victory was a disgraceful defeat. And even later on, even after the successes of Trajan, my father, in conversations with Scaurus, had often expressed, in my hearing, still lingering apprehensions of a time when the barbarians might break in like a flood upon the northern borders of the empire—if ever the imperial throne were cursed with a second Domitian. Patriotism would be even more needed then, he said, than when Marius beat back the Cimbri. All this gave additional weight to Scaurus's remarks. "Artemidorus," I said, "shall be my model. I will try to be a good soldier and a good Stoic in one." So I locked up the note, still sealed.

Here I may say that afterwards, when I did open it, it did not greatly influence the course of my thoughts. By that time, I had come to think that Scaurus was right, and that Epictetus had really borrowed from the Christians. I opened it, therefore, not because I distrusted the fairness and soundness of his judgment, but because I trusted it and looked to him for information. As a fact, it rather confirmed his hypothesis of borrowing, but did not demonstrate anything. The real influence of that little note in my cabinet amounted, I think, to little more than this. In the period I am now about to describe, while daily studying the works of Paulus the Christian, I was beginning to ask myself "If Paulus the follower of Christus was so great a teacher, must not Christus have been greater?" In those days, when taking out Paul's epistles from my bookcase, I used often to see that packet lying there, with WORDS OF CHRISTUS on it, and the seal unbroken. Then I used to say "If only I could make up my mind to open you, you might tell me wonderful things." This stimulated my curiosity. It was one of many things—some little, some great—that led me toward my goal.

The reader may perhaps think that I, a Roman of equestrian rank, must have been already more prone to the Christian religion than I have admitted, if I attempted to procure a copy of Paul's epistles from a bookseller in Nicopolis frequented by my fellow-students. But I made no such attempt. Possibly our bookseller there would not have had a copy. Probably he would not have confessed it if he had. In any case, I did not ask him. It happened that I needed at this time certain philosophic treatises (of Chrysippus and others). So I wrote to a freedman of my father's in Rome, an enterprising bookseller, who catered for various tastes, giving him the titles of these works and telling him how to prepare and ornament them. Then I added that Æmilius Scaurus had sent me some remarkable extracts from the works of one Paulus, a Christian, and that the volume seemed likely to be interesting as a literary curiosity. This was perhaps a little understating the case. But not much. With Flaccus, my Roman bookseller, I felt quite safe. Rather than buy Paul's epistles from Sosia in

Nicopolis, I am sure I should not have bought them at all. Such are the trifles in our lives on which sometimes our course may depend—or may seem to have depended.

Meantime I had been attending lectures regularly and had become familiar with many of Epictetus's frequently recurring expressions of doctrine. They were still almost always interesting, and generally impressive. But his success in forcing me to "feel, for the moment, precisely what he felt"—how often did I recognise the exact truth of this phrase of Arrian's!—made me begin to distrust myself. And from distrust of myself sprang distrust of his teaching, too, when I found the feeling fade away (time after time) upon leaving the lecturer's presence. When I sat down in my rooms to write out my notes, asking myself, "Can I honestly say I hope to be ever able to do this or that?" how often was I obliged to answer, "No!"

I could not trust his judgment about what we should be able to do, because I could not trust his insight into what we were. Two causes seemed to keep him out of sympathy with us. One was his own singular power of bearing physical pain—almost as though he were a stone and not flesh and blood. He thought that we had the same, or ought to have it. Another cause was his absorption in something that was not human, in a conception of God, whom (on some evidence clear to him but not made clear by him to us, or at all events not to me) he *knew* (not trusted or believed, but *knew*) to have bestowed on him, Epictetus, the power of being at once—not in the future, but at once, here on earth, at all times, and in all circumstances—perfectly blessed. Having his eyes fixed on this Supreme Giver of Peace, our Master often seemed to me hardly able to bring himself to look down to us, except when he was chiding our weakness.

Passing over several of the lectures that left me in the condition I have endeavoured to describe, I will now come to the one in which Epictetus alluded to Christians. "Jews" he called them. But he defined them in such a way as to convince Arrian that he meant Christians. Even if he did not, the impression produced on me was the same as if he had actually mentioned them by name. The lecture began with the subject of "steadfastness." "A practical subject, this," I said to myself, "for one in training to be a second Artemidorus." But the "steadfastness" was not of the sort demanded in camps and battlefields. The essence of good, said the lecturer, is right choice, and that of evil a wrong choice. External things are not in our power, internal things are: "This Law God has laid down, *If thou wilt have good, take it from thyself.*" Then followed one of the now familiar dialogues, of which I was beginning to be a little tired, between a tyrant threatening a philosopher, who points out that he cannot possibly be threatened. The tyrant stares and says, "I will put you in chains." The wise man replies, "It is my hands and feet that you threaten." "I will cut off your head," shouts the tyrant. "It is my head that you threaten," replies the philosopher. After a good deal more of this, a pupil is supposed to ask, "Does not the tyrant threaten *you* then?" To this the lecturer replies, "Yes, if I fear these things. But if I have a feeling and conviction that these things are nothing to me, then I am not threatened." Then he appealed to us, "Of whom do I stand in fear? What things must he be master of to make me afraid? Do you say, 'The master of things that are in your power'? I reply, 'There is no such master.' As for things not in my power, what are they to me?"

Epictetus had a sort of rule or canon for us beginners, by which we were to take the measure of the so-called evils of life: "Make a habit of saying at once to every harsh-looking apparition of this sort, 'You are an apparition and not at all the thing you appear to be. Are you of the number of the things in my power, or are you not? If not, you are nothing to me.'" Applying this to a concrete instance, our Master now dramatized a dialogue between himself and Agamemnon, who is supposed to be passing a sleepless night in anxiety for the Greeks, lest the Trojans should destroy them on the morrow.

"*Epict.* What! Tearing your hair! And you say your heart leaps in terror! And all for what? What is amiss with you? Money-matters?

"*Ag.* No.

"*Epict.* Health?

"*Ag.* No.

"*Epict.* No indeed! You have gold and silver to spare. What then is amiss with you? That part of you has been neglected and utterly corrupted, wherewith we desire etc. etc."

Here Epictetus—after some customary technicalities—turned to us like a showman, to explain the royal puppet's condition: "'How *neglected*?' you ask. He does not know the essence of the Good for which he has been created by nature, nor the essence of evil. He cries out, 'Woe is me, the Greeks are in peril' because he has not learned to distinguish what is really his own etc. etc." After this apostrophe, which I have condensed, he resumed the dialogue:

"*Ag.* They are all dead men. The Trojans will exterminate them.

"*Epict.* And if the Trojans do not kill them, they are never, never to die, I suppose!!

"*Ag.* O, yes, they'll die. But not at one blow, not to a man, like this.

"*Epict.* What difference does it make? If dying is an evil, then, surely, whether they die all together or one by one, it is equally an evil. And do you really think that dying will be anything more than the separating of the paltry body from the soul?

"*Ag.* Nothing more.

"*Epict.* And you, when the Greeks are in the act of perishing, is the door of escape shut for you? Is it not open to you to die?

"*Ag.* It is.

"*Epict.* Why then bewail? Bah! You, a king! And with the sceptre of Zeus, too! A king is never unfortunate, any more than God is unfortunate. What then are you? A shepherd in truth! For you weep, like the shepherds—when a wolf carries off one of their sheep. And these Greeks are fine sheep to submit to being ruled over by you. Why did you ever begin this Trojan business? Was your desire imperilled etc. etc.?" [Here I omit more technicalities.]

"*Ag.* No, but my brother's darling wife was carried away.

"*Epict.* And was not that a great blessing, to be deprived of a 'darling wife' who was an adulteress?

"*Ag.* Were we then to submit to be trampled on by the Trojans?

"*Epict.* Trojans? What are the Trojans? Wise or foolish? If wise, why make war against them? If foolish, why care for them?"

I doubt whether Epictetus quite carried his class with him on this occasion. He certainly did not carry me, though he went on consistently pouring out various statements of his theory. For the first time in my experience of his lectures, I began to feel that his reiterations were really tedious. My thoughts strayed. I found myself questioning whether my model soldier and philosopher, Artemidorus, could possibly accept this teaching. Would Trajan, I asked, have been so sure of beating Decebalus, if he had considered the disgrace of Rome a matter "independent of choice," and therefore "nothing to him," "neither good nor evil"?

From this reverie I was roused by a sudden transition—to a picture of a well-trained youth going forth to a conflict worthy of his mettle. And now, I thought, we shall have something more like the ideal of my first lecture, a Hercules or Diogenes, going about to help and heal. But perhaps Epictetus drew a distinction between a Diogenes and mere well-trained youths, mere beginners in philosophy. At all events, what followed was only a kind of catechism to prepare us against adversity, and especially against official oppression. "Whenever," said he, "you are in the act of going into the judgment hall of one in authority, remember that there is also Another from above, taking note of what is going on, and that you must please Him rather than the authority on earth." This catechism he threw into the form of a dialogue between the youth and God—whom he called "Another."

"*Another.* Exile, prison, bonds, death, and disgrace—what used you to call these things in the Schools?

"*Pupil.* I? Things indifferent.

"*Another.* Well, then, what do you call them now? Can it be that *they* have changed?

"*Pupil.* They have not.

"*Another.* You, then—have *you* changed?

"*Pupil.* I have not.

"*Another.* Say, then, what are 'things indifferent'?

"*Pupil.* The things outside choice.

"*Another.* Say also the next words.

"*Pupil.* Things indifferent are nothing to me.

"*Another.* Say also about things good. What things used you to think good?

"*Pupil.* Right choice, right use of phenomena.

"*Another.* And what the end and object?

"*Pupil.* To follow thee.

"*Another.* Do you say the same things still?

"*Pupil.* I say the same things still.

"*Another.* Go your way, then, and be of good cheer, and remember these things, and you will see how a young and well-trained champion towers above the untrained."

I wanted to hear him explain why he spoke of "*Another*," instead of Zeus, or God. It struck me that he meant to suggest to us that in this visible world, whenever we say "*this*," we must also say, in our minds, "*another*," to remind ourselves of the invisible counterpart. "Especially must we say '*Another*'"—this, I thought, was his meaning—"when we speak about rulers. Visible rulers are mostly bad. We must prevent them from encroaching on the place that should be filled in our hearts by the Other, the invisible Ruler."

Instead of this explanation, however, he concluded his lecture by warning us against insincerity, or "speaking from the lips," and against trying to be on both sides, when we ought to choose between two contending sides. This he called "trimming." And here it was—while addressing an imaginary "trimmer"—that he used the word "Jew."

"Why," said he—addressing the sham philosopher—"why do you try to impose on the multitude? Why pretend to be a Jew, being really a Greek? Whenever we see a man trimming, we are accustomed to say, 'This fellow is no Jew, he is shamming.' But when a man has taken into himself *the feeling of the dipped and chosen*"—these were his exact words, uttered with a gesture and tone of contempt—"then he is, both in name and in very truth, a Jew. Even so it is with us, having merely a sham baptism; Jews in theory, but something else in fact; far away from any real feeling of our theory, and far away from any intention of putting into practice the professions on which we plume ourselves—as though we knew what they really meant!" I could not quite make out this allusion to Jews. But there was no mistaking his next sentence, and it was the last in the lecture, "So, I repeat, it is with us. We are not equal to the fulfilment of the responsibilities of common humanity, not even up to the standard of Man. Yet we would fain take on ourselves in addition the burden of a philosopher. And what a burden! It is as though a weakling, without power to carry a ten-pound weight, were to aspire to heave the stone of Ajax!"

Thus he dismissed us. I went out, feeling like the "weakling" indeed, but without the slightest "aspiration to heave the stone of Ajax." Perhaps Arrian wished to encourage me. For after we had walked on awhile in silence, he said, "The Master was rather cutting to-day. I remember his once saying that we ought to come away from him, not as from a theatre but as from a surgery. To-day the surgeon used the knife, and we don't like it."

"But what good has the knife done us?" I exclaimed. "If only I could feel that the surgeon had cut out the mischief, a touch of the knife should not make me wince. But the mischief within me seems more mischievous, and my strength for good less strong, for some things that I have heard to-day. Is a Roman to say, when fighting against barbarians for the name and fame of Rome, 'These things are nothing to me'? Is Diogenes, healing mankind, his brethren, to say, 'Your diseases are nothing to me'? And that fine phrase in the Catechism, 'follow thee'—is it not really a disguised form of 'follow myself'? Does it not mean, 'follow the *logos* within me, my own reason, or my own reasonable will,' or 'follow my own peace of mind, on which my mind is bent, to the neglect of everything else'?"

"It does not mean that, for Epictetus himself, I am convinced," said Arrian. "I believe not, for him," said I; "but it has that meaning for me. His teaching does not teach—not me, at least, however it may be with others—the art of being steadfast. And what about others? Did not he himself just now admit that his *logos* was less powerful than the *pathos* of the Jews to produce steadfastness? What, by the way, is this *pathos*? Does it mean passionate and unreasonable conviction? And who on earth are these Jews that are 'dipped and chosen'?"

My friend's face brightened. Perhaps it was a relief to him to pass from theology to matter of literary fact. "I think," he replied, "that he must mean the Jewish followers of Christus— the Christians, about whom we were lately talking." "Then why," said I, "does not he call them Christians?" "I do not know," replied Arrian, "He has never mentioned either Christians or Christus in my hearing; but he has, in one lecture at all events, used the term 'Galilæans' to mean the Christians. And I feel sure that he means them here, because the other Jews do not practise baptism, except for proselytes, whereas the Christians are all baptized." "But," said I, "he does not call them 'baptized.' He calls them 'dipped'." "That is his brief allusive way," said Arrian. "You know that we provincials, and sometimes even Athenians too, speak of *dipping* the hair, or, if I may invent the word, *bapting* it, where the literary people speak of *blacking* or *dyeing* it. That is just what our Master means. These Christians are not merely *baptized*; they are *bapted*. That is to say, they are permanently and unalterably stained, or dyed in grain. They are. We are not. That is his meaning. Afterwards, as you noticed, he dropped into the regular word '*baptism*,' and spoke of us as *sham-baptists*."

"But he also called them *chosen*," said I, "—that is to say, if he meant *chosen*, and not *caught* or *convicted*." Arrian smiled. "You have hit the mark without knowing it," said he. "I noticed the word and took it down. It is another of his jibes! These Christians actually call themselves '*elect*' or '*chosen*.' I heard all about it in Bithynia. They profess to have been 'called' by Christus. Then, if they obey this 'calling,' and remain steadfast, following Christus, they are said to be '*chosen*' or '*elect*.' But our Master believes this '*calling*' and '*choosing*' to be moonshine, and these Christian Jews to be the victims of a mere delusion, *caught* by error. So he uses a word that might mean '*chosen*' but might mean also '*caught*.' They think themselves the former. He thinks them the latter."

I hardly know why I refrained from telling my friend what Scaurus had told me about the probability that Epictetus had borrowed from the Christians. Partly it was, I think, because it was too long a story to begin just then; and I thought I might shock Arrian and not do Scaurus justice. Partly, I was curious to question Arrian further. So after a short silence, during which my friend seemed lost in thought, I said to him, "You know more about the Christians than I do. Do you think Epictetus knows much about them? And what precisely does he mean by '*feeling*,' when he speaks of 'taking up the *feeling* of the dipped'?"

"As for your first question," said Arrian, "I am inclined to think that he knows a great deal about them. How could it be otherwise with a young slave in Rome under Nero, when all the world knew how the Christians were used to light the Emperor's gardens? Moreover his contrast between the Jew and the Greek seemed to me to come forth as though it had been some time in his mind, though it had not broken out till to-day. He spoke with the bitterness of a conviction of long standing. If—contrary to his own rules—he could be 'troubled,' I should say our Master felt a real 'trouble' in being forced to confess that the Jew is above the Greek in steadfastness and constancy. As to your second question, I think he means that, whereas Greeks attain to wisdom through the reason (or *logos*) these Jews follow their God, or Christus, through what we Greeks call emotion or affection (*i.e. pathos*). And I am half disposed to think that this word *pathos* was used by him on the other occasion when he spoke of the Christian Jews as Galilæans." "Could you quote it?" said I. "No, not accurately," said Arrian, "it is rather long, and has difficulties. I should prefer you to have it exactly. Come into my rooms. I am going out on business, so that we cannot talk about it at present. But you shall copy it down."

So I went in to copy it down. Arrian left me after finding the place for me in his notes. "You will see," he said, "that the Galilæans are there described as being made intrepid '*by habit*.' Well, that is certainly how I took the words down. But I am inclined to think it might have been '*by feeling*'— which seems to me to make better sense. But read the whole context and judge for yourself. The two phrases are easily confused. Now I leave you to your copying. *Prosit!* More about this, to-morrow."

CHAPTER VI

PAUL ON THE LOVE OF CHRIST

THE lecture from which I was transcribing was on "fearlessness." What, it asked, makes a tyrant terrible? The answer was, "his armed guards." A child, or madman, not knowing what guards and weapons mean, would not fear him. Men fear because they love life, and a tyrant can take life. Men also love wealth, wife, children. These things, too, a tyrant can take; so men fear him. But a madman, caring for none of these things, and ready to throw them away as a child might throw a handful of sand—a madman does not fear. Now came the words about "custom" and "Galilæans" to which Arrian had called my attention: " Well, then, is not this astonishing? Madness can now and then make a man thus fearless! *Custom can make the Galilæans fearless!* Yet—strange to say—reason and demonstration cannot make anyone understand that God has made all that is in the world, and has made the world itself, in its entirety, absolutely complete in itself and unimpeded in its motions, and has also made its separate parts individually for the use of all the parts collectively!"

The context made me see the force of Arrian's remark. Epictetus appeared to be mentioning three influences under which men might resist the threats and tortures of a tyrant. In the first place was the "madness" of a lunatic. In the third place was the "logic," or demonstration, of philosophy. In the second place, it would make good sense to suppose that Epictetus meant "feeling," or "passionate enthusiasm." This passage would then accord with the one mentioned above. Both

passages would then affirm that the Christian Jews or
Galilæans can do under the influence of "feeling" what the
Greek Philosophers, or "lovers of wisdom," cannot do with all
the aid of reason (or "logos"). "Custom" would not make
good sense unless the "Galilæans," or Christians, had made a
"custom" of hardening their bodies by severe asceticism. This
(I had gathered from Arrian) was not the fact. In any case, it
seemed clear that Epictetus was here again contrasting some
kind of Jew with the Greek to the disadvantage of the latter.

Curiosity led me to read on a little further. The text dealt
with Man's place in the Cosmos, or Universe, as follows: "All
the other parts of the Cosmos except man are far removed from
the power of intelligently following its administration. But
the living being that is endowed with *logos*, or reason, has
therein a kind of ladder by which he may reason the way up to
all these things. Thus he, and he alone, can understand that
he is a part, and what kind of part, and that it is right and fit
that the parts should yield to the whole." This reminded me
of the saying I have quoted above, "Will you not make a
contribution of your leg to the Universe?" I think he meant
"Will you not offer up your lameness, as a decreed part of the
whole system of things, and as a sacrifice from you to the
Supreme?"

This reasonable part of the Cosmos, this "living being that
is endowed with *logos*," Epictetus declared to be "*by nature*
noble, magnanimous, and free." Consequently, said he, it
discerns that, of the things around it, some are at its disposal,
while others are not; and that, if it will learn to find its profit
and its good in the former class, it will be perfectly free and
happy, "being thankful always for all things to God."

This puzzled me not a little. I could not understand how
Epictetus explained the means by which these "noble, magnanimous, and free" creatures, created so "*by nature*," had
degenerated into the weaklings, fools, profligates, and oppressors,
upon whom he was constantly pouring scorn. Was not each
man a "part" of the Cosmos? Was not the Cosmos "perfect
and exempt from all disorder or impediment in any of its
motions"? Did not each "part" in it—and consequently

Chapter 6] ON THE LOVE OF CHRIST

man—partake in this perfection and exemption, being "made for the service of the whole"? What cause did Epictetus find for the folly, vice, and injustice that he so often satirised and condemned as "subject to the wrath of God"? Man was a compound of "clay" and "logos." The fault could not lie in the "logos." Was it, after all, the mere "clay" that caused all this mischief? And then, lost in thought, turning over the loose sheets of Arrian's notes, one after the other, I came again on the passage I have quoted above from Epictetus, "If I could have, I would have"—laying the fault, as it seemed, upon the "clay." I could not help asking, "If God 'could' not remedy it, how much less 'could' I, being 'clay,' remedy myself, 'clay'?"

Musing on these things I returned to my rooms, and was sitting down to write to Scaurus, when my servant entered with a parcel, from Rome, he said, forwarded by Sosia our bookseller. It contained the books I had ordered from Flaccus, with a letter from him, describing in detail the pains he had taken in having some of the rolls of Chrysippus and Cleanthes transcribed and ornamented, and saying that in addition to the "curious little volume containing the epistles of Paulus," which, as I no doubt anticipated, were "not in the choicest Greek," he had forwarded an epistle to the Hebrews. "This," he said, "does not include in the commencement the usual mention of Paulus's name, and it is not in his style. But I understand that it originated from the school of Paulus."

There was more to the same effect, for Flaccus and I were on very friendly terms; and he was a good deal more than a mere seller of books. But I passed over it, for I was in haste to open the parcel. At the top were the copies of Cleanthes, Chrysippus, and others, in Flaccus's best style. At the bottom of all were two rolls of flimsy papyrus. The larger and shabbier of the two fell to the ground open, and as I took it up, my eye lit on the following passage:—"*Who shall separate us from the love of Christ? Shall tribulation or suffering or persecution or hunger or nakedness or peril or the sword? As it is written:*
  '*For thy sake are we done to death all the day long:*
  We were accounted as sheep of the shambles.'

Nay, in all these things we are more than conquerors through Him that loved us. For I am persuaded that neither death, nor life, nor angels, nor sovereignties, nor things present, nor things to come, nor powers, nor height, nor depth, nor anything in all creation, will be able to separate us from that love of God which is in Christ Jesus our Lord."

"This, at all events," said I, "Scaurus cannot say that Epictetus has borrowed from Paul. Never have I heard Epictetus mention the word 'love'; and here, in this one short passage, Paul uses it twice!" My next thought was that Scaurus was quite right in his estimate of Paul's style. It was indeed terse, intense, fervid, strangely stimulating and constraining. "There is no lack of *pathos*," I said, "Let us now test the *logos*." So I sat down to study the passage, trying to puzzle out the meaning of the separate words and phrases.

"*The love of Christ.*" Well, Christus was their leader. The Christians still loved him, and clung to his memory. That was intelligible. But "that love of God which was in Christ" perplexed me. I read the whole passage over again. Gradually I began to see that the passage implied the Epictetian ideal—according to Scaurus, not Epictetian but Pauline or Christian—of a Son of God standing fearless and erect in the face of enemies, tyrants, oppression, death. But it also suggested invisible enemies—"angels and sovereignties" that seemed to be against the sons of God. And still I could not make out the expression, "that love of God which is in Christ Jesus."

So I turned back to the words at the bottom of the preceding column:—"*If God is for us, who is against us? He that spared not His own Son but delivered him up for us all, how shall He not also, with him, freely give us all things? It is God that maketh and calleth us righteous: who is he that shall condemn? It is Christ Jesus that died—or rather that was raised from the dead, who is on the right hand of God, who also maketh intercession for us.*" And so, coming to the end of the column, I looked on again to the words with which I had begun, "*Who shall separate us from the love of Christ?*"

Now I could understand. "This," said I, "is a great battle. There are sovereignties of evil against the good. The Son of

Chapter 6] ON THE LOVE OF CHRIST

the good God is supposed to devote himself to death, fighting against the hosts of evil. Or rather the Father sends him into the battle and he goes willingly. This Christus of the Galilæans is regarded by them as we Romans might think of one of the Decii plunging into the ranks of the enemy and devoting himself to death for the salvation of Rome. Philosophers might ask inconvenient questions about the nature of the God to whom the brave man devotes himself—whether it is Pluto, or Zeus, or Nemesis, or Fate. No philosopher, perhaps, would approve of this theory. But, in practice, the bravery stirs the spirits of those who believe it. Even if the sacrifice is discreditable to the Gods accepting it, it is creditable to the man making it."

Turning back still further, I found that Paul imagined the Cosmos—or "creation" as he called it—to have gone wrong. He did not explain how. Nor did he prove it. He assumed it, looking forward, however, to a time when the wrong would be made right, and even more right than if it had never gone wrong: *"For I reckon that the sufferings of this present season are not fit to be spoken of in comparison of the glory that is destined to be revealed and to extend to us. For the earnest expectation of the creation waiteth intently for the revealing of the sons of God. For the creation was made subject to change, decay, corruption—not willingly but for the sake of Him that made it thus subject—in hope, and for hope: because even this very creation, now corrupt, shall be made free from the slavery of corruption and brought into the freedom of the glory of the children of God. For we know that the whole of creation groaneth together and travaileth together—up to this present time."*

This struck me as a very different message from that of Epictetus about Zeus. Both Paul and Epictetus seemed to agree as regards the past, that certain things had happened that were not pleasing to God, taken by themselves. But whereas the Greek said about God, "He would have, if He could have; but He could not," the Jew seemed to say, "He can, and He will. Only wait and see. It will turn out to have been for the best."

Reading on, I found something corresponding to Epictetus's doctrine of the indwelling Logos, namely, that each of us has in himself a fragment of the Logos of God,—but Paul called it Spirit—in virtue of which we may claim kinship with Him, being indeed God's children. Epictetus, however, never said that we were to pray to our Father for help. He seemed to think that each must derive his help from such portion of the Logos as each possessed. "Keep," he said, "that which is your own," "Take from yourselves your help," "Within each man is ruin and help," "Seek and ye shall find within you," or words to that effect. Paul's doctrine was different, teaching that we do not at present possess salvation and help to their full extent, but that we must look forward in hope: "*And not only so, but we ourselves also, though possessing the firstfruits of the Spirit—we ourselves also, I say, groan within ourselves, waiting earnestly for the adoption, namely, the ransoming and deliverance of our body*"—as though a time would come when that very same clay, which (according to Epictetus) the Creator would have wished to make immortal but could not, would be transmuted and transported in some way out of the region of flesh into the region of the spirit.

Moreover, besides looking onward in hope, we must also (Paul said) look upward for help. Epictetus, too, as I have said above, sometimes spoke of looking "upward," and of the Cynic stretching up his hands to God. That, however, was not in prayer but in praise.

Epictetus never used the word "prayer" in my hearing except of foolish, idle, or selfish prayers. But Paul represented the Logos, or rather the Spirit, within us, as an emotional, not a merely reasonable power. "It searcheth all things, yea, even the deep things of God," he said to the Corinthians; and by it (so he told the Romans in the passage I was just now quoting) the children express to the Father, and the Father receives from the children, their wants and aspirations: "*For by hope were we saved. But hope that is seen is not hope. For who hopeth for that which he seeth? But if we hope for that which we fail to see, then in patient endurance we earnestly wait for it. And in the same way the Spirit also taketh part with our*

Chapter 6]   ON THE LOVE OF CHRIST   71

weakness. For as to what we should pray for, according to our needs, we do not know. But the Spirit itself maketh representation in our behalf in sighings beyond speech. Now He that searcheth the hearts knoweth what is the mind and temper of the Spirit, because, being in union and accord with God, it maketh representation in behalf of the saints."

This passage I only vaguely understood. For I started with the preconception that the spirit or breath or wind, must be only another metaphor—like "word"—to describe a "fragment" of God (as Epictetus called the Logos in man). I did not as yet understand that this Spirit might be regarded as, at one and the same moment, in heaven with God and on earth with men, representing the love and will of God to man below, and the love and prayers of man to God above. Still I perceived that in some way it was connected with the Christian Christ; and that the Father and the Spirit and Christ were in some permanent relation to each other and to man, by which relation man and God were drawn together. And this led me back again to the words, "Who shall separate us from the love of Christ?" and "We are more than conquerors through Him that loved us."

Comparing this "love" with the friendship felt by the Epictetian Diogenes for the whole human race, I found the latter thin and poor. The Greek philosopher, being a "friend" of the Father of Gods and men, seemed to me to be friendly to men in the region (so to speak) of the Logos, "because"—I was disposed to add—"the Logos within him, in a 'logical' way, commanded him to be friendly to them, for consistency's sake, as being 'logically' akin to him." Perhaps some reaction against the constant inculcation of loyalty to the Logos during the last few weeks led me to be a little unfair to the Epictetian ideal. But, fair or unfair, these were my thoughts at the moment, while I was turning over the letters addressed by this wandering Jewish Diogenes to some of the principal cities of Greece and Asia, coming every now and then on such sentences as these: "*I have strength for all things in Him that giveth me inward power*": "*Being made powerful with all power, in accordance with the might of His glory, so that we rejoice in* endurance and longsuffering, being thankful to the Father": "*Be ye made powerful in the Lord and in the might of His strength.*" Here I noted that he did not say (as Epictetus did) "take power from yourselves." Moreover Paul added "*Put on the panoply of God.*" Then I turned back again to the Roman and Corinthian letters; and still the same thoughts and phrases met me, about "*power*" in various contexts, such as "*demonstration of Spirit and power,*" and "*abounding in hope through the power of the Holy Spirit.*" "*Love,*" too, was represented as an irresistible power. "*The love of Christ constraineth us,*" he said. And then he added, "*One died for all*" and "*He died for all, that the living should be living no longer to themselves, but to Him that for their sake died and was raised up from death.*"

There was a great deal in this Roman letter that was almost total darkness to me at first. The references to Abraham—and, still more, those to Adam, coming abruptly in the phrases, "death reigned from Adam," and "the transgression of Adam" —perplexed me a great deal till I perceived that the Jews fixed their hopes on God's promise to their forefather Abraham, just as Romans—if they believed Virgil—might fix theirs on the forefather of the Julian race. As Æneas was the divine son of Anchises, so Isaac, by promise, was the divinely given son of Abraham. Paul, I thought, might draw a parallel between our Æneas and his Isaac, as though both were receivers of divine promises of empire extending over all the nations of the earth. At this Jewish fancy (so I called it) I remember smiling at the time, and quoting Virgil from a Jew's point of view:

"Tantæ molis erat *Judæam* condere gentem."

But I soon perceived, not only that Paul was in serious earnest, quite as much as Virgil, but also that his scheme, or dream, of universal empire for the seed of Abraham was compatible with the fact of universal empire for the seed of Anchises. Rome, the new Troy, claimed dominion over nothing but men's bodies. The new Jerusalem claimed it over men's souls.

I did not fully take all this into my mind till I had read the story of Abraham and Isaac in the scriptures, as I shall describe later on. But, with Virgil's help, and Roman traditions, I partially understood it even now; and I remember asking myself, "If Virgil were now alive, would he be as sanguine as this Jew? Is not Rome on the wane? Ever since the Emperor cried to Varus, 'Give me back my legions!' have we not had qualms of fear lest we should be beaten back by the barbarians? Do not even the wisest of our rulers say, 'Let us draw the line here. Let us conquer no more'? But this Jew sets no limits to his conquests. His projects may be mad. But at least he has some basis of fact for them. If he has conquered so far, why not further?"

As to "the transgression of Adam," I remained longer in the dark. But I perceived from other passages in the epistles (and from the Jewish scriptures soon afterwards) that the story of Adam and Eve resembled some versions that I had read of the story of Epimetheus and Pandora, who caused sins and pains to come into the world, but "hope" came with them. Adam and Eve did the same. But Paul believed that the "hope" sprang from a promise of a higher and nobler life than would have been possible if Adam and Eve had never gone wrong. I took this for a mere legend, but a legend that might represent the will of Zeus—namely, that man should not stand still, but that he should go on growing, from age to age, in righteousness, which, as Plato says, is the attribute of man that makes him most like God.

Thus I was led on to higher and higher inferences about Paul's "power." First, it was real power, attested by facts—facts visible in great cities of Europe and Asia. In the next place, this power was based on faith and hope. Lastly, this faith and this hope—although they extended to everything in heaven and earth (since everything was to be bettered, purified, drawn onward or upward to what Plato might call its *idea* in God, that is, its perfection)—were themselves based on Christ, as having once died, but now being alive for ever in heaven.

But not only in heaven. For Paul seemed to think of Christ as also still perpetually present with, and in, his disciples on earth. Socrates in the Phædo says "As soon as I have drunk this poison I shall be no longer remaining among you, but shall be off at once to the isles of the blessed." But

Paul spoke of Christ's love, and spirit, and of Christ himself, as still remaining amongst his followers. I knew that the common people think of Hercules as descending from heaven now and then to do a man a good turn; and at this I had always been disposed to laugh. But Paul's view of Christ as being always in heaven, and yet also always on earth, among, or in the hearts of, those who loved him—this seemed to me more noble and more credible; though I did not believe it.

Now I was to be led a step further. For while I was repeating Paul's words "one died for all," and again, "one died," it occurred to me "Yes, but he does not say *how* he died. Is he ashamed to speak of the shamefulness of the death, the slave's death, death upon the cross?" So I looked through the Roman letter, right to the end, and I could find no mention of the "cross" or of "crucifying." But in the very next column, where the first Corinthian letter began, I found this passage: "*Christ sent me not to baptize but to preach the Gospel, not in wisdom of 'logos' (i.e. word), lest the cross of Christ should be emptied of its power. For as to the 'logos' of the cross, to those indeed who are going the way of destruction, it is folly: but to us, who are going the way of salvation, it is the power of God. For it is written:*

'*I will destroy the wisdom of the wise*

And the subtlety of the subtle will I bring to naught.'

Where is the 'wise'? Where is the learned writer? Where is the 'subtle' discusser and disputer of this present age?"

Then followed some very difficult words: "*Hath not God made foolish the wisdom of the Cosmos? For since, in the wisdom of God, the Cosmos, through that wisdom, recognised not God, God decreed through the foolishness of the proclamation of the gospel to save them that go the way of belief: for indeed Jews ask for signs and Greeks seek after wisdom, but we proclaim Christ crucified; to the Jews, a stumbling block; to the other nations, a folly; but, to the called and summoned—Christ the power of God and the wisdom of God.*"

I have translated this literally so as to leave it as obscure to the reader as it was to me when I first read it. Even when I had read it over two or three times, there was a great deal that

Chapter 6]   ON THE LOVE OF CHRIST   75

I could not understand. But it appeared to me to be ironical. It suggested that the "logos" of God may be different from the "logos" of men, or at all events, the "logos" of Greek philosophers. I had for some time been drawing near to a belief that "logos" might include feeling as well as reason. But this strange contrast between the unwise "wisdom of logos" and the wise "logos of the cross" came upon me as (possibly) a new revelation. As for the saying "the Greeks seek wisdom," it reminded me how Epictetus used to deride the man of mere logic, words without deeds, the futile spinner of syllogisms. "Epictetus," I said to myself, "would agree with this accusation." But then I reflected that Paul would perhaps class Epictetus himself among these futile Greeks; and had not my Master himself confessed that the Jew, by mere force of "pathos," outclassed the Greek in resolution and steadfastness, although the latter was backed by "logos"? The conclusion fell upon me, like a blow, "Here is Paul boasting as a conqueror what my Master confesses as a man conquered! Both agree that the 'feeling' of the Jew is more powerful in producing courage than the 'reasonableness' of the Greek!"

I did not like this turn of things. But I was intensely interested in it; and it quite decided me to continue the investigation. The question turned on "logos" and I quoted to myself Plato's precept, "Follow the logos." Epictetus made much of "logos." Well, I would "follow the 'logos,'" in its fullest sense, and would try to find out whether it did, or did not, indicate that "feeling," as well as "reason," may help us towards the knowledge of God. Dawn was appearing when I rolled up the little volume and placed it in my cabinet by the side of Scaurus's sealed note with WORDS OF CHRISTUS on it. That reminded me of my old friend. What would he think of all this?

I sat down at once and wrote to him that I had not opened his note. If I ever did, it would be, I said, because I accepted his verdict. Epictetus really did seem to have borrowed from Paul. The subject was very interesting to me from a historical as well as a literary point of view; and I hoped he would not think it waste of time if I investigated it a little further. At the same time, I sent a note to Flaccus. Æmilius Scaurus, I said, had sent me some "words of Christus" extracted from Christian books, and I desired to receive the books themselves. As for the "scriptures" from which Paul so frequently quoted in their Greek form, I knew that I should have no difficulty in procuring copies of all or most of them from Sosia. This I resolved to do on the morrow, or rather in the day that was now dawning. It was not a lecture-day. Even if it had been, in the mood in which I then was, I should have thought a lecture or two might be profitably missed.

CHAPTER VII

DAVID AND MOSES

THE Greek translation of the Scriptures shewn me by Sosia was in several volumes of various sizes and in various conditions. Unrolling the one that shewed most signs of use, I found that, although it was in prose, it was a translation of Hebrew poems, mostly very short, and of a lyrical character. One of them had in its title the name of "David," which I had met with in Paul's letter to the Romans. Sosia told me that he was the greatest of the ancient kings of the Jews. Ordering the other volumes to be sent to my rooms, I took this back with me, and began to read it immediately, beginning with the poem on which I had chanced in the shop.

It was a prayer for purification from sin: "Pity me, O God, according to thy great pity, and according to the multitude of thy compassions blot out my transgression. Cleanse me still more from my crime, and purify me from my sin." So far, the poem was intelligible to me. I was familiar with the religious rites of cleansing from blood-guiltiness—mentioned in connexion with Orestes and many others by the Greek poets and recognised in various forms all over the world. So I said, "This king has committed homicide. He has been purified with lustral rites and sacrifices. But he needs some further rites: 'Cleanse me still more,' he says. The poem will tell me, I suppose, what more he needs."

After adding some words to the effect that the transgression was against God, against God alone, the king continued, "For behold, in transgressions was I created at birth, and in sins did my mother conceive me. For behold, thou hast ever loved truth; thou hast shewn unto me the hidden secrets of thy wisdom. Thou wilt sprinkle me with hyssop and I shall be purified; thou wilt wash me and I shall be whiter than snow." Here I was at a stand. It seemed to me a great and sudden descent to a depth of superstition, to suppose that this particular additional rite of "cleansing with hyssop" could satisfy the king's conscience. Moreover I thought that "wisdom" must mean the wisdom of the Greeks. It was not till afterwards that I discovered how great a gulf separates our syllogistic or rhetorical or logical "wisdom" from that of the Jews—which means "knowledge of the righteousness of the Creator based upon reverence." Thence comes their saying, "Reverence for God is the beginning of *wisdom*."

These two misunderstandings almost led me to put down the book in disgust. But the passionateness of the king's prayer made me read its opening words once again. Then I felt sure I must have done him injustice. So I read on. Presently I came to the words, "Create in me a clean heart, O God, and renew a right spirit within me. Cast me not away from thy countenance, and take not thy holy spirit from me." These made me ashamed of having taken "hyssop" literally. I saw now that it was just as much metaphorical as "whiter than snow," and that it meant a deep and inward purification—of the heart, not of the body. Still more was I ashamed when I came to the words, "If thou hadst delight in sacrifice I would have given it to thee, but thou wilt take no pleasure in whole burnt-offerings. The sacrifice for God is a broken spirit. A broken and contrite heart God will not despise."

This was all new and strange doctrine to me. The graceful lines of Horace about the efficacy of the simplest sacrifice—of meal and salt—from the hand of an innocent country girl, and about its superiority to the proffered bribe of a hecatomb from a man of guilt, these I knew by heart; but they did not touch the present question, which was as to how the man of guilt could receive purification, without a hecatomb, without the blood of bulls and goats. And the question went even beyond that. For the king said that he had been "in sins" even from the beginning, even before birth. Did he speak of himself alone, or of himself as the type of erring mankind? I thought the latter. He seemed to me to say, "Man is from the first an animal, born to follow appetite. In part (no doubt) he is a divine being, born to follow the divine will; but in part he is an animal, born to follow animal propensity." So far this agreed with Epictetus's doctrine about the Beast. The Beast, at the beginning, tyrannizes over the divine Man, so that the human being may be said to be in sin—and indeed is in sin, as soon as he becomes conscious of the tyranny within him. "No lustral rites, no blood of bulls and goats," the king seemed to say, "can purify this human heart of mine now that it has been tainted and corrupted by submitting to the Beast within me. A moment ago, my prayer was 'Purge me with hyssop,' but now it is 'Destroy me and create me anew,' 'Take away my old heart and give me a new heart.'"

These last words were quite contrary to the doctrine of Epictetus, who taught us that we are to receive strength and righteousness from that which is within our own hearts. And, thought I, is not the king's prayer superstitious? The witches in Rome suppose they can draw down the moon by incantations. This king David in Judæa supposes he can draw down "a clean heart" and "a right spirit" by passionate invocation to the God of the Jews! Are not the two superstitions parallel? Would not Epictetus say so? Would not all the Cynics say so? I thought they would: and, as I was rolling up the little book, I said, "It is a fine and passionate poem, but the prayer is not one for a philosopher." Then, however, it occurred to me that there was a true and a deep philosophy—though I knew not of what school—in the doctrine that the true and purifying sacrifice for guilt is a penitent heart. That set me pondering the whole matter again and reflecting on some of the things in my own life of which I was most ashamed, things that I would have given much to forget, and a great deal more to undo. In the end, I found myself thinking—not saying, but thinking of it as a possible prayer—"In me, in me, too, create a clean heart, O thou God of forgiveness!" It might not be a prayer for philosophers, but I could not help feeling that it might be a good prayer for me.

While I was placing my new volume by the side of Paul's epistles it occurred to me that the words I had just been reading might throw some light on a passage in the epistle to the Romans at which I had glanced last night. Then I could make nothing of it. Now I read it again: "I know that in me, that is, in my flesh, there dwelleth no good thing. To will [that which is good] is present with me, but to do is not present. I will to do good and I do it not. I will not to do evil, and I do it." This now seemed to me a truer description of the state of things (within me at all events) than the view mostly presented to us in our lecture-room. Epictetus often talked as though we had merely to will, and then what we willed—at least so far as concerns the mind and the things in the mind's province—would at once come to pass. True, he did not always say this. Sometimes he insisted on the need of training or practice, and then he likened the Cynic to an athlete preparing for the Olympian games. But it seemed to me that he habitually underrated the difficulty of conforming the human to the divine will: and he never—never even once, as far as I know—recognised the need or efficacy of repentant sorrow.

My immediate conclusion was that, although it was not for me to decide between the "feeling" of the Jews and the "reason" of the Greeks in general, yet one thing was certain—I had a good deal to learn from the former. So I welcomed the arrival of Sosia's servant bringing the rest of my new books. A good many of them I unrolled and cursorily inspected at once. Both from their number, and from the variety of their subjects, it was clear that I should only be able to study a few. I resolved to confine myself to such parts as bore on Paul's epistles, and to dispense with lectures for a day or two. Then it occurred to me that Arrian, who had proposed to resume to-day our conversation on the Jews and Galilæans, might come in at any moment. I put away the Jewish books and went to his lodging, thinking that I could perhaps tell my friend of my new studies in order to explain to him my non-attendance at lecture. Instead of Arrian, however, I found a note informing me that he had been obliged to go suddenly to

Corinth (in connexion with some business of his father's) but hoped to return before long.

This saved explanation; and I spent several days (during his prolonged absence) in studying my new volumes. They led me into a maze—or rather, maze after maze—of bewildering novelties. Sosia had told me that my first volume, containing five books, was called by the Jews "the Law." But it included pedigrees, poems, prophecies, histories of nations, and stories of private persons. The legal portion of it was largely devoted to details about feasts and purificatory sacrifices—the very things that David appeared to call needless. However, when I came to look into the Law more closely, I found that its fundamental enactments were humane and gentle—so much so as to give me the impression of being unpractical. It enjoined on the Jews kindness to strangers as well as to citizens. While retaining capital punishment, it prohibited torture. At least I took that to be a fair inference from the fact that it even forbade the infliction of more than forty blows with the scourge, on the ground that a "brother"—that was the word—must not be so far degraded as to become "vile" in the eyes of his fellow-citizens. It also placed some limitations on the right of masters to punish slaves, even when the latter were foreigners.

Having been accustomed to regard the Jews as unique for their moroseness and unneighbourliness I was all the more astonished at these things. It occurred to me then, as it does sometimes now, that the Law was almost too humane to have been ever fully obeyed by the greater part of the people. For example, even the slaves, even the beasts of burden, were to have one day in seven as a holiday, on which all labour was forbidden. Periodic remission of debts was enacted by law! This surprised me most of all. To think that the revolutionary measure—so our Roman historians called it—for which our tribunes of the people had contended in vain under the Republic, should here be found legalised by the Law of Moses—and this, too, not as an exceptional and isolated condonation, but as a regular remission after a fixed number of years!

"How," I asked, "could the Lawgiver expect people to lend money to borrowers if the creditor knew that in the course of a few months the obligation to pay the debt would cease?" Was he blind to the most manifest tendencies of human nature? No, I found he was not blind to them. He simply said that they must be resisted: "Beware," said he, "that there be not a base thought in thine heart, saying, The seventh year, the year of release, is at hand."

This notion of forbidding an action, or abstinence from action, in a code of laws as being "base"—not as being "subject to a penalty of such a kind," or "a fine of so much," was quite new to me. I had given some time to the study of Roman law, and had always assumed that when the law says "Do this," it adds a punishment in some form or other, "Do this, or you shall suffer this or that." But here, embedded in the Law of Moses, was a law, or rather a recommendation, without penalty. And presently I found that the last of their Ten Greater Laws—if I may so call them—was of the same kind. It could not possibly be enforced—for it forbade "coveting"! Only a few days ago, before I had bought these books from Sosia, I had read in Paul's epistle to the Romans "I should not have known covetousness if the law had not said, *Thou shalt not covet*"; and these words had puzzled me a good deal. I had thought that they must refer to some "law" of a spiritual kind, such as we might call "the law of the conscience" or "the law of our higher nature," or the like. Yet I felt that this interpretation did not quite agree with the context. Now I found, to my utter astonishment, that this was the very letter of the first clause of the tenth of the Greater Laws, "Thou shalt not covet."

To crown all, I found that elsewhere the whole of the code was based by the Lawgiver on two fundamental precepts. The first was, "Thou shalt love the Lord thy God," and this love was to call forth all the powers of mind and soul and body. The second was, "Thou shalt love thy neighbour as thyself." How was either of these to be enforced? "Love," say all the poets, "is free." The Law neither prescribed nor suggested any means of enforcing these two Great Commandments of "loving." And how could "love" be at once "free," as poetry protests, and yet a part of the Law, as Moses testified? There seemed no answer to this question, unless some God could make us willing and eager to enforce the two commandments on ourselves, constraining us (so to speak) by love to love both Him and one another. "Truly," said I, "this Law of Moses is very ambitious." It seemed to aim at more than Law could accomplish. It reminded me of a sentence I had found in one of my new volumes, entitled "Proverbs," "The light of the Lord is as the breath of men; He searcheth the storehouses of the soul."

Somewhat similar was a saying imputed to Epictetus—which I had not heard from Arrian but from a fellow-student—reproving one of his disciples in these words, "Man, where are you putting it? See whether the basin is dirty!" The disciple, though an industrious scholar, was of impure life; and Epictetus meant that, if the vessel of his soul was foul, all the knowledge put into that vessel would also become foul. The moral was, "First cleanse the vessel!" So the Jewish Proverb seemed to say, "The light of the Lord must first search the storehouse of the soul: then the food taken out from the storehouse will be pure and wholesome." This brought me back to the words of David, who seemed to think that the searching and cleansing must come from God and not from man alone, "Create in me a clean heart, O God, and renew a right spirit within me!"

Comparing these two fundamental or Greatest Laws of Moses with the fundamental law of Epictetus, "Keep the things that are thine own," I thought at first that the Jew and the Greek were entirely opposed. On second thoughts, however, I perceived that in "the things that are thine own" Epictetus would include justice and kindness, and all social so-called virtues so far as they did not interfere with one's own peace of mind—for he would perhaps exclude pity, and certainly sympathy in the full sense of the term. But Epictetus thought that people could be sufficiently kind and just and virtuous without other aid than that of the "logos" *within* them. David did not, in his own case, unless that which was within him had been cleansed or renewed by a Power regarded as *outside* him, to whom he prayed as God. There seemed to me, in this difference of "within" and "outside," more than a mere difference of metaphor. But I had no time to think over the matter. For, just as I was regretting that Arrian was not with me to talk over some of these subjects, Glaucus, coming in to borrow a book, informed me that he had met my friend late in the previous night coming from the quay. I had intended to stay at home that morning. But now, finding that Glaucus was on his way to the lecture, I resolved to accompany him, expecting to meet Arrian there.

CHAPTER VIII

EPICTETUS ON SIN

WHEN we reached the lecture-room, a little late, we found it unusually crowded. My place was taken, and I could not see Arrian in his customary seat. Epictetus was in one of his discursive moods. He began with the assertion—by this time familiar to me, but somewhat distasteful now, fresh as I was from the atmosphere of the Jewish writings—that Gods and men alike seek nothing but "their own profit." As in most of his epigrams, he meant just the opposite of what he seemed to assert. He hated high-flown language as much as he loved high thought and action. Even when he mentioned "the beautiful"—on which most Greeks go off into rhapsodies—he almost always subordinated it to the "logos" or told us that we must look for it in ourselves. So here again. Man, he declared, must give up all things—property, reputation, children, wife, country, if they are incompatible with his true "profit." Then, of course, he shewed that man's "profit" is virtue, so that we need not give up these blessings unless their possession is incompatible with virtue.

What he said next was new to me. A father, losing a child in death, must not say "I have lost my child," but "I have given it back." When I say "new," I mean new in his teaching. But I had recently met something like it in my books of Hebrew poems, "The Lord hath given, the Lord hath taken away. Blessed be the name of the Lord." Later on, I heard Epictetus repeat this almost in the same form. This seemed to me not only beautiful and devout but also consistent with reasonable faith.

But I could not follow him when, in reply to the objection, "He that took away this thing from me is a villain," he said, "What does it matter to you by whom the Giver asked back the gift?" It seemed to me that a recoil from villainy, as well as delight in virtue, ought to find a place even in the calmest of mankind. No philosopher, he said, can have an "enemy," because no one can do him any harm or touch anything that really belongs to him. This was true—in a sense. Its reasonableness contrasted with the passionate poetry of the Jews, which I had found full, too full, of talk about enemies. And yet, the more I meditated on the contrast, the more this "What does it matter to you?" seemed to become a cold-blooded, unnatural, and immoral question. Surely it ought to "matter" to us a great deal whether we suffered loss from some neighbour's forgetfulness or from some enemy's premeditated and malignant treachery. He went on in the same chilling style. "Desire," said he, "about that which is happening, that it shall happen. Then you will have a stream of constant peace." I seemed to see Priam "desiring that which was happening" when he saw Troy burned and the women ravished! His son, Polites, was being butchered by Pyrrhus before his eyes, and the old king was standing by, placidly enjoying "a stream of constant peace"!

Then Epictetus said, "An uneducated man blames others for his own evils. A beginner blames himself. An educated man blames neither others nor himself." After this, he introduced what he called the law laid down by God. "Right convictions make the will and purpose good. Crooked and perverse convictions make the will bad. This law," he said, "God has laid down, and He says to each of us, 'If you will have anything that is good, take it from yourself'." Then came another mention of the law—"the divine law" he now called it. It was connected with "right convictions," as to which he asked "What are these?" His reply was, "They are such as a man ought to meditate on all the day long. We must have such a conviction as will prevent us from attaching our feelings to anything that is other than our own—whether companion, or place, or bodily exercise, or even the body itself.

We must remember the law and have it always before our eyes."

This phrase, "meditate all the day long," reminded me of some words of David, which I had been reading the day before, "Oh how I love thy law! It is my meditation all the day." Other Hebrew expressions also came into my mind concerning the sweetness and fragrance of the Lord's commandment, how the poet "opened his mouth and drew in his breath" to taste its delight. These I could understand, when they applied to a law of love, a law of the emotions, a "feeling." But I wondered what Epictetus could produce for us of a nature to kindle such enthusiasm. He continued, "And what is the divine law? It is this. First, Keep the things that are your own. Secondly, Do not claim things not your own; use them, if given; do not desire them, if not given. Thirdly, When anything is being taken from you, give it up at once in a detached spirit, and with gratitude for the time during which one has used it."

"Keep the things that are your own!"—This he placed first, and on this he laid most emphasis, dwelling on each syllable. I fancied that he knew he was disappointing us and almost took pleasure in it as though he were administering to us a wholesome but bitter medicine. "You find this sour," he seemed to say: "Sour or not, it is the truth, the only solid and safe truth. It is not the dream of a poet, or the scheme of a student. It is the plan of a man of business, practicable for all—for slaves as well as free men, for individuals in a desert as well as for communities in a city. 'Love your neighbour'— that is expecting too much. 'Do not covet what is your neighbour's'—that is expecting too little. 'Keep that which belongs to you!' There you have a rule that makes you independent of all neighbours." I was miserably disappointed; yet I could not help respecting and admiring our Master's unflinching frankness, his determination to force us to face the austere truth, and his contempt for anything that seemed incapable of being put into practice at all times and in all circumstances.

He spoke next of "sin" or "error." Some of his language strangely resembled Paul's, but with great differences. He made mention of a "conflict," but he seemed mostly to mean "a conflicting state of things," "logical contradiction," or inconsistency. It might be called self-contradiction, taken as including actions, and not words alone. He also used the very same phrase as Paul's "that which he willeth he doeth not," but not in the same way, as may be seen from the following extract which I took down exactly: "Every error includes self-contradiction. For since the person erring does not wish to err but to go straight, it is clear that what he wills to do he does not do.... Now every soul endowed with 'logos' by nature is disposed to dislike self-contradiction. As long as a man has not followed up the facts and perceived that he is in a state of self-contradiction, he is in no way prevented from doing things that are self-contradictory; but, when he has followed them up, he must necessarily revolt from the self-contradiction.... Here then comes in the need of the teacher skilled in 'logos'...but the teacher needs also power to refute what is wrong and to stimulate the pupil to what is right. This teacher will give the erring man a glimpse into the self-contradiction in which he errs, and will make it clear to him *that he is not doing that which he wills to do and that he is doing that which he wills not to do.* As soon as this is made clear to the person in error, he will, of himself and of his own accord, depart from his error."

Then he supposed a case where a man had relapsed from philosophy into a profligate and shameless life. And first he tried to shew the offender how much he had lost in losing modesty and decency and true manliness. "There was a time," he said, "when you counted this as the only loss worth mentioning." Next, he shewed each of us how to regain what we had lost. "It is you yourself," he exclaimed, "you yourself, no other whom you have to blame. Fight against yourself! Tear yourself away to seemliness, decency, and freedom."

Lastly, he appealed—as I had never heard him do before—to the feelings of loyalty and affection that we might entertain for himself. I thought he must be recalling his old days in Rome, when he, a boy and a slave, in the house of Epaphroditus, might be exposed to the temptations and coercions to which such slaves were subject; and he asked his pupils to imagine their feelings if someone came to them reporting that their Master, Epictetus, had been forced to succumb.

"If," said he, very slowly and deliberately, with emphasis on each syllable, "if someone were to come and tell you that a certain man was compelling *me*"—here he hurried onward— "to lead the sort of life that you are now leading, to wear the sort of dress that you wear, to perfume myself as you perfume yourself, would you not go off straightway and lay violent hands on the man that was thus abusing me? Rescue yourself, then, as you would have rescued me. You need not kill anyone, strike anyone, go anywhere. Talk to yourself! Persuade (who else should do it better?)—persuade yourself."

Never, in my experience, had Epictetus more nearly fulfilled the promise made in his behalf by Arrian—that he would always make his hearers feel, for the moment, precisely what he wished them to feel. There were two or three in the class notorious for their profligacy; but the appeal went home to others as well, conscious of minor derelictions. "Persuade yourself!" There was no need of it. We were all, to a man, already persuaded. Infants and babies though we were, we could all stand up and walk—for the moment. He proceeded in the same spirit-stirring tone, as though—now that we had all resolved to go on this arduous journey with him as a guide— he would go first and shew us how to push our way through the forest.

"First of all," said he, "give sentence against the present state of things." He did not say "*against yourselves.*" That would have been too discouraging. We were to condemn "*the present state of things*"; that is, our present self. "In the next place," he continued, "do not give up hope of yourself. Do not behave like the poor-spirited creatures who, because of one defeat, give themselves up altogether and let themselves be carried downward by the stream. Take a lesson from the wrestling-ring. That young fellow yonder has had a fall. 'Get up,' says the trainer, 'Wrestle again, and go on till you get your full strength.' Act you in the same spirit. For, mark you, there is nothing more pliable than the human soul. You must *will*. Then the thing is done, and the crooked is made straight. On the other hand, go to sleep; and then all is ruined. From your own heart comes either your destruction or your help."

He concluded with a word of warning. Perhaps some of us might appeal to his own *dictum* about seeking our own "profit," as being the only right and wise course. He met it as follows: "After this, do you say 'What good shall I get by it?' What greater 'good' do you look for than this? Whereas you once were shameless, you will now have received again the faculty of an honourable shame. From the orgies of vice you will have passed into the ranks of virtue. Formerly faithless and licentious, you will now be faithful and temperate. If you seek any other objects better than these, go on doing still the things you are doing now. Not even a God can any longer save you."

CHAPTER IX

ARRIAN'S DEPARTURE

WHEN we came out from the crowded room, as Arrian was nowhere to be seen, I went at once to his lodging. To my surprise, he was busy packing, amid books and papers, and a student's other belongings. "Thanks, many thanks," he said, "for this timely visit. This is my last day in Nicopolis. I was just coming round to wish you good-bye. You know I had to go to Corinth. Well, when I got there, I found a letter from my father bidding me wait a few days for further news from him; and on the fourth day came a message that I was to conclude my studies at once and return to Bithynia, as his health had quite given way and his affairs required all my attention. I had intended to start to-day at the fifth hour; but I have just learned that the vessel will not sail till the eighth. So sit down. Epictetus there is not time to call upon. When I write to you I shall ask you to deliver him a letter from me. Sit down, and begin by telling me about the lecture I have just missed, while it is fresh in your memory."

When I had finished, he said, turning over the papers he was sorting, "I remember another of his lectures in which he warned us against a licentious and effeminate life. Here it is, and these are his exact words: 'Do not, in the name of the Gods, do not you, young man, fall back again! Nay, rather go back to your home and say, now that you have once heard this warning, *It is not Epictetus that has said this. How should he? It is some God wishing well to me and speaking through him. It would never have come into the mind of Epictetus to say this, for it is never his custom to make personal appeals. Come, then, let us obey the voice of God, lest we fall under God's wrath.'* I have never forgotten these words, and I trust I never shall. I think a God speaks through Epictetus. Do you not agree with me?"

"I do indeed," said I, "but I am not convinced that God speaks all that Epictetus says, and that there is not more to be spoken. For example, he says, 'You have but to will and it is done.' Is that a common experience? Is it yours? He says, 'Take from yourself the help you need.' Do you find in yourself all the help you need? When you fall, he says, 'Get up,' as though we were boys in the wrestling-ring. But what if we have been stunned? What if one's ankle is sprained or a leg broken? Do you remember what you said to me at the end of my first lecture, 'Will it last?' You also said that Epictetus could make us feel just what he wished us to feel—as long as he was speaking. Well, while I was sitting on the bench in the lecture-room, I felt that getting up from vice was as easy as sitting on that bench. When I walked out, it began to seem less easy. Now that I am quite away from the enchanter, talking the matter quietly over with you, the feeling has almost vanished; and I am obliged to repeat your question about this, and about much more of our Master's doctrine, 'Will it last?'"

"Some of it will last," said Arrian, "We must not expect impossibilities. I have heard him admit that it is impossible to be sinless already, but he bade us remember that it is possible to be always intent on not sinning." "Did he mean," asked I, "by 'already,' that we could not be sinless in this life, but that we might be sinless at what he calls the feast of the Gods, after death?" Arrian did not at once reply. Presently he said, "I do not think so. I believe he meant that we must not expect to be sinless as soon as we have reached the intermediate stage of what he calls 'the half-educated man.' We must wait till we have reached the further stage, that of complete education, where, as you said just now, a man never blames himself, because he does not find in himself any fault that he could blame."

ARRIAN'S DEPARTURE

Here Arrian made a still longer pause. Then he continued, in his usual slow, deliberate way, but with a touch of hesitation that was not usual with him, "I have here a few duplicates of my notes. Among them are some on the subject on which your remarks bear, and about which (I gather) you would like to question me—the immortality of the soul. In my hearing, he has seldom used that precise phrase. And, when he has used the epithet 'immortal,' it has generally applied to life like that of Tithonus—I mean, a deathless life in this present world. To desire such a life, deathless and free from disease, he thinks unreasonable. But I remember his saying once, that he was prepared for death, '*whether it were the death of the whole or of a certain part*'—that was his expression. And I think he may possibly believe that the Logos within us is reabsorbed, after death, into some kind of quintessential or divine fire from which it sprang. But I cannot say that this satisfies me."

Neither did it satisfy me. But I said nothing. Arrian, too, was silent, turning over some of his papers and marking passages for my perusal. But presently, rousing himself, "Did you agree with me," he said, "about the passage you transcribed, when we last met, concerning that sect of the Jews which he called the Galilæans?" I could see that Arrian wished to divert the conversation to "the Galilæans," as being a subject of a less serious character than the doctrine of the immortality of the soul. But the subject of the Galilæans or Jews had become much more serious for me now than it had been when we last conversed together. How much more, I shrank from telling him, in the few minutes at our disposal. He was good, just, a truthful scholar, a gentleman, and a kind friend. Given a few days more—even a few hours—in one another's company, and I should not have kept my secret from him. But how could I hope, in so brief an interval, and amid so many preoccupations, to make him understand what a vast continent of new history, religion, literature—and, above all, "feeling" as opposed to "logic"—had emerged before my mind's eye, during my recent voyages of exploration in the scriptures and in Paul's epistles? So I replied briefly that I agreed with his view.

Epictetus, I said, seemed to me to be speaking, not of the Galilæan "custom," but of their "feeling," as also in the case of the Jews. "And indeed," I added, "the force of this 'feeling' in producing courage appears to me most remarkable." With these words I rose to go.

"Well," said he, "I fear we shall hardly meet again in Nicopolis. But I shall always cherish the recollection of the hours we have spent together here, and of our common respect for our common Master, whom you already love, and whom, if you come to know him as I do—in his home, and in his kindness to those who need kindness—you will (I trust) love still more." "I do love him," said I. "But tell me, do you love all his teaching about indifference to what is happening? You know how our Master scoffs at the agony of Priam looking on the ruin of Troy. Well, suppose you were a Roman citizen, as I am sure you will be before long. Or, rather, suppose you were our new Emperor Hadrian, and saw the northern barbarians not only at our gates but inside our walls, and the City in flames, and the Dacians doing in Rome what the Greeks did in Troy to the Trojan men and women, would you, our Emperor Hadrian, feel it right to say, 'All this is nothing to me'?"
"By the immortal Gods," exclaimed Arrian, "I should not."
"And if Epictetus were in Hadrian's place, or Priam's place, do you think he could say it?"

I had to wait for an answer. "What I am going to say," he replied at last, "may seem to you monstrous. But I really cannot reply No. I cannot tell what he would say. I am not able to judge him as I should judge others." Then he proceeded, with an animation quite unusual in him, "Of any other Hadrian or Priam I should say that such an utterance stamped him as either liar, or beast, or stone. But Epictetus—absorbed in Zeus, devoted to His will, resolved to believe that His will is good, and seeing no way out of the belief that all things happen in accordance with His will—might not Epictetus conceivably feel, in moments of ecstasy, that all these fires and furies, massacres and outrages, cannot prevent him from believing in Zeus and being one with Zeus, so that he himself, Epictetus, might be, nay, must be, in the bosom of Zeus (so to speak) at the very moment when not only Rome, but all the cities, villages, and hamlets of the world—nay, when the universe itself was being cast into destruction? Well, I am out of my depth. I confess it. But will you not agree with me thus far, that *if* Epictetus said that he felt thus, he would really feel thus?"

"Yes," replied I, "I am sure that he would not say it unless he felt it. But I am not sure that he might not feel it merely because he had forced himself to feel it. However, let us say no more now on such subtle matters. It is no small help to have been lifted up by such a teacher above the mere life of the flesh. We part, do we not, in full agreement that Epictetus has been, for both of us, a guide to that which is good?" And thus we did part. I accompanied him to the quay. "May we meet again," were my last words. "May it be soon," were his.

But we never met. The death of his father plunged him almost immediately into domestic cares and matters of business. When the pressure of private affairs relaxed, it was soon followed by affairs of state. This was due in part perhaps to his having been a pupil of Epictetus. The new emperor, long before he became emperor, had always admired our Master; whose recommendation (I am inclined to think) had something to do with Arrian's subsequent promotions. At all events, when I was on service in the north, I heard without any surprise, and with a great deal of pleasure, that my former fellow-student—known now to literary circles as Flavianus, a Roman citizen, and author of the Memoirs of Epictetus—had been appointed governor of Cappadocia.

From time to time we corresponded. But it was not upon the topics that used to engross us in old days. He took a great interest in geography. Military service, at one time in the north and then in the east, gave me some knowledge of this subject, which I was glad to place at his disposal. He also studied military affairs with a view to writing on Alexander. Here again I was of use to him. But we never resumed in our letters that subject about which he had once said to me, "More of this to-morrow." Our paths had branched off, leading us far away from each other in everything except mutual good will and respect. He had become a Roman magistrate. Subsequently he was a priest of Demeter. I had become a Roman soldier, but—a Christian. Many of my friends knew this and I have little doubt that Arrian guessed it. Privately I feel sure he always loved me. Officially he must have been forced to disapprove. Hadrian, it is true, discouraged informations against the Christians, and I had been hitherto connived at: but could I condemn my old friend if he shrank from opening up old speculations that might lead him into unofficial, suspected, and dangerous results? Much more might I myself rather feel condemned for keeping silence. Sometimes I have felt thus. But not often. More often I feel that it was better for him not to know what I know, than to know it, in a sense, and to reject it. Presented in mere writing, I felt sure that it would have been rejected. Writings and books brought me on the way to Christ, but something more was needed to make me receive Christ.

Arrian, I think, avoided such opportunities as presented themselves for meeting. I am sure I did. If we had met, surely I should have been constrained to open my mind to him. Once, at least, I touched (in a letter) on our old conversation about "logos" and "pathos." He replied that, in his new career, both "logos" and "pathos" had to give place to *pragmata*, "business," which, he thought, was likely to take up all his energies during the rest of his life.

Even if I had opened my mind, I cannot help thinking that his would have remained unchanged. One thing, however, I do not think about, but know—namely, that, if we had met, Arrian and I would still have had common ground, as of old, in our love of truth and justice, and that we should still have esteemed, respected, and loved each other. For myself, love him I always shall, not for his own sake alone, but also because he helped me directly and immediately to understand Epictetus, and indirectly and ultimately to perceive the existence of something beyond any truth that Epictetus could teach.

CHAPTER X

EPICTETUS ON DEATH

RETURNING to my rooms, I sat down to think out my problems alone. Presently, on taking up the lecture-notes Arrian had given me, I found that the title of the first was, "What is meant by being in desolation or deserted? And who can call himself deserted?" The subject suited my mood, and I began to read it, as follows: "Desolation is the condition of a man unhelped. To be alone is not necessarily to be deserted. To be in the midst of a multitude is not always to be undeserted. A man may be in the centre of a crowd of his own slaves. But still, if he has just lost a brother, he may be deserted. We may travel alone, yet never feel deserted till we fall into the midst of a band of robbers. It is not the face of a man that delivers us from desolation; it is the presence of someone faithful and trustworthy, thoughtful and kind, good and helpful."

I liked this. But afterwards the lecture strayed into what seemed to me controversial theology or metaphysics, "If being alone suffices to make you deserted, then say that Zeus Himself is deserted when the final fire comes round in its cycle, consuming the universe. Say that He bewails His loneliness exclaiming 'Alas, me miserable! I have no Hera now! No Athene! No Apollo! Not a single brother, son, or relation!' Some people actually do assert that Zeus behaves like this in the final fire!" I gathered that he was attacking some philosophic tenet. But it did not interest me any more than his subsequent assertion—or rather assumption—that "Zeus associates with Himself, reposes on Himself, and contemplates the nature of His own administration." I have never felt drawn towards the conception of a self-admiring, or a solitary God.

Arrian's next note bore on the peace of the universe, a peace proclaimed by the Logos, a peace resembling, but far surpassing, the peace proclaimed by the Emperor, such a peace that every man can say, even when he is alone, " Henceforth no evil can befall me. For me, robbers and earthquakes have no existence. All things are full of peace, full of tranquillity. Whether I am travelling on the high road, or living in the city, whether in public assemblies or among private friends and neighbours, nothing can harm me. There is Another, not myself, who makes it His care to supply me with food. He it is that clothes me. He, not myself, gave me the perceptions of my body. He, not myself, bestowed on me the conceptions of my mind."

Then followed a passage about death, which Arrian, during our last conversation, had marked for my special attention: *" But if at any moment He ceases to supply you with the things needful for your existence, then take heed! In that moment He is sounding the bugle for you to cease the conflict. He is saying to you, ' Come!' And whither? Into no land of terrors. Simply into that same region from which you entered into being. Into the company of such existences as are friendly and akin to you. Into the elements. Such part as was fire in you will depart into fire; such part of earth as was in you, into earth; such part of air or wind as was in you, into air or wind; of water, into water. No Hades! No Acheron! No Cocytus! No Pyriphlegethon! All things are full of Gods and dæmons!"* By this I think he meant " good Gods and guardian angels." He concluded thus, *" Having such thoughts as these in his heart, looking up to the sun, the moon, and the stars, and enjoying the earth and the sea, man has no more right to call himself deserted than to call himself unhelped."*

It was not clear to me how I could continue to call myself " helped " when I was on the point of being dissolved into the four elements. If I were a criminal, successful in escaping punishment on earth, I might deem it "help" (after a fashion) to know that I should be equally successful after quitting the earth, because I need not fear Hades and its three rivers as enemies. But where were the "friends"? The four elements promised but cold friendship! Arrian's comment rose to my mind, and a second time I assented to it, "I cannot say that this satisfies me." Epictetus was so averse from anything like cant or insincerity of expression that I was amazed—as I still am—that he could use, in such a context, the words "friendly and akin." Surely Sappho's cry was truer, when she wandered alone through the woods where she had once been loved by Phaon—

"This place is now dead dust. He was its life."

What would it profit that my "fiery part" should return to fire? It might as well go astray into water, or earth, or into extinction, as far as I cared. To be still loved would have been to be still in some kind of home. But who would love my four elements? I should be "not I," but only four severed portions of what had once been "I," fragments incapable even of mourning, wandering among "dead dust," no better than "dead dust" themselves! How infinitely should I have preferred that Epictetus—if he could not honestly accept the confident hope of Socrates concerning a life after death,—should have said simply this, "As to what Zeus does with our souls after death, others think they know much. I know nothing, except that He does what is best."

Reviewing passages in which Epictetus had mentioned the "soul," I was more perplexed than ever. For in those he distinctly recognised the "*soul*" as "*better than the flesh*," or "*better than the body*," and as using the body as its instrument. When, therefore, he spoke of God as saying to man, "Come!" he ought to have supposed God to be addressing *the whole man, soul as well as body, or perhaps the soul alone,* (using the body, or the flesh, as its instrument). But if God said to the human soul "Come!" how could He go on to say "Such part as was fire in you" and so on, just as though we knew, without proof, that the *soul* was composed of nothing but fire, earth, air and water? We knew no such thing. On the contrary, Epictetus continually assumed that we have within ourselves "mind" and "logos." He also said that "The being of God" is "mind, knowledge, right logos." Now he could hardly suppose that "mind" and "logos" were composed of fire, earth, air, and water. For my part, I did not feel that I knew anything certain about the distinctions between "mind," "soul," "logos" and "I." But those who made distinctions appeared to me under an obligation to say what they meant by them.

It appeared to me that our Master had been inconsistent. As a rule, he dealt with each of us as having a soul that was our real self, and a body that was the tool of the soul. "Tyrants," he would say, "can hurt your *body* but they cannot hurt *you*." Might not a pupil of his go on consistently to say, "Death can kill your *body* but it cannot kill *you*"? This, at all events, was what Socrates meant, when he said, "As for me, Meletus could not hurt me....He might kill, or banish, or degrade," for he certainly meant "kill" the *body*, not "kill" the *soul*.

Subsequently, when I came to read the Christian gospels, I found two of them making this distinction in the words, "Be not afraid of them that kill the body." One of them added, "but cannot kill the soul," the other added "but cannot do anything more." Then I understood more clearly why Epictetus said nothing about what became of the soul after death. For these two Christian writers spoke of a possibility that the soul might be "destroyed in hell" or "cast into hell." Now this was just what Epictetus did not himself believe, and wished to make others disbelieve. He preferred to give up the belief of Socrates that the good "go to the islands of the blessed" after death, rather than believe also that the bad go to a place of the accursed. Hence he dropped all thought of the essential part, or parts, of man, namely, the soul, mind, and logos, as soon as he came to speak of man's death.

The consequence was that Epictetus confused us by an ambiguous use of "*you*." As long as we were alive he said to us, "*You* must regard your body as a mere tool," where by "you" he meant the incorporeal part of man. As soon as we were on the point of death, he said to us, " Do not be alarmed. *You* are going into the four elements," where by "you" he apparently meant our corporeal part. I felt sure then (as I do now) that he did not intend to confuse us. He seemed to me to have been confused by his own intense desire to persuade himself that men must do good without hope of any reward at all except the consciousness of doing good in this present life. I had not at that time read the Christian gospels ; but several passages in Paul's epistles occurred to me as contrary to this doctrine of Epictetus, and I thought that our Master might have been biassed in part by Paul (as Scaurus had suggested) —only not, in this instance, imitating Paul, but contradicting him. So I took up the epistle to the Romans intending to read what Paul said there about Christ's death and resurrection.

CHAPTER XI

ISAIAH ON DEATH

I TOOK up the epistle to the Romans, but I did not read it long. Another subject stepped in to claim immediate attention in the first words on which I lighted. They were these, "Isaiah cries aloud on behalf of Israel, *Though the number of the sons of Israel be as the sand of the sea, the remnant [alone] shall be saved*," and then, "Even as Isaiah has foretold, *If the Lord of Sabaoth had not left seed to us, we should have become as Sodom and should have been made like unto Gomorrah.*" Previously when I had read these words I could neither understand them nor see the way to understand them, not knowing the meaning of "Sodom" and "Gomorrah," nor even "Isaiah." But now, knowing that Isaiah was one of the principal Hebrew prophets, I began to see that many obscure passages of Paul might become clearer to me if I first studied this prophet. This view was confirmed when I found Paul, later on, quoting him again, "But Isaiah is very bold and says, *I was found by them that sought me not, I became manifest to them that consulted me not*; but with reference to Israel he says, *All the day long, I stretched out my hands to a people disobedient and gainsaying.*" The name also occurred toward the close of the epistle thus, "Isaiah says, *There shall be the root of Jesse, and he that is raised up to rule over the nations; on him shall the nations set their hope.*" These last words reminded me of the doctrine of Epictetus about Diogenes "to whom are entrusted the peoples of the earth and countless cares in their behalf."

But I did not know what "root of Jesse" meant. The name, "Jesse," I faintly remembered reading in the poems of David; but where it was I could not recall. Hence the phrase was obscure. I determined to put off the further study of Paul for the present, and to glance through the book of Isaiah in the hope of meeting this and other passages quoted above. Accordingly I unrolled the prophecy and began to read it from the beginning.

At first, the language was clear—though the Greek was as bad as in the poems of David. The "children" of God, said the prophet (meaning the ancient Jews or Hebrews, whom he often spoke of as "Israel") had rebelled against their Father and were being punished with fire and sword by hostile nations executing God's vengeance on their impiety. Then came the sentence I quoted above, from Paul, about the "remnant." After this, the prophet introduced "the Lord"—that is the God of the Jews—as saying that He cared no longer for their incense or their offerings because they came from hands stained with blood. This was somewhat like the saying of Horace about Phidyle mentioned above. But what followed was not like anything in Horace: "Wash you, make you clean; cease to do evil, learn to do good; seek judgment, relieve the oppressed, judge the fatherless, plead for the widow." If they would act thus, then, said God, "though your sins be red as scarlet, they shall be as white as snow." As though the nation were molten metal in a crucible, and He Himself were refining them with fire, the Lord said to the whole people of Israel, "I will purge away thy dross...afterwards thou shalt be called the city of righteousness."

I had begun to hope that I should be able to understand this author as easily as Euripides and much more easily than Æschylus. But now came obscurities. First I read of a golden age. People were to "beat their swords into ploughshares," and not to "learn war any more." Then I found a mention of general destruction as by a universal earthquake. Then came, without any chronological or other order apparent to me, the following pictures, or predictions:—a land without a ruler governed by children and women; a picture of luxurious ladies of rank, a list of their dresses, ornaments, jewels and cosmetics; a "branch of the Lord, beautiful and glorious"; a purifying with a "spirit of burning"; "a song of my beloved touching his vineyard"—all confused together (so it seemed to me at the time) like the prophecies of the Sibyl.

As far as I could see, most of these prophecies dealt with the internal corruption of the nation. The "vineyard" of the Lord was the people of Israel. When He visited the vineyard, looking for fruit, said the prophet, "He looked for judgment but behold oppression." After this, came a vision of the Lord's glory, and then predictions of external calamities, and invasions of foreign nations. But yet there was a promise of the birth of a Deliverer, a Prince of Peace, to sit "upon the throne of David." Following this, at some interval, were the words for which I was searching, about "the root of Jesse." And now I could understand them, for they were preceded by this prediction, "There shall come forth a shoot out of the stock of Jesse, and a branch out of his roots shall bear fruit." Just before that, there had been a description of an invading army, coming as the instrument of the Lord's wrath and "lopping the boughs with terror" and hewing down "the high ones of stature."

Then all was clear to me. I perceived the connexion between the "child" that was to sit on "the throne of David," and the "shoot out of the stock of Jesse." The two together brought back to my mind that passage which I could not before recall from the Psalms, "The prayers of David the son of Jesse are ended." The words of Isaiah were like those of Sophocles where he is speaking of the destruction of the royal house of Laius. Sophocles calls the surviving child the "root," and laments because the axe of Fate was destroying it just when a branch was on the point of "shooting up" from the "stock" so as to produce fruit. So now, but in an opposite mood of hope and joy, Isaiah said that the royal house of David the son of Jesse would not be exterminated, though many of its scions would be cut off. A "branch" would "shoot up" and the succession to the kingdom would be maintained.

In the same way, I perceived, the great Julius, or the

Emperor Augustus, being descended from Iulus, the son of Æneas, might be called "the shoot out of the stock of Anchises," transported from Asia to Europe so as to "shoot up" into a new kingdom more glorious than the old. This, too, explained the word "remnant" used by Paul. As the Trojan followers of Æneas were a "remnant," so too must be the Jewish followers of this "child," a remnant left from defeat, disaster, and captivity, after a great "lopping of the boughs with terror." Virgil sang about the empire of the house of Iulus not as a prophet, but as a poet, prophesying, so to speak, after the event. Isaiah appeared merely to predict empire as a prophet, and a false prophet, prophesying what had not been, and never would be, an "event." The tree of the empire of Rome was erect for all the world to look on. The tree of the kingdom of Jesse appeared to me as extinct as the house of Laius. So I thought then.

Yet I knew that Paul looked at the matter differently and regarded these prophecies as having been, or as about to be, fulfilled. And when I looked more closely into the sayings of Isaiah about the future kingdom, I saw that many of them were capable of two meanings. Sometimes the prophet appeared to be contemplating a kingdom established in the ordinary way by force of arms—a conquest achieved, or at all events preceded, by fire, sword, and desolation. But, for the most part, it seemed to be an empire of peace to be brought about by some kind of persuasion, or feeling. A sudden conviction was to take hold of all the nations of the earth, so that they were to exclaim, with one consent, as at the sound of a trumpet, "Come ye and let us go up to the mountain of the Lord," meaning the Temple in Jerusalem.

In this kingdom, however brought about, the Lord was to be King, and there was to be a "covenant" between Him and all the citizens or subjects, a covenant of righteousness. The subjects were to obey the King and the King would give them a righteous spirit. In some respects the covenant of obedience was to resemble that philosophic oath which Epictetus had enjoined on us, namely, to consult our own interests, to be true to ourselves (meaning, to the spirit of righteousness within us).

But the prophet regarded righteousness as loyalty, or truth, not to ourselves, but to our King.

That seemed to me one great difference between the Greeks and the Hebrews in their notions of worship. The Greeks, when they lifted their thoughts above themselves, looked, in the first place, each man to his several city, and in the next place, to the Gods. They did not think in the first place of the Gods. For the Gods were many, while the City was one. But the ancient Jews, the men of Israel, or at least their prophets, looked to their Lord God as their King—the Father, or sometimes the Husband, of Israel. Although they were many tribes, they had but one God, the Lord God, who had delivered them from the land of Egypt. This Lord God was a God of justice and truth, hating oppression, a defender of the widow and the fatherless. To be loyal to Him was righteousness.

And herein—as I soon began to perceive—was the great difference between the view of righteousness or justice taken by Isaiah and that taken by our Roman lawyers, or any lawyers bound to a written law. The lawyer's righteousness was legality; the prophet's was loyalty. Epictetus and Isaiah agreed together in aiming at loyalty, not legality. Both disliked obedience paid to mere rules and commandments of men. But the former for the most part inculcated loyalty that seemed like loyalty to oneself; the latter, loyalty to God. This precept of Isaiah agreed with the fundamental law prescribed in the code of Moses that the men of Israel were to "love" the Lord their God.

After searching carefully to see what the prophet said concerning the immortality of the soul (about which Moses seemed to be silent) I could find little of a definite kind. In one passage I read "The dead shall arise and they that are in the tombs shall be roused up." But the preceding lines said "The dead shall assuredly not see life"; so that it was not clear whether the words meant that one nation should be destroyed for ever and another nation should be raised up from destruction to life. The prophet appeared to be thinking of the nation collectively, more often than of separate citizens. The metaphor of the Vine of Israel seemed to be almost always in his thoughts. And his hope seemed to be, not concerning separate branches, that every branch should remain; but that, in spite of being cruelly pruned and cut down almost to the ground, the tree, as a whole, would yet grow up and bear fruit. I noticed also that a certain king called Hezekiah, when praying to be delivered from a disease likely to prove fatal, spoke as though there were no life after death.

But there was one passage, of very mysterious import, which seemed to point to a different conclusion. It spoke about a "servant of God," of mean aspect but destined to be a great Deliverer—such as Epictetus had described—"bearing upon him the cares" of multitudes. He was to grow up "as a root in the thirsty ground," which suggested that he was to be "the root of Jesse" above mentioned. But he was not to be like Æneas, "the root" of Anchises. For Æneas divided the spoils in Italy as the prize of his sword. But this Deliverer—so the prophet declared—was "despised and reckoned as naught." He was "delivered over" to the enemies of his nation as a ransom to save his fellow-countrymen, and it was by their wickedness that "he was led to death." Yet in the end, said the prophet, "He will inherit many men, and will divide the spoils of the strong, because his soul was delivered over to death, and he was reckoned among criminals, and he carried the sins of many and he was delivered over on account of their crimes."

This was altogether beyond my comprehension at the time. But I saw that I should have to return to this prophecy hereafter; for I recognised its last words as having been quoted by Paul in writing to the Romans. I found afterwards that the passage in Paul spoke about "believing in Him that raised up Jesus our Lord from the dead, who was *delivered over for the sake of our transgressions,* and was raised up for the sake of our being made righteous." For the present, however, the passage in Isaiah about the "servant" of God seemed to me important, for this reason mainly, because it indicated a belief in a life after death. And so did another difficult passage—if Paul had interpreted it rightly. My copy of the prophecy said, "Death by its strength hath swallowed up"; but the margin said

"Death is swallowed up in victory," and these latter words, too, I recognised as being quoted by Paul; and this, or some similar, sense appeared to be required by the context.

It was growing late and I was obliged to break off. But I resolved to return to the book next morning before lecture. So far as I had read, it appeared to me that the prophet did not formally recognise the immortality of the soul in general. But in the case of the Suffering Servant he did seem to recognise it. Having the Servant in my mind, I unrolled the book of Isaiah to other passages using the same word, such as, "for my *servant* David's sake," "But thou, Israel, art my *servant*," "My *servant* whom I have chosen." At last I came to "the seed of Abraham my *friend*." In all these passages, God was supposed to be speaking. Then it occurred to me, "Did the prophet make an exception for the Suffering Servant only? Did he not also believe that Abraham's soul was immortal?" It seemed to me impossible that if the God of the Jews were asked, "Where is Abraham thy friend?" He would reply—or that the prophet would regard Him as replying—"Resolved into the four elements." On the whole, I was led to the conclusion that Isaiah implied, though he did not express, some kind of doctrine of human immortality dependent on the relation between man and God.

CHAPTER XII

ISAIAH ON PROVIDENCE

EVEN when I was in the act of rolling up the book of Isaiah, very late at night, it occurred to me that the question "Is there a life after death?" might be connected with another, "Is there to be hereafter a reign of righteousness?" I tried to give my mind rest by thinking of other things; but this second question came back to me again and again both before and after I retired to rest. Epictetus spoke about "the sceptre and throne of Diogenes": but I knew he would not assert that the philosopher's "sceptre" implied any present kingdom except over his own mind and the minds of a small band of Cynics—small in comparison with Stoics and Epicureans, and nothing at all in comparison with the non-philosophic myriads. As for a kingdom of righteousness after death in another world, I was now certain that Epictetus did not expect it; and I began to doubt whether he expected such a kingdom at any time in this world. If to believe in Providence means to believe in a God who foresees and prepares that which is best—I could not understand where Epictetus could find a basis for such a belief.

With the Jews, it was otherwise. They, I could see, had received a special training, which made them, more than any other nation known to me, begin by expecting a reign of righteousness on earth. Beginning thus, and being largely disappointed, they might be led on to expect a reign of righteousness in heaven. Their history was like a collection of stories for children, teeming with what a child might call surprises, but a prophet judgments—evil, uppermost, suddenly cast down; humble patient goodness, chastened by pains and trials, lifted up to lordship over its past oppressors. Examples occurred to me before I slept, and many more during the night, in my waking moments. I had not noticed them so clearly when reading the Law consecutively. Now, grouped together, they came almost as a new revelation—if not of history, at all events of legend, and of a nation's thoughts, and of the training through which the Jew Paul must have passed in his childhood and youth.

First, there was Abraham—Abraham the homeless, going out from unbelievers to worship the one God, and receiving a promise that he should be the father of blessing, for multitudes in all the nations of the earth; Abraham the childless, rewarded with the child of promise; Abraham the kind and yielding, who gave way to his kinsman Lot, so that the older patriarch was content with the inferior pastures while the younger chose the fertile lands of Sodom and Gomorrah; Abraham the father of the one child that embodied the truth of the one God, offering up that child on the altar, and receiving him back as if from Hades; Abraham the landless, without a foot of ground in the land promised to him, buying with money a cave to bury his family. "Surely," I said, "the story of Abraham, in itself, is a compendium of national history not indeed for Rome, but for a nation of peace (if only the nation could live up to it!) most fit for training a child to become a citizen in the City of Righteousness!"

If the life of Abraham was full of surprises or paradoxes, so too were the lives of the other patriarchs and leaders of the nation. Isaac, "laughter," laid himself down to die in appearance, but to "laugh" at death in reality. Esau was the "elder," yet he was to "serve the younger." Jacob was promised lordship over his brother in the future, but he bowed down before him in the present. The same patriarch, a poor man, with nothing but his "staff," became rich and prosperous. Yet, because he had deceived his father, he in turn was deceived by his children and sorely tried by their contentions. Through Samuel, the little child, God rebuked Eli the high priest; and the little one became the prophet and judge of Israel. David, the despised and youngest of many brethren, became the greatest of Israel's kings.

Such was the history of the great men of the ancient Jews—tried, but triumphing over trial. On the other hand, the history of the mass of the common people, from the time when they were a family of twelve sons, shewed them as going astray, lying, quarrelling and rebelling. For this they were punished by plagues and enemies; then, delivered by judges or prophets; but only, as it seemed, again to fall away, and to be delivered again; so that the reader of the histories, apart from the prophecies, might well suppose that these ebbs and flows were to go on for ever; that Israel was to be always imperfect, always liable to rebellion; and that the promise to Abraham was never to be fulfilled. More especially might a reader of the histories anticipate this when he saw the great empires of the east, Assyria and Babylon, leading the tribes away into captivity and destroying Jerusalem and the Temple.

Such were my thoughts by night concerning the Law and the Histories of Israel. Resuming the study of the prophecy early next morning, I perceived that in the sins and backslidings of the people there was yet another and far deeper illustration of what might be called "the law of paradoxes." Not only came prosperity out of adversity but also righteousness out of sin, and out of punishment promise. Some of Isaiah's most comforting prophecies arose from the invasion of Israel by Assyria. In this connexion there came a promise about a "child" that was to be "born," of whom it was said "the government shall be upon his shoulder." These things reminded me of passages in the poems, where the poet—musing on the chastisements and deliverances that followed the sins of Israel—exclaims "His mercy endureth for ever," or "I remember the days of old, I meditate on all thy doings." In the history of Greece and Rome I could find comparatively few stories of such "doings." How indeed could I reasonably expect them? Romans and Greeks worship many Gods, but only one Father of Gods and men. Athens might claim Athene, and other cities might have their special patrons among the Gods. But how could it be supposed that the Father of Gods and men would make any one nation His peculiar care? Virgil says that Venus was on the side of the future Rome, and that Jupiter favoured Venus; but Juno intervenes for Carthage. Then Jupiter has to compromise between Juno and Venus, or to conciliate Juno by laying the blame on fate! "How different," I exclaimed, "all this is from the Hebrew egotism that represents the one God as continually saying to Israel 'Thee have I chosen'!"

Yet I had hardly uttered the word "egotism" before I felt inclined to qualify it, adding, "But it is not 'egotism' from Paul's point of view." For indeed Paul seemed to think that God chose Abraham, not for Abraham's own sake—or at all events not merely for Abraham's own sake—but for the sake of "all the nations of the earth," to bring light and truth to them. Epictetus spoke of Diogenes as "bearing on himself the orb of the world's vast cares." Somewhat similarly—when I took up the Law of the Jews to revise the thoughts that had come to me in the night—I found the Law describing the life of Abraham the friend of God. For I did not find Abraham blessed or happy—as the world would use the terms "blessing" and "happiness."

Abraham begins as a homeless wanderer, going forth from his kindred at the bidding of the one true God; and a homeless wanderer he remains to the end. He is a father of kings but no king himself, not even a landowner! He has to buy with money land enough to bury his dead! His life is one of intercession as well as concession. Abraham intercedes for the dwellers in Sodom and Gomorrah, feeling it a painful thing that even a few righteous should suffer with the many. Once indeed Abraham becomes a soldier. But it is not for himself. It is for his kinsman and for the rescue of captives. Abraham makes himself a servant, waiting at table upon his guests. Abraham offers to God the life of his only son. If Paul was right, and if the children of Abraham mean the men that do such things as these in such a spirit as this, and if "the seed of Abraham" is the man that incarnates this spirit, then, I thought, there was perhaps no egotism when the prophet of

Israel represented God as saying to the descendant of Abraham, "Thou, Israel, my servant, Jacob whom I have chosen, the seed of Abraham my friend." For it may mean "I have not chosen the rich, I have not chosen the great and strong. I have chosen the good and kind and truthful and courageous; him only have I chosen." And soon afterwards God says, "I have chosen thee in the furnace of affliction," that is to say, "I have not chosen thee to make thee selfishly happy and prosperous, but to make thee my servant, like Abraham, for the service of all the world."

The same truth appeared to apply to Moses, who, next to Abraham, might be called the greatest of the "servants of the Lord." Even from the cradle he was in peril of death. He delivered his countrymen, as it were, against their will. The burden of their rebellions pressed on him through his life, and caused him to be cut off from the land of promise in the moment of his death. He saw it from afar off but was not allowed to enter it. He was prohibited because of his sin; and his sin fell upon him because his people sinned. "The Lord was wroth with me," said Moses, "for your sakes." That was the greatest burden of all. With the lives of Abraham and Moses before me, it seemed that the greatest servants were also the greatest sufferers.

Having this fresh light, I turned again to the description of the Suffering Servant in Isaiah. Did the prophet mean some particular prince of the house of David who was actually "chosen in the furnace of affliction" in order to deliver Israel? Or did he mean Israel itself, scattered through the world and afflicted in order that it might deliver the world? Plato modelled his Republic in the form of a man: had Isaiah any such double meaning? Did he predict a second David delivering sinful Israel, and also a purified Israel delivering a sinful world? Was he carried, so to speak, by the past into the future? That is to say, had he in mind some prince actually tortured and imprisoned, and as good as dead, for the sake of the people, and did the prophet regard this prince as destined to be raised up from the darkness of the prison house and to reign on earth? Or else was the prince, though actually killed, destined to be raised up and to reign after death in his own person, or to reign in the person of his descendants?

About all these questions I felt that it was not for me to judge. I did not know enough about the history of the people and the language of their poets and prophets. But there remained with me this general truth, as being not only at the bottom of this prophecy, but also pervading the history of Israel, namely, that in order to make a great nation, great men must die for its sake. And I began to conceive a possibility that the greatest of all men, some real "son of Abraham"— I mean some spiritual son of Abraham, not necessarily a Jew— might arise in the history of the world, who might be willing to die not for one nation alone but for all the nations of the empire. But how? And against what enemies? As soon as I asked myself these questions, the conception faded away. I thought of Nero enthroned in Rome, and of the Beast enthroned in the heart of man. Against either of these foes I did not understand how the death of any "son of Abraham," or "servant of God," could avail. How could such a Servant "divide the spoils of the strong, because his soul was delivered over to death"? This was beyond me.

For the rest, Isaiah appeared to me to carry on throughout the book of his prophecies that thread of unexpectedness about which I spoke above—I mean, that what prophets (foreseeing them) call judgments, men of the world (not foreseeing) call surprises. Yes, and even prophets and righteous men—not foreseeing enough—often lift up their hands in amazement, exclaiming, "This hath God wrought!" or "The stone that the builders rejected hath become the headstone of the corner!" But there was a dark as well as a bright side in these surprises. The disappointments were often most strange. For example, Isaiah saw a vision of the Lord "high and lifted up." But with what result? The prophet himself was straightway cast down with the thought of being "unclean." Even afterwards, when his lips had been cleansed with the coal from off the altar so that he might deliver God's message, the message was, "Hear ye, indeed, but understand not!"—because his warning was to be rejected. And so it was throughout, paradox on paradox! Israel was "chosen" in one sentence, "backsliding" in the next. The "despised and rejected" servant was to be "lifted up." The transgressions of the world were to be taken away by a deliverer, who was to be "reckoned among transgressors." Sometimes, as if despairing of the noble and learned among his own people, the prophet seemed to appeal to the poor and simple, according to the words of David, "Out of the mouths of babes and sucklings hast thou ordained strength!" Sometimes he even seemed to turn away from Israel itself—at all events from the majority of the nation—to the remnant, and to the pious among other nations, as though they, yes, even foreigners, might receive the fulfilment of the promise made to the seed of Abraham!

Amid all these (to me) perplexing paradoxes, one thing was clear—constituting a great difference between Isaiah and Epictetus. The former saw God in history. The latter did not. Epictetus said (as I have shewn in a previous chapter) that, up to the time of death, man can always find peace by following the "logos" within himself during life; after death he ceases to exist. "Bearing these things in mind," said he, "and seeing the sun and moon and stars, and enjoying the earth and sea, man is not deserted any more than unhelped." These words now returned to my mind, and I perceived the force of what they did *not* say. They said that God was to be seen in the sun and moon and stars; but they did *not* say that He was to be seen where Isaiah saw Him, in the nations of the earth controlled by the Supreme. It is true that Isaiah, too—like Epictetus—bade his readers look up to the stars as witnesses to God. But Isaiah seemed to me to reckon men superior to stars.

David certainly did so. David had "considered" all the glories of the visible heaven. Yet he counted them inferior to "man," who was "made but little lower than God," and inferior to the "son of man," who had received "dominion" over God's works. In the same spirit, Isaiah, as it seemed to me, spoke of the Maker of the heavenly bodies as being adorable, not because He had made them multitudinous and bright, but because He led them like a flock—as though even a star might wander but for the kindness of the divine Shepherd. Moreover God seemed to him to be controlling the mighty powers of the heaven for the service of man, " *Behold, the Lord, the Lord, He cometh with strength, and His arm with lordship. Behold, His reward is with Him, and His work before Him. As a shepherd shall He shepherd His sheep, and with His arm He shall gather the lambs, and encourage those that are with young. Who measured out the water with His hand, and the heaven with a span, and all the earth with His fingers? Who established the mountains by measure and the valleys with a scale? Who hath known the mind of the Lord and who hath become His fellow counsellor so as to instruct Him?*"

Thus, according to the prophet, there was to be a great advent in which God was to "come" with "reward." He predicted a future "shepherding" of the "sheep" and "gathering" of the "lambs," corresponding to the past "measuring" of the "heaven." According to the philosopher there was to be no such future. All things were to go round and round. Instead of "sheep" or "lambs," bubbles in an eddy seemed a more appropriate metaphor to describe the results of human life in accordance with the general tendency of Epictetian doctrine.

CHAPTER XIII

EPICTETUS ON PROVIDENCE

It was now almost the third hour and I was on the point of rolling up the volume, when a fellow-student suddenly entered to borrow some writing materials. Thrusting the book in my garment I supplied him with what he needed, and we hastened together to the lecture-room.

We conversed, about trivial subjects, but my mind was not in them. It was with Isaiah. I could not help marvelling that a native of so small and weak a country should take so wide and imperial a view of the movements of the nations. In a Roman, I could have understood it better; or in a Greek of the days of Alexander. But that a Jew—whose people was as it were the shuttlecock between the great empires surrounding it—that a Jewish prophet should think such thoughts filled me with astonishment. Then I wondered what Epictetus would say on the administration of the world if he ever dealt with it fully. " He," I said, "was a Phrygian and a slave. Is it possible that he, too, like Isaiah, could speak in this imperial fashion?" Arriving somewhat late, we found the room almost filled; but my seat was vacant, and I was glad to find Glaucus next to me, in the place vacated by Arrian's departure.

Epictetus was just beginning his first sentence. I will give it as Glaucus took it down, exactly: "Be not surprised if other animals, all except ourselves, have ready at hand the things needful for their bodily wants provided for them, not only food and drink but also bedding, and no need of sandals or blankets or clothes—while we have need of all these additional things." He proceeded to say that the beasts were our servants, and that it would be extremely inconvenient for us if we had "to clothe, shoe, and feed sheep and asses! As if," said he, "a colonel had to shoe and clothe his regiment before they could do the service required of them! And yet men complain, instead of being thankful!" Any single created thing, he said, would suffice to demonstrate Providence to a grateful mind. Then he instanced the production of milk from grass and of cheese from milk. Thence he passed from the "works" of Nature to "by-works," such as the beard, distinguishing man from woman. This (I think) was one of his customary digressions against the fashion of smooth-skinned effeminacy: "How much more beautiful than the comb of cocks! How much more noble than the mane of lions! Therefore it was our duty to preserve God's appointed tokens of manhood: it was our duty not to give them up, not to confuse (so far as lay in us) the classes, male and female, distinguished by Him."

"Are these," he continued, "the only works of Providence in our behalf? What praise can be proportionate to our benefits? Had we understanding, we should be ever hymning the graces He has bestowed on us. Whether digging, or ploughing, or eating, ought we not to sing the appropriate hymn to God, saying 'Great is God, because He hath given us tools wherewith to till the ground,' 'Great is God, who hath given us hands, and the power of swallowing, and a stomach, and a faculty of growing in stature painlessly and insensibly, and of breathing even when we sleep'? Hymns and praises such as these we ought to sing on each occasion. But the greatest and most divine hymn of all should be sung in thanks for that power"—he meant the Logos—"which intelligently recognises all these blessings, and which duly and methodically employs them. But *you* are silent. What then? Since you, like the common herd, are blind to God's glory, it was but fit that there should be some one herald, though it be but one, to fill the place left empty by your default, and to chant the hymn that goes up to God in behalf of all. What else am I fit to do, a halting old man like me, except to sing the praises of God?"

And so he drew toward the conclusion of the first part of

his lecture. Were he a nightingale or a swan, he said, he would do as a nightingale or a swan—that is to say, utter mere sounds, songs without words, songs void of reasonable thoughts, without Logos—" But as it is, I am endowed with Logos. Accordingly I must sing hymns to God. This is my special work. This I do. Never will I abandon this post of duty, as long as it is given to me. And I invite and urge you also to the same task of song." From this he proceeded to speak of "the things of the Logos," or "the logical things," as being "necessary"; and he spoke of the Logos as that which "articulates"—by which he meant, distinguishes the joints and connexions of all other things—and also as being that which accomplishes all other things. He appeared to mean that this Logos was reason; and he assumed that it is "impossible that anything should be better than reason." But he refused to enter into the question, If the Logos within us goes wrong, what shall set it right? His language at this point was very obscure. The impression left upon me was that Logos, with him, meant two different things and that he did not distinguish them. When he sang hymns to God in accord with the Logos, I thought he must intend to include something more than reason; but when he passed on to say that "the things of the Logos" (or "the logical things") are necessary, he seemed to mean "reason" alone.

Later on, he returned to his first subject: "When you are in the act of blaming Providence for anything, reflect, and you will recognise that it has happened in accordance with Logos." Then, taking the case of some man supposed to have been defrauded of a large sum of money, he placed in his mouth the objection that, if the fraud is "in accordance with Logos," it would seem that injustice is "in accordance with Logos." For, said the objector, "the unjust man has the advantage." "In what respect?" asked Epictetus. "In money," says the objector. To which Epictetus replied, "True, for he is better than you are for this purpose"—he meant, for making money—"because he flatters, he casts away shame, he is always unweariedly working for money. But consider. Does he get the better of you in respect of faithfulness and honour?" Then he rebuked us, would-be philosophers, for being angry with God for bestowing on us His best gifts, namely virtues, and for allowing bad men to take away from us what was not good in itself, namely, our worldly possessions.

This view of Providence and of wealth seemed to differ from the one assumed in Isaiah and often stated by Moses and David. For they had taught me that righteousness, and truth, and obedience to parents, and neighbourly kindness, tend to "length of days" and to peace and prosperity on the earth—for the righteous man himself as well as for the community; and they also distinguished honest wealth, acquired by labour, from dishonest wealth acquired by greediness and injustice. But Epictetus here made no such distinction.

The Jewish poems recognised it as being, at all events on the surface, a strange thing that a righteous man should be subjected to exceptional, crushing, and continuous calamities by the visitations of God. Epictetus appeared to teach us that God had ordained some men to be restless, pushing, shameless, and greedy, that they may take away the wealth acquired honestly by the good and honest and just. God had made these rascals "better" than the virtuous—in rascality! Then he called on us to admire or accept this ordinance or law: "Why fret, then, fellow? You have the better gift. Remember, therefore, all of you always, and have it by heart and on the lips, *This is a Law of Nature that the better should have—in the province in which he is better—the advantage of the inferior.* Then none of you will fret any more."

In his general theory, Epictetus was careful to separate himself from those who maintain that the Gods do not interfere with the affairs of men, or never interfere except on great and public occasions, and he approved of the words of Ulysses to the Allseeing, quoted by Socrates, "Thou seest my every motion." If man, he said, can embrace the world in his thought, and if the air and sun can include all things in their influence, why cannot God? But this seemed to lead to the conclusion that the influence of God is being perpetually and ubiquitously exerted on men in order to produce knaves, slaves, tyrants, and fools: for such our Master appeared to deem the majority of mankind.

Chapter 13]   ON PROVIDENCE   121

In practice, Epictetus avoided such a blasphemy against God, by drawing no inference as to Providence from any of the laws or institutions of men, for he appeared to regard human institutions as radically bad. At all events he allowed his pupils—as I have shewn above—to say that the rulers of the world are "thieves and robbers" and that the courts of justice are "courts of injustice." His belief in Providence was —I seemed to see clearly—based on nothing but the consciousness of the Logos within himself. The Logos in the vast majority of mankind appeared to him to have done them no good: so he could not argue from that.

When someone mentioned the fate of the Emperor Galba as disproving a belief in Providence, Epictetus implied a scornful disavowal of any intention to base belief on any such historical event. Nor did he ever refer to God as controlling the movements of nations. In answer therefore to my silent question, " Does our Master see God in the history of individuals or nations?" his teaching seemed to reply " No, I see it in nothing except Socrates, Diogenes, and a few other philosophers, and also in myself. Beyond this little group of souls, though I feel myself able to infer God in everything, I cannot really infer Him in anything mental or spiritual. Hence I am driven to such physical instances as butter, cheese, stomachs, and beards!"

On leaving the lecture-room I chatted with Glaucus and tried hard to be cheerful. But how I missed Arrian! I felt inclined to turn Epicurean. The " careless " gods of Epicurus seemed at least less unloveable than the Providence of Epictetus. Too much depressed for any kind of study, I did not return to my lodging but walked out into the country by unfrequented paths, resting after mid-day in a little village inn. Coming out, toward the close of the afternoon, I found an acquaintance of mine, Apronius Rufus, standing in the porch and amusing himself by throwing figs and nuts to a crowd of boys just emerging from the doors of a neighbouring school. From scrambling and scuffling the boys had come to fighting—all but two or three, who held aloof with an air of sulky superiority; and one, I think, saw the schoolmaster in the distance. My acquaintance was attending the Epicurean classes in Nicopolis. We Cynics called the followers of Epicurus "swine," and I could not resist the temptation of saying, " Rufus, you are making converts. When they grow up, these little pigs will do you credit." He laughed good-humouredly : " Not all of them, Silanus ! A few, as you see yonder, remain of your persuasion, true Cynics, that is to say, puppies or prigs. But we do pretty well. Nature is for us, though you and the schoolmaster are allied against us. By the way, I think I see your ally coming round the corner. I will be off. Two against Hercules are one too many. Farewell!" " Farewell!" said I, " Your wit is as much stronger than mine as your philosophy is weaker."

"But *is* it weaker?" thought I, as he strode back to Nicopolis, and I in the opposite direction. Was not Apronius right in saying that Nature was on his side ? Does not Providence, like Circe, throw down figs and nuts for us human creatures to make us swine ? Is she not always saying to us, " Push, and be greedy! Then you will get what you want"? And did not Epictetus acquiesce in this, in effect, saying to the two or three non-pushers, " Be content. The others, the masses of men, are ' better ' than you are for pushing and for kicking and for fighting like greedy swine " ? But who made them " better " ? Was it not Nature ? And how could I feel sure that this same Nature or Providence that made "grass " (as Epictetus said) to produce " milk and butter and cheese," did not make man to produce scrambling and scuffling and fighting —a spectacle for some amused God, who watches from the windows of heaven, like Apronius Rufus from the inn-door on earth ?

After a long circuit, returning to Nicopolis, I sat down to rest in a copse when the sun was drawing towards the west. Tired out by my walk, I fell asleep. When I awoke, the sun had set and the evening star was shining. As I sat in silence gazing upon it, better thoughts were brought to me. " Five minutes," I said, " with Hesper teach more about Providence than an hour with Epictetus." Then it occurred to me, " But, were I Priam, and were this the evening before Troy was taken, would not Hesper shine as brightly before me? What does Hesper prove?" Presently, the lesser stars began to appear, growing each moment in number. Then I remembered how Moses represents the Lord God appearing to Abraham (when he was as yet childless) and saying to him, " Look up to the heaven and number the stars, if thou art able to number them all. So shall thy seed be." And what had come of it all ? A nation that was no nation, a race of captives, known to us in Rome chiefly as hating pork and strangers no less than they loved their sabbaths. Then I thought, " Had Hesper any more favour for Abraham than for Priam ? Perhaps the stars promised peace and prosperity to both and broke their promise ! What Troy is, that Jerusalem is. Nay, worse. Troy has produced a New Troy. Where is the New Jerusalem ? And where is the great nation promised to Abraham ? A flock (or flocks) of exiles, fanatics, and slaves ! "

Just then came into my mind the memory of some words about the stars in Isaiah. I had taken the book with me to lecture. So I unrolled it till I came to them : " *Lift up your eyes on high and see. Who hath appointed all these ? He that leadeth forth His host in a numbered array. He will call them all by name. Because of thy great glory, and in the might of thy strength, not one escapeth from thine eye.*" Then the prophet declared that, even as the stars of heaven are made visible in the darkness, so the seed of Abraham was not hidden by any darkness from God's eye : " *Say not, O Jacob (ah, why didst thou dare to say it, O Israel ?*) ' *My way is hidden from God, and my God hath taken away judgment and hath departed from me.' Hast thou not even now found out the truth ? Hast thou not clearly heard it ? The God eternal, the God that framed and fashioned the earth, even to its furthest corners, He will not faint for hunger, nor is there any fathoming of His wisdom. To them that hunger He giveth strength—but sorrow to them that have no grief. For hunger shall fall on the youths, and weariness on the young men, and the chosen warriors shall utterly lose strength; but they that wait patiently for God shall renew their strength ; they shall put forth wings like eagles ; they shall run and not be weary ; they shall walk erect and shall not faint for hunger.*"

I could not believe all this. But neither could I disbelieve it. One voice said to me, " The poet is casting on the God of the stars the mantle that he has borrowed from the God of Abraham, Isaac, and Jacob." But another voice kept saying to me, "Wait patiently for God: He shall renew thy strength." In the afternoon, when I had thrown myself down to rest, I had thought that I would give up the search after truth, get rid of all my books, leave Nicopolis, and go at once into the army. Now I was more hopeful. But I could not give any logical reason for my hope. Isaiah had not convinced me. Far from it! The promise to Abraham seemed still to me to have resulted in failure. I had broken off my study of Paul, almost at its commencement, in order to study Isaiah. And Isaiah, without Paul, presented many difficulties that might perplex wiser minds than mine. "Grant," said I, "that David the son of Jesse was a great poet. Grant that Isaiah was a great prophet. Yet what were their poems and prophecies except so many pillars of vapour, or, if of substance, then substantial failures; pillars with the capital gone and the shaft broken, no longer sustaining anything? Their temple is burned a second time, never to be rebuilt; the rod of Jesse, cut off from the very root, with no life left in it, 'despised indeed and rejected' but with no compensation of being 'exalted' or of 'dividing the spoils of the strong'!"

All these things I said over and over again to myself. But still another voice, deeper than my own, seemed to be repeating "Wait patiently on God and He will renew thy strength! Wait patiently! Wait!" Up to the moment of retiring to rest that night my mind was in a state of oscillation. On the one hand, Scaurus might be right, and my best course might be to give up the study of philosophy, and to prepare myself for a military career. On the other hand, there appeared nothing in these poems or prophecies of Isaiah that would make a man less fit to be a soldier. My last thought was, "I should like to see how the modern Jew, Paul, takes up the teaching of the ancient Jew, Isaiah. I have but glanced at his quotations as yet." So I decided to examine this point on the following day.

CHAPTER XIV

PAUL'S CONVERSION

HITHERTO my study of Christian or Jewish literature had never followed my intentions. I had intended to read Paul continuously. But first Isaiah, then David, then Moses, and then Isaiah again, had intervened. I was going forward all the while, but by a winding course, like a stream among hills and rocks. Now again I have to describe how—although I sat down with a determination to digress no more but to read through the epistles from the beginning to the end—I was led off to another investigation.

The first phrase in the volume did not long occupy me. True, I had greatly disliked it when I first glanced at it, a few days ago—"Paul a *slave* of Jesus Christ." "Slave" was always used by Epictetus in a bad sense, and I had then thought it savoured of servility. But now I knew that the translation of Isaiah often used it to denote a devoted servant of God; and it seemed to me that Paul had perhaps no other word that could so well express how he felt bound to service by Christ's "constraining love."

Nor did the next words now cause me much difficulty:—
"*Called* to be an *apostle, set apart* to preach the *good tidings* of God, which He promised beforehand through His prophets in the holy scriptures." Scaurus had told me how Epictetus had borrowed from the Christians this notion of being "called" to bear testimony to God. Whether he was right or wrong, he had prepared me to find "called" in such a passage as this. It was connected here with an "apostle," that is, someone "*sent*" by God. This, too, seemed natural. Though Epictetus did

not use the noun, he often used the verb to describe his ideal Cynic—and especially Diogenes—as being "*sent*" to proclaim the divine law. "Set apart" I understood to mean "set apart" by special endowments of body and mind such as Epictetus frequently attributed to Socrates and Diogenes.

As to the "good tidings," I knew that Epictetus would have considered it to be a message from God to this effect, "Children, I have placed your true happiness in your own control. Take it from yourselves, each of you, from that which is within you." But what was Paul's "good tidings"? Isaiah had described God's messengers as "proclaiming good tidings," namely, that God was coming to the aid of men: "As a shepherd will He shepherd His flock and with His arm will He gather the lambs." Epictetus, as I have shewn above, scoffed at this metaphor of "shepherd." But I could not help liking it. Homer used it about kings, Isaiah about God. I thought Paul meant, in part, that God would manifest Himself as the righteous King.

But I knew that Paul must also mean more, and that he would not have claimed the attention of the Romans for a mere repetition of an ancient written prophecy. Any child able to read could have repeated that. Paul must have more good news—either about the Shepherd, or about the time, or about the certainty of His coming. At this point, it occurred to me, "Why wait for the gospels that Flaccus is to send me? Why not search through the epistles to find out what Paul's gospel is?" But I checked myself, saying, "No more digressions." The next words were these: "Concerning His Son, who came into being from the seed of David according to the flesh; who was defined Son of God, in power, according to the spirit of holiness, from the resurrection of the dead, Jesus Christ our Lord." These words I have translated literally and obscurely so as to indicate to the reader how exceedingly obscure they seemed to me. "I must pass on," I said, "I can make nothing of this. What follows may make things clearer."

I began to read on, but soon desisted. The words that followed took no hold of my mind. I tried, and tried again, but was irresistibly dragged back to "resurrection of the dead," and "power," and "spirit of holiness," and "defined"—especially to "resurrection." What kind of "resurrection"? During my childhood I had heard my father tell a story or legend how, just before the battle of Philippi, the spirit of the great Julius appeared to Brutus, saying "Thou shalt see me at Philippi." There Brutus slew himself. And Scaurus had remarked that a similar fate had overtaken others of the conspirators; so that some might declare that Julius had power to rise from the grave and turn the swords of his assassins against themselves. That, if true, was an instance of the power of a man, or a man-god, rising from the dead in a spirit of vengeance. But Paul spoke of "resurrection of the dead," and "power," in connexion with a "spirit of holiness." Paul (I knew that already from the epistles) had been an enemy of Christ, as Brutus had been of Cæsar. Comparing the two conquests, I asked whether more "power" might not be claimed for Christ's "spirit of holiness" than for Cæsar's spirit of vengeance. For Paul, instead of being killed by Christ, had been made a willing and profitable "slave." Brutus had been forced to turn his sword against himself; Paul had been constrained by love to turn his new sword, "the sword of the spirit," against the enemies of his new Master.

What light did this passage throw on the causes of Paul's conversion? I read it over again. Christ, he said, "came into being," or was born, "of the seed of David according to the flesh." Well, that might be one cause. A Jew would be more likely to accept as king a descendant of the house of David. And besides, Jews might think that such a birth fulfilled the prophecy above mentioned about "the root of Jesse." But there might be many born "of the seed of David according to the flesh." That which "defined" Christ to be "the Son of God" was "the resurrection of the dead"; and the "defining" was "in power" and "according to the spirit of holiness." By these last words, Paul seemed to separate Christ's resurrection from any such apparition as that of Julius, or other ghosts and phantasms; which may appear to this man or to that, and then vanish, either caused by evil magic, and doing an evil and magical work, or doing no work at all; whereas the rising again of Christ was caused by a holy power and resulted in a work of abiding power and "holiness."

This it was that led me into a new digression. Recalling how the spirit of Cæsar was said to have appeared and spoken to Brutus, I desired to know what words the spirit of Christ said to Paul, and when and how Christ appeared to him. I wished also to inquire about the nature of Paul himself, before and after his conversion; and whether he shewed signs of restlessness, and of ambition to become a leader in a new sect. Perhaps I should have spared myself this searching. if I had known that, along with the gospels, Flaccus was sending me Luke's Acts of the Apostles. But the results of the search were helpful to me. So I will set them down in case they may be helpful to others.

First, then, I found that, before his conversion, Paul had been a Jew of the strictest kind. "Ye have heard," he said to the Galatians, "how that beyond measure I used to persecute the church of God and laid it waste, and I advanced in the Jews' religion beyond many of mine own age among my countrymen, being more exceedingly zealous for the traditions of my fathers." That expression "ye have heard" clearly shewed that it was a matter of notoriety. The writer meant (I thought) not only "ye have heard from me," but also "from others," perhaps meaning his enemies, the Judaizers (often mentioned in this epistle), who pointed at him the finger of scorn, saying, "This is the man that changed his mind. This man thought once as we do." To the Philippians also Paul said that he had every claim to be confident "in the flesh," being "A Hebrew of Hebrews; as to the law, a Pharisee; as to zeal, persecuting the church; as to the righteousness that is in the law, blameless." So also he said to one of his assistants, Timothy, that he, Paul, had been "the chief of sinners" because he had persecuted the church.

Elsewhere I found him writing to the Romans that his heart sorrowed for his countrymen and that he could almost have prayed to be "accursed from Christ" for their sake, for they, he said, had the Patriarchs, and to them were made the promises; and he expressed a fervid hope that in the end the nation would receive the promises, though for a time they were shut out. What he said to the Romans convinced me, in an indirect way, almost as strongly as what he said to the Galatians and Philippians, that Paul had been a genuine patriot, observing the traditions, as well as the written law, of the Jews, and persecuting the Christians with all his might because he thought (as we also were wont to think in Rome) that they were a pestilential sect, destructive of law, order, and morality. So much for what Paul was before his conversion.

Next, as to what happened to him at the moment of his conversion. First I turned to the Corinthian letter describing the appearances of Christ after death, to see whether anything had escaped me in the context—any words uttered by Christ to Paul, for example, at the time. But there was nothing except the bald statements, by this time familiar to me, " He is recorded to have been raised on the third day according to the scriptures; and he appeared to Cephas; then to the twelve; afterwards he appeared to above five hundred brethen, of whom the greater part remain till now, but some are fallen asleep; then he appeared to James; then to all the apostles; and last of all, as unto one born out of due time, he appeared to me also. For I am the least of the apostles, that am not meet to be called an apostle because I persecuted the church of God." All this Paul had previously delivered to the Corinthians—so says the letter—as a " tradition," and as a part of his " gospel."

This gave me no help. All that I could infer from it was that Christ probably " appeared " to his enemy Paul in the same way in which he had " appeared " to his friends and followers, and that the " appearing " must have been of a cogent kind, since it convinced an enemy. Nor did I gain much more from the Galatian account, which was as follows: " But when it was the good pleasure of God—who set me apart for this service even from my mother's womb, and called me by His grace—to reveal His Son in me that I might make it my life's work to preach the good tidings about him among the nations, immediately I conferred not with flesh and blood, neither did I go up to Jerusalem to those that had been apostles before me, but I went away into Arabia, and turned back again to Damascus."

Here I was in doubt whether "reveal His Son *in me*,"

meant "reveal *by my means*," or "reveal *in my heart*," that is, "unveil in my soul the image of the Son, which up to that time I had smothered with self-will and obstinacy"—as though "the Son" had been all the while in Paul's heart, but he had been refusing to acknowledge him. This latter interpretation I preferred. But still there was no mention of any words uttered by Christ to Paul at the moment of his conversion. Only, as Paul implies elsewhere that he had not seen Jesus in the flesh, that is, in person, I presumed that there must have been some such utterance as "I am Jesus," or "I am the crucified":— else, how would Paul have recognised the appearance?

As to the place of conversion, however, some light was afforded by the words "I turned back to Damascus," shewing that he had been near Damascus when it happened. And the epistle to the Corinthians said that he had been let down in a basket from Damascus so as to escape the Jews. It appeared that he was persecuting the Christians up to the time of his conversion; that he was doing this in or near Damascus when he was converted; and that the Jews living in that city turned against him after his conversion, so that he had to escape from them.

Hereupon I tried to imagine Paul the persecutor, in his course of "persecuting the church," suddenly stopped by an apparition of Christ. In respect of his acts, Paul—though he could not possibly have been so cruel—might be compared to Nero, who also persecuted the Christians. But in respect of righteousness and truth and fervour, Paul was like Epictetus. Then I recalled the story recently told me by Scaurus, how he and his father had come suddenly upon the young Epictetus, in the Neronian gardens, staring upon the Christians in their torments, and how Scaurus had remarked upon the ineffaceableness of the impression produced on his own mind and (as he believed) on that of my future Teacher. That I could well understand. But Scaurus and Epictetus were merely passive spectators. Paul was a perpetrator. "How much deeper," I said, "and all the more deep and terrible in proportion to his sense of justice and truth, must have been the impression on Paul's mind, when he suddenly woke up to the fact that he had been persecuting the followers of Truth, the disciples of the Suffering Servant of God, predicted by the prophets!"

Then it appeared to me that perhaps the precise *words* uttered by Christ in that moment of Paul's shock and agony were not of so much importance as the *feeling* of shock and agony itself, followed by a great wrenching away of prejudices and misconceptions, and by a sudden influx of a dazzling light on eyes habituated to darkness. Looking again at the Philippian letter, I perceived how much Paul had to give up, how lightly he regarded the sacrifice of all his prospects of prosperity and promotion among his own people: "*But whatever things were once gains to me, these I have counted as loss for Christ's sake. Nay, more, I count all things as loss for the sake of the preeminence of the knowledge of Christ Jesus my Lord; for whose sake I suffered the loss of all that I had, and I count it all as refuse, in order that I may gain Christ and be found in Him—not having as my own righteousness that which is of the law, but that which is through faith in Christ, the righteousness that is from God based on that faith—that I may know Him, and the power of His resurrection and fellowship with His sufferings, being conformed with His death; if by any means I may attain to the resurrection of the dead! Not that I have already received, or am already perfected. But I pursue the chase, if by any means I may seize as a prize that for which I was also seized as a captive by Christ Jesus!*"

These last words made me understand how Paul might have regarded Christ as manifested *in* him rather than *to* him. Isaiah saw God uplifted on high *outside* him. But Paul felt the Son of God enthroned as sovereign *within* him: I remembered reading in some drama how the wife of a dethroned and submissive sovereign goads him to rebel against his successor, saying—

"Hath he deposed
Thine intellect? Hath he been *in thy heart*?"

This was just what Paul experienced and exulted in avowing. Christ had "deposed" Paul's former self, and substituted a new self of his own as viceroy, to rule Paul, "in his heart." A soldier might say that Christ, in the moment of taking Paul prisoner, had (so to speak) given him back his sword, saying "Use it on my side among all the nations of the earth, that they also may receive the good tidings of the forgiveness of sins." But in fact (according to Paul's view) Christ had done much more than this. He had given Paul a new sword, "the sword of the spirit." He had also made his whole nature anew, according to Paul's own saying, "If any man be in Christ, he is a new creature, behold all things are made new."

Not that I was as yet convinced that Christ had actually risen from the dead. For I did not yet feel sure that Paul might not have been deceived by himself and by the Christians. But I did now feel sure that Paul was honest and did not knowingly deceive his readers. And it was becoming more and more difficult to believe that self-deception or Christian deception could have produced effects on multitudes of men so great and permanent as those which were plainly discernible in the epistles.

I remember at this time trying to prevent my growing admiration for Paul's work from blinding me to his defects. Such phrases as "let him be anathema," and "dogs," and "whose belly is their glory," and "I would that those who are thus desolating you would even emasculate themselves"—these and others I marked with red in my volume. I knew Epictetus would have condemned them. But I soon perceived that these fiery flashes of wrath were reserved for those whom Paul regarded as proud and greedy ensnarers and oppressors of helpless souls; proud of knowledge that was no knowledge; greedy of money and influence to which they had no right; shutting their eyes against the light, and dragging back poor pilgrims just as they were on the point of entering into the City of Truth. Towards others, even if they might have appeared as rivals, he seemed to me to feel no rivalry, merging all such feeling in allegiance to Christ. Some, he said to the Philippians, preached Christ "thinking to add affliction" to his bonds, out of jealousy and spite. "What then?" he says, "Whatever may be the motive, Christ is preached, and I rejoice. Yea, and I will rejoice." In the same spirit he wrote to the church of Corinth concerning those among them who said, "I am of Apollos," "I am of Cephas," "I am of Paul"—condemning all partisanship, although he gently reminds them of his singular relation to them, "Even though ye have ten thousand tutors in Christ, yet ye have not many fathers: for in Christ Jesus through the Gospel I begot you."

Another detail interested me. Paul (I found) differed greatly from Epictetus in physical constitution. Epictetus used to teach us that a Cynic had no business to be "infirm" of body. At all events, he said, no such person can do the work of a Cynic Missionary. When he extolled "the sceptre of Diogenes," he used to tell a story of the way in which that philosopher, lying by the roadside, sick of a fever, called on the wayfarers to admire him. It was the road to Olympia, and people were on the way to the games: "Villains!" he shouted to them, "Stay! Are you going all that way to Olympia to see athletes fight or perish, and will you not stay to behold a contest between a man and a fever?" But this contest, I think, ended in Diogenes's death. As a rule, both he and Socrates had been perfectly and robustly healthy: and Epictetus seemed somewhat to despise those who were otherwise.

Paul, on the other hand, frequently spoke of his "weakness," meaning physical infirmity or sickness. It was "owing to *weakness*," he told the Galatians, that he preached the gospel for the first time among them; and he called it a "temptation (or, trial) in the flesh." This I took to mean that he had been delayed in Galatia by some sickness, and had founded the Church there while in that condition. So to the Corinthians he said, "In *weakness* and in fear and in trembling did I come addressing myself to you." But that letter went on to say, "And my word and my preaching were not in the persuasive words of wisdom, but in demonstration of the spirit and *power*"—so that "power" went hand in hand with "weakness." Once at least I found Paul praying to be delivered from "weakness." "I will not boast about myself"—so he writes to the Corinthians—"except in my weaknesses." And then he went on to explain the "boasting" as being quite different from that of Diogenes. For the Cynic cried, in effect, "Come and see how strong I am!" But Paul meant that he would "boast" because, when he felt weakest, then his Master came to his aid and made him strong. This he expressed in a way that perplexed me at first: "*There was given to me a thorn in the flesh, an angel of Satan, to buffet me, that I might not be lifted up above measure. About this, I besought the Lord thrice that it might depart from me. And He said unto me, My grace sufficeth for thee, for in weakness is Power made perfect.*"

For some time I could not understand this phrase, "*an angel of Satan.*" But afterwards I found Paul writing to his Thessalonian converts that, when he wished to come to help them, "Satan *hindered* him," so that Satan appeared to be a *hinderer* of the gospel. Then it seemed to me that among the Jews and Christians certain diseases might be regarded as demons, or the work of demons—just as, in Rome, "Fever" is worshipped as a divine and has temples. This fact I had heard Epictetus mention; and he also condemned those who pray to be delivered from fever. The right course was, he said, "to have the fever rightly." Paul seemed to say, "first pray to be delivered from fever, if it seems to hinder you from doing the work of the Lord. Then, if it be revealed to you as the will of the Lord that you should bear the fever, be sure that He will make your bodily weakness spiritually strong. Thus the temptation from Satan, the Hinderer and Adversary, shall be turned into a strengthening trial from God, your Helper and Friend."

Summing up the marvellous changes that seemed to have come about for Paul in consequence of Christ's "appearing" to him, I was more than ever disposed to believe that it was of a divine origin and a great deal more than a mere "appearing." I thought it must have been an "appearing" to the inner eye, the spirit, as well as to the outer eye.

When we Romans and Greeks use the word "spirit," we mostly think of a shadowy unreal appearance of the dead. We should not call Jupiter, or Zeus, a "spirit." But I perceived that, with Paul, "spirit" was more real—and, if I may so say, more eternally solid—than "body." It was the real "person." The word "person" in Greek, as also in Latin, means a "mask" or "character." There is, with us, no one word to express "real person." Common people think the body real, but the spirit unreal. Paul used the name "spiritual body" to describe a "real person," raised from the dead in Christ. Well, then, it seemed to me that the power of Christ on Paul might be described, not only as an "appearing" but also as the grasp of a "real person," "taking hold of" Paul's spirit with a spiritual hand so as to strengthen and direct him. What else was it that made him so strong?

The strength of Epictetus in bearing trials and sufferings had long excited my admiration. But now the strength of Paul seemed greater. Epictetus bore—or at least professed to bear—only his own burdens. As for those of others, he said, "These are nothing to me." Paul was like a gentle nurse or tender mother with the weaklings among his converts. "Who," he asked, "is made to stumble, and I burn not? Who is weak, and I am not weak?" And yet, in his weakness, he was a very Hercules or Atlas, strong enough to bear "the care of all the churches"! This "weak" man was always fighting, always craving to fight, and always conquering—up to the time of his impending departure, when he exclaimed that he had "fought the good fight"! And through what an extent of the civilised world! "From Jerusalem to Illyricum"—so he wrote to the Romans! In that same letter he announced his intention of carrying the eagles of the New Empire into Rome itself, and of passing onward from Rome to the invasion of Spain! No wonder that he felt able to say, "I take pleasure in weaknesses, in outrages, in straits and necessities, in persecutions and hardships, in Christ's behalf; for in the moment when I am weak, in that moment I am strong."

"I am strong"! Yes. Rolling up the volume as I retired to rest that night, I was constrained to agree with that, at all events. "About some things," said I, "or perhaps about many things in your letters I am doubtful; but assuredly you are strong. I myself am also certain that you are honest. But that you are strong—and that, too, with a strength that comes from faith in the resurrection of your Master—this not even an atheist or Epicurean could deny."

CHAPTER XV

EPICTETUS'S GOSPEL

I WENT somewhat unwillingly to the next day's lecture. It would probably be interesting, I thought; but I could no longer deny that I was beginning to feel doubtful about that. And certainly I was more interested in Paul's letters. Soon after I was seated, Glaucus came in. He looked worn and haggard, but there was no time to ask him questions. The subject of the lecture was, How are we to struggle with adversity? The answer was, By bearing in mind that death is no evil; that defamation is nothing but the noise of madmen; and that only the rich, the lords and rulers of the earth, are the subjects of tragedies. But the main point was that "the door" is always open: "Do not be more cowardly than children. The moment they are tired, they say, 'I won't play any more.' Say you the same, 'I won't play any more.' And be off. But if you stay, don't keep on complaining." This topic had become familiar. What followed, though not quite novel, interested me more, because it seemed to bear on the Jewish Law.

First came a general descant on the advantages of being absolutely free from fear. Why should a man fear? Had he not power over everything that might cause him fear? Then a pupil was supposed to ask for more rules of life, saying, "But give me commandments." The reply was, "Why am I to give you commandments? Has not Zeus given you commandments? Has He not given and appointed for you what is your own, unhindered and unshackled; but what is not your own, hindered and shackled? Well, then, what is the commandment? Of what nature is the strict injunction with which you have come into the world from Zeus? It is this, 'Keep in all ways the things that are yours, desire not the things that are for others'.... Having such suggestions and commands from Zeus, what further commands can you crave from me?" He finished this section of his discourse thus, "Bring these commandments, bring your preconceptions, bring the demonstrations of the philosophers, bring the words you have often heard and have often yourself spoken, read, and pondered."

I could not feel sure whether "bring" meant "bring to bear on each point," or "bring to your aid"; but, in either case, this conclusion, to me at least, was disappointing. "It is all very true," I thought, "and strictly according to reason. We are sure we have 'preconceptions.' We are not sure that we receive strength, in this or that emergency, from any being except ourselves. And yet how tame—and, in emergencies, how flat and unhelpful—such an utterance as this appears in comparison with the oracle that the Christian believed he had heard from his Lord, 'My grace is sufficient for thee. For Power is made perfect in weakness'!"

The rest of the lecture was more lively and expressed with more novelty, but old in substance—addressed to those who wanted to enjoy the best seats in the theatre of life but not to be squeezed by the crowd. His prescription was, "Don't go to see it at all, man, and then you will not be squeezed. Or, if you like, go into the best seats, when the theatre is empty, and enjoy the sun there." Then he added something that made my companion Glaucus shrug his shoulders and cease taking notes, "Remember always, *We squeeze ourselves, we pinch ourselves.* For example, we will suppose you are being reviled. What is the harm in that? Why pinch yourself on that account? Go and revile a stone. What harm will you do the stone? Well then, when you are reviled, listen like a stone. And then what harm does the reviler do you?"

We went out together, Glaucus and I. I think I have said before that Glaucus had some troubles at that time in his home at Corinth, but of what kind I did not exactly know. "Silanus," he said presently to me, with a bitter smile, "I am pinching myself with my shoe." "Then take it off," said I. "By the immortal Gods," he exclaimed, "I wish I could! But what if my shoe is the universe? What if it is——" He stopped. I replied at once, like a faithful disciple of Epictetus, "Not the universe, Glaucus, but your opinions about the universe." "Well then," said he, "my 'opinions about the universe.' What if my 'opinions about the universe' include 'opinions about' certain persons and things—home, father, mother, sister, and other such indifferent trifles? To put an imaginary case, could I by 'taking off' my 'opinion about' my father, take my father out of prison, or save him from death, or others from disgrace worse than death? No, Silanus, I am beginning to be a little tired of hearing 'Remember always, *You pinch yourselves.*' Often it is so. But not always. What say you?"

What ought I to have said? I knew exactly what was the correct thing to say. "In such cases, give up the game. The door is open. Do you say the universe pinches you? Then take off your shoe by going out of the universe." This would have been the orthodox consistent answer. But I was inconsistent, not indeed in words, but in a heretical glance of sympathy, which Glaucus—I could see—interpreted rightly. We parted. As I walked slowly back to my rooms, I had leisure to reflect that the gospel of Epictetus had no power to strengthen Glaucus, and—I began to fear—no power to strengthen me, except to bear comparative trifles. It was not strong enough—at least in me—to stand up against the great and tragic calamities of human life.

With these thoughts, I sat down once more to study Paul's epistles from the beginning. Once more (but now for the last time) I was led into a digression. It was the word "gospel" that thus dragged me away, coming upon me (in Paul's first sentence) just when I had been deploring the failure of the "gospel" of Epictetus. Reading on, I found that Paul's "gospel" had been "promised beforehand, through God's prophets, in the holy scriptures concerning His son." A little later, the writer said, "I am not ashamed of the gospel. For it is God's power tending to salvation for every one that hath faith, Jew first, and then Greek. For God's righteousness is therein revealed, from faith tending to faith, even as it is written, 'Now the righteous shall live by faith'."

The next words surprised me by mentioning "God's wrath" as a part of the gospel: "For there is revealed therein *God's wrath* from heaven against all ungodliness and unrighteousness of men that hold down the truth in unrighteousness." But I immediately perceived that it might be regarded as "gospel" or "good tidings" to be informed that God does really feel "wrath" at unrighteousness, or injustice, and that He will sooner or later judge and punish it. Accordingly I was not surprised to find Paul, soon afterwards, connecting "gospel" and "judging" thus: "In the day when God shall judge the secrets of men according to my gospel, through Jesus Christ."

From this I perceived that Paul's gospel promised a righteous judgment as well as immortality. But how could it be proved that there would be this righteous judgment? Paul said that it was "revealed *from faith to faith.*" He added, "*as it is written*"; and a note in the margin of my MS. shewed me that he was referring to a certain prophet named Habakkuk. I unrolled the passage. It seemed that this Habakkuk was living in times when his nation was grievously oppressed. The oppressors were like fishermen catching the oppressed at their pleasure. The prophet, standing on a tower, said to the people, "Wait and have faith. The righteous shall live by faith." Paul meant that if we would begin by having some faith in a righteous God, in spite of appearances on the surface of things, we should be helped to rise "from faith to more faith," and consequently that we should "live"—that is have *real* life. Faith seemed to Paul needful for life. Life without faith seemed to him no real life but a living death.

As I read on, I saw that this kind of "faith" was regarded by Paul as the foundation of all righteousness. He quoted scripture thus, "Abraham had faith in God, and it was reckoned unto him for righteousness." Then I remembered that he had quoted the same passage in writing to the Galatians, in order to prove to them that the seed of Abraham did not obtain righteousness by doing the works prescribed in the code of Moses, but by following in the faith of their forefather. Now this faith, in the case of Abraham, had seemed to me at first of a narrow and selfish nature:—"God will keep His promise to *me*, God will give *me* a child in my old age." But Paul shewed that the promise concerned "all the nations of the earth," and that Abraham was not selfish in his faith—any more than in his pleading with God for such righteous people as might be in Sodom and Gomorrah when he said, "Shall not the judge of all the earth do right?" This faith in God's truth and righteous judgments was at the bottom of Paul's gospel, and Paul taught that it was at the bottom of all righteousness both of Jews and Gentiles.

But here came a great difficulty and obstacle in the way of faith, because, when men departed from God's righteousness, God Himself (so Paul taught) departed from them for a time, allowing them to do the unrighteousness that was in their hearts and to judge unjustly. For this cause (according to Paul) God introduced Law into the world, and especially the Law of Moses. The Law was brought in to represent His righteousness in a poor rough fashion, until the time should come when He would send into the world the real righteousness or justice, the real judge or spirit of judgment. Such a judge (according to Paul's gospel) was Jesus Christ, judging the world already to some extent, but destined to judge it in complete righteousness, "in the day when God shall judge the secrets of men according to my gospel," said Paul, "through Jesus Christ."

At this point came the doctrine of the immortality of the soul, enabling Paul to say, "Wait, and you will see justice done"; whereas Epictetus was forced to say, in effect, "Justice will never be done,"—not at least what a plain man would call justice—"since the justice of this life was, is, and will be, oppression, and no second life is ever to exist."

The only passage in which Epictetus (as far as I could recollect) described a good judge, was one in which the philosopher was supposed to hold a dialogue with the Censor, or Judge, of Nicopolis. The man was an Epicurean; and Epictetus, after representing him as boasting that he was "a judge of the Greeks," and that he could order imprisonment or flogging at

Chapter 15] EPICTETUS'S GOSPEL

his discretion, replied that this was coercing, not judging. "Shew us," said he, "the things that are unprofitable for us and we shall avoid them. Make us passionate imitators of yourself, as Socrates made men of himself. He was really a ruler of men. For he, above all others, so framed men that they subordinated to him their inclinations, aversions, and impulses."

This seemed to me, at first, a fine ideal of a spiritual judge. I contrasted it with Paul's picture of the Lord as Judge taking vengeance in fire upon His enemies; and Epictetus seemed to have the advantage. But on consideration it appeared that Epictetus was confusing his hearers by passing suddenly from a judge to a ruler. According to his own account elsewhere, Socrates did not persuade a thousandth part of those to whom he addressed himself. On the other hand Paul distinguished two aspects of Christ. In one, He appeared as constraining His subjects to love Him and to become "passionate imitators" of Him. In the other, He appeared as a judge, making the guilty shrink from their own guilt, and feel pain at their own sin, when the light of judgment reveals them to themselves. Paul spoke of "fire" according to the metaphors of the scriptures. He appeared to be describing the Supreme Judge as destroying the evil while purifying the good—as fire may destroy some things but purify others.

This was not the only occasion when the gospel of Epictetus seemed to me—not at first, but upon full consideration—inferior to the gospel of Paul in recognising facts fairly and fully. For example, Paul, in the epistle I was now reading, adopted the ancient Jewish tradition that death came into the world as a result of the sin of the first man Adam. According to this view, death was a "curse." Now Epictetus appeared to be directly attacking this doctrine when he spoke as follows, "If I knew that disease had been destined to come upon me at this very moment, I would rush towards it—just as my foot, if it had sense, would rush to defile itself in the mire. Why are ears of corn created? Is it not that they may be parched and ripened? And are they to be parched and ripened, and yet not reaped? Surely, then, if they had sense, the ears of wheat ought not to pray never to be reaped. Nay, this is nothing short of a curse upon wheat—never to be reaped! So you ought to know that *it is nothing short of a curse upon men, not to die.* It is all the same as not being ripened—not to be reaped."

How much finer, thought I at first, is this doctrine of Epictetus than the doctrine of Paul! And how superstitious is that Hebrew story about a serpent, causing death to fall upon man as a curse from God! But coming back to the matter again after I read some way in the epistle, and thinking over what "death" meant to Epictetus and what it meant to Paul, I began to waver. For Epictetus thought that "death" meant being dissolved into the four elements. And how was this like "being ripened and reaped"? When corn is reaped, men get good from it. But when I am "reaped," that is to say, distributed into my four elements, who will get any good from that? So, once more, the gospel of Epictetus, as compared with the gospel of Paul, seemed to be deficient not only in power but also in directness and clearness of statement.

It reminded me of the saying of Paul when he said that God sent him to preach the gospel "*not in wisdom of word*" lest the cross of Christ should be made of no effect." "Wisdom of word" appeared to mean "calling old facts by new names without revealing any new truth." So far as I could understand the gospel of Epictetus, his language about my being "ripened and reaped" was like that other earlier promise that I should find "friends" in the four elements when I passed into them in the dissolution of death. It was all "wisdom of word."

CHAPTER XVI

PAUL'S GOSPEL

IN contrasting Epictetus with Paul to the disadvantage of the former, I was far from imagining that the latter had unloosed the knot of the origin of sin. But at all events he recognised the existence of the knot. Epictetus ignored it, or failed to recognise it. He spoke in the same breath of God's ordaining "vice and virtue, winter and summer," as though God's appointing that some men shall be bad caused him no more difficulty than His appointing that some days shall be cold.

Paul, on the other hand, treated death as though it were a curse in the intention of Satan, but a blessing (or step towards blessing) through the controlling will of God. He also spoke of a spiritual body rising out of the dead earthly body, as flower and fruit rise out of the decaying seed. I did not at first feel sure what he meant by this. Flower and fruit resemble seed in that they can be touched. Did Paul mean that the spiritual body resembled the earthly body in being tangible, besides being more beautiful? I thought not. It seemed to me possible that a person in the flesh, dying, might become a person in the spirit, living for ever. A man's actions and sufferings, sown in the transient flesh, might after death become part of the flower of the imperishable spirit, the real man, the spiritual body. That, I thought, was what Paul meant. This belief I found also stimulative to well-doing, according to the saying of Paul himself, "I press on, if by any means I may attain to the resurrection of the dead." Moreover I remembered the "angel of Satan" appointed for Paul to keep him from pride, and how he prayed against it, and received a revelation "My grace is sufficient for thee." If prayer and strength were brought about for Paul by an "adversary" of prayer, might not righteousness be brought about for the human race by the "adversary" of righteousness? I did not myself at that time believe in the existence of such an "adversary"; but Paul's belief seemed to me not unreasonable.

This turned me to other passages in the epistles concerning "Satan," or the "angels of Satan," or "principalities and powers." And I contrasted them with what Epictetus had said, "All things are full of Gods and daemons," meaning good daemons. Once more, the words of Epictetus seemed the nobler. But were they true? What did they amount to in fact? Nothing except "wisdom of word," calling the four elements "friends"! Thus in the end—though very slowly and reluctantly—I was brought, first, to understand, and then to favour, Paul's opinion, namely, that so far as we can see the truth in the "enigma" of the "mirror" of this world, there is being waged a battle of good against evil, order against disorder, light against darkness, life against death.

What Isaiah said concerning the stars and God's "leading them forth" gave me some help, just when I was thinking about the "conflict between light and darkness." For how, I thought, does God bring forth the stars except through the hand of His angel of darkness? Yet we, men, mostly speak of "darkness" as an enemy. And so, in a sense, it often is. Yet it is revealed in the aspect of a servant of God when besides bringing us the blessing of rest and sleep it leads forth the hosts of glories that (except for darkness) would never have been perceived. So, darkness brings God's greatness to light. Paul certainly predicted that the same truth would hereafter be recognised about death and about the apparent disorder of Nature, and her "groanings and travailings"; and it seemed to me that he extended the same doctrine even to sin.

The result was that I found myself content to accept—in a manner, and provisionally—what Paul said about "Satan" and about "principalities" and at the same time what he said to the effect that all things are from God and through God and to God, and, "For them that believe, all things work together for good." In my judgment, it was better—yes, and more reasonable, in Paul's sense of the word "reason"—to feel that I was in the Universe fighting a real fight against evil but looking up to God as my Helper, than to feel that there was no evil or enemy for me anywhere except in myself, and no friend either. So in the end I said, " Better to have been under the curse of death with Paul, if the curse may lead to a supreme blessing of life eternal in the presence of the Father, than to pass out of life with Epictetus, without any experience of curse at all, as so much earth, air, fire and water, into the nominal friendship of Gods and daemons ! "

In allowing myself thus to be led away by my new Jewish teacher I was not influenced by his letters alone, but by legends and traditions—to some of which he referred—in the Hebrew histories, visions, and prophecies. Some of these taught, predicted, prefigured, or suggested that, while man and the brute forces of man and nature blindly imagine that they are moving the wheel of the universe, God alone is really moving it, and is using them to move it, towards His own decreed and foreordained purpose.

To the most beautiful of all such visions I was drawn by these words of Paul, " Know ye not what the scripture saith of Elijah ? " Here a marginal note in my MS. referred me to the whole story, how Elijah, having slain with the sword the adversaries of God, was himself forced to flee from the sword of King Ahab, to Mount Horeb or Sinai, where the Law had once been given to Israel amid lightnings and thunders. And here the prophet was taught that God is not in the principalities of Nature, not in the tempest or fire or earthquake, but in " the still small voice." This agreed with a passage in Isaiah concerning the Deliverer, " He shall not cry aloud." In comparison with these and other similar poems and prophecies, the best things that the Greeks have written began to appear to me like mere " wisdom of word."

As regards the time when Paul's " good news " or " gospel " of " the righteous judgment " of God was to be fulfilled, I gathered that the judgments of God had been revealed to the apostle as having been working from the beginning of the world—seen, as it were, through openings in a veil—in the deluge, in the destruction of Sodom and Gomorrah, in the punishment of the Egyptians for persecuting Israel, in the punishments of Israel during and after the Exodus, and especially in their captivity and the destruction of their temple. But he seemed to believe that he had received also some special revelation about a judgment to fall upon the Jews, or upon all mankind, as soon as the gospel had been proclaimed to the world, but not before.

His language, however, varied. To the Philippians he spoke as though he were in doubt whether to desire to depart and to be with Christ, or to "remain in the flesh" for the sake of his converts. This shewed that he contemplated the possibility of his dying before the Lord's coming. And this was made still clearer in some of his sayings to Timothy, such as "I have fought the good fight," if taken with their contexts. But to the Thessalonians he wrote somewhat differently. It appeared that certain of them were grievously disappointed because some of their brethren had died before the Lord's coming. Paul wrote to console them, saying that they, too—that is the dead brethren—would be raised up. "We that are alive," he said, "shall in no wise precede them that are fallen asleep"—as though he anticipated that, on the day of the Coming, the greater number of the brethren, and he among them, would be still "alive."

From several of these passages, and from similar words in the prophets, I gathered that, had he lived long enough to witness it, Paul would have considered the destruction of Jerusalem by Titus to have been a "day of the Lord" or "day of judgment." But he was assured that the greatest day of all would not arrive till the sins of mankind had come to a head. Also it appeared to me that Paul did not profess to know when the last "judgment" would come to pass, and that he, like other Christians, at first expected it to come soon, and afterwards changed his mind.

Summing up the results of my study, I found that Paul's

gospel appeared to be good news in a double aspect, first outside us, then inside us. First, it said that man was made by a perfectly good God to be, in the end, perfectly good, but was allowed by the Maker to fall into imperfection, through Satan, as a step towards perfection. This could be seen in the history of God's judgments from the beginning, but most of all in the fact that the Son of God, having been sent into the world as a son of David, for the salvation of all the nations of the earth, and having been killed by the Jews, had been raised from the dead to save and judge mankind in righteousness. Secondly, it said that there was in every human being a faculty of faith in the goodness and love and righteous judgments of God, and that this faith, when fixed on the Saviour, enabled men to receive His spirit of righteousness and His love, to await His judgments, and to lead a life of righteousness on earth followed by an immortality of blessedness in heaven.

Comparing this with the gospel of Epictetus I could not but feel that Paul's was far more helpful, but also more difficult to believe. Yet it was not incredible. Epictetus himself recognised in Socrates some traces of a power to frame men to his own will. If Socrates the Athenian, and Diogenes the Sinopian, and others, whom God called "His own sons," had this power in some degree, in proportion to their possession of a share of the divine Logos, why might not Jesus the Jew be regarded as possessing this power to the fullest extent, having the fulness of the Logos so that he could succeed where Socrates and Diogenes and Epictetus failed?

I write here "Jesus the Jew," to shew that, at that time, I did not know that Jesus was called the Nazarene, nor had I any notion that he was born otherwise than naturally "of the seed of David." But I clearly perceived that Paul placed Jesus far above all patriarchs and prophets. Also I think (but am not quite sure) that I already understood Paul to believe that the Son of God was Son from the beginning of the world, before taking flesh as "the seed of David"—but not in any miraculous way. About this point I did not employ my thoughts. The question for me was, Had this Jesus the power attributed to him by Paul's gospel—to conform men to himself? I was obliged to answer, "Yes, with some men." For the epistles had long ago compelled me to give up the notion that the Christians were a vicious, immoral, and rebellious sect. It was clear to me that they were above the average in morality. And as for Paul himself, I felt sure that Jesus had exerted this power over him, and, through him, over vast multitudes in various nations.

Now, too, having a clearer conception of Paul's gospel, I began to understand better something that had perplexed me a good deal on the first reading—I mean Paul's description to the Galatians of the course he took immediately after his conversion. I had expected that he would have said something to this effect, "You Galatians are revolting from my gospel. But it is the true gospel. I have told you the truth about all Christ's words and deeds. It is true that I did not know Him —or hear Him, or even see Him—in the flesh. But after I was converted, I took great pains to ascertain as soon as possible, from those who had known Him in the flesh, all that He did and said. I wrote down these traditions at once, and read them again and again till I knew them by heart. These are the traditions I gave you." This is what I had expected Paul to say. But what I found him actually saying to the Galatians was this: "*I make known unto you brethren, as to the gospel preached by me, that it is not on any human footing, nor did I receive it from any human being, nor was I taught it as teaching, but [it came to me] through revelation of Jesus Christ.*"

What he meant by "gospel" was—I now perceived—*not Christ's teaching before the resurrection, but His teaching after the resurrection.* And this included an unfolding of the will of God as revealed in the scriptures and in all the history of Israel. This appeared in what followed. The Galatians all knew (he said) how bitterly he had persecuted the Christians. For he had been a most bigoted and bitter zealot of strict Judaism. But, said he, "*When it pleased God to reveal His Son in me that I might preach His good tidings among the nations, straightway I conferred not with flesh and blood, nor went I up to Jerusalem to those that were apostles before me, but I went away to Arabia."* Afterwards (but not in this context) he spoke of "Mount Sinai in Arabia." Sinai being the place where Moses received the revelation of the old Law, and where Elijah, too, received the revelation of the "still small voice," I had assumed (at the time of reading the epistle) that Paul went to Mount Sinai in Arabia that he also might receive his revelation of the new Law of Christ. Perhaps, however, it merely meant that he wished to be alone. If so, I was wrong. But it does not seem to me, even now, wrong to infer that, all through that sojourn in Arabia, Paul was in communion with that same Jesus Christ, who had recently appeared to him, and who had converted him from an enemy into a friend.

The same Galatian letter described Paul as not going up to Jerusalem till "three years" had elapsed. Even then he remained only "fifteen days" in Jerusalem, and saw (as I gathered) only one or two of the apostles, and did not go up again till "after the space of fourteen years." All these details about time he appeared to add, not out of any jealousy of the older apostles, but to shew that he did not attach importance to the things that Christ had said "in the flesh," before death, in comparison with the things that He had said after death, "being raised up according to the spirit of holiness." And who could be surprised at this? The things that Christ said after death, when He had been "defined as Son of God from the resurrection of the dead"—how should not these be more deeply impressed upon the mind of the hearers, and also be most deep and spiritual in themselves, being reserved till the disciples were spiritually prepared to receive them?

So the gospel of Paul resolved itself into this, that God, having decreed from the beginning that men should love Him as Father and one another as brethren, had sent His Son into the world to enable them to do this, by dying for them, and by imparting to them His Spirit. The Son dictated no code of laws to obey. All that He asked was faith in Himself as the Son of God, dying for men, and victorious over sin and death. This seemed simple, but its simplicity did not deceive me into imagining that I believed it. "That is all that is needed," said I, as I closed the volume of the epistles; "but it is more than I possess, or can possess. Paul's gospel is not a message but a person. It is, as he says somewhere, 'Christ, dwelling in the heart through faith.' I feel no such indwelling. In the gospel of Epictetus I am neither able nor willing to believe. I might perhaps be willing, but I am not able, to believe in the gospel of Paul."

CHAPTER XVII

EPICTETUS CONFESSES FAILURE

FROM such thoughts about my own desires and inabilities it was a relief to turn to some definite matter of fact. I had been spending several hours in attempting to find out what Paul's gospel was. But what was Christ's gospel, so far as it could be gathered from the epistles? This I had made no attempt to discover. "Epictetus," I reflected, "though he does not profess to teach a gospel of Socrates or Diogenes, yet frequently quotes from them. Might I not expect to find at least a few words of Christ—whether uttered before or after the resurrection—quoted here and there in some at least of these numerous letters?" Hitherto I had met with none. But now, on rapidly unrolling the volume and searching onwards from the end of the epistle to the Romans, I came to a quotation that had escaped me. It was in the first of the Corinthian letters, following immediately after some details (not of great interest) about women's head-covering. I had just time to note that the passage contained the words "the Lord Jesus said," and "on the night on which he was delivered over," when my servant announced that Glaucus wished to see me, and I put the book aside.

Ostensibly Glaucus had come to compare some of his lecture notes with mine. But I soon found that his real object was to forget his troubles in the society of a friend. To forget them, not to reveal them. He avoided anything that might lead to personal questions, and I respected his reticence. When, however, he rose to go, he made some remark on the difficulty of retaining the imperturbability on which Epictetus was always insisting, "under the sword of Damocles." Knowing vaguely that his alarm was not for himself but for others, I suggested that he might return at once to Corinth. "I would do so," he said, "but my father expressly bids me remain at Nicopolis." He said this uneasily, and with a wistful look, as though he suspected that something was amiss and longed for advice. "If action of any kind is possible," said I, "take it. If not——." Then I stopped. "Well," said he, "'if not'——." He waited for me to complete my sentence. I would gladly have left it uncompleted. For the truth was that I had begun the sentence in one mood and was being called on to complete it in another. When I said, "If not," I had a flash of faith coming with a sudden memory of Isaiah's message about God as the Shepherd of the stars and his exhortation to "wait patiently on the Lord." But it had vanished and left me in the dark. "'If not'——," repeated Glaucus for the second time. I ought to have replied, "Then at least keep yourself ready for action." What I did say, or stammer out, was, something about "waiting and trusting."

Glaucus looked hard at me. "'*Wait and trust!*' That is to say, '*Wait and believe.*' That is not like you, Silanus. You don't mean it, I see. It is not like you to say what you don't mean. I would sooner have heard you repeat your old friend Scaurus's advice, which was more like '*Wake and disbelieve.*' 'Wait,' say you, 'and trust.' Trust whom? Wait for what? Wait for the river of time to run dry? I have kept you up too late. Sleep well, and may sleep bring you better counsel for me!" So saying, he departed, but turned at the door to fling a final jibe at me, "Silanus, you are a Roman and I am only a Greek. But you must not think we Greeks are quite ignorant of your Horace. And what says he about waiting? *Rusticus expectat:* 'Hodge sits by the river.' Farewell, and sleep well."

This was bitter medicine; but I had deserved it, and it did me good. My cheeks burned with shame as I recalled his words "It is not like you to say what you don't mean." Had I come to this? Was this the result of my study of these Jewish writings? And yet, did I not "mean" it? Was not the fact rather this, that in my own mind I did to some extent mean

Chapter 17] EPICTETUS CONFESSES FAILURE 153

and believe it? But it was a dormant belief. And I had no power to communicate it to others. Then I perceived the reason. I had said "Wait and trust." But Isaiah said "Wait thou *upon the Lord.*" In preaching my gospel to Glaucus I had left out "*the Lord*"—the life and soul of the precept! If "the Lord" had been in me, as He was in Isaiah and in Paul, I could not have left Him out. But I left Him out because He was not in me. The truth was that I had no true gospel to preach.

In great dejection I was on the point of retiring to rest when it occurred to me that I had left unfinished, and indeed hardly begun, the study of Christ's words in the Corinthian epistle. Too weary to resume it now, I extinguished the light and flung myself down to forget in sleep all thought of study. But I could not forget. All through the dreams of a restless and troubled night ran threads of tangled imaginations about what those words would prove to be, intertwined with other imaginations about the words of Christ to Paul at his conversion. Along with these came shadows or shapes, with voices or voice-like sounds :—Epictetus gazing on the burning Christians in Rome, Paul listening to the voice of Christ near Damascus, Elijah on Horeb amid the roar of the tempest. Last of all, I myself, Silanus, stood at the door of a chamber in Jerusalem where Christ (I knew) was present with His disciples, and from this chamber there began to steal forth a still small voice, breathing and spreading everywhere an unspeakable peace—when a whirlwind scattered everything and hurried me away to the Neronian gardens in Rome.

There, someone, masked, took me by the hand and forced me to look at the Christian martyrs whom he was causing to be tortured. I thought it was Nero. But the mask fell off and it was Paul. The martyrs looked down on us and blessed us. Paul trembled but held me fast. I felt that I had become one with him, a persecutor and a murderer. They all looked up to heaven as though they saw something there. At that, Paul vanished, with a loud cry, leaving me alone. Fear fell upon me lest, if I looked up, I should see that which the martyrs saw. So I kept my eyes fixed on the ground. But the blessings of those whom I had persecuted seemed to enter into me taking me captive and forcing me to do as they did. Then I too looked up. And I saw—that which they saw, Jesus the crucified. I tried to cry out " I see nothing, I see nothing," but my voice would not speak. I struggled to regain control over my tongue, and in the struggle I awoke.

I had dreamed long past my usual hour for rising; and the lecture was already beginning when I took my seat next Glaucus. It was a relief to me to find him there; for his late outbreak of bitterness had made me fear that he might prove a deserter. Epictetus was describing man as being the work of a divine Artist, a wonderful sculpture, he said, superior to the Athene of Phidias. Appealing to us individually, " God," he said, " has not only created you, but has also trusted you to yourself alone, and committed the guardianship of you to yourself, saying ' I had no one more trustworthy than yourself to take charge of yourself. Preserve this person for me, such as he is by nature, modest, faithful, magnanimous ' "—and he added many other eulogistic epithets. Here Glaucus passed me his notes with a bitter smile, pointing to the words " preserve me this person such as he is by nature." He had marked them with a query. Nor could I help querying them in my mind. I felt that at all events they were liable to be interpreted in a ridiculous way. My thought was, " Paul bids us trust in God or in the Son of God. Epictetus never does this. But here he says that God trusts us to ourselves. Does He then trust babies to preserve themselves ? And if not, when does He begin to trust us—whether as boys or as youths or as men—to preserve ourselves as we are by nature ? " And here I may say that, as regards belief, or trust, or faith, Epictetus differed altogether from Paul. The former inveighed against babblers, who "trust" their secrets to strangers, and against the Academic philosopher for saying "*Believe* me it is impossible to find anything to be *believed* in." But he never insisted (as Paul does) on the marvellous power possessed by a well-based belief or faith to influence men's lives for good. For the most part Epictetus used the word " belief," like the words " pity " and " prayer," in a bad sense.

But to return to the lecture. In order to illustrate his favourite topic of the necessity of seeking happiness in oneself, Epictetus, as it were, called up Medea on the stage, expostulating with her for her want of self-control: "Do not desire your husband, then none of your desires will fail to be realised." She complained that she was to be banished from Corinth. "Well," said he, "Do not desire to remain in Corinth." He concluded by advising her to desire that which God desires. "And then," said he, "who will hinder or constrain you any more than Zeus is constrained?" To me, even as a dramatic illustration, such advice seemed grotesque. Nor was it a good preparation for what followed, in which he bade us give up desires and passions relating, not only to honour and office, but also to country, friends, children: "Give them all up freely to Zeus and to the other Gods. Make a complete surrender to the Gods. Let the Gods be your pilots. Let your desires be with them. Then how can your voyage be unprosperous? But if you envy, if you pity, if you are jealous, if you are timid, how do you dare to call yourself a philosopher?"

I could perceive that Glaucus was ill pleased at this, and especially at the connexion of "pity" with "envy"—though it was not the first time, nor the last, that I heard Epictetus speak of "pity" in this contemptuous way. Perhaps others were in the same mood as Glaucus, and perhaps our Teacher felt it. If he did, he at all events made no effort to smooth away what he had said. Far from it, he seemed to harden himself in order to reproach us for our slackness and for being philosophers only in name. "Observe and test yourselves," he exclaimed, "and find out what your philosophy really is. You are Epicureans—barring perhaps a few weak-kneed Peripatetics. Stoic reasonings, of course, you have in plenty. But shew me a Stoic man! Shew me only one! By the Gods, I long, I long to see one Stoic man. But perhaps you have one—only not as yet quite completed? Shew him, then, uncompleted! Shew him to me a little way towards completion! I am an old man now. Do me this one last kindness! Do not grudge me this boon—a sight that up to this day my eyes have never enjoyed!"

We were all very quiet at this outburst, so unusual in our Teacher. Two or three youths near my seat seemed stimulated rather than depressed. But to me it seemed a sad confession of failure, amounting, in effect, to this, "I have taught from the days of Vespasian to the second year of Hadrian. My business has been to produce Stoics. Up to this day, a real Stoic is "—these were his words—" *a sight that up to this day my eyes have never enjoyed.*" What a contrast, thought I, between *my* Teacher (for "mine" I still called him) and that other, the Jew, Paul, (whom I refused to call "mine") who numbered his pupils by cities, and whose campaigns from Jerusalem to Rome, through Asia and Greece, had been a succession of victories, leading trains of prisoners captive under the banner of the Crucified!

What followed amazed me, forcing me to the conclusion that Epictetus was profoundly ignorant of human nature, at all events of our nature, and perhaps of his own. For instead of saying, "We have been on the wrong road," or "You have not the power to walk, and I have not the power to make you walk," he found fault with himself and us, without attempting to shew what the fault was. At first it seemed our lack of noble ambition. "Not one of you," he exclaimed, "desires, from being man, to pass into becoming God. Not one of you is planning how he may pass through the dungeon of this paltry body to fellowship with Zeus!" But then he shifted his ground, saying, in effect, "I am your teacher. You are my pupils. My aim is so to perfect your characters that each of you may live unrestrained, uncoerced, unhindered, unshackled, free, prosperous, blessed, looking to God alone in every matter great or small. You, on your side, come here to learn and to practise these things. Why, then, do you fail to do the work in hand, if you on your side have the right aim, object, and purpose, and *I on my side—in addition to right aim, object, and purpose—have the right preparation*? What is deficient?"

Here was our Master assuming as absolutely certain that he had "*the right preparation*"! But that was just the point on which I had long felt doubtful, and was now beginning to feel absolutely certain in a negative sense. However, he continued

Chapter 17] EPICTETUS CONFESSES FAILURE 157

with the same perfect confidence in himself and in the practicability of his theory, "I am the carpenter, you the material. If the work is practicable, and yet is not completed, the fault must rest with you or with me. Then he concluded with the following personal appeal; these were his exact words, "Is not this matter"—he meant the art of living as a son of Zeus, free, and in perfect peace—"capable of being taught? It is. Is it not in our own hands? Nay, it is the only thing that is in our own hands. Wealth is not in our own hands, health is not, reputation is not. Nothing is—except the right use of our imaginations. This is the only thing that is by nature ours, unpreventable, unhinderable. Why do you not perform it then? Tell me the reason. Your non-performance is either my fault, or your fault, or the natural and inherent fault of our business. Now our business, in itself, is practicable, and is indeed the only business that is always practicable. It remains, then, that the fault rests either with me, or with you, or, which is nearer the truth, with both of us. What is to be done, then? Are you willing that we should begin together, at last though late, to bring this purpose into effect? Let bygones be bygones. Only let us begin. Believe me, and you will see."

With that, he dismissed us. I was curious to know what Glaucus thought of it, so I waited for him to speak. To my surprise, he said, "It is not often that the Master speaks in this way or suggests that he himself may be in fault. Who knows? He may have something new in store. I felt so angry with him at the beginning of the lecture that I was within an ace of going straight out. But now, as he says, 'Let bygones be bygones.' I shall go on with him a little longer. What say you? For the most part he is too cold for me, always talking about the Logos within us, and the God within us, as though I, Glaucus the son of Adeimantus, who need the help of all the Gods that are, were myself all the God that I needed! He chills me with his Logos. But when he appealed to us in that personal way 'Believe me,' he gave me quite a new sensation. Did it not stir you? I don't think I ever heard him say that before."

"It did stir me," said I, "and I am sure I never heard him

say it before. Plato represents Socrates as always persuading his hearers to 'follow the Logos,' not to follow Socrates; and Epictetus, for the most part, uses similar language. For the rest, I am not sure that our Master will do me all the good I had hoped. But I shall do as you do. We shall still sit, I hope, together." So we parted.

I had not said more than the truth. Epictetus had stirred me, but not in the way in which he had stirred Glaucus. "Let bygones be bygones"—the "bygones" of nearly forty years! Why were they to be "bygones"? Had they no lesson to teach? Did they not suggest that for forty years Epictetus had been on the road to failure and that he had consequently failed? Could I believe that during all that time Epictetus himself had been deficient in "purpose"? Not for a day! Not for a moment!

As I sat down to revise the notes of my lecture, it occurred to me that Glaucus—who was of a much less settled temperament than Arrian—must have heard better news from home, and that this helped him to take a brighter view of things in general and of philosophy in particular. "If my old friend were here," said I, "would he not regard Glaucus's change of mood as one more instance of Epictetus's power to 'make his hearers feel precisely what he desired them to feel'? But what if I went on to say that this 'power' was mere rhetoric, not indeed 'wisdom of word' in the sense of hair-splitting logic, but 'wisdom of speech,' the knowledge of the language and imagery best fitted to stir the emotions? What would Arrian say to that?"

I mentally constructed a dialogue between us. "There is something more, Silanus." "But what more?" "That I do not know. Only I know there is something more behind." Then Scaurus's explanation recurred to me of that "something more behind." For Scaurus had asserted that Epictetus had been touched by what he called the Christian superstition, which, although he had shaken it off, had left in his mind a blank, a vacant niche, which he vainly tried to fill with the image of a Hercules or a Diogenes. That brought back to my thoughts Scaurus's first mention of "Christus"; and then it

Chapter 17] EPICTETUS CONFESSES FAILURE

came upon me as a shock that I had spent half-an-hour in my rooms, musing over Epictetus and Glaucus and Arrian, and there, on the table before me, was Paul's first epistle to the Corinthians containing his only quotation of the words of the Lord, and I had taken no notice of it. So I put my notes aside and unrolled the epistle.

CHAPTER XVIII

PAUL'S ONLY RECORD OF WORDS OF CHRIST

THE first words of the sentence were, "For *I* received from the Lord"—he emphasized "*I*," as though it meant "*I myself*," or "Whatever others may have received, *I* received so and so"— "that which I also delivered over to you, that the Lord Jesus, on the night on which he was to be delivered over...." Here I paused and looked back, to see what "for" meant (in "*for* I received") and why Paul was introducing this saying of the Lord. I found that the apostle had been warning the Corinthians thus, "Ye meet together, not for the better, but for the worse." In the first place, he said, there were dissensions among them, and in the next place, "When ye come together it is not possible to eat the Lord's Supper, for each one taketh his own supper, and one is hungry while another is drunken." Then I understood that the Lord's Supper meant that same Christian feast of which Arrian had spoken. This interested me because in Rome, as a boy, I had heard it said that the Christians partook of "a Thyestean meal," that is, they killed children and served up the flesh to the parents. This I do not think I had myself believed, except perhaps in the nursery; but it was commonly taken as truth among the lower classes in Rome.

Now I perceived that the meal was to have been a joint one—like that of the Spartan public meals or syssitia, where all fed alike. But in that luxurious city of Corinth many of the Christians had introduced Corinthian luxury and turned the public meal into a group of private meals, so that some

Chapter 18] PAUL AND WORDS OF CHRIST

had too little and others too much. Paul tried to bring them back to better things by telling them what Christ said to his disciples on the night of his last meal, "the night on which he was to be delivered over." He implied that their meal ought to have been like Christ's last meal; and now the question for me was, what that, the Lord's Supper, was like.

But first I had to ask myself the meaning of Christ's being "delivered over." About this I had no doubt that it referred to the prophecy in Isaiah concerning the Suffering Servant, who "was *delivered over* on account of our sins." These words Paul had quoted in the epistle to the Romans, and he elsewhere spoke of God, or the Father, as " giving," or "*delivering over*," the Son for the salvation of mankind. Now both Isaiah and Paul had made it quite clear that the Servant, or Son, thus "delivered over" by the Father, goes voluntarily to death, and this I assumed to be the case here. But I did not know by what agency God was said to have "delivered him over." I thought it might be by a warning or dæmonic voice, as in the case of Socrates, bidding him surrender himself to the laws of his country. Or Christ's own people, the citizens of Jerusalem, might have delivered him up to Pilate, to procure their own exemption from punishment on account of some rebellion or sedition. Or he might be said to have been delivered over by a decree of Fate, to which he voluntarily submitted.

So much was I in the dark that for a moment I thought of Christ as fighting at the head of an army of his countrymen and giving himself up for their sakes, like Protesilaus or the Decii; and I tried to picture Christ doing this, or something like this. But I failed. Still I was being guided rightly so far as this, that I began faintly to recognise that this "delivering over" might be not a mere propitiation of Nemesis, occurring now and then in battles, but part of the laws of the Cosmopolis, occurring often when a deliverance is to be wrought for any community of men. Of such a propitiation Protesilaus was the symbol, concerning whom Homer says,

> "First of the Achæans leaped he on Troy's shore
> Long before all the rest."

He leaped first, in order to fall first. But his country rose by his fall. His wife sorrowed, "desolate in Thessaly," and his house was left "half built." But in the minds of men he abides among the firstfruits of the noble dead, who have counted it life to lay down life for others. This legend I now began to apply to spiritual things. I was being prepared to believe that the sons of God in all places and times must needs be in various ways and circumstances "delivering themselves over" as sacrifices to the will of God, in proportion to their goodness, wisdom, and strength—the good spending their life-blood for the evil, the wise for the foolish, the strong for the weak.

After this, came a sentence that perplexed me greatly, "This is my body, which is in your behalf. Do this to my remembering or reminding." Not being able to make any sense at all of this, I read on, in hope of light: " In the same way also the cup, after supper, saying, This cup is the new covenant in my blood." The word "covenant" helped me a little, because I had found Paul speaking elsewhere to the Corinthians in his own person about a "new covenant." and an "old covenant." Also to the Galatians he mentioned "two covenants," one of which, he said, "corresponds to Mount Sinai." So I turned to the scripture that described how God made a "covenant" with Israel that they should obey the Law given to them from Mount Sinai. It had these words : "And Moses, having taken the blood "—that is, the blood from a " *sacrifice of salvation*" consisting of bullocks—"sprinkled it on the people and said, 'Behold the blood of the covenant that the Lord has covenanted with you concerning all these words'." The blood of the old covenant (I perceived) was blood of "sprinkling," purifying the body. David prayed for something more than that, when he said, "Create in me a clean heart, O God, and renew a right spirit within me." So it occurred to me that the "new covenant" was to purify, not the body but the heart and the spirit, entering into man and becoming part of him so as to cleanse him from within.

This seemed to agree with Paul's opinion, and with what I had read in Isaiah, that the sacrifices of bulls and goats cannot make the heart clean. Now, therefore, going back again to the first words "This is my body, which is in your behalf," I inferred that Christ was speaking about Himself as being the "*sacrifice of salvation*" above mentioned, and that He used these words, purposing to devote Himself to death for the people, in order to redeem them from sin by purifying their hearts.

I am writing now in old age. Forty-five years have passed since the night when I first read, "This is my body, which is in your behalf." During that interval I have done my best to ascertain the exact words spoken by the Saviour in His own tongue. And now it is much more clear to me than it was then that the Lord Jesus was herein giving Himself, His very self, both as a legacy to the disciples and also as a ransom for their souls. But even then I perceived that some such meaning must be attached to the words, and that they could not have been invented by any disciple; and they made me marvel more than anything else that I had met with in the Jewish scriptures or Paul's epistles. Such a confidence did they shew in the power of His own love, as being stronger than death! I do not say that I believed that the words had been fulfilled. But I felt sure that Christ had uttered them in the belief of their being fulfilled; and, just for a few moments, the notion that He should have been deceived seemed to me so contrary to the fitness of things, and to the existence of any kind of Providence, that I almost believed that they must have had some kind of fulfilment. I did not stay to ask, "How fulfilled?" I merely said, "This is divine, this is like the 'still small voice.' This is past man's invention. This must be from God."

Then I checked myself, doubt rising up within me. "Paul," I said, "was not present on the night of the Last Supper. He says concerning these words, 'I received of the Lord that which I also delivered unto you.' Is it not strange that the oracles or revelations supposed by Paul to have been delivered to him by Jesus after the resurrection should have included matters of historical fact, and historical utterances, which could have been ascertained from the disciples that heard them? I must wait till I receive the Christian gospels from Flaccus."

Then this also occurred to me. "Socrates, too, like Christ,

was unjustly condemned. Socrates might have escaped from death, but he refused. The dæmonic voice that told him what to do and not to do, bade him remain and die, and he obeyed. In effect, then, this voice from heaven '*delivered over*' Socrates to death. Or he may be said to have '*delivered himself over.*' Now what were the last words of Socrates? Did he leave any such legacy to his disciples? Might I not find some help here? For assuredly Socrates, like Christ, endeavoured to make men better and wiser." I remembered hearing Epictetus say—and I recognised the truth of the saying—"Even now, when Socrates is dead, the memory of the words and deeds of his life is no less profitable to men, perhaps it is more so, than when he lived." So I turned over Arrian's notes and found several remarks of our Master about Socrates and his contempt for death; and with what a humorous appearance of sympathy he accepted the jailer's tears, though he himself felt they were altogether misplaced. At last I came to a passage where Epictetus compared Socrates, on his trial, and in his last moments, to a man playing at ball: "And what was the ball in that case? Life, chains, exile, a draught of poison, to be parted from a wife, to leave one's children orphans. These were his playthings, but none the less he kept on playing and throwing the ball with grace and dexterity."

This was enough, and more than enough. It was hopeless, I perceived, to search in Epictetus for what I sought—some last legacy of Socrates to his disciples, implying that he longed to help them after death. Epictetus would have rebuked me, saying, " How could he help them when he was dissolved into the four elements? What could Socrates bequeath to them beyond the memory of his words and deeds?"

Failing Epictetus, I took out from my bookcase such works of Plato and Xenophon as might contain the last thoughts of Socrates. Both of these writers believed in the immortality of the soul. Yet I could not find either of them asserting, or suggesting, that Socrates felt any trouble or anxiety for his friends and for their faith, nor any token of a hope that his soul might help theirs after his death—or rather, to use his phrase, after he had "transferred his habitation." When I tried to find

Chapter 18]   OF WORDS OF CHRIST   165

such a hope, I could not feel sure that I was interpreting the
words honestly. It seemed to me that I was importing something of the Jewish *pathos*, or feeling, into an utterance of the
Greek *logos*. I still retained the conviction that Socrates, in
his last moments, had his disciples at heart, and that, in
enjoining that last sacrifice to Æsculapius, he wished to stimulate them to something more spiritual and more permanent
than that single literal act. But I longed for something more.
I thought of Christ's "constraining love," and how a man might
be "constrained" in a natural way by the love of the dead—
the love of a wife, father, mother, or child. Such a love
I said, might be no less powerful, for help and comfort, than
the hate of Clytemnestra following Orestes for evil. Æneas
(I remembered) used the word "*image*," speaking to the spirit
of Anchises, "Thy *image*, O my father, constrained me to come
hither." But Anchises replies that he himself had been all the
while following his son in his perilous wanderings, so that it
was not a mere "*image*." It was a *presence*. "Is it possible,"
I asked, "that Christ, not in poetry but in fact, thought of
bequeathing to His disciples such a *presence*, to follow and help
them after His death?"

Yes. It seemed quite possible, nay, almost certain—that
Christ thought this. But who, except a Christian, would
believe that the thought was more than a dream? "Scaurus,"
I said, "who often jests at me as a dreamer, would now jest
more than ever. Here am I, pondering poetry, when I ought
to be studying history! Yet how can I study history in Paul,
when Paul himself tells me that he received these words from
one that had died—presumably therefore in a vision? The
right course will be to wait till Flaccus sends me the gospels.
These may chance to be historical biographies—not records of
things seen, or words heard, in visions." And then Scaurus's
saying recurred to me, that no two writers agree independently
in recording a speech or conversation for twenty consecutive
words that are exactly the same. "And this," said I, "I hope
to test before many days are over, with regard to these
mysterious words of Christ."

But before rolling up the book it came into my mind that

Paul said somewhere to the Romans "I beseech you therefore by the compassionate mercies of God to present your bodies a *living sacrifice*, holy, acceptable to God." Having found these words and read them carefully over, I thought that the writer must have had in view some allusion to the sacrifice of Isaac. For that was the only "living sacrifice" that I could find (and indeed it is the only one) mentioned in scripture. Then I turned to the first book of the Law and there I found that God's promise of Isaac to Abraham had been called a covenant, and this, said Paul to the Galatians, was, so to speak, the real *thought* of God. The covenant of Sinai was only an afterthought. The sign of Abraham's covenant by promise was in the blood of circumcision stamped permanently on man's body. The sign of the covenant of Sinai was in the blood of bullocks merely sprinkled on the body. Also there was yet another covenant between God and man, earlier than both of these. This, the earliest covenant of all, was with Noah. Now the sign of this was not on man at all, but on the sky, being the rainbow. And in the covenant with Noah there was no mention of blood (either of man or beast) except this—that man was not to taste the blood of beasts when he ate their flesh, and that he was not to pour out the blood of men, much less to taste of it.

Then it seemed to me that the words and thoughts of Christ, being a Jew, must be studied in the light of the words and thoughts of his countrymen the ancient Jews. The first covenant, that of Noah, said, "The blood is the life, therefore ye shall not taste of blood; and whosoever shall taste of blood, whether of man or beast, shall die; and whosoever shall pour out the blood of man, his blood shall be poured out and he shall die." This was confirmed by the Covenant of Moses the Lawgiver. Then came a second covenant, that of the Son, saying, "I have changed all that. I am the New Covenant. The New Covenant is in my blood, that is, in my life. My blood is truly my life. Ye shall taste of my blood. It shall be poured out for all, as a living sacrifice. Whosoever shall taste of my blood shall not die but shall live for ever, even as I live."

Looking back now to that moment, I seem to perceive that

I was being led on by the Spirit of God, far beyond my own natural powers of thought and reason, in order that I might have some foretaste of the revelation of the Lord's sacrifice, so as to be strengthened and prepared for the trial that was shortly to fall upon me, when I was to be dragged away from the shore that I had just touched, back again into the tumultuous deep. For a long time I continued musing on this mystery, and turning over passage after passage in Paul's epistles describing how believers are all one "in Christ," and "Christ in them," and how they are made righteous, or brought near to God, "in the blood of Christ."

So passed the greater part of the day, up till the ninth hour. Then came a reaction. The thought of Scaurus returned, and of his criticisms. "He is right," I said, "I am a dreamer. I will go out into the fields." So I went out, taking my Virgil as company. When I came into the woods I sat down in the warmth of the westering sun. There, for a time, listening to the songs of the thrushes and the cooing of the doves, I felt at peace, and opened my Virgil, intending to read about the bees and the fields. But I had brought the Æneid by mistake, and the first words I met were these:

"Si nunc se nobis ille aureus arbore ramus
Ostendat nemore in tanto!"

Then back again came suggestions of doubt. For I recognised it as a kind of oracle from the Gods, that I must still be seeking for the light of the truth in the dark forest of error, and that I could not find it without divine help. "But," said I, as I started up to return home, "it shall be such help as a Roman may accept without shame. The faith of Junius Silanus shall never be constrained by spells, or incantations, or by anything except reasonable conviction and the force of facts."

Returning home as the sun was sinking I found letters awaiting me. Among these, one was from Flaccus, saying that he had sent me three little Christian books called "gospels," in accordance with my order. After his usual fashion, addressing me as the son of his old master, but also as a companion in the fellowship of book-lovers, he added some remarks on the contents of the parcel. "The third of these books," he said, "is written by a man of some education, named Lucas, a companion of Paulus (whose works I recently sent you); and he has published a supplementary volume, which I have ventured to add although you did not order it. The supplement is entitled 'The Acts of the Apostles,' that is, of the missionaries sent out by Christus. The 'gospel,' as you probably know, is a record of the acts and words of Christus himself. Also, as you are interested in this sect, I have sent you a book called the Revelation of John. It is written in most extraordinary Greek, without pretensions to grammar, much less to style. But it has some poetic touches in it. Of the eastern style, of course. But that you will understand. This John was himself—(I am told)—one of their 'apostles,' and a man of note among the Christians. He is said to have written it soon after the reign of Domitian."

There was also a letter from Scaurus, or rather a packet of letters. Out of it fell a separate note of the nature of a postscript, and I read that first, as follows: "Two things I forgot to say. First, if you decide to open my sealed note about the similarities of Paul and Epictetus, I shall not now feel hurt. For the reasons I have given in my letter, I hope you will not open it, because I trust you will turn your mind to other matters. But I do not now regard that note as important. By this time, you probably have the books of the Christians. You also know more than you did about Epictetus, so you have been able to judge for yourself whether I have not spoken the truth. But now—I repeat—my advice is to put the whole investigation aside. Go to Illyria and see whether you cannot find an opening there for a military philosopher."

As to the sealed note, I have explained above that, when I opened it, I found it was, as Scaurus said, of very little importance to me—knowing what I then knew. Such effect as it had on me was produced before I had opened it, because it provoked my curiosity and stimulated me to study the books of the Christians.

The postscript continued as follows. "The second thing,

much more important, concerns a fundamental matter in this Christian superstition. You know, I am sure, from Paul's letters, that the ancient Jews—better called Israelites—have always claimed that God has honoured them above all nations by making a special 'treaty' or 'covenant' with them. Well, Paul admits this for Jews, but claims for Christians that they have a still better 'treaty' or 'covenant,' which he calls 'new,' as distinct from that of the Jews, which he calls 'old.' He represents his leader, Christ, as making or ratifying this 'new covenant' with his blood, on the night on which he was betrayed. Not only this, but he gives the exact words uttered by Christ—and, mark you, *this is the only occasion on which he quotes any words of Christ at all.* Not only this, but he says that he received them from his leader; 'I received from the Lord that which I also delivered over to you.' Now, Silanus, look for yourself. Do not believe me. Look in Paul's first epistle to the Corinthians, some way after the middle, and see whether he does not quote these words, 'This cup is the new covenant in my blood. Do this as often as ye are drinking, to my remembering.' What the words mean I do not precisely know. But there they are. Next look in the three gospels———"

"Now," said I, "I shall get light." I put down the letter and took up the three gospels—the packet from Flaccus. But a glance shewed that it would be a long and difficult business to find the passage in them, and to compare their three versions with the one in Paul's epistle. So I turned to the postscript again, "Next look in the three gospels and prepare to be surprised. You will find the following four facts. First, none of them contain the words 'Do this to my remembering.' Secondly, the latest gospel (that of Lucas) makes no mention of a 'covenant.' Thirdly, the two earliest gospels do not call the covenant 'new.' Fourthly, the Greek word may mean not 'covenant' at all, but 'testament'; and the meaning may be that their leader bequeaths them his blood—whatever that may mean—by his last will and testament.

"Now I put it to you, Silanus, as a reasonable man, whether it is worth while investigating a superstition as to which the earliest documents disagree concerning such a fundamental fact (or rather allegation). These Christians—for I am informed they mostly take Paul's view—assert that their Founder made a '*new covenant*' between them and God on a special night. Three of them give accounts—detailed accounts—of all manner of things that happened on that night. A fourth, Paul, professes to give the very words of the Founder of the Covenant, as he received them from the Founder himself, not alive of course but dead! And he, Paul, *alone of the four, mentions the phrase 'new covenant.*' What do you think of this?"

Indeed I did not know what to think of it. And Scaurus's next words almost decided me to take his view of the whole matter, to put away all my Jewish and Christian books and to have done with every kind of philosophy. "Spare me," so the postscript proceeded, "for the sake of the immortal Gods, my dearest Quintus, spare me the pain—during the few years or months of life that may still remain for me—of seeing the son of my dearest friend ensnared in the net of a beguiling superstition that must lead you away from your duty to your country. Be kind to me and to your father."

Not having read the preceding part of his letter, I was amazed at this outburst of alarm in my behalf. But I perceived that, with his usual sympathetic insight, he had read some of my thoughts almost before I was conscious of them myself, and I was grateful to him. If he had stopped there, I sometimes think things might have happened differently. But he continued, "*Truth*, as Sophocles says, *is always right*. Be true to the truth. Be true to yourself. Amid all the shifting fancies and falsehoods around you, esteem the knowledge of yourself the only knowledge that is certain and unchangeable. In that respect the old philosophers were right. 'Know thyself' is the only divine precept. On self-knowledge alone is based the only covenant—if indeed it is fit to imagine any covenant—between God and man."

From these last words I found myself in absolute revolt. During the past few days I had come to think that perhaps the only certain and unchangeable truth was that self-knowledge without other knowledge is impossible, or, if possible, most harmful. Dissenting from these last words I went back to dissent further, or rather to draw a different inference. "Truth is always right." Then could it be right for me to give up the search for truth, lest I should pain myself or Scaurus? From my father, one of the most just and honourable of men, how often had I heard the maxim, *Audi alteram partem*! Why should I not "hear the other side" since that very day had placed at my disposal (thanks to Flaccus) the means of doing this? Scaurus had indirectly challenged me to do it. My father had, in a sense, commanded it. Before I retired to rest that night, I resolved to devote the whole of the next day, and as much time as I could spare afterwards, to the examination of the Christian gospels.

CHAPTER XIX

HOW SCAURUS STUDIED THE THREE GOSPELS

BEGINNING with the passages that described the Lord's Supper, I soon found that Scaurus was correct in saying that the words of the Lord quoted by Paul were not in any of the gospels. But my copy of Luke—an old one, having been transcribed in the reign of the emperor Nerva as the scribe stated—contained a note in the margin, not in the scribe's handwriting, "After '*my body*,' some later copies have these words, '*which is being given in your behalf. Do this to my remembering; and the cup likewise, after supping, saying, This cup is the new testament in my blood which is being shed for you*'." Now these words were very similar to Paul's quotation, and Flaccus had told me that Luke was a companion of Paul. So I reflected that Luke must often have partaken of the Christian Supper with Paul, and must have heard these words from Paul. Why therefore were the words omitted in Luke, except in "some later copies"? Mark, Matthew, and Paul agreed in inserting some mention of "covenant." Why did Luke, Paul's companion, alone omit it?

Looking into the matter more closely, I found that Luke, though he omitted the phrase about "covenant," *inserted in his context some mention of "covenanting," or "making covenant,"* as follows: "I *covenant* unto you as my Father *covenanted* unto me." The "covenant" was "a kingdom, that ye may eat and drink at my table." Also, in the same context, Jesus said, "The kings of the nations lord it over them, and those who play the despot over them are called"—I think he meant, "called" by their flatterers—"benefactors. But you, not so."

And Jesus went on to say, "He that ruleth must be as he that serveth," and, "I am among you as he that serveth." The words "my Father covenanted unto me" appeared to mean a covenant of sacrifice, namely, that the Son was to sacrifice Himself for the sins of the world, and to pass, through that sacrifice, into the Kingdom at the right hand of the Father. And the other words meant that Jesus "covenanted" with the disciples that they should sacrifice themselves in like manner, taking Him as it were into themselves, by drinking the blood of the sacrifice (that is, His blood) and eating its flesh or body (that is, His body). And thus they, too, being made one with Him, were to pass into the Kingdom.

Such a "covenant" as this, would, I perceived, be so "new" that it might be described as turning the world upside down—all the kings serving their subjects, all the masters waiting on their servants. This was indeed strange. But it was not peculiar to Luke. Mark and Matthew (I found) had a similar doctrine, though not in this passage; only, instead of "I am among you as he that serveth," they had, "to give his soul as a ransom for many." This accorded with what was said above, namely, that the "covenant," or condition, on which the Son came into the world, was, that He should be the "servant," or "sacrifice," or "ransom," for mankind. All three names expressed aspects of one and the same thing. David had said, "The sacrifice of the Lord is a contrite spirit." That meant, contrite for *one's own* sins. Jesus seemed to go outside a man's self, and to say, "The sacrifice of the Lord is a spirit of service *to others.*" Romans, I reflected, would call this doctrine either an impracticable dream, or—if practicable, and if attempted—a pestilent revolution. But once more the thought recurred that the Jew would say to us, as the Egyptian said to Solon, "You Romans are but children," and that, although Rome had the power (as Virgil said) of "subjecting the proud oppressors in war," it might not have what Epictetus described as the power of the true Ruler (which this Jewish Ruler seemed to claim), namely, to draw the subjects towards the ruler with the chain of "passionate affection."

Scaurus next asserted that some disagreements here between

the evangelists arose from translating Hebrew into Greek. Where Mark has "and they drank," Matthew has "drink ye." Scaurus said that the same Hebrew might produce these two Greek translations. "Also," said he, "supposing Jesus to have said in his native tongue, *This is my body for you*, some might take 'for you' to mean 'given *to you* as a gift,' but others 'given *for you* as a sacrifice'." Hence he inferred that it was hardly possible to discover what Jesus actually said, because, besides differences of memory in the witnesses, there might be differences of translation in those who remembered the same words. But on the other side, if Scaurus was right, the facts shewed the independence of the witnesses, as well as their honesty and accuracy. If Jesus used one Jewish phrase that might imply two meanings, it seemed natural that his disciples should try to express both meanings in Greek. The nearness of the Passover (at the time when the words were uttered), and the connexion in scripture between "covenant" and "sacrifice," and many things that I had read in Paul's epistles, made me believe that "sacrifice" was implied. Why should not the disciples suppose that their Saviour bequeathed a legacy *to* them that was also a sacrifice *for* them? This seemed to me a beautiful and intelligible belief.

The result was that I resolved not to give up the study of these books. Repeating my father's maxim, *Audi alteram partem*, "Scaurus," I said, "shall be on one side, and the three gospels"—which I spread out on the table—"shall be on the other." I soon found, however, that my task was not so simple. There was not merely "the other side," there were often three "sides"—so strangely did the gospels vary. Scaurus made a fourth, or, rather, a commentary on the three. From my youth up (thanks largely to Scaurus) I had some skill in comparing histories. It was necessary first (I perceived) to have the three gospels side by side. For this purpose, the penknife and the pen—the former for transposing, the latter for transcribing—had to be freely used. Mark's gospel I preserved intact. Extracts from Matthew and Luke—copying or cutting them out—I placed parallel to the corresponding passages in Mark. I also made use of marginal notes in my MS.

referring me to parallel passages in the other gospels or in the scriptures. Some days were spent in this labour. After that, I determined to attend lectures regularly, but to devote all my leisure to a close examination of the gospels with the help of Scaurus's comments. Now I must speak of his letter.

It began, as his postscript had ended, with a personal appeal, warning me against a tendency to dreaming, "which," said he, "I think you must have inherited from my Etrurian grandmother, whose blood runs in your veins—through your dear mother—as well as in mine. I myself, at times, have to fight against it." Then he cautioned me against the Jews. "They are all of them," he said, "dangerous people, though in different ways. There are two sorts, plotters and dreamers; the plotters, all for themselves; the dreamers, all for someone else, or something else (the Gods know what!) outside themselves. Now a dreamer in the west, mostly a Greek (for a Roman dreamer is a rare bird) is a harmless creature—dreaming passively. But the Jewish dreamer dreams actively. He is, to use the Greek adjective, *hypnotic*. If I might invent a Greek verb, I would say that he '*hypnotizes*' people. He makes others dream what he dreams. And his dreams are not the dreams of Morpheus, 'golden slumbers' on 'heaped Elysian flowers.' No, they are often dreams like those of Hercules Furens—destroying himself and his friends while he thinks he is destroying 'powers of evil'! I have known several Jews, some very good, more very bad; only one, perhaps, half-and-half. That was Flavius Josephus, whose histories you have read. He could be all things to all men in a very clever way, mostly for his people, sometimes for himself.

"Paul was all things to all men in a very different way, and always the same way. Paul, as you know, frankly warns his readers, 'I am become all things to all men that I may by all means save some,' and 'I became to the Jews a Jew that I might gain the Jews'—not for himself, of course, but for his Master, the King of the Jews. I have never told you, before, something that I will tell you now—to warn you against these Jews, especially the Christian Jews. I once saw this Paul, only once. I was but a boy. He was standing, chained, in a corridor in the palace, waiting to be heard. One of the Prætorian guard was talking to him and Paul was replying, while my father and I were passing by; and my father, having something to say to the guardsman, made some courteous remark to Paul about interrupting their talk. Paul stood up. He was rather short, and bent down besides with the weight of his chains; and the guardsman (quite against regulations) had put a stool for him to rest on. He reached up his face to my father's as though he could not see very distinctly: but it was not exactly the eyes, but the look in them, the unearthly look, that I shall never forget. No doubt, he was thankful for the few syllables of kindness. It seemed to me as if he wished to return the kindness in kind. He said something. What it was I don't know. Probably bad Greek or worse Latin. Thanks of some sort, no doubt. But it was the look—the look and the tone, that struck me. Struck! No, rather, bewitched. For days and nights afterwards I saw that man's face, and heard his voice in my dreams. I did not like the dreams. But he made me dream. He was a retiarius. If he had had me alone for a day or two, I feel even now that he would have caught me in his Christian net. I don't want you to be caught."

Then Scaurus went on to speak of himself at some length. I will set down his exact words for two reasons. First, they shew what pains he had taken to prepare himself for the work of a critic. Secondly, his letter seemed to me to explain in part why he was so set against what he called the soporific or hypnotic art of Paul. He and I approached the apostle in different circumstances. I came to Paul before coming to the gospels. He read the gospels first, and found it impossible to believe them. Then, with a mind settled and fixed against belief, approaching Paul, he found—this I believe to be the fact—that Paul was drawing him towards Christ. He resisted the constraint, thinking that he was resisting a sort of witchcraft. Yes, and even to the end of his life, he fought against the truth, seeing it masked as falsehood. Yet assuredly he loved the truth and spared no pains to reach it. Let my old friend speak for himself in what I will call—

SCAURUS'S AUTOBIOGRAPHY

"While I am in the mood for telling secrets I may say that, for me, too, this Christian superstition has not been without attractions; and, had there been anything solid in it, I think I should have ascertained it. You must know that in the last year or two of Domitian this sect was brought into notice in Rome among the highest circles by rather painful circumstances —painful, I mean, to me. I had retired from the army. As soon as I had recovered from my wounds, enough to be able to limp about, I looked round me for something to do. I was not in favour with the Emperor. He had lost reputation in the Dacian war; and he was supposed to dislike those officers— there were only a few—who had done creditably in that most discreditable business. I was supposed to be one of the few. At all events, in the 'regrettable incident' of Fuscus, I brought off most of my men safe, and we did not run away. Well, I thought I had better lead a retired life. So under the plea of disablement—which was unfortunately only too true, as I was lamed for life—I kept at home in Tusculum all through the reign of Domitian, giving myself up to literature.

"Even as a boy, I was very fond of Greek, and I liked learning it in my own way and not according to the ways of my masters. My way was to commit to memory—and to keep in memory by constant repetition, a very different thing from mere 'committing'—great masses of such literature as I liked best. Many and many a time have I met and passed a friend or schoolfellow in the Via Sacra, and heard his voice behind me, 'Are you going to cut me, Scaurus?' But I had not been 'Scaurus' when I passed him. I had been Medea frantic, or Demosthenes haranguing the Athenians, or Plato describing Thales on the well's brink, or—for I was an eclectic—Thucydides recording his personal experiences of the plague. I kept this up, even in the army. Many a long night in Dacia has been shortened in the company of my friends, the great Greek authors. The result of all this was, that when I reached consular age, and, instead of going in for consulships, went in for lameness and literature,

I was well provided, so far as concerned the Greek raw material, for critical studies.

"Well, as time went on, extending the course of my reading, I happened to pick up in Flaccus's shop a Greek translation of the Hebrew book of Job. It was a chaos, with occasional lucidities—some of them magnificent. On my shewing it to a learned Jew (whom Josephus had recommended to me) he explained to me that the Greek translators had often been misled by similarities of Hebrew words. Hebrew is a queer language. It has vowels but does not write them. I saw at once what an abundant source of error this might be. Even in Latin, where vowels are written, I have known Greeks go wrong by rendering *amnis* as though it were *omnis*. How much more, if there were no vowels! My rabbi—that is their name for 'teacher'—informed me that even the Greek-speaking Jews were now beginning to be dissatisfied with the Seventy (that is the name they give to their authorised version). Several new translations of some of the books were floating about, he said, and a good and faithful translation of the whole would probably be produced before long. This interested me. Under his guidance I studied the parallelisms in the two books of Esdras and other books of theirs. I learned just enough Hebrew to understand how it would be possible for an expert to go back to a lost Hebrew original from two extant parallel Greek translations. You see what I mean. A very little knowledge of Latin might enable anyone to see, that, in two Greek documents, '*oaks*' and '*flintstones*,' being parallel, point to a Latin '*ilices*' or '*silices*'—the reading being doubtful—from which two Greeks have been translating.

"Now I must pass to the last year or last but one of Domitian. You have heard your father speak of Flavius Clemens (not exactly a strong man, but a good one) who was put to death by his uncle, the Emperor, for 'Judaism' (so it was called) and his poor wife exiled. 'Judaism,' with our people, was only a more respectable name for 'Christianism,' though the two superstitions are poles asunder. Poor Domitilla was a downright Christian. Her husband Clemens was at all events Christian enough for Domitian's purposes. He was put to death and his effects confiscated. I bought a few of his books as memorials of my old friend, and among these were certain Christian publications called 'gospels.'

"Every Christian missionary is supposed to 'preach the gospel'; so, of course, there might be, theoretically, as many gospels as missionaries, and 'a gospel according to' each missionary, if each chose to write down what he preached. Accordingly I gather from Flaccus that there have been a great number of these 'gospels'; but only three are now in large demand among Christians in Rome—the three he sent you. The earliest of these is 'The Gospel according to Mark.' That it is the earliest you can see thus. Put them (that is, of course, the parallel parts of them) in three columns, Mark in the middle. Then imagine three schoolboys seated together— Sinister, Medius, and Dexter—writing a translation of Homer. Suppose Sinister and Dexter to be cribbing from Medius, who sits between them. The experienced schoolmaster will speedily discover that, whenever Sinister and Dexter closely agree, it is because they cribbed from Medius. Similarly Matthew and Luke largely copied—not 'cribbed,' for they did it honestly enough, no doubt—from Mark. Consequently (subject to certain exceptions, which I will state later on) Matthew and Luke *never agree together—in those parts of the gospel where there are three parallel narratives—without also agreeing with Mark.* Don't trust me for this. Try it yourself."

I did try it. And I found that—subject to the exceptions defined by Scaurus in another letter—his statement was correct. His letter continued, "So I began with Mark. Do not suppose that I began with any prejudice against him. On the contrary, your old friend, whom you are so fond of calling Misomythus, must plead guilty, I fear, to a latent desire of the philomythian kind—that Mark might contain truth and not myth. But hereby hangs another tale, and I must begin another confession.

"Among Domitilla's slaves was one especially dear to her, her librarian, whom she would (no doubt) have manumitted if she had anticipated the blow that was soon to fall on her husband and his household. He was an old man, of Alexandrian extraction, and of some education, simpleminded as a child,

12—2

perfectly honest, giving an impression of firmness, gentleness, and dignity, quite unusual in a slave. I liked old Hermas—that was his name, you must have seen him, I think, in your childhood—for his own sake, as well as for his love of literature. When I bought the books I bought him at the same time. He was nearly seventy and ailing. The calamities of his mistress helped him to his grave, and he died a few days after he had come to my household. We had very little talk together, and least of all at our last meeting; but what we had then, I never forgot. It happened thus. One afternoon, when he came into the library a little later than usual—slowly, and painfully, and leaning on his staff—I happened to have Domitilla's three gospels rolled out on the table before me. There were some notes in the margin of Matthew. These were in his neat small handwriting and I was looking at them. 'Not Domitilla's hand, I think,' said I, with a smile. He shook his head, opened his lips as if to speak, looked long and wistfully at me, as if he would greatly have liked to talk about something more than mere librarian's business. But all he said was, 'Will my lord give his instructions for the day's work?' I gave them. They were that he should go to bed and keep there till he was fit for business. He bowed, moved slowly toward the door, turned and looked at me a second time with that same expression, only more intense; then left the room without a word. I felt strangely drawn towards the old man, and had almost called him back. But I did not. 'To-morrow,' I said, 'to-morrow.'

"Unexpected business took me from Tusculum late in that afternoon and kept me away for three days. On my return I was told that Hermas was no more. He had earnestly desired to see me, they said; and when he found that I had left Tusculum, and that my return might be delayed, and that his voice was failing, and death perhaps imminent, he had spent his last strength in writing a letter, which, by his request, was to be left by his side until he was carried to the funeral pyre—in case I might come to take it. I went at once to his bedside and read it there. I keep it still. But I will not transcribe it for anyone, not even for you, Silanus. It is a confidence

Chapter 19]   THE THREE GOSPELS   181

between me and old Hermas, a private confession of a dream of
his. A dream fulfilled and to be fulfilled, he says. All a dream,
I say. Who shall decide ? Though I will not give you the
words, you shall have the substance of his letter.

"Well, then, if I might believe this letter, he, old Hermas,
lying dead on the couch before my eyes, was not really dead,
but only on the way to a beautiful city of justice and truth, to
which all the just, honourable, and truthful might attain,
Roman, Greek, Jew, Scythian, rich and poor, bond and free,
high-born and low-born. No franchise was needed except a
patient and laborious pursuit of virtue. In this city no one
citizen was greater than another. If anyone could be called
greatest, it was the one that made of least account his own
pleasures, his own wealth, fame, and reputation, serving the
state and his fellow-citizens in all things. Yet it was not a
republic, for it had a king. But this king was not a despot like
the kings of the east, abhorred by Greeks and Romans. The
kingdom was a family at unity with itself, the citizens being
closely bound by affection to their king as father and to their
fellow-citizens as brethren. 'And if,' said Hermas, 'you desire to
be drawn towards that king and to become one with all the
fellow-citizens of the City of Truth, I beseech you, my dear lord
and benefactor—being, as you are, a lover of truth—to study
with all patience those books of my dearest mistress Domitilla,
which I saw before you on that day on which you spoke to me
your words—your last words to me, so God wills it—words of
kindness following deeds of kindness, for which may the Father
in heaven be kind to you for ever and ever.'

"A postscript added a further request, that I would search
for other papyri, which contained the epistles of Paul, and
which, he said, belonged to Domitilla's library, though he had
been unable to find them. 'These,' he said, 'give a clue to the
meaning of many things that are obscure in the gospels; for in
the gospels traditions derived from different documents or
witnesses, are sometimes set down without uniform arrangement,
and without proportion; so that, in Mark, a whole column of
forty lines might be given, for example, to the exorcism of some
evil spirit, and only three or four lines to some principal and

fundamental saying of Christ. But Paul, though he was neither an eye-witness nor an ear-witness, understood spiritual things, according to his saying, *We have the mind of Christ.*'

"This was written on the day before his death. Another postscript, added on the following day, contained nothing but a hope or prayer that he might meet me in the City of Truth. I should add that I searched at the time in vain for Domitilla's copy of Paul's letters. It was not till three years afterwards that I read them, having procured a copy from another source. Sometimes I regret this and ask myself whether Hermas might have been right in thinking that Paul would have led me to understand the gospels better. But I cannot think that the Gods have decreed that those alone shall find the way to the City of Truth who may happen to have studied four Christian papyri in a particular order. Now I must pass from all this prattle about regrets, hopes, prayers, and preconceptions, to describe my exploration of the gospels and my search for historical fact."

CHAPTER XX

SCAURUS ON FORGIVENESS

At this point, Scaurus had drawn two lines, thus:

───────

██████████████████████████████████████

Then the letter continued, "These two lines, my dear Silanus, represent two portions of Mark's '*gospel*'—which word you know, I presume, that the Christians use, as the Greeks do, to mean '*good news.*' Well, the short thin line represents the portion given by Mark to the moral precepts or sayings of Christ. The long thick line represents the portion given to framework—for example, to describing a certain John, called the Baptist, who, so to speak, introduces Christ to the people; to casting out devils; to healing specified diseases, fever, leprosy, paralysis, blindness, deafness, dumbness, lameness; to the raising up of a child apparently dead; to the destruction of a herd of swine by suffering devils to enter into them; to walking on water; to calming a tempest; to a feeding (or rather two feedings) of thousands of men with a few loaves and fishes; to blasting a fig-tree (but that comes later on); to the character of Herod the tetrarch, and his birth-day feasting, ending in the beheading of the above-mentioned John; to the finding of an ass by the disciples in exact accordance with Christ's predictions and precepts; lastly, to very minute details of Christ's trial and crucifixion. There are also a few fables, called parables, likening the good news, or gospel, to seed, which will not grow if sown in wrong places but will grow without man's interference if sown rightly.

But, all this while, about the good news itself, and about its nature, and about the persons to whom the good news is to be brought, and about the good that it will do people—hardly one word! Do not take my word for this. Take your own copy of Mark and look at the first words of Jesus, 'Repent and believe the gospel.' But what gospel? Jesus has not mentioned the word before. This is a specimen of the whole work. It is not a gospel at all. It leaves out essential things. It is only the frame of a gospel."

I did not see at first how to answer this. But on looking into the matter it seemed to me that Scaurus had not noticed Mark's first words, "The beginning of the *gospel of Jesus Christ as it is written in Isaiah the prophet.*" Moreover Christ's first words were not "Repent," but "*The time is fulfilled,* and the kingdom of God hath drawn near. Repent and believe in the gospel." Now the first mention of "preaching the gospel" in Isaiah is in a passage that begins thus: " Comfort ye, comfort ye, my people, saith God...because *her humiliation is fulfilled, her sin is loosed....The voice of one crying in the wilderness, Prepare ye the way of the Lord*...and the glory of the Lord shall appear and all flesh shall see *the salvation of God*..."; and soon afterwards come the words, "Unto a high mountain get thee up, O thou *that preachest the gospel* to Sion." A marginal note in my Isaiah said that—instead of "*her humiliation is fulfilled*"—the right translation was "*her time of service is fulfilled,*" which resembled Mark, "*The time is fulfilled*"—words omitted by Matthew and Luke.

Reviewing Mark and Isaiah together, I came to the conclusion that Mark took for granted that his readers would refer to the passage in Isaiah, and that he meant, in effect, this: "*The beginning of the gospel of Jesus Christ was the fulfilment of Isaiah's gospel* (namely, 'Comfort ye my people because *the time is fulfilled and her sin is loosed*')." John the Baptist, according to Mark, fulfilled *Isaiah's prophecy*. He was the voice crying in the wilderness, "Prepare the way," namely, for this gospel of the salvation of God. Then came Jesus saying, in the words *of Isaiah,* "'*The time is fulfilled,*' that is, *for the gospel of the 'loosing of sins'*; believe in this gospel." Looked at in this way, Mark, though brief and obscure, did not seem to me to have "*left out*" what was (as Scaurus said) "essential," but to have referred his readers to Isaiah for what was essential, if they were not already familiar with the passage, so that they might understand the meaning to be, "Believe in *the gospel of the loosing, or forgiveness, of sins, predicted by Isaiah, and fulfilled now.*"

Scaurus's next objection was this: "Soon after telling us that Jesus called four men away from being fishers of fish to be 'fishers of men'—without explaining the nature or object of this 'fishing,' Mark says, 'Men were amazed at his teaching. For his way of teaching was that of one having authority and not as the way of the scribes.' But what kind of '*authority*'? Listen to the rabble, how they define it (a few lines lower down). 'What is this? A novel teaching! With *authority* does he dictate even to the unclean spirits and they obey him.' Now Flavius Josephus has told me that he himself has known a conjurer or exorcist cast out an unclean spirit or demon—in the presence of Vespasian and his officers—and make it knock over a bucket of water in its exit: but he never told me—and you may be sure he would never have supposed—that the conjurer, on the strength of his exorcisms, would claim to preach a gospel!"

This struck me at first as a very forcible objection. And I was not surprised that Matthew omitted the whole of this narrative; for it is liable to be misunderstood. But I found on examination that Jesus did not (as Scaurus said) "claim to preach a gospel" on the strength of such exorcisms. On the contrary, Mark and Luke say soon afterwards, that Jesus "would not allow the demons to speak because they knew him." Moreover I found that the man from whom the demon was said to have been expelled cried out that Jesus was "the Holy One of God." So it appeared possible that Jesus—if he possessed, like Apollo or Æsculapius, some divine power of healing—might heal lunatics or possessed persons among others, and yet might not claim, on the strength of such exorcisms alone, to preach a gospel. From what I had read in Paul's epistles, and also from my recent reading of Isaiah's prediction of the "gospel," it seemed to me more likely that Jesus would connect his gospel—though what the connexion would be I did not yet see—with the forgiveness of sins.

And this indeed I found to be the subject of Scaurus's next objection; "Then Jesus says that he will cure a man of paralysis in order that the spectators 'may know that the Son of man hath authority on earth to forgive sins.' Now this is the first mention of 'the Son of man.' Who, or of what nature, is this Son of man? There is no answer."

Scaurus spoke thus, perhaps, because he had in his mind some passages in the Jewish scriptures where a "son of man" is described as coming on the clouds to judge mankind, and others where a "son of man" means "son of a mere mortal." He may have thought that Mark ought to have explained which of the two was meant.

But Paul's epistles had shewn me that, when he regarded Christ as having authority over all things, he, Paul, was in the habit of quoting one of the most beautiful of David's Psalms, which said, "What is man that thou art mindful of him, and *the son of man* that thou visitest him? For thou hast made him but little lower than the angels." Now here my MS. said, in the margin of the Psalm—as I quoted it above—"*but little lower than God.*" Then David continued, "Thou hast *subjected all things under his feet.*" These words "subjecting all things" are frequently applied by Paul to the reign or lordship of Christ over mankind. And "to subject" was precisely the word used by Epictetus concerning the ideal ruler, when he taught us that Socrates had the power "so to frame his hearers" that they would "*subject*" their wills to his. It seemed to me, then, that if Scaurus had said to Mark "Why did you not explain which *son of man* Jesus meant?" Mark might have replied, "*Because the Lord Jesus did not recognise two 'sons of man.'* He taught us that the son of man on earth is intended by God to be the son of man in heaven, and that the son of man, even on earth, is superior to the moon and the stars, having 'authority over all things'."

Afterwards I found that Jesus (in Matthew) quotes elsewhere part of another passage in this same psalm of David, namely, "Out of the mouth of babes and sucklings hast thou established strength, because of thine adversaries, that thou mightest still the enemy and the avenger." Paul taught that the "adversaries" of the Lord are the angels of Satan, and the "enemy" is the devil, and these are like wild beasts seeking to devour the soul of man. David, therefore, might be interpreted spiritually as meaning that God has given "authority" to the Son of man, not only over the visible "beasts of the field" but also over the invisible "beasts" that attack the heart of man. "Over these"—Paul might say—"hath the Son of man received authority that he may still the enemy and avenger," that is to say, that he may put Satan to silence by delivering man from the bondage of sin. Some thought of this kind occurred to me at the time. And I was confirmed in it afterwards when I found in the gospels elsewhere mention of "authority" to "trample on, or rule over," wild "beasts" of various kinds. The facts seemed to shew that Jesus often meditated on this beautiful poem of David and on the power given by God to "the Son of man" and to "babes and sucklings"—to whom Jesus appears often to refer under the title of "the little ones."

These considerations to some extent met Scaurus's next objection: "Now as to *authority to forgive sins*—what is meant by this? I can forgive you a *debt* of a thousand sesterces. But I cannot forgive you a *theft* of a thousand sesterces—except in the language of the people. Whether you stole them from me or from somebody else, that makes no difference. You remain a thief—a past thief of course—till the end of your days. Jupiter himself, as Horace in effect declares, cannot unthieve you."

This caused me a great deal of thought. It was logical, yet I felt it was not true. It seemed to me, for example, that if two sons had stolen money from two several fathers, one father might so deal with the child that he might feel himself forgiven, even though he had to pay the money back again; while another father, though not exacting the money, might make the boy feel that he was not forgiven, and that he would be a thief all his life long. Even Epictetus, I remembered, said about Diogenes, "He goes about like a physician feeling the pulses of his patients, and saying, 'You have a fever; you, a headache; you, the gout. You must fast; you must eat; you must not bathe; you must have the knife; you must have cautery.'" He was talking of mental or spiritual diseases. Well, to be slavishly afraid of God—was not this a disease? And to one thus diseased, might not a healing Son of God come with a message from the Father, "He loves you, though He may punish. He will punish as a Father that loves. Steal no more; He will not treat you as a thief. Sin no more; He will not treat you as a sinner."

Epictetus once declared that Diogenes had been sent before us as a reconnoitrer into the regions of death and had brought back his report, "There is nothing terrible there." I never could quite understand on what grounds our Teacher based this assertion, unless it was because the Cynic himself had absolutely no fear of death. It was more easy for me to understand—I do not say, to prove, but to understand—that a great prophet might bring a similar report from the Father of men, "I come from the House of God to tell you that there is nothing terrible there—except for the cruel and base. There is nothing but kindness and justice and true fatherhood." About the alleged "report" of Diogenes, I had felt that—if I believed it—it would deliver me from bondage to the fear of death. Similarly I felt, about the message or gospel of this Jewish prophet, that—if I believed it—it might raise me above fears into a region of love and trust and loyalty to the righteous Father. This was only theory. I did not believe it. But I felt the possibility of believing and of being strengthened by the belief.

Scaurus next objected to the words, "I came not to call the righteous but sinners." This was in Mark and Matthew. "Luke," he said, "adds 'to repentance'; and that of course is meant. Now it is quite right that 'sinners' should be 'called' to 'repentance.' But is that 'good news'? Is that 'gospel'? And, if it is, what about 'the righteous'? They, it seems, are not 'called.' There is no 'gospel' for them!"

Here Scaurus seemed on strong ground. And I felt that

he might urge against Mark what Epictetus says about Diogenes, namely, that the ideal physician inspects others, besides those who are manifestly diseased, in order to see who are healthy and who are not. But then I asked myself, "Who are 'the righteous'?" And the answer Paul put into my mouth was, "None are righteous except through faith in God's Son." That is to say, "None are righteous save through the Spirit of Sonship. None are righteous through the Law." Moreover, on examining the context, I found that the words "I came not to call the righteous" were uttered to unrighteous, envious people, the Pharisees, who grudged forgiveness of sins to the sinners. Elsewhere Luke described the Pharisees as "counting themselves to be righteous and despising others." That is, they were "righteous" in their own estimation. In reality, then, Jesus regarded all men as in need of health, that is to say, in need of righteousness. Also, what Jesus called "repenting" was what the prophets call "turning to Jehovah." So the message of the gospel was, "Turn ye to the Lord and He will forgive you and will grant health to your souls." This was addressed to all that needed better health, that is, to all the nation. But some made themselves blind to their own sinful acts and deaf to the sinful utterances of their own hearts. These could not hear the gospel. The "call" of the gospel did not come into their ears. But it was not the gospel's fault but theirs.

The more I thought over Scaurus's trenchant criticism, the stronger grew my suspicion that Romans and Greeks might be inferior to the best of the Jews in the knowledge of the depths of human nature. I knew from Paul's epistles that the apostle recognised a certain mysterious power of forgiving sins and infirmities by bearing them. This Paul called "the law of Christ," saying, "Bear ye one another's burdens and so fulfil the law of Christ," and again, "If anyone be overtaken in a fault, do ye, who are spiritual, restore such a one in a spirit of meekness." This word, "restore," came into my mind when Scaurus said, "Once a thief, always a thief." It seemed to me truer to say that a father might "restore" his child, after the theft, so that he might be honest for the rest of his life. This power of "restoring" was (as indeed it still is) a great mystery to me. But it is a mysterious fact, not a mere imagination.

Also Scaurus himself said, "It is very likely that many of the poorer Jews were called 'sinners' by the Pharisees for breaking small and perhaps disputed rules about purification or about the exact observance of the sabbath. This my rabbi admitted, although he did not care to say much about it. I can understand that Christ might deal epigrammatically (so to speak) with poor creatures of this kind by pronouncing them 'forgiven' or 'righteous.' But they would be just as 'righteous' as before; neither more righteous nor less righteous; his 'pronouncing' would make no difference. The Jews closely connect 'pronouncing righteous' and 'making righteous,' as though the sentence of the judge is anything more than the expression of the judge's opinion! But it is a pure delusion."

I did not think Scaurus was right. It did not seem to me that the voice of the true Son of man, saying, "I pronounce you righteous in the name of the Father of men," would be of the same kind or efficacy as the voice of a lawyer, saying, "Having in view sect. 3 of chap. 4 of such and such a Code, I pronounce you not guilty." I had come to feel that the Son of man represented the "authority" of humanity—divine humanity, such humanity as commends itself (without support from statute law) to the consciences of mankind. The Pharisees (I thought) might have *made* some of these poor men really *unrighteous* by making them frightened of God—as though He were an austere lawgiver or hard taskmaster. The Son, delivering them from this servile terror, and raising them into a wholesome fear, that is to say, into a free and loving reverence for a righteous God, might bring the Spirit of the Father into their hearts, thus *making* them *righteous*. If so, Christ's voice, saying "I forgive you," would not be a mere judge's "sentence," or expression of "opinion." It would be a power, causing the guilty to feel, and to be, forgiven.

Scaurus then said, "Now pass on, and you will find nothing worth mentioning except a wilderness of wonders and portents until the twelve apostles are sent out to 'preach the gospel.' And now, say you, Jesus must surely tell his missionaries what this 'gospel' is. But no. Not a word about it. Mark himself says, 'They preached that men should repent.' Wholesome tidings, no doubt, but hardly *good* tidings!" Here, as before, Scaurus (as it seems to me) had failed to see that Jews would understand Mark's meaning to be "They preached that men should turn to God and receive forgiveness"—which would be "good tidings." Moreover he had omitted Christ's doctrine that "the Son of man is lord even of the sabbath," to which Mark alone (I found) prefixed "The sabbath was made for man and not man for the sabbath." According to this doctrine God seemed to say to men, "Priests, temples, sacrifices, fasts, sabbaths, rites and ceremonies, psalms, hymns, and prayers—all these I have given you for your own sake, to draw you nearer to me." This, in a way, was like the doctrine of Epictetus, that each man must take an oath to himself to think of his own interest. But in another way it was different. For Matthew added, "I desire kindness, not sacrifice." That went to the root of the difference between Epictetus and Christ. The former said, "Think of your own virtue"; the latter, "Think how your neighbour needs your kindness." According to the gospel, the rule of God was, "Draw near to me." Then, in answer to men's question, "How draw near?" the reply was, "Draw near to one another. That is the best way. Drawing near to me by sabbaths or sacrifices is a second best way. The second best must not interfere with the first best."

It appeared to me that Scaurus dealt with Mark more severely than he would have dealt with Plato. Plato regards "justice," not as obedience to the written laws, but as "doing that which is best for all." If therefore retribution of good and evil comes on the welldoer and on the evildoer, severally, as being "the best thing" for each and for all, this is "justice." But Scaurus quoted Mark, "In the moment when ye stand praying, forgive, if ye have any charge against anyone, that your Father also in heaven may forgive you your trespasses," and then said, "This is not just. If I forgive my slave for robbing me or for cruelly maiming one of his fellow-slaves, does it follow that Jupiter should forgive me for theft or murder? Not in the least. He ought to punish me twice over, first, for

unjustly forgiving crime, and then for being a criminal myself."
Here Scaurus was thinking of remitting penalty, whereas Mark meant bearing the burden of sin. And, although the matter was not then as clear to me as it is now, I could see how a man wronged, and prosecuting the wrong-doer, not as offending against society and justice but as offending against himself—a man that does not wish to "do the best thing" for offenders and for the community—creates for himself an image of a God bad and selfish and unforgiving like himself; so that either he trembles before his bad God and is a slave; or else he regards himself as the favourite of a bad God, and becomes confirmed in his own badness.

On the whole, though I was forced to admit the justice of many charges that Scaurus brought against Mark—and especially the charge of disproportion, and of neglecting great doctrines while emphasizing small details of narrative—still I was satisfied that Mark did contain a gospel, namely, the good tidings of the forgiveness of sins. Scaurus called Mark's gospel a mere frame. It seemed to me that it would have been less untrue to call it a picture in which the principal figure was not clearly seen because of intervening objects and inferior figures. Or it might be called a drama in which the leading character is too often absent from the stage; or, when present, he speaks too little, while minor characters are allowed to speak too much.

CHAPTER XXI

SCAURUS ON THE CROSS

SCAURUS continued, "I pass over a good many columns in Mark before I come to anything of the nature of a precept. Then I find the following, 'There is nothing outside the man, entering into him, that can defile him.' Now you might suppose that this would have been good news, addressed as it is, to the needy multitude. For it would have enabled them (you may say) to eat pork like their Greek neighbours and would have saved them trouble and expense in preparing food.

"But look at the context. Jesus is upholding the written law of Moses against the teachers of unwritten traditions. These teachers told people that if a particle of this or that came off their hands into their mouths while they were eating, they were defiled. These traditions also prescribed minute regulations about preparing meat, and about avoiding meat sold in the markets of Greek cities. Look at Paul's Corinthian letters about this. These regulations must have been very inconvenient for the poor Jews in the Greek cities of Galilee. Jesus stood up for the poor, and for the written law, which said nothing about such details. Long after the crucifixion, Peter was told by 'the Lord' in a vision (you will find it in the Acts) that he might eat anything he liked, pork included. But Jesus said nothing of the kind before his death. Turn to the Acts and you will find it as I have said."

I turned, and found, as usual, that Scaurus was right, though there was no special mention of pork in the Acts, but only of "beasts and creeping things," which Peter calls "unclean." Scaurus continued, "Now look carefully at what follows in Mark and Matthew. Mark represents the disciples—but Matthew represents Peter—as questioning Christ privately about this startling saying. The questioners are said to have called it a 'parable.' There was no 'parable' about it at all. But the fact was that, *after the resurrection, it was revealed to Peter, or to the disciples,* that the meaning of the saying 'Nothing outside defileth' went far beyond its original scope; so that it swept away the whole of the Levitical ordinances about things 'unclean.' If you examine Mark's words carefully you will see that he inserts a comment of his own (which Matthew omits) namely that Jesus *uttered these words 'purifying all kinds of food.'* If by 'purifying,' Mark meant 'purifying *in effect,*' or 'purifying, *as the disciples subsequently understood,*' then he was right. If he meant 'purifying *at once,*' or 'purifying *in such a way as to abrogate immediately the Levitical prohibitions,*' then he was wrong; for that was not the meaning.

"What indeed do you suppose would have happened, if Jesus and his disciples had sat down to a dinner of pork on that same day? They would have been stoned by the multitude. The meaning was limited as I have said above. Mark has probably mixed together what occurred before, and what occurred after, the crucifixion. It was very natural. How many of the 'dark sayings' or 'parables' of Jesus might remain 'dark' to the disciples, till they reflected on them after his death! Moreover the evangelists believed that Jesus, after his death, rose again and appeared on several occasions to the disciples, apart from the rest of the world—that is, 'in private'—and that he explained to them after death what had been dark sayings during his life. How inevitable for biographers—writing thirty, forty, or fifty years after the events they narrated—sometimes to confuse explanations, or other words of Christ, uttered 'in private' after death, with those uttered before death, whether in private or not! I shall have to mention other instances of such confusion. It is not surprising that Luke omits the narrative."

I could not deny the force of this. But, though it derogated from Mark as a witness, it did not seem to me to derogate from Christ as a prophet. I felt that no wise teacher could have desired, thus by a side-blow, to sweep away the whole of the national code of purifications. So I was ready to accept Scaurus's view, at all events provisionally.

"I pass over," said Scaurus, " the precept, 'Beware of leaven,' which was certainly metaphorical; and two narratives of feeding multitudes with 'loaves,' which in my opinion are metaphorical; and a mention of 'crumbs,' which my reason leads me to interpret in one way, while my desire suggests another. About this I shall say something later on, as also about predictions of being killed and rising again. Now I reach these words, ' If anyone wishes to come after me, let him disown himself, and *take up his cross and follow me.* For whosoever desires to save his life shall lose it, and whosoever will lose his life for the sake of me and the gospel shall save it.' Note that these words are preceded by a prediction that the Son of man must be 'killed.' Also remember that the ' cross ' is a punishment sanctioned by Roman but not by Jewish law. Bearing these facts in mind, imagine yourself in the crowd, and tell me what you would think Christ meant, if he turned round to you and said, ' You must take up your cross.' Do not read on to see what I think; for I doubt whether Christ used these words. But, if he did use them, tell me what you think he meant by them."

I was taken aback by this. For I perceived that the sense required a metaphorical rendering, and, at the same time, that such a metaphor was almost impossible among any Jews, *before Christ's crucifixion.* At first I tried to justify it from Paul's epistles, which declared that, in Christ's death, "*all died*"—meaning that all, by sympathy, died to sin and rose again to righteousness. Paul said also "I have been crucified with Christ," and " our old man"—meaning "our old human nature " —" has been crucified with Him," and " the world has been crucified to me and I to the world." But these expressions were all based on the Christian belief that the " cross " was the way to " resurrection." They were quite intelligible after the resurrection, but not before it.

Then I tried to imagine myself in the circle of disciples

surrounding Socrates in prison, and the Master, with the bowl of poison in his hands, preparing to drink it, and looking up to us and saying, "If you intend to be disciples worthy of me, you too must be prepared to take up the hemlock bowl." What, I asked, should I have understood by this? It seemed to me that the words could only mean "You, too, must be prepared to be put to death by your countrymen."

Now as the hemlock bowl was the regular penalty among the Athenians, so the cross (as Scaurus had said) was the regular penalty among the Romans *but not among the Jews*. So, when I tried honestly to respond to Scaurus's appeal, and to imagine myself in the crowd following Jesus, and the Master turning round to us, and saying, "Take up your cross," I was obliged to admit, "I should have taken the Master to mean, 'If you are to be worthy followers of mine, you must be prepared *to be put to death as rebels by the Romans*'."

Scaurus took the same view. "Well," he continued, "I will anticipate your answer, for it seems to me you can only come to one conclusion. You, in the crowd, would take the words to mean that you must follow your Master to the death against the Romans. But all intelligent readers of the Christian books ought to know that he could not have said that. He was a visionary, and utterly averse to violence, so averse that he was on one occasion reproached for his inaction by John the Baptist—who once said to him, in effect, 'Why do you leave me in prison? Why do you not stir a hand to release me?' Moreover, if Jesus had said this, what would the chief priests have needed more than this, to get Pilate to put him to death: 'This man said to the rabble, If you are intending to follow me, you must go with the cross on your shoulders'? 'Can you prove this?' would have been Pilate's reply. They would have proved it. Then sentence would have followed at once as a matter of course. And who can deny that it would have been just?"

I certainly could not deny it. Then Scaurus pointed out to me how Luke avoided this dangerous interpretation, by inserting "daily," so as to give the words a metaphorical twist, "Let him take up his cross *daily*." But this, he said, was manifestly an addition of Luke's. If Jesus had inserted "daily" why should Mark and Matthew have omitted it? "Daily" would make no sense till a generation had passed away, so that "to be crucified with Christ" had become a metaphorical expression for mortifying the flesh. On this point, at all events, Scaurus seemed to me to be right.

He continued as follows, "I am disposed to think that Mark has misunderstood a Jewish phrase as referring to the cross when it really referred to something else. You know that, in Rome, a rascally slave, regarded as being on the way to crucifixion, is called '*yoke-bearer*,' which means practically '*cross-bearer*.' Mark, who has a good many Latinisms, might regard '*take the yoke*' as meaning '*take the cross*'—*if the former expression could be proved to have been used by Jesus.* Still more easily might '*take the yoke*' be regarded as equivalent to '*take the cross*' *if it could be proved that the Jews themselves connected 'taking the yoke' with martyrdom*.

"Both these facts can be proved. In the first place, Christ actually said to the disciples, '*Take my yoke* upon you.' It is true that this saying is preserved by Matthew alone; but its omission by others is easily explained, as I will presently shew. In my judgment, it is certain that Christ did give this precept, and that it had nothing to do with crucifixion. The context in Matthew declares that the kingdom of heaven is revealed only to 'babes'—whom Christ elsewhere calls 'little ones' or those who make themselves 'least' in the kingdom of God—and soon afterwards come the words, '*Take my yoke upon you* and learn from me, for I am meek and lowly in heart.' This is the fundamental truth of Christ's teaching, that those who make themselves the humblest of servants to one another are greatest in his 'kingdom.' In order to reign, one must serve, or '*take the yoke*.'

"The next fact is that Jews of the present day—so I am credibly informed—would say of a Jewish martyr that he '*took the yoke* upon himself,' when he made a formal profession of obedience to the Law just before death. This I must ask you to take for granted. It would be too long to prove and explain." I suppose Scaurus heard this from the teacher he called "his rabbi." It was confirmed, to my own knowledge, by something that happened nearly thirty years ago when one of the most famous Jewish teachers, Akiba by name, was put to death under Hadrian. I heard it said by a credible eyewitness that "they combed his flesh with combs of iron," and another added "Yes, and Akiba, all the while, kept *taking upon himself the yoke of the Kingdom of Heaven*," by which he meant repeating the profession of faith.

"A third fact," said Scaurus, "is that the Christians, from a very early period, used the word '*yoke*' in a depreciatory sense to mean the 'bondage'—as they called it—of the Law of Moses. Paul calls the latter '*the yoke of bondage*.' The Christians, at their first public council, speak of it as '*a yoke*'; and a Christian writer named Barnabas says that 'the new law' is '*without the yoke of necessity*.' I suspect that among the Greeks and Romans the servile associations of 'yoke' have also tended to the disuse of the term among the Christians of the west. You may object that the associations of 'cross' are still more disgraceful than those of 'yoke.' But I do not think they would be so for Christians, who regarded the disgrace of the cross as a step upward to what they call 'the crown of life.' Indeed I am rather surprised that Matthew's tradition 'Take my yoke upon you' has been retained at all, even by a single evangelist."

Most of this was new to me. But, even if it was true—as seemed to me not unlikely—the same conclusion followed as above. The mistake derogated from Mark, not from Christ. Indeed Scaurus's interpretation seemed to me to exalt Christ. For might not some people, of austere and fanatical minds, find it easier to "*take up the cross*," that is, to lacerate and torture themselves, than to "*take up the yoke*," that is, to make their lives subservient to the community in a spirit of willing self-sacrifice? Indeed Scaurus himself said, "If I am right, the Christians have lost by this misunderstanding. When I say 'lost,' I mean 'lost in respect of morality.' For some may '*take up the cross*' like the priests of Cybele, finding a pleasure in gashing themselves—such is human nature. But it is not so exciting a thing to '*take up the yoke*' if it implies making oneself a drudge for life to commonplace people."

This seemed very true. And afterwards I was not surprised to find that the fourth gospel contains no precept to "take up the cross." But it commands Christians to "love one another"— a precept that nowhere occurs in Mark. Also what Scaurus said about "making oneself a drudge" was, in effect, inculcated by the fourth gospel where it commands the disciples to "wash one another's feet." Sometimes I have asked why this gospel did not restore the old tradition about "yoke." Perhaps the writer avoided it as he avoids "faith," and "repentance," and other technical terms that might come between Christians and Christ. Scaurus himself said, "There seems to me more morality in the old rule of Moses, 'Love thy neighbour as thyself' than in either 'Take up the cross' or 'Take up the yoke.' If ever this Christian superstition were to overrun the world, I could conceive of a time when half the Christians might fight with the war-cry of 'the yoke,' and the other half with the war-cry of 'the cross,' cutting one another's throats for these emblems. But I could not so easily conceive of a time when men would ever cut one another's throats with the war-cry, 'We love one another'."

These words of Scaurus seemed to me at the time to be quite true. Now, forty-five years afterwards, they seem to me true as to fact, but not quite true as to interpretation. For, since what Scaurus called "the old rule of Moses" included "Love God," as well as "Love thy neighbour," it followed that the Lord Jesus, in saying "Take my yoke," meant "Serve God," as well as "Serve man." And, in order to serve God, must not one be prepared to suffer, as God also is called "longsuffering"? And of such "suffering" can there be any better emblem than Christ's cross?

I cannot honestly deny the force of the evidence adduced by Scaurus to prove that the Saviour did not really utter the precept of "taking up the cross," and that He did utter the precept of "taking up the yoke." But I can honestly accept the former as an interpretation of the latter, an interpretation fit for Greeks and Romans when the gospel was first preached, and likely to be fit for all the races of the world till the time of the coming of the Lord. If Scaurus is right, only the precept of the yoke was inculcated by Christ in word. But all agree that the precept of the cross was inculcated by Christ in act. Both metaphors seem needed, and many more, to help the disciples of the Lord to apprehend the nature of His Kingdom, or Family.

CHAPTER XXII

SCAURUS ON MARK

SCAURUS continued as follows: "I now come to a passage where Mark represents Christ as saying, 'Whosoever shall be ashamed of me and of my words, the Son of man also shall be ashamed of him.' This suggests to me for the first time (re-perusing these strange books after an interval of more than twenty years) that I may have been blaming Mark for not doing what, as a fact, he had no intention of doing—I mean, for not giving a collection of Christ's utterances in connexion with the 'good news.' If we were to question Mark about the expression 'me and my words,' and to say, 'What words do you refer to?' perhaps he might reply, 'I do not profess to give Christ's *words*, but only their tenor.' Perhaps Mark has in view a person, or character, rather than any gospel of 'words.' And I think I ought to have explained that, at the very outset of his work, Mark described a divine Voice (a thing frequently mentioned in Jewish traditions of the present day about their rabbis) calling from heaven to Christ, 'Thou art my beloved Son.' It is this perhaps that Mark may consider a 'gospel,' namely, that God, instead of sending prophets to the Jews, as in old days, now sends a Son."

This did not seem to me a complete statement of the fact. "Gospel," as I have said above, seemed to me to have meant, in Mark, the gospel of forgiveness of sins promised by Isaiah. And Scaurus himself was justly dissatisfied with his own explanation, for he proceeded, "Still, this is not satisfactory. For ought not the Son to have a message, as a prophet has?

Nay, ought not the Son to have a much better message? The Voice from heaven is repeated at the stage of the gospel at which we have now arrived. But both before and now, it is apparently heard by no unbelievers. Nor does Christ himself ever repeat it to unbelievers. He never says, 'I am *the Son of God*,' nor even, 'I am *a Son of God.*' He simply goes about, curing diseases, and saying 'The sabbath is made for man,' and, on one occasion, 'Thy sins are forgiven thee,' and, 'The son of man hath authority on earth to forgive sins,' and a few more things of this sort. What is there in all this that would induce Christ to use such an expression as, 'Whosoever shall be ashamed of me and of *my words*'? I could understand his saying 'of me,' but not 'of *my words*.' Surely it would have been better to say, 'Whosoever shall be unjust, or an adulterer, or a murderer, I will be ashamed of him'."

Here it seemed to me that Scaurus had not quite succeeded in his attempt to do justice to Mark by reconsidering his gospel in the light of the words "Thou art my beloved Son." For suppose a Son of God to have come into the world, like an Apollo or Æsculapius of souls. Suppose Him to have had a power, beyond that of Moses and the prophets, of instilling into their hearts a new kind of love of God and a new kind of love of neighbour. Lastly, suppose this Son of God to feel quite contented, and indeed best pleased, to call Himself Son of man, because He regarded man as the image of God, and because He felt, within Himself, God and man made one. Would not such a Son of God say, just as Epictetus might say, "Preserve the Man," "Give up everything for the Man," "Save the Man within you, destroy the Beast"? Only, being a Jew, He would not say "Man," but "Son of man," exhorting His disciples to be loyal to "the Son of man" and never to disown or deny "the Son of man."

I was confirmed in this view by a mention (in this part of Mark) of "angels" with "the Son of man," thus: "The Son of man also shall be ashamed of him when he shall come in the glory of his Father with the holy angels." This seemed to say that the Son of man although, as David said according to one interpretation of the Psalm, "*below the angels*" on earth, will be manifested in the glory of the Father *with the attendant angels* in heaven—thus reconciling the two aspects of the Son of man described by David and Daniel.

I noticed, however, that Matthew, in this passage, does not say (as Mark and Luke do) "the Son of man will be ashamed"; and it occurred to me that, where Christ used the phrase "Son of man," and spoke about "the coming of the Son of man," different evangelists might render these phrases differently so as to make the meaning brief and clear for Greeks. Indeed Scaurus himself suggested something of this kind, saying that some might use "I" or "me" for "Son of man" (in Christ's words). He also added that "the Son of man" might sometimes be paraphrased as "the Rule, or Law, of Humanity"; and, said he, "Matthew has a very instructive parable, in which the Son of man in his glory and with his angels is introduced as seated on his throne, judging the Gentiles at the end of the world. Then those who have been kind and helpful and humane are rewarded because—so says the Son of man—'Ye have been kind to *me*.' 'When have we been kind to *thee*?' they reply. The Son answers, 'Ye have been kind to *the least and humblest of my brethren*. Therefore ye have been kind to me.' This goes to the root of Christ's doctrine. The Son of man is humanity and divinity, one with man and one with God, humanity divine."

Scaurus went on to say that Mark's sayings about the Son of man would have been much clearer if some parable or statement of this kind had been inserted making it clear that Christ as it were identified himself with the empire of the Son of man mentioned by the prophet Daniel, against the empire of the Beasts. "There is always a tendency," said Scaurus, " among men of the world, and perhaps among statesmen quite as much as among soldiers—yes, and it exists among some philosophers, too, spite of their creeds—to deify force. I own I admire Christ for deifying humanity. But his biographers—Mark, in particular—do not make the deification clear. If I were to lend my copy of Mark to a fairly educated Roman gentleman, I really should not be surprised if he were to come to me, after reading it right through from beginning to end, and ask me, 'Who *is* this Son of man?'" These words impressed me at the time; but much more afterwards when I actually met this very question in the fourth gospel, asked by the multitude at the end of Christ's preaching, "Who *is* this Son of man?"

"After this," said Scaurus (not speaking quite accurately, for he omitted, as I will presently shew, one short but important saying of Christ) "comes a statement that a certain kind of lunacy cannot be cured by the disciples unless they fast as well as pray. But here, I am convinced, Mark has made some mistake through not understanding 'faith as a grain of mustard-seed,' which the parallel Matthew has. That is a very interesting phrase, which I must go into another time.

"Close on this, occurs a prediction, with part of which I will deal later on. But about part of it I will say at once that I find it quite unintelligible. It is, 'The Son of man is on the point of being betrayed into the hands *of men*.' Why '*of men*'? Surely he could not be betrayed into the hands of anyone else! I observe that Mark and Luke say, 'They were ignorant of this saying,' and I am not surprised. I presume it is simply a repetition of Christ's prediction of his violent death, introduced in order to emphasize his foreknowledge of the treachery of one of his own disciples. But I do not understand '*of men*'."

As to this, I have shewn above that the word rendered by Scaurus "betrayed," occurs in Isaiah's description of the Suffering Servant, "He was *delivered over* for our transgressions," and that it is quoted from Isaiah by Paul. I had always rendered it "delivered over." And now, too, it appeared to me much more likely that the Lord Jesus used the word in that sense. If so, it would have no reference to treachery, but would mean "delivered over by the Father." This would explain "*of men*," because it would mean that the Father *in heaven* delivers over His Son "into the hands *of men*" *on earth*. I have heard that one of the brethren, a learned man, explains "*of men*" as being opposed to "of Satan," but "men" seems to me more likely to be in antithesis to "God." I found afterwards that in the gospels the word "deliver over" is regularly used about Judas Iscariot "delivering over" Jesus to the Jews. So Scaurus may be right. But Paul's rendering seems to me to make better sense in Christ's predictions.

I had been prepared by Paul and by Isaiah to recognise that Christ might have had in view the thought that the Son was to be "delivered over" to death by the Father for the salvation of men. Scaurus had not been thus prepared. Otherwise I think he would have been more patient with obscurities in Mark. Mark seemed to me to assume that his readers would know the general drift of " the gospel " as Isaiah predicted it, as Christ fulfilled it, and as the apostles preached it. Hence he was not so careful as the later evangelists to make his meaning clear to those who had no such knowledge. Take, for example, the words "If any one desires to be first he shall be last." "This," said Scaurus, "might mean ' He shall be degraded so as to be last'." Scaurus also attacked the saying that whosoever receives a child in Christ's name receives Christ, and, "Whosoever shall not receive the kingdom of God as a little child shall surely not enter therein." "I suppose," said he, "this means we are to put aside the vices of youth and manhood and to start afresh. But that is more easily said than done. And there is nothing in Mark to shew how it can be done."

Here Scaurus seemed to me not to have quite done justice to Mark, because he had not given weight to the precept at the very beginning of his book. It was very short, and might easily have escaped me but for Paul's guidance. Paul, I knew, taught that Abraham was "made righteous" by "having faith" in God's good tidings. Hence I had noted, what Scaurus had not noted, that *Mark, alone of the evangelists, placed the precept "Have faith," in the first sentence uttered by Christ, saying "Have faith in the gospel."* This, then, I perceived—this "faith in the gospel" was supposed by Mark to have power to "make men righteous."

This seemed, from a Christian point of view, to answer Scaurus's objection, "'Start afresh' is more easily said than done." The answer was—not my answer, but such an answer as I thought a Christian might make—"Yes, it is much more easily said than done. But the Son of God has authority both to say it and to give power to do it. He says, in effect, '*Be thou able to start afresh*,' and the man *is* ' able to start afresh '."

Then, if Scaurus replied, " Prove this," Paul came forward saying, " I at all events have received power to ' start afresh.' Even my enemies will attest what I have been, a persecutor of the Christians. Now I have been ' forgiven ' by Him that has authority to forgive. The old things are passed away. Behold, they are become new." And if Scaurus had said, " But have others been enabled to ' start afresh ' ? " Paul would have answered, " Yes, multitudes, from the Euphrates to the Tiber. Do not trust me. Take a little journey from Tusculum into the poorest alleys of Rome, and judge for yourself." Here I felt Paul would have been on such strong ground that Scaurus would have given way. " Paul "—he might have said—" is superstitious, and under hallucinations, but I must frankly confess he has the power to help people to ' start afresh '." That is just what I, too, felt. It was quite different from the feeling inspired in me by my own Teacher. When Epictetus said " Let bygones be bygones," " Let us start afresh," " Only begin and we shall see," I felt, almost at once, that he was imagining impossibilities. When Paul said " There is a new creation," I felt that he was describing not only a possibility but also a fact—a fact for himself and for multitudes of others; not indeed a fact for me, but, even for me, a possibility.

To return to Scaurus. " At last," said he, " I came upon a definite precept to shew how perfection could be obtained. A rich young man asks Jesus how he can inherit eternal life. Jesus replies, ' One thing is lacking to thee. Go, sell thy substance, and give to the poor, and thou shalt have treasure in heaven, and come, follow me.' Definite enough ! But is it consistent with morality ? Is it not entirely against Paul's protest, ' Though I give all my goods to the poor and have not love, I am nothing ' ? " Here Scaurus did not seem to me so fair as usual. For, knowing the gospels as well as he did, he was aware that Jesus did not enjoin this rule on all, for example, on Zacchæus. He laid down no rules. One man He bade go home, another He bade follow Him. Moreover

Scaurus, who accused Epictetus of borrowing from Christ, knew that Epictetus inculcated poverty and unmarried life, not on all his disciples, but on any Cynic wishing to go as a missionary; and therefore he ought not to have inferred that Jesus inculcated poverty on all His disciples because He gave it as a precept in answer to the question, " What lack I yet ? " For my part, although I was not at that time a Christian, yet when I read Mark's words, " Jesus, looking upon him, loved (or embraced) him and said, *One thing is lacking to thee* "—I could understand that, for this particular man, the "one thing lacking" really might be that he should "sell all that he had," and that Jesus, knowing this, gave the precept out of His great love. Scaurus called this " a definite precept to shew how perfection could be obtained." But I found only Matthew saying " If thou wouldest be perfect." Mark and Luke did not here use the word " perfect."

Scaurus proceeded thus : " Little remains to be added in the way of precepts. There is a repetition of 'whosoever desires to be great, he shall be your servant.' And this is supported by the saying that 'the Son of man came not to be ministered unto but to minister.' Then comes a most startling statement, ' All things that ye pray and ask, believe that ye received them and they shall be unto you,' and, ' In the moment when ye stand praying——' but I have spoken of that above. I really do not think that I have omitted anything of importance. Does not this amaze you ? "

About the "startling statement" I will speak later on. But here I may say that Scaurus had omitted one short precept "Have salt in yourselves." And this, to some extent, answered one or two of his objections. For, as I understood it, " Have salt in yourselves " corresponded to a saying of Epictetus, who bade us seek help from "the Logos within us." On one occasion (noted above) Epictetus, rebuking one of our students for saying, " Give me some precepts to guide me," replied, " Have you not the Logos to guide you ? " Mark appeared to me to represent Christ as saying, " Take into your hearts the spirit of the Son, which the Son gives you. It will be the salt of life, life for you and life passing from you to others, purifying all your words and actions by imbuing your heart." Elsewhere, also, Mark represented Christ as condemning the Pharisees (in the words of Isaiah) because, though they honoured God with their lips, their heart was far from Him and they "taught as doctrines the commandments of men." Mark seemed to say " Obey the commandments of the Logos," not " of men." Still, I could not but admit that this brief metaphor, overlooked by Scaurus, might easily be overlooked or underrated by hundreds of other readers less careful and candid; and I was forced to sympathize—though not wholly to agree—with the outburst of disappointment which concluded his letter. "O that my old friend Plutarch had had the writing of the life of this Jewish prophet! Or that at least he had been at Mark's elbow, to check him when he began descanting on extraneous matters and to remind him that his readers wanted to hear what he had to say about Christ, not about John the Baptist or Herod Antipas! Many of my friends think but poorly of Plutarch; but he would have been at all events infinitely superior to Mark. I do not wish to be hard upon the latter. The chariot of the gospel, so to speak, was already moving before he was harnessed to it, and he (not being a disciple of special insight or information) had to go the chariot's way. Although his book hardly ever quotes prophecy it is based on prophecy and continually alludes to prophecy. It does not deal with Christ's life as the ancient Jews dealt with the lives of Moses, Samuel, and David. Though it plunges into the midst of things like a book of the prophets—Jeremiah, for example, or Ezekiel—it does not give the words of the prophet in full, but runs off into all sorts of minor matters.

"You remember what Plutarch says about the importance of expression in biography. Mark occasionally attempts to represent a sort of expression—mostly by means of such phrases as 'being moved with compassion,' 'being grieved,' 'looking steadfastly at him,' 'turning round,' and so on. But the deeper sort of 'expression,' the prophet's attitude towards God and man, towards the past and the future, towards the kingdom of God and the kingdoms of men—this he does not represent. Not at least consciously. Perhaps he does, sometimes, unconsciously, when he preserves Christ's darker sayings where the later writers alter or omit them. For this, he deserves thanks. But, in spite of this, Mark's gospel remains, *me judice*—regard being had to the greatness of the prophet whose life he is writing—the most inadequate of all the biographies I know."

So far Scaurus. But his admission that Mark "sometimes preserves Christ's darker sayings where the later writers alter or omit them" suggested to me that, in summing up, he felt that he might have passed over some of Mark's unique traditions. And, as a fact, he had omitted "every one shall be salted with fire," and three passages declaring that "*all things are possible.*" He also omitted the precept "Be at peace with one another." Matthew and Luke omit all these, except that Matthew once has "*all things are possible.*"

This last tradition presents manifest difficulty. I have heard unbelievers scoff at it and ask whether "evil things" are "possible" for God. Moreover Scaurus himself urged on one occasion that not even God can undo the past. Later on, when I studied the gospels with more leisure, it seemed to me that, in saying "all things," the Lord Jesus had constantly in view "the things of the invisible world" or "the things pertaining to the redemption of man." So I found "all things" used in Paul's epistle to the Philippians, declaring that the Lord Jesus Christ was to "fashion anew the body of our humiliation that it may be conformed to the body of his glory, according to the working whereby *he is able even to subject all things unto himself.*"

When I came to read the fourth gospel (called John's), finding how often it supports Mark against Luke, I looked about for this word "possible" or "able" (for one and the same Greek adjective represents the two meanings). But John nowhere uses it. So I thought, "This then is an exception." But I soon found that John expressed Mark's saying, though in a different way. It is in a paradox, saying that the Son is "*able to do nothing from himself.*" This looks like a confession of *not* "*being able.*" But the sentence proceeds, "*unless he sees the Father doing something*"; and, after this, "The Father loveth the Son and sheweth him all things that He Himself is doing." So the meaning really was, "*The Son can do all that the Father is doing and wills the Son to do.*" John did not therefore deny the power of the Son. He asserted it. But he disliked speaking of "power." He avoided all words that mean "able," "strong," "powerful"—meaning "might" as distinct from "right." He prefers "authority," as when he says that the Son has "*authority* to lay down his life and to take it again."

My conclusion was that Mark had recorded the actual words of Jesus, "all things are possible," assuming that his readers, being instructed in the teaching of the apostles, would understand that the words had a spiritual meaning, "All things are put by the Father under the feet of the Son of man." But sometimes, as in the Healing of the Lunatic, the meaning might be ambiguous, or the context might not be so given as to make the words clear. Hence Luke always omitted or altered them, as being obscure and likely to be misunderstood. John paraphrased and explained them. If these facts were correct, it followed that a great debt was due to Mark for preserving the difficult truth when there must have been a great temptation to omit it or to alter it into what was easy but not true. Scaurus gave some weight, but hardly weight enough (I thought) to this merit in Mark.

CHAPTER XXIII

SCAURUS ON SOME OF THE MIRACLES

"AND now," continued Scaurus, "I will tell you how the vision of the City of Truth and Justice, conjured up for me by that dear old dreamer Hermas, vanished into thin air. I intended to have spoken first about some of the miracles; but I will come back to them afterwards. For the present, turn over your Mark till you come nearly to the middle, and you will find a story about an act of healing at a distance. I have heard a Greek doctor tell stories of a man's being influenced by the death of a twin brother at a distance. He invented the word *telepatheia* to express it. Well, I will invent an analogous word for healing at a distance—*teliatreia*. However, it is not from the miraculous point of view that I wish to discuss the story, but simply as a question of morality.

"It contains these words, 'It is not fit to take the children's bread and to cast it unto the dogs.' Who says this? Jesus. To whom? To a poor woman, called 'Greek, Syrophœnician by extraction.' What is her offence? She has been asking Jesus to cast an evil spirit out of her daughter. Now what do you think of that? The Greeks, of old, affected to call all non-Greeks barbarians. But would their philosophers, would Socrates, or gruff Diogenes, or any respectable Greek philosopher, say such a thing to any non-Greek woman? I admit that Jesus ultimately granted this poor creature's request. But that was only because she answered with the tact and patience of a Penelope, acquiescing in the epithet 'dogs' and replying, 'Yea, Lord, yet even the dogs beneath the table eat of the crumbs of the children.' Had it not been for her almost superhuman gentleness, she would have retired rejected, gaining from her petition nothing but the reproach of 'dog.' I write bitterly. I confess I felt bitter when I saw so noble and sublime a character as that of this Jewish prophet apparently degraded and polluted by an indelible taint of national uncharitableness."

I was beginning to investigate the passage, when my eyes fell on a note that Scaurus had appended at the bottom of the column. "Since writing this, I have looked into the passage again, to see whether I could have been misled. And I notice that Luke omits the whole narrative. Also, while Mark represents the *woman* as coming to Jesus and 'asking him' to heal the child, Matthew represents the *disciples* as coming to Jesus and 'asking him' to send her away. I should like to be able to believe that the woman was really a Jewess turned Gentile, that the disciples tried to drive the woman away, calling themselves 'the children' and her 'the dog,' that Jesus replied, as in Matthew, 'It was precisely these lost degraded ones that I was sent to restore.' In order to obtain this meaning, the changes of the text would not be very great. But I fear this cannot be maintained."

I caught at Scaurus's explanation, and was sorry that he himself did not hold to it. For I was more troubled by this objection of his than by anything else that he had said; and I thought long over it. Finally, I came to the conclusion that Scaurus was nearly right; that this woman, though called "a Syrophœnician by extraction," was a Jewess (as Barnabas the Jew is called "a Cyprian by extraction") and that she had fallen away into Greek idolatry and an evil life, so that Jesus—being, like Paul, all things to all men and women—was on this one occasion cruel in word in order to be kind in deed, stimulating her to better things. This agreed with Paul's use of the word "dogs," which assuredly he would not have applied except to "evil-doers." If, however, it should be demonstrated that the woman was not a Jewess, and not leading an impure life, and that Jesus (not the disciples) used these words to her, then I should still believe in the kindness of Jesus, although these words were apparently unkind. No one would suspect cruelty, in a man habitually kind, except on very strong evidence. Here the evidence was not strong. The witnesses were two, not three; and the two narratives disagreed in important details. This was the conclusion to which I then came.

If Scaurus had read the epistles before the gospels, approaching the latter with some feeling of Christ's constraining "love," he could hardly have stumbled (so I thought and so I think still) at this single narrative. Jesus did not call the centurion a "dog." Jesus had also supported the law of kindness against the law of the sabbath. He had said that "that which goes into the mouth" does not defile a man. He had eaten and drunk with publicans and sinners. How was it possible that a prophet of such broad and lofty views as these could call a poor afflicted woman a "dog" simply because she was not a Jewess? I longed to be near my old friend and to appeal to his common sense and justice, and I felt sure that I should have convinced him. Even if Jesus bade the missionaries at first go only to "the lost sheep of the house of Israel," that seemed to me quite consistent with a purpose that in the end the gospel should be proclaimed to all nations.

In another narrative, which had caused me difficulty of the same kind, Scaurus gave me help. It is not in Mark. But I will set it down here because it bears on kindness. Matthew and Luke represented a disciple as asking to be allowed, before following Christ, to "bury" his father, and as not being allowed. "As to this," said Scaurus, "I have no doubt that the man meant, 'Suffer me to wait at home till I have seen my aged father into the grave and have duly buried him.' Similarly Esau says, in effect, 'My father will die before long. I will wait till I have mourned for him before killing Jacob.' So, in Latin, we say 'I have buried them all,' meaning 'I have survived and buried all my relations.' My rabbi confirms me in this view. Christ always defends nature and natural affection against man's conventions, so that it seems to me absurd to suppose that he would enjoin anything really inhuman."

Scaurus next proceeded to attack the miraculous part of Mark's narrative. Mark, he said, considering the smallness of his gospel, describes many more miracles, relatively, than Matthew and Luke. "As to miracles," said he, "I am ready to believe in anything, miraculous or non-miraculous, on sufficient evidence. But the evidence about Mark's miracles leads me to two conclusions. Some of them occurred but were not miraculous. The rest, although they were honestly supposed to have occurred, did not occur.

"Let us take the first class first. Mark calls them 'powers,' *i.e.* works of power. That is a good name for them. But Mark seems to think that, if a man has 'power' to cast out demons and perform cures without medical means, such a one must be a great prophet or even a Son of God. To that I demur. I remember, when I was in Dacia, one of my men was down with fever, and bad fever, too. But when the bugles sounded out one night, and the enemy came on, beating in our outposts and pouring into our camp on the backs of some of our cowardly rascals, this brave fellow was up and doing, without helmet or armour, in the front with the best of them. Next morning, he was none the worse. Nor was there any relapse. He was quite cured. I think I have told you how Josephus described to me the casting out of a demon in the presence of Vespasian. And I might remind you of Tacitus's story about the cure of a blind man by the same emperor. I suspect, however, that the former was a mere conjuring trick and that the latter was got up by the priests of—Serapis, I think it was. So I lay no stress on either. But I have spoken to many sensible physicians, who tell me that paralysis and some kinds of fever can be cured by what they call an emotional shock. Often the cure does not last. Some of these physicians go a little further and ascribe to certain persons a peculiar power of quieting restless patients and pacifying or even healing the insane. But I entirely refuse to believe that, if a man has such a power, he can consequently claim to be a Son of God."

About the objection thus raised by Scaurus I have said enough already. It seemed to me that the power of permanently healing the paralysed, and permanently pacifying and healing the insane, was quite different from that of startling a paralysed man into a temporary activity. The former appeared

Chapter 23] ON SOME OF THE MIRACLES 215

to me allied with moral power and with steadfastness of mind, and likely to be an attribute of the Son of God. Still I was sorry that Mark devoted so much space to it. Here I agreed, in part, with Scaurus.

He then passed to the second class of miracles, "those that were honestly supposed to have occurred, but did not occur." "If," said he, "I assert that Mark turned metaphorical traditions into literal prose, you must not suppose that I accuse him of dishonesty. All the ancient Jews did it. Look at the story of Joshua, describing how he stopped the sun. Perhaps also you have read how God caused a stream to spring up from the Ass's Jawbone (originally a hill of that name, like the headland or peninsula called *Ass's Jawbone* in Laconia, which you and I passed together some five or six years ago). The second (the jawbone miracle) is somewhat different in origin from the first (the sun miracle). There are many shades of verbal misunderstanding capable of converting non-fact into alleged fact. There was all the more excuse for this error in Christian Jews (such as Mark and others) because of two reasons. In the first place, the prophets had predicted that all manner of disease (blindness, deafness, lameness) would be cured in the days of the Messiah (using even such expressions as 'thy dead men shall awake'). In the second place, Christ did actually—as I have admitted—cure some diseases, such as insanity, fever, and paralysis. How, then, could it be other than a difficult task, in such circumstances, to distinguish the literal from the metaphorical traditions about the cures effected by Christ?"

I could all the less deny the force of these remarks because I had been studying the words, "Whatsoever things ye ask, praying, believe that ye have received them and they shall be unto you." These words, if applied literally—to bread, for example, or money—were manifestly not true. Indeed they were absurd. How could a man honestly believe that he had received a thousand sesterces in the act of praying for them? But if applied spiritually, as in Paul's prayer concerning the thorn in the flesh, they might (I felt) be true for one endowed with great faith. Paul prayed that the "thorn" might "depart" from him. In one sense it did not depart. But in another sense, it did depart because God so increased his strength that the "thorn" became as nothing.

Now in this same passage of Mark I found the following: "Whosoever shall say to this mountain, 'Be lifted and thrown into the sea,' and shall not doubt in his heart but believes in that very moment that what he says is happening, it shall be unto him." Luke also elsewhere had, "If ye have faith as a grain of mustard-seed, ye would say to this sycamine-tree, 'Be uprooted and be planted in the sea,' and it would have obeyed you." I took for granted that "mountain," "mustard-seed," and "sycamine-tree," must all have been metaphorically used.

Scaurus confirmed this view, saying that the Jews were in the habit of calling a learned interpreter of the Law an uprooter of mountains, *i.e.* of spiritual obstacles blocking the path of the students of the law. But then he added something that amazed me, "Matthew has, 'If ye have faith, and doubt not, ye shall not only do the deed of the fig-tree, but even if ye say to this mountain, Be lifted and thrown into the sea, it shall come to pass.' Now, 'mountain' being metaphorical, you might naturally anticipate that Matthew intended 'fig-tree' to be metaphorical. But if you look back a little, you will find that *Matthew actually imagines that there was a literal fig-tree in question.* So does Mark. He and Matthew turn the metaphor into a literal miracle, as follows.

"In the first place, Jesus comes to a literal fig-tree, seeking literal fruit. He finds none. Consequently, say Mark and Matthew, a curse of barrenness was pronounced on it by Jesus. What followed? The tree was at once 'dried up,' or (according to Mark) 'dried up from the roots.' Now first note that the Hebrew word that means 'barren' means also '*root up,*' '*cut off,*' or '*cut down.*' Then pass to Luke. He omits the whole of this *miracle* about a fig-tree. But he has a *parable* about a fig-tree. The Lord of a vineyard comes to a barren fig-tree, and gives orders that it shall be '*cut down.*' The vinedresser intercedes for it that it may be spared for one year more in case it may bear fruit."

I looked and found that the story in Mark and Matthew

was as Scaurus had described it. But another detail astonished me. It was a phrase that followed the words, "While they were passing by early in the morning"—*i.e.* the morning after the curse had been pronounced—" they saw the fig-tree dried up from the roots." Instead of writing that they were all amazed at the speed with which the curse had been fulfilled, Mark wrote, "And *Peter, remembering it,* says to him, 'Rabbi, behold, the fig-tree that thou cursedst is withered up'." Trying to put myself in the place of Peter, I asked, "What should I have done when I approached the spot? How could I fail to be on the alert to note the tree that my Master cursed yesterday? How could any of my companions fail? How was it possible that any of us could forget? How could I possibly talk about '*remembering*' it? How, therefore, could a historian suppose it needful to insert that I, or any of us, '*remembered*'?"

Turning to Matthew, I found that he got rid of "remembering," and of "Peter" too, by making the miracle occur instantaneously, thus, "He said unto it [*i.e.* to the tree], 'Let there be no fruit from thee henceforward for ever.' And immediately the fig-tree withered away. And when the disciples saw it, they marvelled, saying, 'How did the fig-tree immediately wither away'?"

Scaurus explained the whole matter as follows: "Look at Ezekiel's saying, 'I the Lord have *dried up the green tree,*' and its context. You will find that '*the green tree*' is Tyre. Elsewhere Luke has a proverb about 'the green tree and the dry,' where 'the dry' refers to the destruction of Jerusalem by the Romans. So here, the fig-tree, green but barren, is Jerusalem. Luke has given the parable correctly. The Lord of the vineyard, he says, comes to a fig-tree, *i.e.* Jerusalem, in the vineyard, that is, in Judah. He does not say that it is green, but we may imagine that. However, it has no fruit. 'Let it be *cut down,*' says the Lord. Well, I have shewn you that 'Let it be cut down' might mean, in Hebrew, 'Let it be *barren* so that none may eat fruit from it,' or 'Let it be *dried up.*' As a historical fact, the fig-tree was *cut down,* or *dried up,* when Jerusalem was destroyed by Titus. But that was not immediate. It was long after the resurrection. *When Jerusalem was destroyed*, the disciples *remembered*"—this explained my difficulty above mentioned—"that the Lord had pronounced this curse on Jerusalem. I could shew you, if space allowed, that the name 'Peter' (which would be in Hebrew 'Simon') might be confused (in Hebrew) with our Latin phrase 'qui cum eo erant' meaning 'those that were with him,' *i.e.* Christ's disciples, and also that Mark's phrase 'passing by *early*' may be an error for 'passing along to *inspect, visit,* or *seek* fruit.' Having regard to the fact that Peter died a year or two before the city was destroyed, I am inclined to think that it was 'the disciples,' not 'Peter,' that 'remembered.' But there is no space for details. It must suffice to have shewn you how a *parable* of Jesus, about *cutting down* a fig-tree, '*remembered*' by his disciples long afterwards as referring to Jerusalem, has been converted by Mark and Matthew into a portentous miracle about *withering* a fig-tree instantaneously (according to Matthew) or by the following morning (according to Mark)."

This explanation of "*remembering*" seemed exactly to meet my difficulty. I accepted it at once. Subsequently I found that the fourth gospel twice represents the disciples as "*remembering*," after Christ's resurrection, things that He had said or done before the resurrection, which things, at the time, they had not fully understood. Moreover that gospel declared that, up to the evening before Christ's crucifixion, His words had been "dark sayings" to them, but that the Spirit would "call them back to their minds," or "remind them" of their meaning. This confirmed me in the conclusion that the Withering of the Fig-Tree was a parable, not a history, and that the disciples "*remembered*" it, and were reminded of its meaning by the Holy Spirit, after the Lord had risen from the dead.

Scaurus added a reference to a lecture of Epictetus, which, he said, I must have heard, and which bore on the story of the fig-tree. I had heard it and remembered it well. The subject was, in effect, "The Precocious Philosopher." Epictetus likened him to a precocious fruit-tree. "You have flowered too soon," he said; "The winter will scorch you up, or rather you are already frostbitten. Let me alone! Why do you wish me, before my season"—he meant, blooming before the seasonable preparation—" to be withered away as you are withered yourself?" This, Scaurus said, was perhaps borrowed from Mark. I examined the text of the lecture, and it seemed to me that his conjecture was by no means improbable.

Scaurus proceeded, "I could go through Mark's other miracles in the same way—those I mean that are not acts of healing—and shew you that they are all metaphors misunderstood. But I have given too much space to these unimportant matters. At least I consider them unimportant except so far as they shew Mark to be historically untrustworthy. Now I must pass to more important things, merely adding—as an instance of this man's curious want of all sense of proportion—that while giving—how often must I repeat this!—a whole column to Herod Antipas's birthday and its consequences, he does not give one line, or one word, to Christ's resurrection—except in predictions made by Christ himself or in statements made by angels. I am not a Christian, nor a half-way Christian. But I have an immense admiration for Christ and an immense curiosity to know the exact facts about his life, death, and subsequent influence on his disciples. To me therefore, simply as a historian—or as a mere man interested in the affairs of men—this absolute silence about that which should have been most fully stated and supported by the evidence of eyewitnesses, is nothing short of provoking. Will you not agree with me, after this, that Mark is the most inadequate of biographers?"

I could scarcely believe my eyes when I read this. "Scaurus," I said, "must for once have made a mistake, or his copy of Mark must have been defective." But my copy confirmed his. It ended with the words, " For they were afraid." This was too much for me. Perhaps I was overwrought with long and close study and with the strain of attempting to grapple with Scaurus's criticisms. I remember to this day—and not with entire self-condemnation, for it was Mark, not Mark's subject, that disappointed me—that in a sudden storm of passion I threw the gospel down and vowed I would never look at it again.

CHAPTER XXIV

SCAURUS ON CHRIST'S BIRTH

ON the following morning my indignation against Mark began to seem certainly hasty and possibly unjust. True, his book was apparently without beginning or end, disfigured by superfluities and omissions, and extraordinarily disproportioned. But what if he had no time to revise it? What if it was a collection of notes about Christ's mighty works and short sayings, which he was intending to combine with a collection of Christ's doctrine when he died—died perhaps suddenly, perhaps was put to death? I tried to find excuses for his work. Still, I could not deny that, if Scaurus was right as to the story of the fig-tree, the earliest of the evangelists shewed a deplorable inability to distinguish the things that preceded Christ's resurrection from the things that followed it. I resolved, however, that this should not deter me from continuing my study of the other gospels. My disappointment with Mark increased my admiration—it was not then more than admiration —for Christ, whom he seemed to me to have failed to represent. "Perhaps," said I, "Matthew and Luke will do more justice to the subject." So I took up their gospels. The resurrection was what I most wanted to read about. But I decided to begin at the beginning.

"In style, proportion, arrangement, and subject-matter," said Scaurus, "Matthew and Luke are much more satisfactory than Mark, although Mark often preserves the earliest and purest form of Christ's short sayings. When I say 'Matthew,' you must understand that I do not know who he is. I am

Chapter 24] SCAURUS ON CHRIST'S BIRTH 221

convinced that Matthew the publican, one of Christ's twelve apostles, is not responsible for the work called by his name. Flaccus—whom I more than suspect of Christian proclivities— knows a good deal about these matters. Well, according to Flaccus, ' Matthew ' wrote in Hebrew. ' Everyone agrees about it,' he says. An early Hebrew gospel would naturally be attributed to Matthew. He, being a 'publican,' or tax-collector, would necessarily be able to write. Peter and John are said to have been ignorant of letters. There are more styles than one in Matthew—a fact that suggests compilation. Luke, an educated man, and perhaps identical with a ' beloved physician ' mentioned in one of Paul's epistles, certainly compiled his books from various sources ; ' Matthew ' almost certainly did the same. Later on, I will speak of their versions of Christ's discourses. Now I must confine myself to their accounts of a very important subject—Christ's supernatural birth."

Up to this point I had been reading with little interest, doubting whether it would not be better to pass on to the accounts of the resurrection. As I have explained above, my study of Paul's epistles had not led me to believe that there would be anything miraculous about the birth of Christ. The phrase " supernatural birth," therefore, came on me quite unexpectedly. What followed, riveted my attention : " Mark, as you know, says nothing about Christ's parentage. First he gives, as title, ' The beginning of the gospel of Jesus Christ '— where, by the way, old Hermas has written, in my margin, 'some add, *Son of God.*' Then there is a Voice from heaven, at the moment of Christ's baptism, heard (apparently) only by John the Baptist and Jesus, ' Thou art my beloved Son.' A similar Voice occurs later on. Mark represents a blind man as calling Jesus ' son of David,' and his fellow-townsmen say, ' Is not this the carpenter, the son of Mary ? ' This might indicate merely that Joseph the carpenter was dead. But 'Son of Mary' might be used in two other ways. The enemies of Jesus might use it to suggest that he was a bastard. The worshippers of Jesus might use it (later on) to shew that he was a Son of God, not born of any human father. Matthew has, ' Is not this the carpenter's son ? ' This, however, Matthew might write not as his own belief, but as that of Christ's fellow-townsmen. Luke, who has 'Is not this Joseph's son?', gives the whole of the narrative quite differently. I should add that the first Voice from heaven is differently given in some copies of Luke." I examined this at once. My copy had a marginal note, " Some have, *Thou art my Son, this day have I begotten thee.*"

"You see," said Scaurus, "in these early divergences, traces of early differences as to the time and manner in which Jesus became the Son of God. Paul appears to me to have believed that the sonship pre-existed in heaven. . . 'God,' he says, 'in the fulness of time, sent forth His son, born of a woman, born under the law, that he might redeem those that were under the law.' In Job, 'born of a woman' implies imperfection, or mortality. In Paul, 'born of a woman' and 'born under the law' imply two self-humiliations undergone by the Son of God. Paul's view is that the Redeemer must needs make himself one with those whom he redeems. Since the Jews were not only 'born of a woman' but also 'born under the law,' the Son of God came down from heaven and placed himself under both these humiliations. Paul, therefore, seems to have regarded the divine birth as taking place in heaven from the beginning, but the human birth as a self-humbling on earth, wherein the Son of God becomes incarnate in the form of the son of Joseph, of the seed of David, after the flesh."

This had been my inference from Paul's epistles, as I have said above. But what followed was quite new to me: "You are aware from Paul's epistles that Christ is regarded by him as preeminently the Seed of Promise, Isaac being merely the type. Well, listen to what Philo, a Jew, somewhat earlier than Paul, declares about the birth of Isaac. Philo says, 'The Lord begot Isaac.' Philo describes Sarah as 'becoming pregnant when alone and visited by God.' It was God also, he says, who 'opened the womb of Leah.' Moses, too, 'having received Zipporah, finds her pregnant by no mortal.' All this is, of course, quite distinct from our popular stories of the love affairs of Jupiter. You may see this from Philo's context: 'It is fitting that God should converse, in an opposite manner to that

Chapter 24]   ON CHRIST'S BIRTH   223

of men, with a nature undefiled, unpolluted, and pure, the genuine Virgin. For whereas the cohabitation of men makes virgins wives (lit. women), on the other hand when God begins to associate with a soul, what was wife before He now makes Virgin again.' I could quote other instances, but these will suffice. Now I ask you to reflect how such language as this would be interpreted in the west, not only by slaves, but even by people of education, unaccustomed to the language of the east, but familiar with our western stories of the births of Hercules, Castor and Pollux, Bacchus and others."

I saw at once that the language would be liable to be taken literally. But on the other hand it seemed to me that no disciple of Paul could accept anything like our western stories. Scaurus had anticipated an objection of this kind in his next words: "You must not suppose, however, that Hebrew literature contains, or that Jewish or Christian thought would tolerate, such stories as those in Ovid. Nor will you find anything of this kind in Matthew and Luke, to whose narratives we will now pass. Matthew says, rather abruptly, that Joseph, finding Mary, his betrothed but not yet his wife, to be with child, and intending to put her away secretly, received a vision of an angel and a voice bidding him not to fear to take to himself Mary his wife, for she was with child from the Holy Spirit, and 'she will bring forth a child and thou shalt call his name Jesus.' Luke, after a much longer introduction (about which I shall speak presently), says that a vision and a voice came to Mary—he does not mention one to Joseph—bidding her not to fear, and saying 'Thou shalt conceive and bring forth a child, and shalt call his name Jesus.' In theory, it is of course possible that two similar visions might come, one to Mary and another to Joseph, bidding both 'not to fear.' But Matthew adds something that points to an entirely different explanation: 'Now all this hath come to pass that it might be fulfilled which was spoken by the Lord through the prophet, saying, *Behold the virgin shall be with child and shall bring forth a son and they shall call his name Emmanuel*'."

These words I had myself read in Isaiah and had taken as referring to a promise made in the context, namely, that in a short time—two or three years, just time enough for a child to be conceived and to be born and to grow up to the age when it could say "father" and "mother"—the kings of Syria and Samaria would be destroyed. Accordingly Isaiah says that he himself married a wife immediately afterwards and that the prophecy was fulfilled. Having recently read these words more than once, I was prepared to find that Scaurus interpreted them in the same way. He added that the most learned of the Jews themselves did the same, and that the Hebrew does not mention "virgin," but "young woman." "This," said he, " I heard from a learned rabbi, who added, 'The LXX is full of blunders, but we are hoping for a more faithful rendering, from a very learned scholar named Aquila, which will probably appear soon'." Here I may say that this translation has actually appeared—it came out about ten years ago—in quite unreadable Greek, but very faithful to the Hebrew; and it renders the word, not "virgin," but "young woman," as Scaurus had said.

It was this very rendering that caused a coolness between me and Justin of Samaria. It happened, I am sorry to say, shortly before he suffered for the sake of the Saviour, in this present year in which I am writing. I chanced to meet him coming out of the school of Diodorus, in his philosopher's cloak as usual, but hot and flustered, not looking at all like a philosopher. Some people—Jews, to judge by their faces— were jeering and pointing after him in mockery. Justin— furious with them, but also (as I thought) worried and uncomfortable in himself—appealed to me: "I have been contending for the Lord," said he, "against these dogs. They flout and mock me for demonstrating how fraudulently and profanely they have mutilated the Holy Scriptures, cancelling some parts and altering others, when translating them into Greek." Then he instanced this very passage, in which he said the Jews had vilely corrupted the rendering of the Hebrew from "virgin" to "young woman." I would have kept silence; but, as he pressed me to say whether I did not agree with him, I was obliged to reply that I did not; and I added that not only Aquila rendered it thus, but other good scholars, many of them Christians. Upon this, he flung away from me in disgust, without one word of salutation, and I never saw him again.

The fact was, he had committed himself in writing, about ten years before, to this false charge against the Jews, and to many other baseless accusations. There was no way out of it now, but either to retract or to face it out. He was a brave man and knew how to face death. But he was not brave enough to allow himself to be conquered by facts. Samaritan by birth, he had something of the Samaritan—but not of the Good Samaritan—in his hatred of the Jews. Had he loved the truth as much as he hated those whom he called truth's enemies, he would perhaps have gone on to cease from his hate, and would have become no less faithful as a Christian than as a martyr.

Now I must return to Scaurus. "Luke," said he, "was an educated man, and saw at once that this prophecy about 'the virgin' did not apply. So he omitted it. This he had a right to do. It was only an evangelist's opinion, not a statement of anything that had actually occurred. But there remained the tradition of *fact*, namely, that an angel had appeared and had announced the future birth of a child begotten from the Holy Spirit. Luke regarded this announcement as made to the mother, like the announcements—not the same of course, but similar— made to Sarah, Rebecca, and the mothers of Samson and Samuel. Moreover in Matthew's account—as I judge from Hermas's marginal notes—there are many variations, some of which leave it open to believe that the utterance to Joseph (like that to Abraham before Isaac's birth) referred merely to God's spiritual generating, so that Jesus, though the Son of God according to the spirit, was yet, according to the flesh, the son of David by descent from Joseph. Luke expresses his disagreement from this view by giving various utterances of Mary and the angel at such length that they may be called hymns or poems. And indeed—if judged liberally and not by the pedantical rules of Atticists or over-strict grammarians—they are poems, by no means without beauty.

"Luke adds another narrative in which he makes the birth of John the Baptist serve as a foil (so to speak) to the birth of

Christ. John, like Christ, was born as a child of promise, after a vision of an angel. But there the likeness ceases. The vision is to the father, not to the mother. The father disbelieves and is punished by dumbness. Elizabeth, the mother, was not a virgin. She, like the wife of Abraham, was barren up to old age. There is no vision to Elizabeth, and no mention of divine generation. If a Jew, Philo for example, were to say to Luke, 'Your Messiah may have been a son of God and yet son of Joseph (as Isaac was son of Abraham)' Luke might reply, 'Read my book, and you will see that it was not so. John the Baptist might be called son of God after this fashion, but Jesus was born in quite a different manner'."

After this, Scaurus went on to treat of Christ's pedigrees, as given by Matthew and Luke, shewing Christ's descent, the former from Abraham, the latter from Adam. These details I shall not give in full. Scaurus had something of the mind of a lawyer and something of the eagerness of a hound hunting by scent, and, as he said himself, when once on a trail he could not stop. "Matthew," said he, "omits three consecutive kings of Judah in one place and a fourth in another. I pointed this out to my old rabbi above-mentioned, and he laughed and said, 'My own people do that sort of thing. History is not our strong point. We like facts to fit nicely, and this writer of yours has made them fit. Does he not himself almost tell you that he is squaring matters, when he says that there are fourteen generations from Abraham to David, and fourteen from David to the captivity, and fourteen from the captivity to Christ? This is symmetrical, but it is not what your model Thucydides would call history.' My rabbi went on to say, 'A more serious blunder, from our point of view, is that this Christian has included in the ancestry of his Christ a king called Jeconiah about whom one of our prophets, Jeremiah, says, "Write ye this man childless, for no man of his seed shall prosper, sitting upon the throne of David and ruling any more in Judah".' Then, seeing the two papyri lying side by side on the table before me, he added, 'I see you have another pedigree there, does that make the same blunder?' 'No,' said I, 'the author was named Luke, a physician, an educated man and a great compiler of documents. He gives quite a different pedigree.' 'I am not surprised,' said my rabbi. 'If he was a sensible man, he could hardly do otherwise'."

So far Scaurus. He did not anticipate what I have lived to experience. Quite recently I heard some Christians use this very mention of Jeconiah in an opposite direction, namely, as a proof that Matthew believed Jesus to have descended from God, but *not* from Joseph after the flesh. In particular, I have heard a young but rising teacher, Irenæus by name, argue as follows, "If indeed He had been the son of Joseph, He could not, according to Jeremiah, be either king or heir, for Joseph is shewn to be the son of Joachim and Jeconiah as also Matthew sets forth in his pedigree." Then he went on to quote Jeremiah's prophecy that Jeconiah should be childless and have no successor on the throne of David. And his argument was to this effect, "Christ is the royal son of David. Therefore He could not have descended from Jeconiah, Joseph's ancestor. Matthew knew this. Therefore Matthew, though giving Joseph's pedigree, did not mean to imply that Jesus was the son of Joseph." And this seemed to convince those who heard him! I also heard this same Irenæus, in the same lecture, say, "If He were the son of Joseph, how could He be greater than Solomon,...or greater than David, when He was generated from the same seed, and was a descendant of these men?" After we had gone out from Irenæus's lecture, I asked the friend sitting next to me to explain this argument to me; for it seemed to me to prove that a man could not be greater than his ancestors. "Ah, but you forget," he replied, "*what* ancestors. They were *royal* ancestors. How could the son of a mere carpenter be greater than David or Solomon?" It seemed to me that the sinless son of "a mere carpenter" might be greater in the eyes of God than a whole world of such royal sinners. But I found it hard to convince him that I was even speaking seriously!

To return to Scaurus. He dealt next with the pedigree in Luke. "You might have supposed in these circumstances," said he, "that Luke would drop the pedigree of Joseph altogether, and give only that of Mary. Well, he has not done this. Another course would have been to state clearly that Jesus was not really, but only putatively, the son of Joseph (being really the son of God) and to add that he gave the pedigree of Joseph, as Matthew gives it, because Joseph was the putative father. Well, he has not quite done this either; but he has done half of it. He has written 'being the son, as was supposed, of Joseph.' But he has also given a pedigree of Joseph differing from that of Matthew in that portion which extends from Joseph to David. What do you think of this?"

I thought that the whole thing was a cobweb and wished Scaurus would pass to something more interesting. But he continued, "My rabbi suggested that Luke had invented a new genealogy. But when I dissented—for I am convinced that neither Luke nor Matthew invented, and that these early writers generally were very simple honest souls—he asked me whether I knew of any instance in the gospels where the name spelt in Greek *Eli* or *Heli* was misunderstood. I replied that there was one instance where Jesus used it to mean *my God*, but the bystanders took it to mean *Elias*. 'Well then,' said the rabbi, 'I should not be surprised if your honest compiler Luke, a learned man perhaps in Greek, but innocent of Hebrew, had got hold of some tradition saying, *Jesus was supposed to be the son of Joseph, being the son of God*. Though in Hebrew there is a difference between the spelling of *El*, God, and the name *Eli*, there is not much difference in Greek. And Luke, having once started on the scent of a new pedigree supposed to connect Jesus with *Heli*, ransacked various Jewish genealogies till he found one containing the name, and adopted it as a substitute for Matthew's.' This was what my rabbi suggested. All I can say is that it seems to me more probable than that Luke invented the genealogy."

Scaurus entered into further details to vindicate Luke's honesty, concluding as follows, "My own belief is that the parents of John and of Jesus were good, pure, simple, noble-minded people, liable to dreams and to the seeing of visions and to the hearing of voices. As to 'dreams,' by the way, look at the earliest account of the Lord's appearing to Solomon,

'In Gibeon, the Lord appeared to Solomon *in a dream...Solomon awoke, and behold it was a dream.*' Then look at the later account in Chronicles, '*In that night did God appear unto Solomon.*' No 'dream' and no 'awaking'! *Verbum sapienti!* The facts above alleged—to which I could add—when combined with the influence of prophecy—seem to me to explain everything in Matthew's and Luke's Introductions as being at once morally truthful and historically untrue."

Later on, Scaurus said, "Luke himself in his story of Christ's childhood, does not seem to me to be so consistent as an educated writer would have been if he had been dishonestly inventing. For he represents Mary as saying to her son, 'Behold, thy father and I seek thee sorrowing.' By 'thy father' she means Joseph. But could she have used this language, or felt this sorrow, if she had realised indeed that her son was not one of the many children of the Father of Gods and men, but that he was unique, God incarnate? This and many other points convince me that Luke (in his account of the birth) is not composing fiction, but only compiling, harmonizing, adapting, and moulding into a historical shape, what should have been preserved as poetic legend."

Scaurus then gave one more detail from Mark, "who," said he, "meagre though he is, often records actual history where later accounts disguise it. Mark says that, when Jesus was preaching the gospel, his own family (literally '*those from him,*' that is, '*those of his household*') 'came to lay hands on him; for they said, *He is beside himself.*' Matthew and Luke omit this. But Matthew and Luke agree with Mark when the latter goes on to describe how the mother of Jesus and his brethren come to the place where he is preaching. Not being able to reach him through the crowd, they send word that they desire to speak to him. Jesus does not go out nor stop his preaching. Those who obeyed the gospel, he said, were his mother and his brethren. I have said that Matthew and Luke omit the attempt of Christ's family to stop him from preaching as being out of his mind. Probably variations in the text enabled them honestly to omit it, believing it to be erroneous. And indeed how could they believe otherwise? How could Matthew and Luke believe that Mary would accompany the brethren of Jesus in an attempt to 'lay hands' on him after recording what they have previously recorded about the supernatural birth? Lay hands on her divine Son, the Son of God, engaged in proclaiming the will of his Father in heaven! The story might well seem to them incredible. But it bears the plain stamp of genuine truth."

Scaurus then pointed out the divergence between Matthew and Luke as to the manner in which Jesus came to be born in Bethlehem. This I omit. But in the course of it he shewed me how Matthew has been influenced by prophecies applied by the Christian Jews to Christ, as being their Deliverer from Captivity, and their Comforter in time of trouble. "For example," said he, "since *Egypt* in Hebrew poetry is often synonymous with *bondage*, the Christian Jews might naturally praise God in their songs and hymns for fulfilling, through Christ, the prophecy, 'Out of Egypt have I called my son,' *i.e.* Israel, meaning that God had called them, the new Israel, out of *bondage* (as Paul often says) into the liberty of the children of God. But Matthew takes this as meaning that, when Christ was a little child, he was literally *'called out of Egypt.'* Hence he is driven to infer that he must have been taken to Egypt. For such a journey he finds a reason by supposing that it was to escape from the sword of Herod. He fits in this story with another prophecy representing Rachel as weeping for her children, and as being consoled by the Lord. Hence Matthew infers a massacre of children by Herod in Bethlehem, corresponding, on a small scale, to the wholesale destruction from which the infant Moses escaped. But such a massacre is not mentioned by any evangelist, or by Josephus, or by any other historian or writer known to me."

I was depressed by this, and eager to pass on to something more satisfactory. So was Scaurus. "I have no desire," he said, "to dwell on these points. I am interested in the biographies of all great teachers, philosophers, and lawgivers, as well as conquerors—*so far as they are true.* Untruth gives me no pleasure, but disappointment—unmixed except for the slight pleasure one may find in tracking an error to its hole and killing it.

"With much greater pleasure shall I turn to Matthew's and Luke's accounts of the words and deeds of Christ. Only I will add that, were I a Christian, I should long for a new gospel that would go back to facts, rejecting these additions of Matthew and Luke. Not that I would go back to Mark. By '*facts*,' I do not mean such facts as John the Baptist's diet of locusts and clothing of camel's hair. But surely a genuine worshipper of Christ—I can conceive such a thing; for after all, what is more worthy of worship on earth, next to God Himself, than 'the man that is as righteous as possible,' concerning whom Socrates says that there is 'nothing more like God'?—I say a genuine Christian, if he were also a philosopher, might surely find it possible to state in a few simple words his conviction that, whereas John the son of Zachariah was sent by the Logos, and contained only a portion of the Logos, Jesus the son of Joseph was actually the Logos incarnate. I wholly reject such a notion myself, partly because I am not sure that I believe that there is any divine Logos at all—having, in fact, given up speculating on these matters. But if I were as sure on that point as your Epictetus is, and if I were a Christian to boot, I am not sure that I should have any great difficulty in believing that some one man might exist—might be 'sent into the world,' I suppose, a Christian would say—as different from ordinary possessors of the Logos as steam is from water—after all, steam is water—superior to Numa the Roman, superior to Lycurgus the Spartan, to Solon the Athenian, yes, superior to Moses the Hebrew.

"You will be disposed to smile at my 'Moses,' as an anticlimax. But let me tell you that this Moses was a very great man. He was a genuine maker of a republic. I don't mention your friend's ideal, Diogenes, for I don't regard him as a maker of anything. I do not even mention my own favourite Socrates. He is not for the man in the street. He is a maker of thinkers. I am speaking of makers of men, and contemplating the possibility of a unique Maker, a Creator of an altogether new social condition. Well, then, suppose I believed in the Logos in heaven and the Logos on earth. Your philosophers would tell me to regard it as a divine flame lighting many human torches without self-diminution. Granted. Then I should believe that every man had his share of the Logos; some, a great share; others, a very great one. Why should I not contemplate the possibility of a unique and complete man, not 'sharing,' but containing or being—a man that might be or contain the totality, or, as Paul says, the fulness, of the Logos? I see weak points in this torch-analogy except as an illustration of the belief; yet the belief itself does not appear to me against reason. But enough of this rambling! I have discerned of late many signs that I am growing old, and none more patent than this tendency to expatiate on my cast-off Christian explorations begun in the years when I was vigorous. I pass, and with great relief, to some things that are real possessions—I mean some portions of Matthew's and Luke's versions of Christ's discourses."

For my part, it was not with unmixed "relief" that I turned to the next portion of Scaurus's letter. His conclusions about Christ's birth had merely accorded with my inferences from Paul's epistles; but he had shaken my faith in Matthew and Luke as trustworthy historians; and I looked forward with misgivings to his further criticism, which, I feared, might prove destructive. In this depression, I endeavoured to recall the words of Paul to the Corinthians about having a "treasure in earthen vessels." Mark certainly was an "earthen vessel." Matthew appeared likely to be no better, so far as I could judge from his story of Christ's birth and childhood. Luke, trying to reduce these legends to historic shape, did not seem to me to have succeeded, in spite of all his pains and sincerity. While I was unrolling the Corinthian epistle to refresh my memory, the thought occurred to me, "Is it possible that any God should choose such writers to set forth the life and character of His Son! How could the All-wise be guilty of such foolishness?" I had hardly uttered the word "*foolishness*" when my eyes fell on the words, "The *foolishness* of God is wiser than the wisdom of men." Then I became more modest. "God's ways," I said, "are not our ways. Perhaps He desires to force us to think and to feel for ourselves." I felt grateful even to Mark because he alone had preserved some of Christ's deep and difficult sayings. And in the end I recurred to the thought that had been of late growing stronger and stronger within me concerning the possible inferiority of Romans and Greeks to Jews in things of the spirit. "Thucydides," I said, "would have surpassed Isaiah in describing exactly the campaign of Sennacherib against Hezekiah. But in describing visions and judgments of the Lord, Isaiah is, perhaps, the man, and Thucydides the babe. I will continue my exploration, with Scaurus as a guide."

CHAPTER XXV

SCAURUS ON CHRIST'S DISCOURSES

"MATTHEW and Luke," said Scaurus, "go even beyond Mark in the inculcation of a doctrine, beautiful after a fashion, but unjust, and impracticable. Mark says, 'Love thy neighbour as thyself.' Surely, that is as far as reason can let us go. I should say it is farther. But Matthew and Luke say, 'Love your enemies.' Now I can recall one passage where Epictetus says that the Cynic must love the men that thrash him, but I am sure that his general view is this, 'The man that treats me thus behaves like a beast, or like a mere scourge in the hand of Zeus, whose pleasure it is thus to try me. How can I hate a beast? Or how can I hate a scourge?'"

Then, after reminding me how he had declared that Epictetus borrowed from the Christians, he said, "This, I think, is an instance. The Christian really loves the beast-like man because he believes the man to be made in the image of God and degraded by Satan. The Christian really pities him; he is troubled for the man's sake. Christ says 'Pray for him'; and the Christian honestly prays, 'This man is behaving like a beast. God help him!' The Epictetian does not recognise prayer or pity; he recognises his own peace of mind as God's supreme gift. 'This man,' he says, 'is behaving like a beast. But it is no evil to me. I must see that it does not interfere with my peace of mind. I must beware of pitying him.' Elsewhere Epictetus says that when you are reviled you are to make yourself a 'stone,' whereas Christ says, 'Bless them that curse you.' This exceptional sentence, then, in which Epictetus speaks about 'loving one's cudgellers' appears to me a case where our friend, while cutting away the Christian foundation, has tried to keep the Christian superstructure. Perhaps the view of Epictetus (at all events in word and in appearance) is somewhat selfish. But certainly the Christian precept is contrary to justice and common sense. One ought no more to love the wicked than to admire the ugly."

This seemed at first convincing, or, at all events, overpowering. But he went on to connect it with the doctrine of forgiveness, which Matthew and Luke included in the Lord's Prayer. "This doctrine," said Scaurus, "I have mentioned above, as being in Mark, although he does not give the Lord's Prayer. It is, in fact, intended by Christ to be the very basis of his community. Now of course, Silanus, you and I and all reasonable people are agreed that we ought to be patient, and equable, and to condone faults to our equals, and not to lose our temper with our inferiors, if (as Epictetus says) a slave 'brings us vinegar instead of oil.' And a magnanimous man will put up with much greater offences than these, sometimes with injustice or fraud, sometimes even with insults, if he feels that his honour is not touched by them, or that society does not require a prosecution of the offence. But there is all the world of difference between this—which any gentleman would do, philosopher or no philosopher—and the extraordinary dishonesty—for I can call it by no other name—reduced to a system by the Christians, of 'letting people off' in the hope that God may 'let you off.' I do not want to be 'let off' by God. I should prefer to say (as Epictetus says to the tyrant) 'If it seem advisable, punish me'."

As soon as Scaurus used this argument, I perceived that he confused the remission of penalty with the forgiveness of sin, that power of "bearing the burdens" of others, and of "restoring" others, which, as I have shewn above, Paul recognised as a fact and which Paul made me recognise as a fact, though a very mysterious fact. Hence, reasoning backward, I saw that this faculty of discerning the image of God in the most sinful of sinners, and of pitying the sinner, yes, and even of loving him, might belong to God Himself, and to men in so far as they are like God. If so, the existence of this power of loving one's enemies was a reality, just as the power of forgiving was a reality. "Scaurus himself," I said, "has and uses this power. He often sees good in people where most men would fail to see it. He likes those in whom others see nothing to like. I can conceive that a Son of God might not only possess but impart a power of this kind, increased to such a degree that it might be justly called a new power."

"The curious thing," said Scaurus, "about this doctrine of loving and forgiving is this. Although it appears unpractical and paradoxical, yet the 'kingdom' (to use the Christian word) based on this doctrine is, I must confess, not unpractical at all, but on the contrary a very solid and inconvenient fact in a great number of our largest cities and among the poorest and most squalid of the populace. Note the difference between the kingdom of the Christian and that of the Stoic. The Christian missionary cries aloud like a herald, 'Repent ye; the kingdom of God is at hand,' the Cynic says '*I am a king*,' or—to quote Epictetus exactly—'Which of you, having seen me, does not recognise in me his natural king and master?' The former prays, and teaches his proselytes to pray, looking up to a God in heaven, 'Thy kingdom come'; the latter neither prays nor enjoins prayer of any kind.

"I suppose no Greek or Roman philosopher would apply the title of king to God quite as freely and naturally as Hebrew and Jewish writers do; for when we Romans say 'king,' we think of 'tyrant.' But apart from that (which is only a superficial difference of word) our philosophers have little or none of that expectation which underlies the words 'Thy kingdom come.' The Christians assert (supported by Matthew and Luke) that Christ himself taught them to pray thus. They anticipate a new kingdom—new family, if you prefer the term—where all the world will be brothers and sisters doing the will of the Father. When they pray 'Thy kingdom come,' they mean 'Thy will be done.' Indeed Matthew has inserted 'Thy will be done' in his version of the Lord's Prayer. Perhaps it was a paraphrase, which Luke has rejected because it was not a part of the original. But in any case, 'Thy will be done' is well adapted to make the meaning of 'kingdom' clear in the churches of the west. If a Christian philosopher were to write a gospel, I should not wonder if he were to go still further and drop the word 'kingdom' altogether, because it is calculated to give a false impression to all that are unacquainted with the Hebrew or Jewish method of speech." Scaurus was nearly right here. When I came to study the fourth gospel, I found that Jesus is represented as never using the word except in explanations to Nicodemus and Pilate.

"Now," said Scaurus, "I do not deny that there are advantages in this scheme of a kingdom over the whole world, where the king is not a despot but a beneficent ruler to whom all may feel heartily and permanently loyal. *As compared with Christ*, such Epictetian 'kings' as Socrates, Diogenes, and Zeno, pass before us like solitary champions, fighting, so to speak, each for his own hand. Or we may liken them to torch-bearers, lighting up the darkness for a time but not succeeding in transmitting the torch to a successor. They depart. There is a momentary wake of light. It disappears. Then we have to wait for a new torchbearer, or a new champion; and the fighting, or the torch-waving, has to begin all over again. Take notice of my qualification—'as compared with Christ.' Even thus qualified, perhaps my remarks about Socrates are too strong. For assuredly his light has not gone out. But to tell the truth, resuming my study of these half-forgotten gospels in the light of Paul's epistles, I find myself sometimes admiring rather to excess that visionary letter-writer and practical church-builder. Our philosophers do not consolidate a kingdom. The Christians do. I am impressed by what Paul calls somewhere their 'solid phalanx.' There is something about it that I cannot quite fathom."

I too was impressed by Scaurus's confession that he had somewhat changed his mind about the gospels in consequence of Paul's epistles. It seemed to me to explain some inconsistencies in his letters. Also I noted that Paul's phrase was "the solid phalanx *of your faith*," and that perhaps "*faith*" explained "*phalanx*." Scaurus now passed to the doctrine of New Birth. "I call it thus," said he, "for brevity. Mark expresses it ambiguously, saying that no man can enter into the kingdom unless he receives it 'as a little child.' Now this might mean 'as he receives a little child.' And this interpretation is rather favoured by the fact that, somewhat earlier, Mark has a doctrine about 'receiving one of such little children.' I suspect some mystical doctrine is concealed in Mark. But Matthew has, 'unless ye turn and become as little children.' There is no mistaking that. Now I say, in the first place, this is impossible; in the second place, it is wrong. First, it is impossible. The Father of heaven, says Horace, may send fair weather to-day and foul tomorrow. But not even He—

'——diffinget infectumque reddet
Quod fugiens simul hora vexit.'

You must agree with me. Jupiter cannot cause what has been done to have been not done. In the next place, it is wrong. A full-grown man has no right to divest himself of full-grown faculties. How much better is the doctrine of Epictetus, 'My friend, you have fallen down. Get up. Try again.' This is possible. This is encouraging. But tell the same man, 'Become a little child,' 'Be born again'! He will think you are playing the fool with him."

I wondered why Scaurus did not see that here again he was inconsistent. He had forgotten the admissions he had made in view of Paul's epistles. In the cities of Asia and Greece, some of the vilest among the vile had been told by Paul, "You must become new creatures in Christ," "You must die to sin and rise again to righteousness." They did not "think he was playing the fool." They had (as Scaurus confessed) been morally "born again." Moreover Paul had met his objection as to "full-grown faculties" by saying, "Be ye babes in respect of malice, but in understanding be full-grown men." Still I was sorry that the gospels had expressed this obscurely. Neither of us had as yet read the fourth gospel. That makes the doctrine quite clear by shewing that what is needed is not to be "born over again"—for one might be "born over again" ten times worse than one was before—but to be "born *from above*." This was quite different from "causing what has been done to have been not done." It meant "created anew," or "reshaped," so that the Spirit of Christ, within the Christian, dominated the flesh. Both here and elsewhere, Scaurus's criticisms would have been very different, if he had known the fourth gospel.

"The next point to be considered," said Scaurus, "is the laws for the new kingdom. Matthew has grouped together a collection of precepts as a code. Some of these contrast what 'has been said,' or 'has been said to men of old,' with what Christ now says. Apparently Matthew intended this code of laws (uttered, he says, on a 'mountain') to correspond to the code promulgated on Mount Sinai. But Luke (who by the way omits the 'mountain' and makes the scene 'a place on the plain') while giving many of these precepts, scatters them about his gospel specifying various occasions on which several of them were uttered; and he never inserts the contrasting clause above-mentioned. The conclusion I draw is, that Christ promulgated no law at all. Law deals almost exclusively with actions. Christ dealt almost exclusively with motives, as the last of the Ten Commandments does. When Christ inculcates actions, they are often metaphorical or hyperbolical, as when he says, 'If you are struck on one cheek, turn the other to the striker,' 'Let not your right hand know what your left hand does,' 'If a man takes your cloak, give him your coat too,' and, 'If anyone wants to make you go a mile with him, go two miles,'—to which last precept, by the way, Epictetus would say, No."

I think Scaurus was referring to a passage where Epictetus said, "Diogenes, if you seized any possession of his, would sooner give it up to you than follow you on account of it." Scaurus went on to say, "Matthew's habit of grouping sentences makes it difficult to distinguish sayings uttered before the resurrection from those uttered after it. For example, he speaks of a power of 'binding and loosing' given to Peter, in connexion with a mention of the 'church.' On another occasion, a similar power is given to the other disciples, again in connexion with the 'church.' Now this 'binding and loosing' is not mentioned by any other evangelist. What does it mean? And when was this saying uttered?

"My rabbi tells me that 'binding and loosing' is regularly

used by the Jews to indicate that a rabbi 'forbids' or 'sanctions' a certain action—for example, the eating of a particular food. Thus in the Acts of the Apostles, the Lord would be said by the Jews to 'loose' the eating of food that was before unclean, saying to Peter, 'Arise, kill and eat.' And I can conceive that a gospel might describe Jesus as saying to Peter, ' I give thee this power of loosing unclean food, that thou and the rest of my disciples may henceforth eat with the Gentiles, and in their houses, asking no questions concerning the food.' But I do not myself believe that Christ used the phrase 'bind and loose' in this sense. I think he connected it with that strange doctrine of forgiveness of sins on which he laid so much stress, and that it was uttered after the resurrection, when the term 'church' might be more naturally used." Scaurus was so far right in this that I afterwards found in the fourth gospel a doctrine, not indeed about " binding and loosing," but about "imprisoning and loosing" or " arresting and loosing"; and this was connected with "sins," and Christ gave this power to the disciples after the resurrection.

Scaurus continued, " Look at Matthew's words in one of these passages, ' But if he refuse to hear the church, let him be unto thee as the heathen and the publican,' and then, at some interval, 'Where two or three are gathered together in my name, I am there in the midst of them.' Then look at the last words of Matthew's gospel, uttered after the resurrection, 'Behold I am with you always.' Does not the saying, ' I am there in the midst of you when you are gathered together,' come more appropriately from Christ, appearing after the resurrection, than from Christ before the resurrection? I think so. The context indicates a tradition of some utterance made after the resurrection, conveyed through some apostle in a Jewish form, promising Christ's presence to the disciples. Paul assumes such a presence, writing to the Corinthians ' When ye are gathered together, and my spirit, together with the power of the Lord Jesus Christ, to deliver over such a one to Satan.' These last words about 'Satan ' I do not profess to comprehend fully; but they seem to me to imply the opposite of 'loosing'— some kind of ' binding ' or 'remanding to prison.' And it is to take place in the presence of Christ, with Paul's spirit, when the church of Corinth is ' gathered together '."

I thought Scaurus was probably right as to the date of this promise. But I was much more impressed by what he said concerning the tradition, in Luke, "*Eat those things that are served up to you.*" This, in Luke, was almost meaningless to me, but it had been full of meaning in Paul's epistle to the Corinthians, where the apostle spoke about meat sold in Gentile markets: "If an unbeliever invites you, and ye desire to accept, *eat everything that is served up to you, asking no questions.*"

Scaurus said, " This tradition about ' *eating what is served up* ' occurs nowhere in the gospels except in Luke's account of the sending of the Seventy, beginning, ' After these things the Lord appointed other seventy.' Now this word ' *appoint* ' does not in the least necessitate the conclusion that Christ appointed the Seventy before the resurrection. Look at the '*appointment*' of the thirteenth apostle in the place of Judas. The Acts says ' Lord, *appoint* him whom thou hast chosen.' Then Matthias is ' *appointed.*' The Lord is supposed to '*appoint*' him in answer to the prayer. Concerning this, Luke might say, '*After these things the Lord appointed Matthias.*' If these words had been inserted in the gospel, they would have given the false impression that Jesus, while living, had appointed Matthias. Well, that is just the impression—a false one—that Luke gives as to the '*appointment*' of the Seventy. The fact is that the Seventy (a number often used by the Jews to denote all the nations or languages of the world) represent the missionaries ' *appointed* ' *after the Lord's death to go to the cities of the Gentiles to prepare them for the Coming of the Lord from heaven.* These were to go into the houses of Gentiles. Though Jews, they were to eat of Gentile food—' *everything that is served up.*' Without this explanation, the tradition has no meaning—or, if any, an unworthy one, ' Do not be fastidious. If you cannot have pleasant food, eat unpleasant food.' This seems to me absurd. But with this explanation, the precept becomes intelligible and necessary."

This convinced me. Moreover Luke's use of "the Lord," for "Jesus"—since "the Lord" would be more likely to be used than "Jesus" after the resurrection—seemed slightly to favour Scaurus's conclusion. He passed next to a tradition of Matthew's about abstinence from marriage "for the sake of the kingdom of heaven." On this he said, "Looking at Paul's advice to the Corinthians about celibacy and marriage, and at the distinction he draws between 'advice,' and 'allowance' and 'command,' and 'not I but the Lord,' I am convinced that Paul spoke on his own responsibility, except as to Christ's insistence on the old tradition in Genesis, 'The two shall be one flesh.' I mean that Christ upheld monogamy against polygamy and against that modified form of polygamy which arose from the husband's unrestricted, or scarcely restricted, right of divorce. Soon after the resurrection, in the midst of persecutions, when the Christians expected that Christ might speedily return and carry them up to heaven, it was natural that the Corinthians should apply for advice to Paul, and other churches to other apostles.

"My belief is that Christ's words extended to only the first half of Matthew's tradition. The disciples complain, in effect, 'If a man cannot divorce his wife when he dislikes her, it is best not to marry.' To this Christ replies, as I interpret him, 'Not all grasp the mystery of the true marriage contemplated from the beginning (namely, "the two shall become one") but only those to whom it is given.' This seems to me to have been explained in a wrong sense in the words that follow about 'eunuchs.' At all events, Paul twice quotes the words quoted by Christ (about the 'two' becoming 'one') as though they were the basis of his doctrine about marriage and also a type of the mysterious wedlock between Christ and the church. I do not think, however, that any confident conclusion is deducible. Christ elsewhere indicates—when dealing with an imaginary case where a woman has married seven brothers consecutively—that the marriage tie does not extend to the next life. By the Jews, marriage is, and was, regarded as honourable, and almost as a duty. But a Jewish sect called the Essenes, or some of them, practised celibacy; and you know how Epictetus inculcates celibacy on his Cynics of the first class. These facts, and the pressure of hard times, and Paul's example, may not only have favoured abstinence from marriage among Christians but also have favoured some tampering with tradition in order to enjoin celibacy. A letter to Timothy speaks of certain heretics as 'forbidding to marry.' Perhaps the only safe conclusion about Matthew's tradition is that no conclusion can be deduced from it."

Scaurus next discussed the question whether Christ inculcated poverty on his disciples. He denied it. Not that he denied Luke to be more correct verbally in saying "Blessed are *the poor*" than Matthew in "Blessed are *the poor in spirit*." But he asserted that Christ meant "*poor in spirit*." Similarly (said Scaurus) Christ meant "hungering *after righteousness*," as Matthew says, though Luke was right verbally in omitting "after righteousness." For, according to Scaurus, "Christ hardly ever used such words as 'bread,' 'leaven,' 'water,' 'hunger,' 'thirst,' 'fire,' 'salt,' 'treasure,' and so on, except metaphorically." Then he quoted the following instance out of Mark's version of Christ's instructions to the twelve apostles, where, he said, Mark's metaphors had been misunderstood literally—and consequently altered—by Matthew and Luke.

"Mark," said he, " has, 'that they should take nothing for the journey, *save a staff only*, no bread, no wallet, no money for the purse.' Matthew and Luke have '*no staff*.' Now turn to Genesis, where Jacob thanks God for helping him on his journey, 'I passed over Jordan with *my staff*.' He *means*, 'with *my staff only*.' Philo explains this '*staff*' metaphorically, as 'training,' *i.e.* the instruction or guidance given by God. David says to God, 'Thy rod and *thy staff* are my help,' or words to that effect—manifest metaphor. My rabbi shewed me a Jewish paraphrase of Jacob's words, 'I had neither gold, nor silver, nor herds, but *simply my staff*.' He also told me that this '*staff*' was supposed by the Jews to have been given by God to Adam from whom it descended to the patriarchs in succession. This shews that Jews might find no difficulty in Christ's metaphor, 'Go forth with *nothing but a staff*,' *i.e.* the staff of Jacob, the rod and staff of God. But Greeks and Romans would naturally take the word literally as meaning 'walking-stick.' Then they would find a difficulty, asking, 'Why should Jesus say, *No bread, no wallet—only a walking-stick?*' Hence many, writing largely for Gentiles, might alter it into '*no walking-stick.*' This is what Matthew and Luke have done. Similarly they altered Mark's metaphor '*but shod with sandals,*' *i.e.* with light shoes fit for the 'beautiful feet' of the preachers of the gospel, into '*no boots,*' or words to that effect. The error is the same. Jewish metaphor has been in each case taken literally by Matthew and Luke."

Scaurus added a few remarks on Christ as a historical character, "dimly traceable," he said, "in the combined testimony of Mark, Matthew, and Luke"—where I thought he might have added, "and in the epistles of Paul." His main thought was that, in spite of all the defects of these three writers, it was possible to discern in Christ a successor of Moses and Isaiah. "This man," said Scaurus, "may be regarded in two aspects. As a lawgiver, he took as the basis of his republic a re-enactment, in a stronger form, of the two ancient laws that enjoined love of the Father and love of the brethren. As a prophet, he saw a time when all mankind—recognising in one another (man in man and nation in nation) some glimpse of the divine image, and of the beauty of divine holiness—would beat their swords into ploughshares, and go up to the City of peace, righteousness, and truth, to worship the Father of the spirits of all flesh. Isaiah had foreseen this. But this prophet was also possessed with a belief, beyond Isaiah's, in the unity of God and man. He was persuaded that the true Son of man was the Son of God, higher than the heavens. I think also that he trusted—but on what grounds I do not know, unless it was an ingrained prophetic belief, found in all the great prophets, carried to its highest point in this prophet—that, as light follows on darkness, so does joy on sorrow, righteousness on sin, and life on death. A Stoic would say that these things alternate and that all things go round. But this Jewish prophet believed that all things in the end would go up—up to heaven. That is how I read his expectation. Feeling himself to be one with God, he placed no limits, except God's will, to the mighty works that God might do for him in his attempt to fulfil God's purpose of exalting men from darkness to light and from death to life.

"It is in some of these mysterious aspirations," said Scaurus, "that I cannot follow this prophet of the Jews. At times he seems to me to act and speak (certainly Paul speaks thus) as though God had caused mankind to take (if I may say so) one disease in order to get rid of another. I am speaking of moral disease. God seems to Paul to have allowed man to contract the disease of sin in order to rise to a health of righteousness, higher than would have been possible if he had not sinned. On these and other mystical notions this Jewish prophet may perhaps base views of forgiveness, and of love, and of the efficacy of his own death for his disciples, all of which perplex me. Sometimes I reject them entirely. Sometimes I am in doubt." These last words of Scaurus seemed to me to explain many inconsistencies in his letters. But how could I be surprised? Was I consistent myself? Was not my own mind at that instant fluctuating like a very Euripus? I could understand his doubts only too well.

He concluded by contrasting Christ with John the Baptist. "The one point," said Scaurus, "in which these two prophets or reformers agreed, was that the Lord God would intervene for the people, if only the people would return to Him. But in other respects they appear to me to have altogether differed. John the Baptist seems to have desired to bring about a remission of debts in accordance with the Law of Moses, as insisted on by previous prophets. He also desired an equalisation of property. That is what I gather from the gospels themselves, interpreted in the light of the ancient Law of the Jews. Moreover Josephus told me that Herod the tetrarch put John to death on political grounds, because he seemed likely to stir up the people to sedition, nor did he ever mention the influence of Herodias as contributing to the prophet's execution. Of course the story about the dancing and the oath may be true, and yet the oath may have been a mere excuse for getting rid of an inconvenient person. John was not unwilling (as I gather) to resort to the sword of Gideon or the fire of Elijah if the word of the gospel did not suffice to establish the new kingdom.

"Jesus, on the other hand, was absolutely averse to violence. Jesus was penetrated with the belief in the power of 'little ones' and 'babes' and 'sucklings.' How far he anticipated the future in store for himself I cannot say. Sometimes I am inclined to believe that he thought God would intervene at the last moment and deliver him from the jaws of death. Sometimes he seems to have deliberately faced death with the conviction that he would be swallowed up by it for a short time, emerging from it to victory.

"The Baptist certainly expected to be delivered by Jesus from the prison in which he was being kept by Antipas, and to have been disappointed by his friend's inaction. It must have been a very bitter moment for the latter when John sent to reproach him, as good as saying, 'Are you, too, a false Messiah? Will you leave me to perish in prison? Are you really our Deliverer, or must we, the whole nation, turn from you as a laggard, and wait for another?' In my opinion, this was the very greatest temptation to which Jesus was exposed. In that moment—as I judge when I try to guess the eastern metaphor corresponding to western fact—Jews would say that Satan said to Christ 'Worship me, and I will give you the empire of the world,' or 'Take the risk! Throw yourself down from the pinnacle! See whether God will save you!' In plain words, the temptation was, 'Appeal to the God of battles! Rouse the people to arms, first against Antipas, and then against the Romans!' For a perfectly unselfish and noble nature, believing in divine interventions, this must indeed have been a great, a very great temptation."

Scaurus finished this part of his letter by quoting a passage that I had long had in mind, but I had forgotten its context, "Do you remember, Silanus, how the old Egyptian priest says in the Timaeus, 'Solon, Solon, you Greeks are always boys'? Then comes the reason, '*You have not in your souls any ancient belief based on tradition from the days of old.*' Well, we Romans are in the same position as the poor Greeks. So are the Egyptians for the matter of that. For it is not antiquity alone, but *divine* antiquity, that counts. None of us have this divine antiquity of ' tradition from the days of old ' going back to such characters as Abraham, Moses, and the prophets. I think we must put up with our inferiority. These things we had better leave to others. We have, as Virgil says, ' arts ' of our own, the arts of war and empire. There, we are men, full-grown men. But as compared with Moses, Isaiah, and above all with this Jesus, or Christ, I must frankly confess I sometimes feel myself a ' boy,' and never so much as now. My conclusion is, *I will keep to the things in which I am not a 'boy.'* Do you the same."

CHAPTER XXVI

SCAURUS ON CHRIST'S RESURRECTION (I)

PASSING next to the subject of Christ's resurrection, "To deal first," said Scaurus, "with Christ's alleged predictions that he would 'rise again,' what strikes me as the strangest point in them is his frequent mention of being '*betrayed.*' For the rest, if Jesus believed himself to be the Messiah or Christ—as I think he did, if not at first, yet soon—or even if he did not believe himself to be the Christ, but thought that he was to reform the nation, I can well understand that he adopted the language of one of their prophets, Hosea by name, who says, 'Come and let us return unto the Lord...he hath smitten, and he will bind us up. After two days will he revive us. On the third day he will raise us up, and we shall live in his sight.' Using such language as this, a later Jewish prophet, such as Christ, might lead his followers up to Jerusalem at the Passover, not knowing whether he should live or die, but convinced that the Lord would work some deliverance for Israel. And the predictions of 'scourging,' and 'smiting,' and 'spitting,' I could also understand, as coming from the prophets. But 'betrayal' is not mentioned by the prophets, and I cannot understand its insertion here."

With this I have dealt above, and with the double sense of the word meaning "deliver over" and "betray." I now found that the evangelists sometimes apply the word to the act of Judas the betrayer (because by his betrayal Christ was "delivered over" to the Jews); and Scaurus regarded it as meaning "betray" here. I could not however believe that Jesus, when predicting His death, used the word in the sense "*betray.*"

It seemed to me that He predicted that His end would be like that of the Suffering Servant in Isaiah, namely, that He would be "*delivered over*" as a ransom for the sins of the people by the will of His Father. Long afterwards, I found that, whereas the Greek in Isaiah has "*delivered over for*," the Hebrew has "*make intercession for*." Then I saw, even more clearly than before, the reason why Christ may have often repeated this prediction, if He foresaw that His death would "make intercession" for the people. The evangelists rendered this so that it might be mistaken for "would be betrayed." But Paul made the matter clear.

Scaurus added that the rising again was predicted as about to occur, sometimes " on the third day," as in Hosea, but sometimes "after three days," corresponding to a period of three days and three nights spent by Jonah (according to a strange Hebrew legend) in a whale's belly. And he also said, " Mark and Matthew represent Jesus as saying, concerning what he would do after death, ' I will go before you *to Galilee.*' But Luke omits these words. Later on, after the resurrection, Mark and Matthew again mention this prediction; but there Luke has 'remember that which he said to you *while yet in Galilee.*' My rabbi tells me that the words 'to Galilee' might easily be confused with other expressions having quite a different meaning. This seems to me probable, but into these details I cannot now enter. I take it, however, that Luke knew Mark's tradition '*to Galilee,*' and rejected it as erroneous. Matthew also says that certain women, meeting Jesus after death, 'took hold of his feet,' and Jesus sent word by them to the disciples to 'depart *into Galilee.*' Here you see '*Galilee*' again. But this tradition is not in any other gospel. Luke makes no mention of any appearance in *Galilee.*"

These discrepancies about "Galilee" might have interested me at any other time; but "*took hold of his feet*"—this was the assertion that amazed me and carried away my thoughts from everything else. I had approached the subject of the Resurrection through Paul, who mentions Christ merely as having "appeared" to several of the apostles and last of all to himself. I had all along assumed that the "appearances" of the Lord to the other apostles had been of the same kind as the appearance to Paul, that is to say, supernatural, but not material nor tangible. Having read what Paul said about the spiritual body and the earthly body, I had supposed that Christ's earthly body remained in the tomb but that His spiritual body rose from the dead, passed out of the tomb—as a spirit might pass, not being confinable by walls or gates or by the cavernous sides of a tomb—and "appeared" to the disciples, now in this place, now in that. That the "spiritual body" meant the *real spiritual "person"*—and not a mere "shade" or breath-like "spirit" of the departed—this (as I have explained above) I had more or less understood. But I had never supposed that the "body" could be touched. And now, quite unexpectedly, Scaurus thrust before me, so to speak, a tradition that some women "*took hold of Christ's feet*" after He had risen from the dead.

"Of course," said Scaurus, "most critics would say at once that the women lied. But in the first place, even if they did lie, that would not explain why Mark and Luke omitted it. For you may be quite sure the evangelists would not believe that the women told a lie; and, if they believed that the women told the truth, why should they not report it? For the fact, if a fact, is a strong proof of resurrection. In the next place, I am convinced that the Christian belief in Christ's resurrection is far too strong to have been originated by lies. I believe it was originated by visions, and that the stories about these visions were exaggerated in various ways, but never dishonest ways. In this particular case, the explanation probably is, that the women saw a vision of Christ in the air and '*would have held* it fast by the feet,' that is, *desired to do so, but could not*. I could give several instances from the LXX where '*would have*' is thus dropped in translation. The belief of the Christians was, that Christ ascended to heaven. The women are perhaps regarded as *desiring to grasp his feet while he was ascending*, but Christ prevents them, sending them away to carry word to his '*brethren*'—for so he calls them—of his resurrection." I had not, at the time, knowledge enough to judge of Scaurus's explanation; but I afterwards found that "*would have*" might be thus dropped, and that the fourth gospel represents a woman as attempting, or desiring, to "touch" Jesus, but as being prevented (by the words "touch me not") because He had "*not yet ascended*"; and Jesus says to her "*Carry word to my brethren.*" Scaurus's explanation was confirmed by these facts.

Scaurus continued as follows, "Mark, the earliest of the evangelists, contains no account of the resurrection, except as an announcement made by angels. He says that the women "were afraid" when they heard this announcement; and there he ends. But in my copy of Mark there is an appendix (not in the handwriting of the same scribe that wrote the gospel) which begins, ' Now having arisen on the first day of the week he became visible at first to Mary of Magdala, out of whom he had cast seven devils.' Then it says that Jesus 'was manifested in a different form' to two of his previous companions, when walking in the country. Then it mentions a third and last manifestation to 'the eleven' seated at a meal." I turned at once to my copy of Mark, but there was no such appendix. It ended with the words "for they were afraid."

Scaurus proceeded, "This appendix is not at all in Mark's style, but it is probably very ancient. Luke mentions no appearance of Christ to women. But he describes an appearance to two disciples walking toward a village near Jerusalem; or rather, not to them while walking, for Jesus did not appear to them at first so as to be recognised; he first walked and talked with them and 'opened their minds to understand the Scriptures.' Then, in the village, during the breaking of bread, he was recognised by them, and vanished. As regards 'walking,' I may mention that the ancient Jews describe God as '*walking with Israel*,' and I have read in a Christian letter, '*The Lord journeyed with me*,' meaning 'enlightened me.' So the word may be used metaphorically. These two disciples expressly mention a 'vision of angels' spoken of by the women, who told them that angels had announced that Christ had risen from the dead; but, according to Luke, the two disciples and their companions disbelieved the women's tale. And not a word is said by Luke, then or afterwards, about any appearance of Christ himself to women.

"You can see for yourself, Silanus, under what a disadvantage this Mark-Appendix placed these poor, simple, ignorant, honest Christians, when it called as their first witness to the resurrection a woman that had been formerly a lunatic. I believe they have been already attacked by their Jewish enemies on this ground. If they have not been, I am sure they will be. Luke, a physician and an educated man, chooses his ground much more sensibly. First, he omits all direct mention, in his own narrative, of manifestations to women. Secondly, he says, in effect—not in narrative but in dialogue— 'The women *did* see an apparition, but it was only of angels.' Thirdly, 'the *men* (and men are not liable to the hysterical delusions of women)—the *men*,' he says, 'treated the women's vision as a mere delusion. The *men* saw Jesus himself.' Possibly Luke was influenced by Paul, who in his list of the witnesses of manifestations makes no mention of women. The Law of Moses does not expressly exclude women's testimony. But Josephus once told me that his countrymen allowed neither women nor slaves to give public testimony. So it is clear that Jewish tradition has interpreted the Law as excluding women, and that Paul, when controverting Jews, would not appeal to the evidence of women, because Jews would not accept it. Perhaps Luke followed in the same path.

"Luke also makes the following attempt to meet the objections of those who might urge that Christ's apparition was not a rising of the actual body from the grave. He represents Christ as saying to the disciples, 'Handle me'—as a proof that he was not a disembodied spirit. Now I do not believe that Luke invented this, although he, the latest of the three evangelists, is alone in recording it. Curiously enough, I have only recently been reading a letter—very wild and extravagant but manifestly genuine—written some four or five years ago by a Christian named Ignatius, which throws light on these very words in Luke. A few months after writing it, the man suffered as a Christian here in Rome, and his letters naturally had a vogue. Flaccus sent me a copy as a curiosity. Well, this letter says that when Christ came to his disciples—Ignatius says '*to those around Peter*' but the meaning is 'to Peter and his companions,' that is, 'to Christ's disciples,' as I have explained above—in the flesh, after his resurrection, he said to them, 'Take, handle me, and see that I am not a bodiless dæmon.' Then Ignatius adds—and these are the words I want you to mark—'Straightway they *touched* him and believed, having been *mixed with his flesh and blood.*'

"Do you remember my laughing at you as a boy because you translated Diodorus Siculus literally, 'They *touched* one another because of extreme need,' when it ought to have been, 'They *fed on* one another'? I quoted to you, at the time, the saying of Pythagoras, 'Do not *touch* a white cock,' *i.e.* 'do not *feed on* it.' There are many instances of this meaning. Well, the Christians believed that they *fed on* Christ. His '*flesh and blood was mixed*' with theirs—or they were '*mixed*' with his—when they *fed on* him in their sacred meal. If there were some Greek traditions saying 'they *touched* him,' meaning 'they *fed on* him,' there would naturally be other traditions about '*touching*' Jesus meaning that they '*handled*' him. The latter would suggest that they touched the wounds in his body inflicted during the crucifixion."

I remembered my boyish mistake, and I saw clearly that Christians would have had much more excuse for making a similar one. Scaurus added, "This also explains Ignatius's curious use of 'take' (as in Mark and Matthew)." At first I could not understand what Scaurus meant; but on looking at Ignatius's Greek, which Scaurus gave me, I perceived that the words were not "*Take hold of me*, handle me," but "*Take*," *i.e.* "*Take* me," or "*Take* my body (as a whole)." Now "*take*" is similarly used by Mark and Matthew in the sentence "*Take*, eat, this is my body," where Mark omits "eat."

"Moreover," continued Scaurus, "Luke goes on to relate that Jesus said to the disciples, 'Have ye anything to eat?' and that *they gave* him some broiled fish, and that he ate in their presence. Christians in Rome have been in the habit—it would take too long to explain why—of using FISH as the emblem of Christ. The sense requires '*he gave*,' not '*they gave.*' I think Luke has confused '*he gave*' with '*they gave.*' The confusion, in Greek, might arise from one erroneous letter."

After giving me several instances of such confusion, he said, "I should not be surprised if some later gospel stated the fact more correctly, namely, that *Christ gave* the disciples 'fish'." This I afterwards found to be the case in the fourth gospel.

Scaurus then proceeded, "I think, however, that Luke's error may have arisen in part from another tradition, which he has preserved in the Acts—somewhat like that of the Christian Ignatius which I have quoted above. Ignatius spoke of '*mixing*,' Luke, in the Acts, speaks of '*incorporating*'—I can think of no better word to give the meaning—saying that Jesus, '*in the act of being incorporated with*' the disciples, bade them not to depart from Jerusalem till they had received the Holy Spirit. Now this word '*incorporate*'—which is used of men brought into a city, hounds into a pack, soldiers into a squadron, and so on—is adapted to represent that close union which is a mark of almost all the Christians, who say with Paul that they are 'one body in Christ' and 'members one of another.' But this compact union of Christians is also represented by their Eucharist, so that Paul says to the Corinthians, in effect, not only, 'Ye are one body,' but also 'Ye are one loaf.' And I rather think that some Christians at the present time, in their Eucharists, pray that, as the grains of wheat scattered in the field are made into one, so the scattered children of God may be gathered into one. I think you must see how easily errors might spring up from metaphors of this kind used in the various churches of the empire, among people varying in language, customs, and traditions, and for the most part illiterate.

"Even in the letter of Ignatius above-mentioned, a scribe has altered the word 'mixed' into 'constrained' in the margin; and I am not surprised. I do not by any means accuse Luke of dishonesty, nor of carelessness. He did his best. But he was probably a physician—a man of science therefore—and liked to have things definitely and scientifically stated. This word above-mentioned, 'being made into one compact body with them,' might easily be supposed to mean 'partaking of salt with them,' that is, 'sharing a meal with them.' That rendering had the advantage of constituting a definite proof of Christ's resurrection with a body that might be called in some sense material, since it (*i.e.* the body) was capable of eating. Then, of course, Luke would adapt his other accounts of the resurrection to this tradition, which he would naturally regard as one of central importance. But, though honest and pains-taking, Luke appears to me to have altered and corrupted what was perhaps, in some sense, a real—yes, I will admit, in some sense, a real—manifestation (if indeed any visions are real) into a mere non-existent physical sign or proof.

"Luke represents Jesus as feeding on his own body in order to satisfy his unbelieving disciples that he is really among them. I can easily imagine how very different may have been the feelings of those simple enthusiasts, the early Galilæan disciples, when they used these words—never dreaming that they would be reduced to dry, evidential prose—in psalms and hymns and spiritual songs, praising the Lord for allowing them to 'sit at His table,' and to 'eat and drink with Him,' or for making them 'sharers in the sacred food of His body' and 'partners of His board.' It was only, after a generation or more had passed away, outside the atmosphere of Galilee—it was only to a compiler laboriously tracing back the truth through documents—that all these phrases would suggest the thought of Jesus proving his reality by partaking of food that his disciples give to him.

"It may be said, as though it were to Luke's discredit, 'He represents Peter as positively testifying to this eating.' Of course he does. You know how speeches are written, even in the most accurate histories. No historian, as a rule, professes to record a speech of any length exactly. If Luke first inferred that Christ ate with the apostles after his death, he would also naturally go on to infer that Peter, in attesting Christ's resurrection, must necessarily have included some mention of this fact. I cannot blame him. I think he was perfectly honest, though in error." I agreed. But it seemed to me an error much to be regretted.

On one point, however, Scaurus seemed to me to be not quite accurate, when he said of Luke, "He represents Peter as positively testifying to this eating." For Peter's speech was to this effect, " God raised him up on the third day and granted that he should be manifested—not to all the people but to witnesses previously appointed by God, namely us, who ate with him and drank with him—after he had risen from the dead." Scaurus regarded this as meaning that "the eating and drinking" of Christ's disciples took place "after his death." Even if that had been so, it might be that Jesus was merely present (not eating and drinking) when the disciples ate and drank: and something of this kind I afterwards found in the fourth gospel. But I punctuated the words differently, and interpreted them differently, as meaning that the "*manifestation*" (not the "eating") *took place after the resurrection*; and that the manifestation was limited to those who had been Christ's intimate companions, or as the Greeks say, "*sharers of his table*," *during his life*.

I remembered also an old remark of Scaurus's about our modern Roman use of "convivo," meaning "I *live with*," and how easily it might be taken to mean the ordinary "convivor," meaning "I *feast with*." Since that, I have found that, in other ways, "*living with*" and "*eating with*" may be easily confused. For these reasons I concluded that the supposition that Jesus ate with the disciples after His resurrection was not justified.

CHAPTER XXVII

SCAURUS ON CHRIST'S RESURRECTION (II)

"I NOW come," said Scaurus, "to one of the most interesting of all the traditions of the resurrection—the 'rolling away of the stone' from the tomb. As to the alleged facts, all the evangelists agree. But Mark alone has preserved traces of what I take to be the historical fact, namely, that the narrative, as it now stands, has sprung from Christian songs and hymns based on Hebrew scriptures and Jewish traditions. I shewed you above how the precept, 'Go forth with the staff alone,' did not mean 'with a walking-stick' but 'with the staff of God,' a metaphor from the story of Jacob in Genesis. Curiously enough, the same story will help us to explain the rolling away of the stone.

"There Jacob rolls away the stone from the well for Rachel in order that her flocks may obtain water. The Jews have many symbolical explanations of this 'rolling of the stone.' One is, that the stone is the evil nature in man. When worshippers go into the synagogue, the stone (they say) is rolled away. When they come out, it is rolled back again. Philo comments fully on the somewhat similar action of Moses helping the daughters of Jethro, taking it in a mystical sense. The scriptures may be regarded as the 'water of life' or 'living water.' The 'stone' prevents the 'water' from issuing to those that thirst for it. You may perhaps remember that Paul says something of the same kind, but using a different metaphor. To this day, he says, a 'veil' lies on the hearts of the Jews when the scriptures are read.

So Luke says—concerning one of Christ's predictions about his resurrection—'it was *veiled* from them.' Luke also relates that Christ, after the resurrection, conversed with two disciples, but did not make himself visible to them till he had 'interpreted the scriptures' to them. Then, when he broke bread, 'their eyes were opened and they recognised him.' This 'interpreting,' the two disciples call 'opening the scriptures.' The '*opening of the scriptures*' might be called '*taking the veil from the heart,*' or '*rolling away the stone.*' But the last phrase might still better be used for '*rolling away the burden of unbelief*'."

All this seemed fanciful to me. But as I knew very little about Jewish tradition I waited to see what traces of this poetic language Scaurus could shew in the Greek text of Mark. Before passing to that, however, Scaurus shewed me, from Isaiah, that "the stone" might be used in two senses, a good and a bad; a good, for believers, as being "the stone that had become the head of the corner"; but a bad, for unbelievers, as "the stone of stumbling and rock of offence." And he said that the stone rolled away by Jacob was called by some Jews the Shechinah or glory of God. According to Matthew, the "stone" at the door of the tomb was "sealed" by the chief priests, the enemies of Christ. There it stood, as an enemy, saying to the disciples, "Your faith is vain. He will come out no more. He is dead." This was "*a stone of stumbling.*" On the other hand Scaurus said he had read an epistle written by Peter, which bids the disciples come to Christ as "*a living stone.*"

"Now," said Scaurus, "taking the accounts literally, we must find it impossible to explain how the women, at about six o'clock in the morning, could expect to find men at the tomb ready and willing to roll the stone away for them; or, if guards were on the spot, how the guards could be induced to allow it. And there are also other difficulties, too many to enumerate, in the differences between the evangelists as to the object of the women's visit. But taking the account as originally a poem, we are able to recognise (I think) two or three historic facts found in Mark alone.

"First, take the statement that the women 'said,' or 'said to themselves,' 'Who *will roll* away the stone for us from the door of the tomb?' I am not surprised that someone has altered this into, 'Who *has rolled* away the stone for us?' Improbable though the latter is, it is at all events conceivable. But it is inconceivable that women, going to the guarded door of a prison, should ask, as a literal question, 'Who will open the door for us?' Taken literally, Mark's text implies something almost as absurd as this. But now take it as a prayer to heaven. Then you may illustrate it by the language of the Psalmist, 'Who will rise up for me against the evil-doers? Who will stand up for me against the workers of iniquity?'— followed by 'Unless the Lord had been my help my soul had soon dwelt in silence.' So the Psalmist says, 'Who will bring me into the fenced city?' and then adds, 'Hast not thou cast us off, O God?' You see in all these cases the question is really a prayer, a passionate and almost desperate prayer, implying 'What man will do this for us? No man. No one but God.' So it is in the Law, 'Who will go up to heaven? Who will go down into the deep?' These last words Paul quotes as the utterance of something approaching to despair. So I take the women's words as having been originally a cry to God, 'Who, if not God, will roll away the stone!'

"Secondly, note that Mark says nothing about any guards at the tomb. According to him, no obstacle was to be anticipated by the women, in their attempt to enter the tomb, except the weight of the stone, which was 'exceeding great.' No other evangelist says this. But I have seen traditions describing the stone as so heavy that twenty men could scarcely roll it, or that it required the efforts of the elders and scribes aided by the centurion and his soldiers. In my opinion the omission of the 'greatness' by Matthew and Luke, and the literalising of it by later traditions, arise from a misunderstanding of its poetical and spiritual character. The 'stone' was 'exceeding great' in this sense, that it could not be moved except by the help of God.

"Thirdly, 'the women *looked up* and saw it (*i.e.* the stone) *rolled upward*,' that is, as I take it, to heaven, in a vision.

The word here used for 'look up' may mean 'regain sight,' as though the women were blind to the fact till they had uttered their aspiration ('who will roll it away?') and then their eyes were opened. Anyhow, it is more than 'looked.' I think it means 'saw in a vision'." I was certainly astonished at this use of "look up," but much more at the "*rolling up*" of the stone.

"As to Mark's '*rolling up*'," said Scaurus, "I have looked everywhere, trying to find his word used by others in the sense of 'roll away,' or 'roll back.' But in vain. Its use here is all the more remarkable because, when Jacob rolls away the stone for Rachel, the word '*roll away*' is used. You may say, 'This shews that the term is not borrowed from Jacob's story.' I cannot agree with that. The Christian hymn might contrast Jacob, the type of Christ, rolling the stone merely on one side, with Christ, the fulfilment, rolling it right up to heaven. I should add that a marginal note in Mark inserts an ascension of angels with Jesus at this point."

In attempting to do justice to this narrative and to Scaurus's criticisms of it, I felt at a great disadvantage owing to my ignorance of Jewish literature and thought; and at first I was much more disposed to put by the whole story as an inexplicable legend than to accept Scaurus's explanation. But afterwards, looking at Matthew's narrative, I found that Matthew described an "angel" as "rolling away the stone," and as saying to the women, "Fear not." This seemed decidedly to confirm the conclusion that the women saw "a vision of angels" (a phrase used by Luke) in which vision the stone was seen rolled away—or (as Mark says) "rolled upward"—when the angels went up to heaven. But all this—though it confused and wearied me—did not prevent me from believing that the spirit, or spiritual body, of Christ had really risen from the dead, since I had all along supposed that this alone was what was meant by Christ's resurrection, in accordance, as it appeared to me, with Paul's statements. Nothing that Scaurus had said, so far, seemed to me to shake Paul's testimony to the resurrection.

But Scaurus's next remarks dealt with this matter, and greatly shook my faith. "I had almost forgotten," he said, "to speak of Christ's appearance to Paul. It was clearly a mere image of Paul's thought, called up by his conscience—nothing more. I need write no further about it. Flaccus has sent you Luke's Acts of the Apostles. If you are curious, look there, and you will find enough and more than enough. My belief is, that, if Stephen had not seen Christ, Paul would not have seen Christ. That puts the matter epigrammatically, and therefore (to some extent) falsely; for all epigrams are partly false. But it is mainly true. There may have been other Stephens whom Paul persecuted. But Stephen, I think, summed up the effect of all. Read what Paul says to the Romans about the persecuted and their conquest of persecutors :—' Bless them that persecute you'; that is, instead of resorting to the fire of vengeance against one's enemy, use, he says, the refiner's fire of kindness, ' for in doing this thou shalt heap coals of fire on his head'; finally, 'Be not conquered by evil, but conquer evil with good.' Read this. Then reflect that Paul 'persecuted.' Then read the Acts and see how he persecuted Stephen, and how Stephen interceded for his enemies. I take it that Paul is writing from experience—that the intercession of Stephen 'overcame' Paul (*he* would say 'overcame,' *I* should say 'hypnotized' him) and compelled Paul to see what Stephen saw, namely, Jesus raised from the dead and glorified. Read the Acts and see if I am not right."

It had not occurred to me before, while I was reading what Flaccus's letter said incidentally about the inclusion of the Acts of the Apostles in my parcel, that this book would probably give me Luke's account of the conversion of the apostle Paul, which had been so much in my thoughts, in my conjectures, and even in my dreams. Now, therefore, although barely a dozen lines of Scaurus's letter remained to read, I immediately put them aside and took up the Acts. Here I found that I had been wrong in most of my wild anticipations about the circumstances of Paul's conversion; but I had been right in supposing that the conversion took place near Damascus, and that the utterance of Christ would contain the words, " I am Jesus." Moreover the words, " Saul, Saul, why persecutest thou me?" accorded (not indeed exactly but as to their general sense) with my dream about the Christian martyrs—

how they looked at me, as though saying, Why didst thou rack me¸? Why didst thou torture me?; and how they blessed me, and looked up to heaven; and how they made me fear lest I, too, should be compelled to look up and see what they saw.

Now therefore once more I was seized with a kind of fellow-feeling for Paul as he journeyed to Damascus. I began again to imagine his efforts to prevent himself from thinking of Stephen, and from seeing Stephen's face looking up to heaven, and from hearing Stephen's blessing. It seemed to me that I, too, should have rebelled as Paul rebelled at first, striving against my conscience, like the bullock that kicks against the goad. Then I asked, "Should I have done what Paul did afterwards? Should I, too, have been 'overcome' as Paul was, being brought under the yoke?" I thought I might have been.

But was it seemly or right that a free man should be brought under a "yoke"? That was the question I had now to answer. I seemed to have come to the branching of the paths. All depended on the nature of the "yoke." What was it? On the one hand, Paul said it was "the constraining love of Christ." He had made me feel that there was nothing base in it, nothing to be ashamed of. Nay, under Paul's influence, this "yoke" had begun to seem an ensign of the noblest warfare, a sign of royalty, the emblem of service undertaken by God Himself, the yoke of the risen Saviour, the Son of God, enthroned by the Father's side in heaven, and in the hearts of men on earth. But on the other side stood Scaurus, maintaining that all these Jewish stories were dreams—not falsehoods, but self-deceits more dangerous than falsehoods. He had also convinced me that the gospels contained an unexpected multitude of errors and exaggerations and disproportions. This I could not honestly deny. Thus the gospels flung me back—or at least, as interpreted by Scaurus, seemed to fling me back—from the faith to which I was just on the point of attaining through the epistles. In my bewilderment I was no longer able to say clearly and firmly as before, "Nevertheless the moral power of the gospel is attested by facts that Scaurus and Arrian both admit, facts that Epictetus would be only too glad to allege for himself—by myriads of souls converted from vice to virtue. Does not this moral power rest on reality?"

The Christians themselves seemed to attach so much importance to "Christ in the flesh" that I began to attach importance too. The evangelists appeared to say, in effect, "If we cannot prove that Christ in the flesh arose from the dead, then we admit that He has not arisen." So they—or rather my impression about them—led me away to say the same thing. A few days ago, I had neither desired nor expected that Christ should be demonstrated to have risen in the flesh. Now I said, " I fear it cannot be proved that Christ in the flesh, that Christ's tangible body, rose from the dead. Nay, more, I feel that the belief in what might be called a tangible resurrection arose from some such causes as Scaurus has specified. So I must give up all belief."

I ought to have waited. I ought to have asked, "All belief in *what*?" "Belief in *what kind* of resurrection?" Scaurus himself had casually admitted that visions, though not presenting things tangible, might present things real. If so, then the visions of Israel might be real, the visions to Abraham and the patriarchs, to Moses, to the prophets. These might be a series of lessons given to the teachers in the east to be passed on to the learners in the west. Among the latest of these was a vision of "one like unto a Son of man." He was represented as "coming" with the clouds of heaven. That was a noble vision. Yet how much better and nobler would be a vision of the Son of man "coming" into the hearts of men, taking possession of them, reigning in them, establishing a kingdom of God in them! Such a Son of man had been revealed to Paul, "defined" as "the Son of God" "from the resurrection of the dead." Being both God and man He brought (so Paul said) God and man into one, imparting to all men the sense of divine sonship, the light of righteousness and spiritual life, triumphant over spiritual darkness and death. This is what I ought to have thought of, but did not.

Such an all-present power of divine sonship Paul seemed also to have in view when he likened belief in the risen Saviour to the faith described by Moses in Deuteronomy. The true believer, said Paul, is not the slave of place, saying, "Who shall go up to heaven?" that is, to bring Christ down to us from the right hand of God. Nor does he say, "Who shall go down to the abyss?" that is, to bring Christ up to us from the dead. The word of faith is "very near." It is "in the heart." It says, "Believe *with the heart* that God raised Christ from the dead." Such belief is not from the "eyes" nor from the "understanding"—as if one saw with one's own eyes the door of the grave burst open by an angel, or heard the facts attested in a lawcourt by a number of honest and competent eye-witnesses incapable of being deceived and of deceiving. To say, " I believe it because Marcus or Gaius believed it," is to avow a belief in Marcus or Gaius, not in Christ, unless the avower can go on to say "and because I have felt the risen Saviour within me."

He alone really and truly believes in the resurrection of Christ whose belief is based on personal experience. If he has that, he can contemplate without alarm the divergences of the gospels in their narratives of this spiritual reality. He will understand the meaning of Paul's words, "It pleased God to *reveal His Son in me*"—not "to me," but "*in me*." For indeed it is a revelation—not a demonstration from the intellect and senses alone—derived from all our faculties when enlightened by God. God draws back the veil from our fearful and faithless hearts and gives us a convincing sense of Christ at His right hand and in ourselves. This "conviction" is derived from no source but the convincing Spirit of the Saviour, coming to us in various ways, and through many instruments, but mostly through disciples whom the Saviour loves, and who have received not only His Spirit but also the power of imparting it to others.

All these things I knew afterwards, but not at the time I am now describing. I had indeed already some faint conjecture of the truth, but not such as I could put into definite words. I was defeated. In the bitterness of defeat I exclaimed, "There is more beyond, but I cannot reach it. I cannot even suggest it. These evangelists give me no help. They take part with Scaurus against me. I am beaten and must surrender." Yet I felt vaguely that I was not fairly beaten. I was like a baffled suitor retiring from a court of justice, crushed by a hostile verdict, victorious in truth and equity, but beaten and mulcted of all his estate on some point of technical law.

In this mood, sullen and sick at heart, weary of evidence and evidential "proofs" that were no proofs, and irritated rather with the evangelists than with Scaurus—who, after all, was doing no more than his duty in pointing out what appeared to him historical errors—I was greatly moved by an appeal to my love of truth with which my old friend concluded his letter. It was to this effect.

"Well, Silanus, now I have really done. I cannot quite understand what induced me to take up so much of my time, paper, and ink—and your time, too, which is worse—and all to kill a dead illusion. Why do I say 'dead' if it was never alive? Perhaps it was once nearly alive even in my sceptical soul. I think I have mentioned before that I, even I, have had moments when the dream of that phantom City of Truth and Justice had attractions for me. Perhaps I fancied it might be possible to receive this Jewish prophet as a great teacher and philosopher—helpful for the morals of private life at all events, even though useless for politics and imperial affairs— apart from the extravagant claims now raised for him by his disciples. But it is gone—this illusion—if it ever existed. The East and the West cannot mix. If they did, their offspring would be a portent. This Christian superstition is a mere creature of feeling, not of reason. I do not say it has done me harm to study it. Else I would not have sent you this letter. It is perhaps a bracing and healthful exercise to remind ourselves now and then that things are not as we could wish them to be, and that we must not 'feign things like unto our prayers.' A truthful man must see things as they are in truth. The City of Dreams has closed its gates against me, and I am shut out. It is warm in there. I am occasionally cold. So be it! Theirs is the fervour of the fancy, the comfortable warmth of the not-true. I must wrap myself in the cloak of truth—a poor uncomfortable thing, perhaps, but (as Epictetus would say) 'my own.' Truth, my dear Silanus, is your own, too—that is to say, truth to your own reason, truth to your own conscience. Never let wishes or aspirations wrest that from you. '*Keep what is your own!*'"

For the time, this appeal was too strong for me. I wrote to Scaurus briefly confessing that the City of Dreams had had attractions for me, as well as for him, but that I had resolved to put the thought away, though I might, perhaps, continue a little longer the study of the Christian books, which I, too, had found very interesting. When I grew calmer, I added a postscript, asking whether it was not possible that "feeling," as well as "reason," might play a certain lawful part in the search after truths about God. My last words were an assurance that, whereas I had been somewhat irregular of late in my attendance at Epictetus's lectures, I should be quite regular in future. This indeed was my intention. As things turned out, however, the next lecture was my last.

CHAPTER XXVIII

THE LAST LECTURE

AWAKING early next morning, two or three hours before lecture, I spent the time in examining the gospels, and in particular the accounts of Christ's last words. So few they were in Mark and Matthew that I could not anticipate that Luke would omit a single one of them or fail to give them exactly. They were uttered in public and in a loud voice. According to Mark and Matthew, they were a quotation from a Psalm, of which the Jewish words were given similarly by the two evangelists. They added a Greek interpretation. Luke, to my amazement, omitted both the Jewish words and the Greek interpretation. Afterwards, Mark and Matthew said that Jesus, in the moment of expiring, cried out again in a loud voice. On this occasion they gave no words. But there Luke mentioned words. Luke's words, too, were from a Psalm, but quite different in meaning from the words previously given by Mark and Matthew.

Still more astonished was I to find what kind of words the two earliest evangelists wrote down as the last utterance of Christ—" My God, my God, why hast thou forsaken me?" That Christ said this I could hardly believe. Reading further, I found that some of the men on guard exclaimed " This man calls for Elias "—because the Jewish word " Heli " or " Eli," " my God," resembles the Jewish " Elias." I wished that these men might prove true interpreters. Then I found that, although Luke mentions neither " Eli " nor " Elias," he nevertheless mentions " Elios " or " Helios," which in Greek means " sun." This occurred in the passage parallel to Eli or

Heli. What Luke said was that there was an "eclipse," or "failing," of "the sun." I thought then (and I think still) that Luke was glad—as a Christian historian might well be without being at all dishonest—to find that Mark's "Eli" had been taken, at all events by some, not to mean "my God." Perhaps some version gave "Elios," or "Helios," "sun." This Luke might gladly accept. Indeed, in the genitive, which is the form used by Luke, the word "Heliou" may mean either "of the sun" or "of Elias."

But, on reflection, I could not find much comfort from Luke's version. For the difficult version seemed more likely to be true. And how could there be an "eclipse" of the sun during Passover, when the moon was at the full? Then I looked at the Psalm from which the words were taken, and I noted that although it began with "Why hast thou forsaken me?" it went on to say that God "hath not hid his face from him, but when he cried unto him he heard him." Also the Psalm ended in a strain of triumph, as though this cry "Why hast thou forsaken me?" would end in comfort and strength for all the meek, so that "all the ends of the earth shall remember and turn unto the Lord." Nevertheless this did not satisfy me. And even the help that I afterwards received from Clemens (about whom I shall speak later on) left me, and still to this day leaves me, with a sense that there is a mystery in this utterance beyond my power to fathom, though not beyond my power to believe.

I was still engaged in these meditations when my servant brought me a letter. It was from Arrian, informing me of the death of his father, which would prevent him from returning to Nicopolis. He also requested me to convey various messages to friends to whom he had not been able to bid farewell owing to his sudden departure. In particular he enclosed a note, which he asked me to give to Epictetus. "Add what you like," he said, "you can hardly add too much, about my gratitude to him. I owe him morally more than I can express. Moreover in the official world, where everybody knows that our Master stands well with the Emperor, it is sometimes a sort of recommendation to have attended his lectures. And perhaps it has helped me. At all events I have recently been placed in a position of responsibility and authority by the Governor of Bithynia. I like the work and hope to do it fairly well. Even the mere negative virtue of not taking bribes goes for something, and that at least I can claim. I am not able, and never shall be able, to be a Diogenes, going about the province and healing the souls of men. But I try to do my duty, and I feel an interest in getting at the truth, and judging justly among the poor, so far as my limited time, energy and intelligence permit.

"In the towns, among the artisans and slaves, I have been surprised to find so many of the Christians. You may remember how we talked about this sect more than once. You thought worse of them than I did. But I don't think you had much more basis than the impressions of your childhood, derived from what you heard among your servants and the common people in Rome. I have seen a great deal of them lately and have been impressed by the high average of their morality, industry, and charity to one another.

"You never see a Christian begging. What is more, they set their faces against the exposing of children. I have often thought that our law is very defective in this respect. We will not let a father strangle his infant son, but we let him kill it by cold, starvation, or wild beasts. Every such death is the loss of a possible soldier to the state. It is a great mistake politically, and I am not sure whether it is right morally. When I first came to Nicopolis I used to hear it said that our Epictetus—one of the kindest of men I verily believe—once adopted a baby that was on the point of being exposed by one of his friends, got a nurse for it, and put himself to a lot of trouble. I sometimes wonder why he did not first give his friend the money to find a nurse and food for the baby, and then give him a good sharp reprimand for his inhumanity. For I call it inhuman. But I never heard Epictetus say a word against this practice. The Jews as well as the Christians condemn it. Perhaps the latter, in this point, merely followed the former; but in most points the Christians seem to me superior to the Jews.

"I am proud to call myself a philosopher, and perhaps I should be prouder than Epictetus would like if I could call myself a Roman citizen; but I am free to confess that there are points in which philosophers and Romans could learn something from these despised followers of Christus. *Fas est et a Christiano doceri.* I have been more impressed than I can easily explain to you on paper by the behaviour of this strangely superstitious sect. There is a strenuous fervour in their goodness—I mean in the Christians, I am not now speaking of the Jews—which I don't find in my own attempts at goodness. I am, at best, only a second-class Cynic, devoid of fervour.

"You may say, like an orthodox scholar of Epictetus, 'Let them keep their fervour and leave me calmness.' But these men have both. They can be seasonably fervid and seasonably calm. I have heard many true stories of their behaviour in the last persecution. Go into one of their synagogues and you may hear their priest—or rather prophet, for priests they have none—thundering and lightening as though he held the thunderbolts of Zeus. Order the fellow off for scourging or execution, and he straightway becomes serenity itself. Not Epictetus could be more serene. Indeed, where an Epictetian would 'make himself a stone' under stripes and say, 'They are nothing to me,' a Christian would rejoice to bear them 'for the sake of Christus.' And even Epictetus, I think, could not reach the warmth, the glow, of their affection for each other. I am devoutly thankful that I did not occupy my present office under Pliny. It has never been my fate to scourge, rack, torture, or kill, one of these honest, simple, excellent creatures, whose only fault is what Epictetus would call their '*dogma*' or conviction—surely such a 'dogma' as an emperor might almost think it well to encourage among the uneducated classes, in view of its excellent results. Farewell, and be ever my friend."

The third hour had almost arrived and I had to hasten to the lecture-room taking with me the note addressed to Epictetus. All the way, I could think of nothing but the contrast between what Arrian had said about the Christians, and what Mark and Matthew had said about Christ's last words—the servants tranquil, steadfast, rejoicing in persecution; their Master crying "My God, my God, why hast thou forsaken me?" It perplexed me beyond measure.

In this bewilderment, I took my accustomed place beside Glaucus, who greeted me with even more than his usual warmth. He seemed strangely altered. It was no new thing for him to look worn and haggard. But to-day there was a strange wildness in his eyes. Absorbed though I was in my own thoughts, I could not help noticing this as I sat down, just before Epictetus began.

The lecture was of a discursive kind but might be roughly divided into two parts, one adapted for the first class of Cynics, those who aspired to teach; the other for the second class, those who were content to practise. The first class Epictetus cautioned against expecting too much. No man, he said, not even the best of Cynic teachers, could control the will of another. Socrates himself could not persuade his own son. It was rather with the view of satisfying his own nature, than of moving other men's nature, that Socrates taught. Apollo himself, he said, uttered oracles in the same way. I believe he also repeated—what I have recorded before—that Socrates " did not persuade one in a thousand " of those whom he tried to persuade.

I remembered a similar avowal in Isaiah when the prophet declares that his message is " Hear ye indeed, but understand not"; and this, or something like it, was repeated by Jesus and Paul. But Isaiah says, "Lord, how long?" And the reply is that the failure will not be for ever. In the Jewish utterances, there was more pain but also more hope. I preferred them. Nor could I help recalling Paul's reiterated assertions that everywhere the message of the gospel was a " power,"—sometimes indeed for evil, to those that hardened themselves against it, but more often for good—constraining, taking captive, leading in triumph, and destined in the end to make all things subject to the Son of God. Compared with this, our Master's doctrine seemed very cold.

In the next place, Epictetus addressed himself to the larger and lower class of Cynics, those who were beginning, or who aspired only to the passive life. These he exhorted to set their thoughts on what was their own, on their own advantage or profit—of course interpreting profit in a philosophic sense as being virtue, which is its own reward and is the most profitable thing for every man. It was all, in a sense, very true, but again I felt that it was chilling. It seemed to send me down into myself, groping in the cellars of my own nature, instead of helping me to look up to the sun. Most of it was more or less familiar; and there was one saying that I have quoted above, to the effect that the universe is "badly managed if Zeus does not take care of each one of His own citizens in order that they like Him may be divinely happy." Now I knew that Epictetus did not use the word *eudæmon*, or divinely happy, referring to the next life, for he did not believe that a "citizen of Zeus" would continue to exist, except as parts of the four elements, in a future life. He meant "in this life." And if anyone in this life felt unhappy—more particularly, if he "wept"—that was a sign, according to Epictetus, that he was not a "citizen of Zeus." For he declared that Ulysses, if he wept and bewailed his separation from his home and wife—as Homer says he did—"was not good." So it came to this, that no man must weep or lament in earnest for any cause, either for the sins or sorrows of others, or for his own, on pain of forfeiting his franchise in the City of Zeus. I had read in the Hebrew scriptures how Noah, and Lot, and others of the "citizens of God," lived alone amongst multitudes of sinners; but they, and the prophets too, seemed to be afflicted by the sins around them. Also Jesus said in the gospels, "O sinful and perverse generation! How long shall I be with you and bear you!" as though it were a burden to him. And I had come to feel that every good man must in some sense bear the sins and carry the iniquities of his neighbours—especially those of his own household, and his own flesh and blood. So I flinched from these expressions of Epictetus, although I knew that they were quite consistent with his philosophy.

Glaucus, I could clearly see, resented them even more than I did. He was very liable to sudden emotions, and very quick to shew them. Just now he seemed unusually agitated. He was writing at a great pace, but not (I thought) notes of the lecture. When Epictetus proceeded to warn us that we must not expect to attain at once this perfection of happiness and peace, but that we must practise our precepts and wait, Glaucus stopped his writing for a moment to scrawl something on a piece of paper. He pushed it toward me, and I read "*Rusticus expectat*." I remembered that he had replied to me in this phrase when I had given him some advice about "waiting patiently," saying that all would "come right," or words to that effect. I did not now feel that I could say, "All will come right." Perhaps my glance in answer to Glaucus expressed this. But he said nothing, merely continuing his writing, still in great excitement.

Epictetus proceeded to repeat that "pity" must be rejected as a fault. The philosopher may of course love people, but he must love them as Diogenes did. This ideal did not attract me, though he called Diogenes "mild." The Cynic, he said, is not really to weep for the dead, or with those sorrowing for the dead. That is to say, he is not to weep "*from within*." This was his phrase. Perhaps he meant that, although in the ante-chamber and even in some inner chambers of the soul there may be tearful grief, and sorrow, and bitterness of heart, yet in the inmost chamber of all there must be peace and trust. But he did not say this. He said just what I have set down above. At the words "*not from within*," Glaucus got up and began to collect his papers, as though intending to leave the room. The next moment, however, he sat down and went on writing.

The lecture now turned to the subject of "distress"— which interested me all the more because I had noticed in the morning that Luke had described Christ as being "in distress" when he prayed fervently in the night before the crucifixion. But it seemed to me that Luke and Epictetus were using the same word for two distinct things. Epictetus meant "distress" about things not in our power, and among these things he included the sins of our friends and neighbours. But Luke seemed to mean "distress" about things in Christ's power, because (according to Luke's belief) Christ had a power of bearing the sins of others. If so, Luke did not mean what Epictetus meant, namely, nervous, faithless, and timid worry or terror, but rather an *agōn*, or conflict, of the mind, corresponding to the *agōn*, or conflict, of the body when one is wrestling with an enemy, as Jacob was said by the Hebrews to have wrestled with a spirit in Penuel.

At this point, after repeating what I had heard him say before, concerning the grace and dexterity with which Socrates "played at ball" in his last moments—the ball being his life and his family—Epictetus passed on to emphasize the duty of the philosopher to preserve his peace of mind even at the cost of detaching himself from those nearest and dearest to him. Suppose, for example, you are alarmed by portents of evil, you must say to yourself "These portents threaten my body, or my goods, or my reputation, or my children, or my wife; but they do not threaten *me*." Then he insisted on the necessity of placing "the supreme good" above all ties of kindred. "I have nothing to do," he exclaimed, "with my father, but only with the supreme good." Scarcely waiting for him to finish his sentence, Glaucus rose from his seat, pressed some folded papers into my hand, and left the room.

I think Epictetus saw him go. At all events, he immediately put himself, as it were, in Glaucus's place, as though uttering just such a remonstrance as Glaucus would have liked to utter, "Are you so hard hearted?" To this Epictetus replied in his own person, "Nay, I have been framed by Nature thus. God has given me this coinage." What our Master really meant was, that God has ordained that men should part with everything at the price of duty and virtue. "Duty" or "virtue" is to be the "*coin*" in exchange for which we must be ready to sell everything, even at the risk of disobeying a father. A father may bid his son betray his country that he, the father, may gain ten thousand sesterces. In such a case the son ought to reply—as Epictetus said—"Am I to neglect my supreme good that you may have it [*i.e.* what you consider your supreme good]? Am I to make way for you? What for?" "I am your father," says the father. "Yes, but you are not my supreme good." "I am your brother," says the brother. "Yes, but you are not my supreme good."

All this (I thought) was very moral in intention, but might it not have been put differently—"Father, I must needs disobey you for your sake as well as mine," "Brother, you are going the way to dishonour yourself as well as me"? Glaucus could not have taken offence at that. However, this occasional austerity was characteristic of our Teacher. Perhaps it was an ingredient in his honesty. He liked to put things sometimes in their very hardest shape, as though to let his pupils see how very cold, reasonable, definite, and solid his philosophy was, how self-interested, how calculating, always looking at profit! Yet, in reality, he had no thought for what the world calls profit. His eyes were fixed on the glory of God. This alone was *his* profit and *his* gain. But unless we were as God-absorbed as he was—and which of us could boast that?—it was almost certain that we should to some degree misunderstand him. Just now, he was in one of these detached—one might almost call them "non-human"— moods.

A few moments ago, I had been sorry that Glaucus went out. But I ceased to regret it when I heard what followed. It was in a contrast between Socrates and the heroes of tragedy, or rather the victims of calamity. We must learn, he said, to exterminate from life the tragic phrases, "Alas!" "Woe is me!" "Me miserable!" We must learn to say with Socrates, on the point of drinking the hemlock, "My dear Crito, if this way is God's will, this way let it be!" and not, "Miserable me! Aged as I am, to what wretchedness have I brought my grey hairs!" Then he asked, "Who says this? Do you suppose it is someone in a mean or ignoble station? Is it not Priam? Is it not Œdipus? Is it not the whole class of kings? What else is tragedy except the passionate words and acts and sufferings of human beings given up to a stupid and adoring wonder at external things—sufferings set forth in metre!"

This seemed to me gratuitously cruel. If ever human being deserved pity, was it not the poor babe Œdipus,

18—2

predestined even before birth to evil, cast out to die on Mount Cithaeron, but rescued by the cruel kindness of a stranger—to kill his own father, to marry his own mother, to beget children that were his brothers and sisters, and to die, an exile, in self-inflicted blindness, bequeathing his evil fate to guilty sons and a guiltless daughter! But Epictetus would not let Œdipus alone: " It is among the rich, the kings, and the despots, that tragedies find place. No poor man fills a tragic part except as one of the chorus. But the kings begin with prosperity, commanding their subjects (like Œdipus) to fix garlands on their houses in joy and thankfulness to the Gods. Then, about the third or fourth act, comes 'Alas, Cithaeron, why didst thou receive and shelter me?' Poor, servile wretch, where are your crowns now? Where is your royal diadem? Cannot your guards assist you?"

All this was in stage-play, the agony of the king and the scoffing of the philosopher so life-like as to be quite painful—at least to me. Then Epictetus turned to us in his own person: " Well, then, in the act of approaching one of these great people, remember this, that you are going to a tragedian. By 'tragedian' I do not mean an *actor*, but a *tragic person*, Œdipus himself. But perhaps you say to me 'Yes, but such and such a lord or ruler may be called blessed. For he walks with a multitude'"—of slaves, he meant—"'around him.' See, then! I too go and place myself in company with that multitude. Do not I also 'walk with a multitude'? But to sum up. Remember that the door is always open. Do not be more cowardly than the children. When they cease to take pleasure in their game, they cry at once 'I will not play any more.' So you, too, as soon as things appear to you to point to that conclusion, say, 'I will not play any more.' And be off. Or, if you stay, don't keep complaining."

This was the end of the lecture, and I felt gladder than ever that Glaucus had gone; for he seemed to me to have been just in the mood to take to heart that last suggestion, "The door is always open." I hastened to his rooms, but he was not there. I found however that he was expected back soon, for he was making preparations for a journey. Leaving word that I should call again in an hour, I determined to use the interval to leave Arrian's note with Epictetus.

The Master was disengaged and gave me a most kindly welcome, asking with manifest interest about Arrian and his prospects, and giving me to understand that he had heard of me, too, from Arrian and others. His countenance always expressed vigour, but on this occasion it had even more than its usual glow. Perhaps he was a little flushed with the exertion of his lecture. Perhaps he was glad to hear that at least one pupil, likely to do good work in the world, was remembering him gratefully in Bithynia. Possibly he thought another such pupil stood before him. I had never seen him close, face to face. Now I felt strongly drawn towards him, but not quite as pupil to master. From the moment of leaving the lecture-room that day, I had been repeating, " Alas, Cithaeron, why didst thou receive and preserve me?" Poor Œdipus! He seemed to sum up the cry of myriads of mortals predestined to misery. And what gospel had my Master for them? Nothing but mockery, " Poor, servile wretches!"

Yet I had felt almost sure, even from the first utterance of the cruel words, that he had not intended to be cruel. Now, as I stood looking down into his face and he up at mine, some kind of subtle fellowship seemed to spring up between us. At least I felt it in myself and thought I saw it in him. And it grew stronger as we conversed. I rapidly recalled the reproach he had just now addressed to himself in his lecture, as coming from one of his pupils, "Are you so hard hearted?" At the moment I had asked "Could it possibly be true?" Now I knew it was not true. Certainly he had been absorbed in God. His God was not the God of Christ. It was a Being of Goodness of some sort, but impersonal, an Alone, not a real Father. Such as it was, however, Epictetus had been absorbed in it. He motioned to me to be seated, and began to question me about friends of his in Rome.

I was on the point of replying, when the door burst open and Glaucus suddenly rushed in, beside himself with fury. Striding straight up to Epictetus, he began pouring forth a tale of wrongs, treacheries, outrages and malignities, perpetrated on his family in Corinth. He took no notice of my presence, and I doubt whether he was even aware of it, as he burst out into passionate reproaches on our Master for teaching that a son must witness such sufferings in a father or mother, brother or sister, and say, " These evils are no evils to me."

It would serve no useful purpose, nor should I be able, to set down exactly what Glaucus said. Let it suffice that he had only too much reason for burning indignation against certain miscreants in Corinth. He had only that morning received news—which had been kept back from him by treachery—that cruel and powerful enemies had brought ruin, desolation, and disgrace upon his family. His father had been suddenly imprisoned on false charges, his sister had been shamefully humiliated, and his mother had died of a broken heart. " Epictetus," he cried, " do you hear this ? Or do you make yourself a stone to me, as you bid us make ourselves stones when men smite us and revile us ? Do you still assert that there are no evils except to the evil-minded ? By Zeus in heaven, if there is a Zeus and if there is a heaven, I would sooner torture myself like a Sabazian, or be crucified like a Christian, or writhe with Ixion in hell, that I might at least cry out in the hearing of Gods and men, ' These things *are* evil, they *are*, they *are*,' than be transported to the side of the throne above with you, looking down on the things that have befallen my father, mother, and sister, and repeating my Epictetian catechism, *I am in perfect bliss and blessedness ; these things are no evils to me!* O man, man, are you a hypocrite, or are you indeed a stone ? " So saying, without waiting for a word of reply, he rushed from the room.

I went with him. I was not sure—nor am I now—whether Epictetus wished me to stay or to go. But I thought Glaucus needed me most. My heart went out to him when I heard for the first time how shamefully he had been deceived and how cruelly his family had been outraged, and I did not know what he might do in his despair. Besides, if I had stayed, could Epictetus have helped me to help my friend ? What would his helping have been? It could have been nothing more—if he had been consistent—than to repeat for the thousandth time that Glaucus's "trouble," and my "trouble" for Glaucus's sake, were mere *dogmas*, or "convictions," and that our "convictions" were wrong and must be given up. Would he have been consistent? Would he have said these things?

To this day I cannot tell. As I followed Glaucus out of the room, while in the act of turning round to close the door, I had my Master at a disadvantage. I saw him, but he did not see me. His head was drooping. The light was gone from his face; the eyes were lacking their usual lustre; the forehead was drawn as if in pain. It was no longer Epictetus the God-absorbed, but Epictetus the God-abandoned. If I had turned to him with a reproach, " Epictetus, you are breaking your own rule. You are sorrowing, sorrowing in earnest," would he have replied, " No, only in appearance, not *from within*"? I do not think he would. He was too honest. To this day I verily believe that for once, at least for that once, our Master broke his own rule and felt real "*trouble.*" And I love him the better for it. That indeed is how I always like to remember his face—as I saw it for the last time, not knowing that it was the last, through the closing door—clouded with real grief, while I was leaving him for ever without farewell, never trusting so little in his teaching, never loving the teacher so much.

CHAPTER XXIX

SILANUS MEETS CLEMENS

WE walked on together, both of us silent, till we came to Glaucus's rooms. "Farewell," said he. I replied that I would come in to see whether I could help him to make arrangements for his journey. He said nothing, but suffered me to enter. For some time I busied myself with practical matters. So did Glaucus. But every now and then he stopped, and sat down as though dazed. I questioned him about his journey and time of starting. Finding that only two or three hours remained, I urged him to rouse himself. "It will be of no use," he said, "but you are right." Then he exclaimed bitterly, "Am I not obeying Epictetus? Am I not making myself a stone?" "Not quite," said I, "for a stone feels nothing. You are worse than a stone. For you feel much, yet do nothing to help those for whom you feel." "Thank you for that," said he. Then he roused himself. He did injustice to Epictetus, yet I perceived, as never before, how harmful this "stone-doctrine"—if I may so call it—might prove to many people.

I have no space, nor have I the right, to describe more fully Glaucus's private affairs, the courage, affection, and steadfastness with which he bore the burdens of his family and saved his father and sister from their worst extremity. His course was different from Arrian's. Arrian remained outside the fold. Glaucus found peace as I did. And I know that many a suffering soul in Corinth suffered the less because Glaucus, having experienced such a weight of sorrow himself, had learned the secret of lightening it for others. He died young, thirty years ago, but he lived long enough to "fight the good fight."

Our last words together, as he was in the act of departing, I remember well: "What was that you said to me, Silanus, about waiting and having one's strength renewed?" It was from Isaiah. I repeated it. Then I added, " But I spoke the words, I fear, because I had once felt them to be true. I did not quite feel them to be true at the moment when I repeated them to you. Perhaps I was not quite honest, or at least not quite frank." " Then you don't hold to them now ? " said he. " God knows," said I. "Sometimes I do, sometimes I do not. For the most part I think I do. I believe that there is good beneath all the evil, if only we could see it, or at least good in the end, good far off." " Then " replied he, " you believe, perhaps, in a good God ? " " I hope I may hereafter believe," said I, "nay, I am almost certain I believe in a good God now. But, if I do, it is in a God that is fighting against evil, a God that may perhaps share in our afflictions and in our troubles." "What?" said he, "you, a pupil of Epictetus, believe that God Himself can be troubled! Then of course you believe that a good man may be troubled?" "Indeed I do," said I. " At least I half believe it about God, and wholly about man." "Then you think I have a right to be troubled. You are a heretic." " We are heretics together," said I. "You have a right to be troubled, and I to be troubled with you." " Thank you, and thank the Gods, for that at least!" said he. "Do you know," said I, "that I am certain that Epictetus felt troubled too, for your sake ? I saw him when he did not see me, as I was leaving the room ; and I could not be mistaken." " Ah ! " said Glaucus, drawing in his breath. Then suddenly, as we were clasping hands in our last farewell, he added "Do not think too much about those scrawls!" And before I had time to ask his meaning, he had ridden away.

Returning to my rooms, I put away my lecture-notes and took out the gospels. But I could not read, and longed to be in the fresh air. As I rose from my seat to go out, my first thought was, "I will take no books with me." But Mark happened to be in my hand, the smallest of the gospels. "This," I said, "will be no weight." But it weighed a great deal in the rest of my life, as the reader will soon see.

Before long, unconsciously seeking familiar solitudes, I found myself on the way to the little coppice where some days ago I had seen Hesperus above the departed sun, and Isaiah had shed on me the influence of his promise of peace. "Now," said I sadly to myself, " I have with me a book that calls itself the fulfilment of that promise. But it fulfils nothing for me." As I spoke, and drew the book from the folds of my garment, several pieces of paper fell on the ground. When I picked them up, I found—what I had completely forgotten—Glaucus's "scrawls." I thought they would contain some requests to perform commissions for him in Nicopolis, or to convey messages to friends, and that he might have written these in the lecture-room when he expected to hear news that might call him suddenly away. But they were something quite different. The first that I opened was entitled "A Postscript," written in verse, rallying me upon my advice about "waiting." It shewed me how Glaucus, too, had been affected, not only by the lecture that drove him from the room, but also by that saying of Epictetus concerning Zeus (" He would have if he could have ") which had disturbed me so much. It was wildly written as Glaucus himself confessed: but I will give it here, because— besides being a rebuke to me, and to all teachers that preach a gospel they do not feel—it shews how Epictetus himself, the perfection of honesty, stirred up in an honest and truthful pupil questionings and doubts that he could not satisfy or silence :

POSTSCRIPT.

If you, my Silanus
(Who think hopelessness heinous,
And lectured me lately
So sweetly, sedately,
Discussing, dilating,
I will not say "prating,"
On the great use of waiting,
You, whom I respected
But never suspected,

> Never, no never,
> Of being so clever)
> Would but do your endeavour
> To find more rhymes for "ever,"
> Then cease would I never
> But rhyme on for ever,
> Like that horrible lecture,
> Our Master's conjecture,
> About Zeus, a kind creature,
> Whose principal feature
> Was his frankly regretting
> That the Fates keep upsetting,
> By their cruel preventions,
> His noble intentions;
> "'Tis not that I would not,
> But I could not, I could not,"
> So said Zeus in a lecture
> Our Master's conjecture.

P.S. Mad, isn't it? But isn't the lecture madder?
P.P.S. I do hope and trust the Master is mad. I must go out.

The larger "scrawl" touched me more nearly because it condemned those who indulge in "self-deceiving" and "call it believing"—a thing that Scaurus dreaded, and taught me to dread; and I was in special dread of it at that time. I have been in doubt whether to give this in full. But I am sure Glaucus, now in peace, would not take it amiss that his wild words of trouble should be recorded if they may help others who have lost peace for a time. So I give it to the reader just as Glaucus gave it to me. Outside was written, in large letters, "RUSTICUS EXPECTAT." Before the verses came a letter in prose as follows:

Rusticus sends greeting to Silanus.

I am scrawling you a little poem, Silanus, to distract myself from this accursed lecture, lest Epictetus should make me absolutely sick with his nauseating stuff about the duty of sons not to be troubled by the troubles of their parents. Some days ago you gave me some edifying advice. Here is the answer to it—a little drama.

Dramatis personae only two:—(1) *Rusticus, for shortness called Hodge, i.e. Glaucus the Rustic, or perhaps Glaucus persuaded by Silanus, so that Glauco-Silanus is the true Rustic, unless you like to take the rôle entirely for yourself. Anyhow Hodge is a great fool;* (2) *The River, i.e. Destiny, alias*

Fate, alias Zeus, alias the God of Epictetus, alias the Whirlpool of the All, alias Nothing in Particular.

The metre is appropriate to the subject matter, i.e. whirlpooly, eddyish, chaotic. There is no villain. The River would be if it could. But it can't —not being able to help being what it is—like Zeus, you know, who said in our lecture-room recently, "I would if I could but I couldn't." Hodge starves or drowns. This should make a tragedy. But he is such a fool that he turns it into a comedy—for the amusement of the Gods. They are intensely amused—which perhaps should turn the thing back again into a tragedy. Comedy or tragedy? Or tragicomedy? Or burlesque? I give it up. The one thing certain is, Chaos!

RUSTICUS EXPECTAT.

Hodge sits by the river
Awaiting, awaiting.
Across he is going
If it will but stop flowing.
But when? There's no knowing.
He dare not try swimming
In those waves full and brimming.
On foot there's no going,
And there's no chance of rowing.
So there he sits blinking
And calling it "thinking"!
God nor man can deliver
His soul from that river,
But Hodge won't believe it
His soul can't receive it!
Himself he's deceiving,
But he styles it "believing"!
So this simpleton artless
To a THING that is heartless
Prays!—yes, takes to praying
In the hope of its staying
His soul to deliver:
"Good river, kind river,
Across I'd be going
If you would but stop flowing
Stay! pity my moping!
I'm hoping, I'm hoping
That you won't flow for ever.
Oh, say, will you never
Cease flowing, cease flowing?
Across I'd be going,

Chapter 29] SILANUS MEETS CLEMENS

> Rest! Flow not for ever!"
> Says the river, deep river:
> "I care not a stiver
> For all your long waiting
> And praying and prating
> And whining and pining
> And hoping and moping.
> Wait, if you like waiting,
> Prate, if you like prating,
> Pray, if you like praying,
> But think not I'm staying,
> Dream not I'm delaying
> For a man and his praying,
> For his smiling or frowning,
> His swimming or drowning.
> Hope, if you're for hoping,
> Mope, if you're for moping,
> I'm not made for consoling
> But for rolling and rolling
>   For ever.
> Time's stream none can sever.
> Then cease your endeavour
> Your soul to deliver
> By coaxing the river.
> Cease shall I never
> But flow on for ever
>   FOR EVER."

I was walking slowly onward, with the paper in my hand, my eyes bent on the ground. Suddenly a shadow, and a courteous salutation, made me aware that a stranger had met me and was passing by. Surprised and startled, I recovered myself after a moment and turned round to answer his greeting. He, too, turned, a man past threescore as I guessed, but vigorous, erect, with a dignity of carriage that appeared at the first glance. He bowed and passed on. The face reminded me of someone, but I could not think who it was. I turned again to Glaucus's paper. "Don't think too much of those scrawls" had been his last words. But how could I help thinking of them? How many myriads were in the same case! The myriads did not say what Glaucus said. But how many of them felt it! They had not suffered perhaps as he had, but they had suffered enough—crushed, maimed, forsaken!

Yes, FORSAKEN! As I uttered the word aloud, there came back to me both the face of the stranger and the face like his, the face that I had not been able to recall. I had been thinking of old Hermas, whom I had seen as a child of five or six and had never forgotten. Scaurus's letters had recently brought him back to my memory again and again, depicting him just as I remembered him, and suggesting to me all sorts of new questions as to the mystery that lay behind those quiet eyes and that strong gentle look, which even in my childhood had left on me an indelible impression. I had been asking myself, What was the secret of it? Now I knew. Hermas was *not "forsaken."* And this man, the man I had just met, he too looked *not "forsaken."* "Yet I wonder," said I, "what that stranger would think if Hermas were to invite him to worship a Son of God whose last words to the Father were, 'Why hast thou forsaken me?' Epictetus, I know, would declare that the words expressed an absolute collapse of faith. How would old Hermas explain them? And what would Scaurus say if I confessed that I found no God anywhere in heaven or earth to whom my heart was so drawn as this 'forsaken' Christ? What would the Psalmist say if I used his words thus, 'Whom have I in heaven but thee? And there is none on earth that I should desire in comparison with thee, O, thou FORSAKEN SON OF GOD!'"

By this time I had reached the wood. Pacing up and down, full of distracting thoughts, I came on the place where I had had my first vision of peace. There, tired out in body and mind, I threw myself down to rest. Presently, feeling in the folds of my garment for the gospel of Mark, I could not find it. Yet I had felt it when I first drew out Glaucus's paper. There was nothing for it but to retrace my steps as exactly as possible in the hope of hitting on the place where I must have dropped it. But I had not gone a hundred paces before I heard a rustling in the bushes, and the tall stranger reappeared and a second time saluted me.

I returned his salutation. Then we were both silent.

Chapter 29] SILANUS MEETS CLEMENS

Nothing was in his hand, yet I felt sure that he had found my book, and I waited for him to speak. But a moment's reflection shewed me his difficulty. Was he, a stranger, to ask a Roman knight whether he had dropped one of the religious books of a proscribed superstition? It was for me, if for either, to begin. I liked the stranger's look even better than before and felt that he could be trusted; so I told him of my loss. He at once placed the volume in my hands saying that he had come back to restore it, believing me to be the owner. I thanked him heartily. He replied that I was welcome, then waited a moment or two, as though to allow me to say more if I pleased. I stood silent, wanting to speak, but as it were tongue-bound—not so much afraid as ashamed. At last, I stammered out something about the wood and its distance from Nicopolis. He smiled as though he understood my embarrassment. Then he repeated that I was welcome and moved away.

I had suffered him to go a dozen paces when a voice said within me, "Why do you let him go? Scaurus let Hermas go and repented it. You said that this man did not look 'forsaken.' Why do you let him 'forsake' you? Why do you make yourself 'forsaken'? Perhaps he can help you." I called him back. "Sir," said I, "pardon me one question. Doubtless you looked at this roll to find some clue to its owner?" "I did," he replied. "I am interested," said I, "in this little book"——. Then I paused. I had grown into the habit of adding—in writing to Flaccus, to Scaurus, and in speaking to myself too—"from a literary point of view," "as a historical investigation," and so on. But now I could not say such things. In the first place, they would not be true. In the second place, I knew instinctively that the man would know that they were not true. Moreover I had a presentiment that he was to be to me what Hermas had almost been to Scaurus. On the other hand, had I the right to ask a perfect stranger whether he had studied a Christian gospel? He read my thoughts. "You desire," he said, "to ask me something more. Am I acquainted with this book? That, I think, is your question? If so, I say, 'Yes'." "There are," said I, very slowly, and almost as if the words were drawn out of me by force, "some few things that I greatly admire and many things that greatly perplex me, in this little book. I think I might understand some of the latter, had I some guidance." "I am but a poor guide," he replied. "Nevertheless, if it is your will, I am quite willing. I have an hour's leisure. Then I must go on my business. Shall we sit down here?"

So we sat down, and I began to question him about Mark and the other gospels. But before I describe our conversation, I must remind my readers that at that time, forty-five years ago, in the second year of Hadrian, the gospels of Mark, Matthew, and Luke, were not regarded as on the same level as scripture, nor as entirely different from other writings composed by pious Christians such as, for example, the epistle of Clemens Romanus to the Corinthians. No doubt, some Christians, even at that date, were disposed to rank the three gospels by themselves as superior to all others past or future; and some of them may have asserted that the number three was, as it were, predicted in the Law. For Moses said, "Out of the mouth of two witnesses" (that might be Mark and Matthew) "or three witnesses" (that would include Luke) "shall every word be established." But if they spoke thus, I do not know of it.

On the contrary, I have heard, that about the very time of our conversation, that is in the second year of Hadrian, there were traditions about Mark (current in the neighbourhood of Ephesus) placing him on a very much lower level than the Hebrew prophets. Some used to accuse him (as I have confessed above that I was perhaps too prone to do) of being disproportioned and lengthy in unimportant detail. An Elder near Ephesus defended Mark. He laid the blame on the necessities of the case, saying that Mark recorded what he had heard from Peter, and that Peter adapted his teachings to the needs of the moment, so that "Mark committed no error" in writing some things as he did. Whether this Elder was right or wrong, his words shewed that neither he, defending Mark, nor his opponents, attacking Mark, regarded the

Chapter 29] SILANUS MEETS CLEMENS

evangelist as perfect. Indeed his gospel was generally underrated, being placed far below that of Matthew and Luke, because people did not perceive that Mark often contained the account that was the truest—although expressed obscurely or in such a way as to cause some to stumble.

At that time it would have been thought profane to put Mark or Luke on the same level with Moses, Samuel, David, Solomon, Isaiah and the prophets, to whom "the word of the Lord" is said to have "come." Luke never says, "The word of the Lord came to me," but, in effect, this: "I have traced things back carefully and accurately, and have thought it well to set them forth in chronological order." Matthew, as being an apostle, might have been placed on a different footing. But as he wrote in Hebrew, and his gospel was circulated in Greek, it was not thought that we had the very words of the apostle. Moreover Matthew's words often differed in such a way from Luke's, that even a child could perceive that two writers were describing the same words of the Lord in two different versions, so that both could not be exactly correct. And, very often, Luke's version appeared better than Matthew's.

Yet even in the reign of Trajan there had perhaps been springing up among a few people the belief that the three gospels above-mentioned were not only superior to others then extant but also to others that might hereafter be written. These men thought that Luke had said the last word on the things that were to be believed, correcting what was obscure in Mark and adding what was wanting. Perhaps it was natural that those who thus favoured Luke's gospel should be for a time averse to a fourth gospel. I believe that my friend Justin of Samaria, who suffered as a martyr in this very year in which I am now writing, always retained a prejudice of this kind, favouring the three gospels, and especially Luke. Even though he could not sometimes avoid using some of the traditions that had found a place in the fourth gospel, he disliked to quote it as a gospel, and, as far as I know, never did quote it verbally in his writings.

On the other hand, some of the younger brethren now go

into the opposite extreme, and maintain, not only that the fourth gospel is to be accepted, but also that the number four was, as it were, predestined. This seems to me as unreasonable as it would have been to maintain, in Trajan's time, that the gospels must be three because of the "three witnesses" prescribed by Moses on earth, and the three in heaven (the Father, the Son, and the Holy Spirit) and the three angels that visited Abraham, and so on. Yet I have actually heard the teacher Irenæus—the young man about whom I spoke above—asserting that the gospels must needs be four to correspond with the four quarters of the globe, the four elements, the four living creatures in Ezekiel, and other quadruplicities.

However, I thank God that, when I was a young man, no such stumbling-block as this lay between me and my Saviour. Nor was any such belief in the necessity of four gospels entertained by my new friend Clemens—for that was his name, though he was not a Roman but an Athenian. He had long accepted the three gospels as containing the truth about Christ and about His constraining love. Recently, he had accepted the fourth gospel as also containing the same truth. But he neither believed nor expected me to believe that every word in these four writings was so inspired as to convey the unmixed truth. It was in these circumstances and with these preconceptions—or perhaps I should rather say freedom from preconceptions—that Clemens and I began our conversation.

CHAPTER XXX

SILANUS CONVERSES WITH CLEMENS

I EXPLAINED to Clemens that I had been attending the lectures of Epictetus. He had taught us, I said, to neglect external things, and to value virtue, as being placed by God in our own power and a possession open to all. "This," said I, "has strengthened me—this and the influence of his character—in the determination to lead a life above the mere pleasures of the flesh. But, on the other hand, Epictetus teaches us that we are never to be troubled, not even by the troubles or misdoings of those nearest and dearest to us. We are to say, 'These things are nothing to us'." I then explained to Clemens how this doctrine had repelled me, and how I had been led by an accident to study the letters of Paul, in which I found a very different doctrine.

"Paul," said I, "counts many external things as evil, and especially the errors and transgressions of his converts. These he feels as evils and pains to himself. Yet he always seems hopeful and helpful, full of strength both for himself and for others. I have felt drawn towards him, and, through him, to the prophet Jesus, or Christ, whom he calls Son of God. Paul speaks of himself as led towards this Jesus by a 'constraining love' filling the heart with joy and peace. I have felt something of this, or at least have felt the possibility of it. In my childhood, 'Christus' was called one of the vilest of the vile, and I believed it. Now I have come to regard him as—I know not what. Just now I said 'prophet.' But Epictetus calls Diogenes God's 'own son.' Christ, in my judgment, stands far above Diogenes and perhaps even above Socrates. When I say 'above Socrates,' I do not mean in reason, but in feeling, and in the power to draw men towards kindness and steadfast welldoing. I think I had come almost to the point of calling this Jesus 'God's own son' in a very real sense, as being above all other men, yes, and more—more than I could understand. And then——."

"And then?" said Clemens. I had paused. He waited an instant longer, questioning, or rather interpreting me, with his eyes. "And then," said he, "something threw you back?"

"Yes," said I, "something threw me back. And what do you think it was? Paul drew me on. But the author of this little book, he, and Matthew, and Luke—these threw me back. It happened in many ways. I must tell you the last first. A friend, a fellow-student, has just now left me for Corinth, crushed to the earth by the most shameful outrages on his family. I wished to give him some comfort, to point him towards some hope, to give him what you Christians—for surely you are a Christian?" He assented. "Well, what you Christians call 'good tidings' or 'gospel.'

"Now if I could believe Paul, I should have a 'gospel.' For then the spirit of Jesus, having risen from the dead, would be travelling about the world everywhere at hand to strengthen His disciples, and to comfort their hearts, and to assure them that all will be well in the end. 'I have prevailed over death' —so His Spirit would say to us—'I will always help the poor and oppressed. I will never forsake them till I have made them sharers in my eternal kingdom.' This it would say to each one of us, 'You, Gaius, or you, Marcus, I will be with you always. I will never forsake you.' But how can I believe these beautiful assurances, when I find Mark declaring (and Matthew agreeing with him) that Christ's last articulate utterance was, 'My God, my God, why hast thou forsaken me?' How can I assure my friend that God never forsakes the oppressed, if He forsook His own Son? And how can I deny that 'forsaking,' when the Son Himself says, *Why hast thou forsaken?* ? Epictetus forbade us to admit that we are ever alone. 'God,' said he, 'is always within you.' Is not that the

Chapter 30] CONVERSES WITH CLEMENS

better and nobler doctrine? If the better and nobler doctrine is not true, does it not follow that the truth is bad and ignoble, and that, in real truth, there is no good and noble power controlling the world? Which of the two is right, Epictetus or Christ?"

"Both, I think," said Clemens. He had been listening with attention and manifest sympathy, but without any change in that steadfast look of peace and trust which his face habitually wore. I seemed to read in his countenance at once pain and faith, pain for my burden, faith that he could help me to bear it or to cast it away. Presently he added, "Do not suppose that by answering so briefly and quickly I wished to cut short your objection or to deny the difficulty. Far from it. You have asked, I think, one of the hardest questions, perhaps the very hardest, that could be put to a worshipper of Christ. Often have I thought of it, and I should not like to answer it hastily. You know perhaps that Luke omits these words, and that he mentions, instead, something about the 'sun'?" "Yes," said I, " but that seemed to me only to shew that Luke was willing to accept a version that removed the difficulty in the original." "I agree with you," said Clemens, "and, if so, that indicates that the difficulty was recognised before Luke compiled his gospel. Certainly, certainly, those wonderful words were really uttered."

Then he said, "First let me give you an explanation that is not unreasonable and may have some truth in it. You know, I dare say, that the words are from the Psalms?" "Yes," I replied, " but the Psalmist changes his mood. He goes on to say, 'He hath not hid his face from him, but, when he cried unto him, he heard him,' and afterwards, 'All the ends of the earth shall remember and turn unto the Lord'." "You have mentioned," said Clemens, "the very words that seem to some of our brethren to answer your question; for they say that the Lord had in mind the whole of the Psalm when He quoted the first words, and that He meant this, 'I cry unto thee, O Father, in the words of scripture *Why hast thou forsaken me?* knowing that thou hast not indeed hidden thy face from me, but thou art hearing me: and all the ends of the earth shall remember my crying and thy hearing and shall turn unto thee'."

"And are not you content with this explanation?" said I. "Not quite," said Clemens. "For, though this may be true, more may be true. I have read in another gospel, later than these three, that the Son did no work on earth and uttered no word, without looking up to the Father in heaven and listening to the Father's voice, which told Him from time to time what to do and to say. And I have heard one of the brethren, a man full of spiritual understanding, and well read in the scriptures, interpret the question as though it were a real question, not an exclamation—the Son questioning the Father as to His will. If that were so, the Son might be conceived as saying, 'For what reason, O Father, hast thou forsaken me for a while and hidden the light of thy countenance from me? Teach me, O Father, in order that I also may be willing to be forsaken, and may desire to be deprived of the light of thy countenance.' And then the Father replies, 'I forsake thee, O my Son, because thou must needs die, and in my presence is the fulness of life. The time hath come for thee to give up thy life, that is, to lose my presence for a brief space, that all men may gain for ever by thy brief loss and be saved from death by thy sacrifice of life.' And after this, said the brother, the Lord cried out a second time. What He said then, Mark and Matthew have not recorded; but they write that He then expired or sent forth His Spirit. The brother I am speaking of believed that the Son, by crying aloud 'Why hast thou forsaken?' prepared Himself to be willingly forsaken, and to be under the darkness of this momentary forsaking just before He gave up His life as a sacrifice for men."

"But you say," said I, "that Epictetus, too, is right." "Certainly," replied Clemens. "Epictetus says that men, God's children, are never 'alone.' And that is true. Indeed I can shew you presently a new Christian gospel—the one I mentioned just now—which represents Christ as saying this very thing, 'Ye shall leave me alone—and yet I am *not alone*, because the Father is with me.' Look at the matter thus. Do we not know that God may be regarded as being in all places at once, so that to speak of Him as 'here and not there' is no less a metaphor than to speak of His 'hiding His countenance,' or 'bearing us in His arms'? God therefore is, as Epictetus often affirms, 'within us.' But is He not also (as I think Epictetus seldom or never affirms) 'outside us'? Is not the Psalmist's metaphor right when he says that God, being outside us, hides His face sometimes from His children? Sometimes He does this because they have sinned, in order that they may seek His face and cease to sin. But does He not also do this when men have not sinned, in order that the righteous may become more righteous and the pure more pure, by longing more than ever for the sight of His countenance and by thirsting anew for His presence?

"I do not quite like to explain the dealings of God with men by anything that frail human creatures do in sport. And yet there is something so sacred (at least I think so) in the relations between parents and young children, that I have been sometimes led to liken God hiding His face from His children to a mother hiding her face from the babe in her arms. She hides it, but only for a moment, only that the child may be the more joyful afterwards. And the arms never let go their embrace." Then, after a pause, he added, "But perhaps you say, 'Do not you Christians believe that Christ was already perfectly righteous, and perfectly pure, and that He already rejoiced to the utmost in the Father's love? Why then should God forsake such a Son? Why should He hide His face from the Holy One, even for a time?' That, I think, is the question you would like to ask?"

Reading assent in my face, he proceeded, "Some might reply that this question has been answered by the brother above-mentioned, who says, in effect, 'The Son was forsaken by the Father, not that the Son might be made purer, or freed from sin, but that He might know the Father's will and might prepare Himself for His imminent self-sacrifice.' But is that— I will not say a complete answer, for who will venture to say that he knows completely all the purpose of the Father in causing the Son to feel forsaken?—is it even an answer that ought rightly to satisfy us? Will you be patient with me, my friend—for friends we are already (are we not?) in our joint search after truth——" "We are indeed," said I, "and I would gladly hear your fullest thoughts on this matter." " Permit me then," said he, " to put another thought before your mind, namely, that the Son of God, being Son of man, may have been forsaken by the Father in order to learn, as a man, the heights and depths of human nature, and to what an abyss of darkness the purest and most faithful saint may sometimes sink ; and how even in that abyss, the saint may feel, through faith, that there are still beneath him the arms of God, not indeed supporting him but ready to support him ; and that he is—as the prophets say about Israel—'forsaken' yet 'not forsaken.' No height in saintliness is higher than such a faith as this.

"The scriptures tell us," he continued, "that man is to love God with all his heart and with all his soul and with all his power, and with all his understanding. You know this?" I nodded assent. "Consider then how you and I will feel in the moments or hours before our departure, if God has decreed that we shall pass away by a slow and tedious passage, with a gradual weakening of our mental and spiritual powers, a chill of the heart, a deadening of the understanding, and a fading away of the fire of the soul; so that it is no longer possible for us, no longer permitted to us by God Himself, to love Him with all our human powers, because our powers themselves are becoming powerless. May we not then perhaps feel our grasp on the hand of the heavenly Father loosening, and our souls slipping back from the supporting strength of His presence, downward, and still downward, into the darkness of the infinite abyss ? Should that hour of trial come upon us, would it not be a very present help in our trouble to know that the Lord, the Saviour, the Eternal Son of God, in the form of man, was troubled likewise ? "

Indeed I thought it would—*if* only I " knew " it. I suppose my face must have shewn this, for Clemens, without waiting for an answer, continued with a kindling countenance, " And now, dearest brother, be still more patient with me while I put one more thought before you. You have been talking to me about 'trouble' and about your friend's 'trouble': and you said that it made you, as well as your friend, feel 'forsaken'." I assented. "And you were not ashamed," he continued, " of feeling his 'trouble' to some extent as yours, nor was your friend ashamed of feeling the 'trouble' of his family? Well, then, believe me, the Lord Jesus Christ felt the troubles of all His disciples, friends, followers, yes, all the troubles of all the sinful children of men, as though they were His own troubles. And in feeling 'troubled' along with others I venture to think that He also felt 'forsaken' along with others.

"This is sacred ground. I fear even to kneel, much less to tread upon it. But I think the Lord Jesus meant this also, amidst a multitude of meanings, 'O Father, why hast thou forsaken me, making me feel one with the sinners whom thou forsakest? Is it that thou art breaking for a time the sensible bond between me and thee in order to bind me to them? Is it that I may be made one with them, so as to make them one with me? Wouldst thou make me to be sin that the world may be made to be righteousness?'"

I remembered the words of Paul, "Him that knew not sin God *made sin* in our behalf": but I had never understood them before. Nor did I now, but I thought I caught a glimpse of their meaning. It was only a glimpse, and I sat silent, afraid as it were to move lest I should lose it. I seemed in a new world, or rather, in a mixed world, in which the old and the new were contending. I could neither see clearly nor move freely as yet. I felt that light and freedom were around and very near, forcing their way towards me, if I would but reach out my hand to them. But I could not do it.

"I feel," said I, "as though, in time, these hard words might become intelligible, or rather, I should say, beautiful and full of comfort to me. But how different they are from the last words of Socrates!" "Most different," replied Clemens. "Often have I pondered on the difference. I was born in Athens, and I admire the literature and language of my native city. But my mother was of Jewish extraction; and when I worship, and pray, and feel sorrow, and seek consolation, it is in the thought and phrase (though not in the language) of my mother's people. And again and again have I reflected on the strange contrast between the two 'last words,' the Jewish and the Greek. These 'last words' represent last thoughts.

Socrates felt righteous, and happy, and not 'forsaken,' and not at all anxious about his friends nor about his doctrine. The Lord Jesus felt forsaken—doubly forsaken. First He sorrowed for His disciples because He knew that they would forsake Him; and He prayed for them that they might not utterly fail. Afterwards He Himself felt forsaken by the Father.

"Perhaps, so far, Socrates may seem to have the advantage. But what has followed? Socrates is enshrined in books, a companion and dear friend of students for ever, but in books. He is not for the crowd in the street, nor for the ploughman in the field, nor for the poor, the simple, and the unlettered. And though he may fortify some of us against the fear of death, he does not bring the deepest consolation to those who are suffering under a perpetual burden of pains or sorrows. But the Spirit of the Lord Jesus moves among all sorts and conditions of life in all the races of mankind, bringing joy to them that rejoice righteously, and wholesome sorrow to those that sin, and strength to the heavy laden, and comfort to all that mourn, and freedom from all servile fear. Yes, He brings freedom, even to those enemies against whom He makes war, turning their consciences against themselves and making them His willing captives to lead others captive in turn. For indeed this captivity is no captivity but an embracing with the arms of a Father revealed in the Son according to the words of Hosea 'I taught Ephraim to walk. I took him in my arms. He knew not that I healed him. I drew him with cords, with bands of love.' Dear friend, it is my firm conviction that those only can relieve pain of the heart who have felt pain of the heart. Those only can save the forsaken who have felt forsaken. It was in fact because Christ had been forsaken that He was enabled to draw Paul towards Him with the cords of His constraining love."

"But," said I, "if love was the foundation of Christ's doctrine, how is it that Mark hardly ever mentions it? Should I be wrong in saying that Mark never mentions 'love' at all except in one place where Jesus, being asked what is the greatest commandment, quotes from the scripture the ancient commandment to love God and one's neighbour?" "Alas," replied Clemens, "you would be only too right! Yet believe me, Christ's doctrine of doctrines was 'love'—and that, too, not the old commandment, but a new commandment, because Christ introduced into the world a new kind of love, a more powerful love, a constraining love. This He imparted through His blood to His disciples, as is made clear in this new gospel"—and here he took a roll out of his garment—"about which I spoke to you lately, and in a letter, by the same author, which is an appendix to the gospel." And then he read to me, from John's gospel, the words, "A new commandment give I unto you that ye love one another," and "By this shall all men know that ye are my disciples if ye have love one to another"; and he pointed out the newness and greatness of the love, reading the words, "Greater love hath no man than this that a man lay down his life for his friends." Lastly, he added, from the epistle, "God is love."

All this astonished me not a little, and I replied, "Here at last, it seems to me, we have the only true gospel, Paul's gospel, the gospel of the constraining love of Christ. But how came it to pass that, whereas this was the true gospel, such a gospel as Mark's, full of marvels, and portents, and exorcisms, should be the first published to the world—so I have been told on good authority—a gospel that gives a whole column to the dancing of the daughter of Herodias and not one line to 'love one another'?"

"Often and often," replied Clemens, "have I asked myself the same question. I think, though I am not sure, that the reason is this. After the resurrection of the Lord, the apostles went forth to the world to attest the resurrection, and to preach the gospel, saying, in effect, what we find Peter and Paul actually saying in their epistles. But perhaps you have not read Peter's epistle?" I had not. "If you had, you would have found that Peter, like Paul, teaches this commandment of love. Doubtless all the apostles did the same. Consequently, before any gospels were written, all the churches were familiar with this doctrine of love, and with the doctrine of the resurrection. These were the important things. These had been handed down by the apostles to the elders, and by the first generation of the elders to the second. These, therefore, the churches knew. But the unimportant things, as Paul deemed them, the things that concerned Christ in the flesh, and His works of healing and of casting out spirits, and His sayings in the flesh to the disciples, and His discussions and controversies with the Pharisees, and how He was delivered over to Pilate, and how He suffered this and that particular humiliation (such as 'spitting' and 'smiting') in exact accordance with the scriptures—these things the churches had not committed to memory in any kind of detail. These therefore the earliest evangelist wrote down. Hence it came to pass that he recorded, in large measure, not the most important but the least important things."

"I understand now," said I, "but is it not to be regretted?" "For all reasons but one," replied Clemens, "I think it is to be regretted. I am often sorry that Mark does not give us the Lord's Prayer. I suppose he omitted it, as being known to everybody. But, as it is, we have two versions, and Matthew's is very different from Luke's. A version by Mark might have taught us whether the two versions are from one original, or whether the Lord gave His disciples two prayers at two different times—perhaps one before the resurrection, one after it. Again, Mark does not give us any account of the Lord's resurrection. Some think that a page of the manuscript of his gospel was lost. I, too, once thought so; but now I am disposed to think that he stopped short here, saying, 'Here begins the testimony of the apostles. It is their part to testify to the Lord's resurrection.' In any case it is to be regretted."

"But," said I, "your expression, just now, was, 'to be regretted for *all reasons but one.*' What did you mean by that?" "I meant," said Clemens, "that if all the evangelists had agreed exactly in their reports of all Christ's words, there might have been, amidst many advantages, this one disadvantage, the danger that the letter of the words of the Lord might have become a second law, like the law of Moses, to be interpreted by lawyers. In that case, what the Lord said about divorce, and marriage, and about the manner of life of the evangelists, and their sustenance, and about giving up or retaining one's possessions—all these things might have been collected into a small code. On this code might have been written a large commentary; on that, perhaps, another commentary, still larger. Thus the Church of Christ might have drifted into the legalities of men far away from the one true law of Christ, as it is defined in Paul's epistles 'Bear ye one another's burdens,' and (in the new gospel that I shewed you just now) 'Love one another with the love with which I have loved you'."

"Tell me more about that new gospel," said I. "I would gladly do so," said Clemens, "if time permitted. But the shadows are lengthening and the hour we were to spend together is past. Most willingly would I stay with you, but my work calls me away. Tomorrow, however, if you would like to come to my lodging in the house of Justus, at the corner of the market-place, soon after sunset, I shall have returned to Nicopolis, and you shall have a sight of the new gospel and such aid as I can give you in explaining it." So we parted for the time, after I had eagerly accepted his invitation.

CHAPTER XXXI

CLEMENS ON THE FOURTH GOSPEL

"How many things I should have asked him if he could only have stayed!" was my first thought, as Clemens disappeared behind the bushes. My next thought was, "How many new things I already have to think about!" Mechanically I turned homewards and took a few steps on the way to the city. Then I sat down to reflect.

Not many minutes had elapsed before I heard footsteps behind me. Presently, a little on my left, Clemens, without noticing me, passed striding hastily onwards in the direction of Nicopolis. I called to him. He turned and came up to me with an exclamation of joy, "I am thankful to have found you so soon. It has been on my mind that I ought to have at least explained to you why I did not offer to lend you this new gospel." "I would not have lent it to anyone had I been in your place," said I. "Yes," said Clemens, "you would have. Trust me, dear friend, if you believed this gospel, as I do, you would long to lend it to those who did not as yet believe it. But the truth is, I did not wish to lend it to you without a few words of introduction, for which I feared there would be no time. I forgot that the moonlight would suffice to guide me to the end of my journey. Have you leisure and desire for a little more conversation? Without it, I fear this little book might make you stumble, might even repel you. It is entirely different from the other three gospels both in its style and in its language. Whether reporting Christ's sayings or relating His actions, it almost always differs from the earlier accounts. It is also largely different in the facts related. What say you?"

"I say 'Thanks,' with all my heart," replied I; then, as we sat down together, "May I ask first, who wrote it?" "You not only may, but ought," he replied. "It is just the question I expected from you, and, alas! just one of the questions that I cannot answer in the usual way by saying 'A the son of B.' It seems to hint the authorship in dark expressions. At the end of the book it says, 'This is the disciple that beareth witness of these things and he that wrote these things'; but the texts vary and it is not quite clear whether the 'writer' and the 'bearer of witness' are one and the same. Nor does it give any name to the witness or the writer, nor any means of ascertaining the name or names, except that it describes him, a little before, as being 'the disciple whom Jesus loved, who also leaned on His breast,' *i.e.* at the last supper. Also, going back further, I find it written concerning a certain flow of blood and water from the side of the Saviour on the cross, 'He that hath seen hath borne witness and his witness is true, and he knoweth that he saith true, that ye may believe.' Going back further still, and comparing the beginning with the end of the gospel, the reader is led indirectly to the conclusion that the disciple that 'hath borne witness' is John the son of Zebedee.

"This John is often referred to as one of the chief apostles, in the three gospels; but his name is not so much as once mentioned in the fourth. Whenever 'John' occurs in this gospel, it is always John the Baptist, even though 'Baptist' is not added. Not till the last chapter does it become clear that the author is one of the 'sons of Zebedee'." "But might it not be James?" said I. "It might," replied Clemens, "but for the following fact. The gospel goes on to say, in effect, that, whereas Peter was to be crucified hereafter, this disciple was to live so long that a report sprang up in the church that he would never die. Now this could not apply to James, as he was beheaded quite early in the history of the church. It follows therefore that the author was John, who, though he became a martyr, or witness, for the Saviour, survived his martyrdom and lived to a great age."

This seemed to me an unsatisfactory way of writing history, and not quite fair to readers. For ought they not to be partly guided, in their judgment of the historian's statements, by their knowledge of his character, and of his opportunities for obtaining information? "How much more satisfactory," said I, "is the honest straightforwardness of the Greek writer, 'This is the third year of the history that Thucydides compiled'." "You are right," replied Clemens, "I cannot deny it. It would have been more satisfactory—if it could have been written with truth—that we should read at the end of this little roll, 'I John, the son of Zebedee, wrote this work.' But what if he did not write it yet had a great part in originating it? What if there was some kind of joint production, revision, or correction, of the work, so that it would not have been true to say, 'I John wrote it'?"

"Is there any evidence of this?" I asked. "A little," he replied. "It is the only one of the four gospels that contains 'we' in its conclusion, thus, '*We* know that his testimony is true.' I have also heard a tradition that it was revealed to Andrew that John was to write the gospel and that his fellow-disciples and bishops should revise it. But the following is more important evidence: John the son of Zebedee wrote a book called the Apocalypse—have you seen it?" I said that I had glanced at it. "It was written when he was a very old man, after he had been sent to the mines in Patmos by Domitian, and it is written in, I will not say bad Greek, but a dialect of Greek entirely different from that of any of the gospels or epistles. Now the fourth gospel is written in very fair Greek and in a style as different as possible from that of the Apocalypse. It is quite impossible that John, after writing the Apocalypse when he was eighty or ninety, should then write a gospel in a style so absolutely different."

"Then why," said I, "should the gospel be called by his name?" "I explain it thus," said Clemens. "When John returned from Patmos a very old man, saved from the fiery trial of the sufferings he had undergone—both before his condemnation and also afterwards in the mines—it was natural that every word uttered by him should be treasured up. I have heard it said that he could hardly be carried into the church, and that, when there, he repeated nothing but 'Little children,

Chapter 31] ON THE FOURTH GOSPEL

love one another.' In time, the brethren grew weary of this and remonstrated with him. This seems to have gone on for a long while. For (as I have said above) a report was current about him that he would 'never die' but would wait for the Lord's coming. There is no record (known to me) of any time, place, or manner, of his departure. I infer that, during the period of his decrepitude, the brethren at Ephesus would collect traditions from him and preach his gospel for him as far as they could. Afterwards, when it was clear that he would die, the gospel would be reduced to writing." "But this," said I, "greatly lowers the value of the gospel as history." "It does," said he, "and its historical value may also be lowered by the fact that, even before the gospel was written, the apostle was a great seer of visions. A seer is not the best kind of historian. He is liable to mix vision with fact. Especially might this be done by a seer that had seen Christ both before and after Christ's death. But still I greatly value this gospel because, like the epistles of Paul, it seems to me to go to the root of the matter. I told you just now that the old man, when he could say nothing else, repeated over and over again the words ' Little children, love one another.' When they asked him to say something else, he said 'that was enough.' And the old man was right. It is ' enough '—if we can receive strength to do it."

"This greatly attracts me," said I. "But, if your explanation is true, a great deal depends upon the apostle's friend, or friends, who wrote down the substance of his traditions and arranged them as a gospel." "A great deal, as you say," replied Clemens. "I have been informed that there was a great teacher near Ephesus, who was called preeminently ' *the Elder* ' —a name given, I believe, by students to their teacher, even in some of the schools of the Stoics. Has that ever fallen within your experience?" "Something of the kind," I replied. "I remember that Epictetus lately spoke of himself as '*the Elder*.' It seemed to me a modest way of saying 'I whom you call your Teacher, or your Master, but I merely call myself your Elder.' He said we ought to be so superior to the fear of death that his great business ought to be to keep us from dying too soon, not to make us fearless of death. 'This,' he said, 'ought to engage the attention of *the Elder* sitting in this chair.' And then he added, 'This ought to be the great struggle of *your Teacher* and *Trainer,* if indeed you had such a one'—as though Elder and Teacher were much the same thing."

"That," said Clemens, "is exactly to the point. Well then, you must know that John the son of Zebedee is commonly supposed to have written not only a gospel but also an epistle, or perhaps three epistles. The first epistle is quite in the style of the gospel, but it mentions not 'John,' nor even 'I,' at the beginning, but '*we*,' 'That which *we* have heard.' The two other letters, which are very short, begin, '*The Elder* to so-and-so.' These two letters are in style similar to that of the first, but some doubt exists as to their authorship, and I have seen it written, in connexion with them, that the Wisdom of Solomon was not written by Solomon but 'by his friends to do him honour.' Whoever wrote that, seems to have believed that '*the Elder*' mentioned in the two epistles was not John the son of Zebedee but one of his 'friends'."

"What was the Elder's name?" said I. "The two epistles do not mention it," replied Clemens. "But the Elder near Ephesus of whom I spoke above, was called by the same name as the son of Zebedee, 'John'; and the tradition that mentions him (along with another teacher named Aristion) appears to distinguish the two Johns, mentioning both in the same sentence. I ought to add that I mentioned this same Elder above as defending Mark on the ground that he was the mere interpreter of Peter. 'Mark,' said the Elder, 'made it his single object to leave out nothing of the things that he heard and to say nothing that was false therein.' Now you will find—I think I have already mentioned the fact—that this new gospel frequently intervenes, where Luke omits, or alters, anything that is in Mark, so as to explain Mark's obscurity or set forth Mark's tradition in different language. This points to the conclusion that the writer of the fourth gospel agreed with the Elder called John in his verdict on Mark, which is, in effect, 'Not erroneous in fact though imperfect in expression.' My own belief is that this tradition about two persons of the same name is accurate; and that, besides John the Apostle, there was also the Elder John, residing in or near Ephesus about the same time."

"But," I asked, "might not 'John the elder' naturally be taken to mean 'older in age' as opposed to 'John the younger'? And is it not strange that, in view of the great age of John the Apostle, such a distinctive appellation should be given to his namesake?" "Perhaps it would be," replied Clemens. "But it is not given. Have you not noticed that I did not speak of '*John the Elder*' but of '*the Elder, John*'? The two are quite different. The former (at least among Christians) would simply mean 'John the Presbyter or Elder' as distinct from 'John the Deacon,' 'John the Bishop,' and so on. But 'the Elder, John'—a phrase twice repeated in my tradition—may imply that the teacher was known during his life among his pupils as '*the Elder*,' and that, after his death, 'John' was added for the sake of clearness. I believe it was the custom to describe the elders near Ephesus in this indefinite way."

The view here taken by Clemens has been somewhat confirmed of late years by a practice that I have noticed—a bad practice, I think—in the young Irenæus. In the course of his lectures, when referring to his authority—instead of mentioning an elder by name, Polycarp, Aristion, Papias, John, as the case may be—he used such expressions as "He that is greater than we are," "The divine old man and herald of the truth," "He that is superior to us," and all these, as far as I could gather, about elders in the province of Ephesus. Concerning this indefiniteness I am in the same mind now as I was when I replied to Clemens, "It is very unfortunate."

"It is," said he, "but I believe it is fact. Well then, according to my view, one particular elder of these Johannine elders—I mean the elders in the region of Ephesus collected round the aged apostle, John the son of Zebedee—was so much superior to the rest that he was called preeminently '*the* Elder.' If 'the Elder' preached and wrote for John the Apostle, and if the Elder's name was John, there would be an additional reason why the writer of the gospel would avoid the name John (except in connexion with John the Baptist) throughout the gospel.

"But my conviction is that the aged apostle, besides preferring oral tradition to books (as you will see from the last lines of his work), shrank from putting himself forward as the author by the name of 'John,' and insisted that, if he was to be mentioned at all, it was to be only by the title, 'the disciple whom Jesus loved.' John the Elder may have accepted this condition because he felt it to express a deep truth—namely, that the Lord Jesus is best known through some one whom He has loved.

"You know how carefully the Greeks distinguish 'voice' or 'sound' from 'word.' Well, this new gospel introduces John the Baptist as testifying to Christ and saying that he was a mere voice, 'I am the *voice* of one crying in the wilderness, *Make straight the way of the Lord.*' To the inferior and preparatory witness is given a distinctive name 'John.' The superior and perfected witness was also called 'John' after the flesh; but the writer of the gospel preferred that the name after the flesh should be dropped, yes, and even his distinctive personality merged, as it were, in the title, 'the disciple whom Jesus loved'."

"But you spoke, above, about 'brethren' as perhaps preaching John's gospel for him during his decrepitude. Now you seem to incline to think that only one man wrote it?" "Yes," replied Clemens, "I used 'brethren' first, to leave the question open. Then I endeavoured to give reasons for thinking it was one brother; and this conclusion is supported by the style. There are some slight differences in this gospel between the words of the Lord and the words of the evangelist, in respect of style. That is natural; indeed, one would expect many more. But, taken as a whole, the gospel does not shew many styles, as Luke's does, but only one style—extending to the words of all characters introduced in the book, so that it is sometimes hard to say where a speaker ceases to speak and the evangelist begins to comment."

"But this is surely astonishing," said I, "that the author should have so little regard for the words of the Lord as not to make it absolutely and always clear where they end, and where his own comments, or the words of someone else, begin."

"It is astonishing," said Clemens, " but I am disposed to think that John the Apostle himself may in some cases have left his friends in doubt; and the Elder—or whoever it was that wrote the gospel—may have thought it best to leave the ambiguity as he found it. I pointed out to you above how the differences between the three gospels had this advantage that they forced the reader to think of the spirit rather than the letter of the words of the Lord. But they also had a danger, namely, that men might be puzzling their brains as to the differences of scribes and reporters instead of refreshing their hearts with the Spirit of Christ. Now if the Elder had, so to speak, simply added a fourth parallel column to the three existing parallel columns of the sayings of the Lord, the result might have been to increase that danger.

"You may say that if the Elder felt sure that he had received the exactly correct form of the Lord's words from John the Apostle, he ought to have set them down thus, whatever might be the consequences. But I do not believe that he did feel sure. More probably he knew that it was impossible, from the old man's reminiscences, to restore the words exactly, as uttered by Jesus, and that it was best not to attempt a restoration, but to prefer paraphrase, giving their spiritual essence. Or else, in cases where the three evangelists differed seriously among themselves, the Elder might think it best to substitute an entirely new tradition on the same subject."

"Is it not possible," said I, " that some part of the gospel may have been written at an earlier date? Are there for example any expressions that shew the Temple to have been still standing at the time of writing?" "I have looked through the volume, searching for such evidence," replied Clemens, "and can find absolutely nothing except a phrase in a rather obscure and corrupt passage about the existence of a pool, an intermittent pool, near Jerusalem. Now of course a pool is not destroyed even when a neighbouring city is utterly destroyed; and parts of Jerusalem continued to be inhabited, after its capture by Titus, although the walls, and a large part of the city, were razed to the ground. The gospel says, 'There *is* in Jerusalem a pool...having five porches.' I have not ascertained whether this pool is still used (as the narrative says it was then) for medicinal purposes, and whether the 'porches' still exist. I must also confess my belief that this is one of several narratives in which perhaps allegory may have modified history. But in any case the phrase 'there is a pool' seems to me to afford no basis, worth calling such, for a hypothesis of date. It seems to me of little more importance than if a writer said 'There *is* a mountain called the Mount of Olives' or 'There *is* a brook called Kedron.' I could, if you liked, discuss the passage with you more fully."

"Let me rather ask you," said I, "about a matter that greatly interests me. The words of Christ at the last supper—does John give them as Mark and Matthew do, or as Luke, or as Paul?" "That is a case," said Clemens, "where John does not correct but substitutes. He does not give these words at all. But he inserts a narrative about Christ's washing the feet of the disciples, and a precept that the disciples are to do the same. The 'washing of feet,' as I could shew you if time allowed, is connected with sacrifice, in Leviticus. As to the partaking of the bread and wine, he says expressly that the Saviour gave some of it to Judas—meaning (I think) to shew that there was no efficacy for good in the food, apart from faith and love."

"And what," I asked, "as to the words about 'forsaking' uttered on the cross, where Luke again differs from Mark and Matthew?" "Here," replied Clemens, "I do not feel sure whether John introduces a new saying altogether, or gives the substance of the old saying in Mark. Certainly he does not agree with Luke. And let me add that I have examined a great number of passages where words of Mark, being obscure or difficult, are altered or omitted by Luke, and I find that in almost every case John intervenes to support Mark—only expressing Mark's meaning more clearly and spiritually.

"Concerning the 'forsaking,' I suggested to you before that it is a metaphor. If so, the reality may be expressed by other metaphors in the scriptures, such as 'I have lost the light of thy countenance,' 'I am cast away from the joy of thy presence,' 'My soul is deprived of the fountain of thy light.' The Psalms say, 'O God, my God...my soul is athirst for thee,' and again, 'My soul thirsteth for God,...when shall I come and appear before God?' The 'thirst' implies absence from God. It will be satisfied by 'coming' to God. Well, John represents Jesus as saying, 'I thirst,' in accomplishment of 'the scriptures.' Then (as I take it) the soldiers misunderstand this thirst as meaning simply literal thirst. They offer Christ vinegar. Christ 'took it,' says the gospel. Then He said, 'It is finished' and 'rested His head'—that is to say, on the bosom of the Father, and 'delivered over His spirit'."

"'Rested His head' is a strange expression," said I. "It is," said Clemens, "but it occurs in Matthew and Luke as follows, 'The Son of man hath not where to rest His head,' meaning 'He hath no home, no resting-place, on earth, but only with the Father above.' One of the ablest Greek scholars among the brethren assures me that John also uses the phrase to mean this; and I believe it is not used in Greek in any other sense. So, too, 'delivered over His spirit' signifies that in the supreme moment the 'delivering over' of the Suffering Servant was not passive but active. He delivered Himself over. But I ought to add that, in Aramaic, the same verb means (in different forms) 'finish,' 'deliver over,' and—the word used here by Mark and Luke—'expire'."

Scaurus had said something of this kind concerning the three gospels, and had argued that it increased the difficulty of ascertaining what Christ actually said. But I had supposed that it would not extend to a gospel written in a Greek city like Ephesus and so long after the other gospels, when Greek traditions might be expected to predominate. I was depressed by this frank avowal on the part of Clemens, and remained in silence for a moment or two weighing its consequences.

CHAPTER XXXII

CLEMENS LENDS SILANUS THE FOURTH GOSPEL

CLEMENS waited patiently for me to resume our conversation. Soon it occurred to me that I had been unreasonable in my expectations if the circumstances were as he had described them. Suppose this new gospel to have originated from the reminiscences of John the son of Zebedee, a fisherman of Galilee, and the aged author of such a book as the Apocalypse. How could such traditions, if set down exactly as they came from the old man's lips, fail to abound in Jewish phrases and thoughts such as I had met with in the apocalyptic work? But these would have made the gospel very unsuitable for Greeks and Romans and indeed for almost all except Jews. It was therefore natural, and indeed almost necessary, that the old man's recollections, after being imparted to his friends, who would probably be the elders of Ephesus, should be freely interpreted, or perhaps paraphrased, in a form fit for all readers. Such interpreters, or such an interpreter, might not always be perfectly successful.

It was foolish of me not to have foreseen this. But still I was disappointed. "This," said I, "adds a new element of uncertainty, if John has sometimes preserved traditions of Christ's words translated from the Jewish tongue." "It does," said Clemens, "and so does another fact that applies both to Greek and to Hebrew or Aramaic. You know that, in Greek, 'he *said*' or '*used to say*,' or 'it *says*,' often signifies 'he *meant*' or 'it *means*.' The same is true in Hebrew. Hence if an evangelist or scribe, after giving Christ's actual words, for example, '*Do righteousness*,' were to add 'But he meant, *Do alms*'—because, in Hebrew, 'righteousness' often means 'alms'—it would be possible to misinterpret the addition as meaning 'But he [also] *said* (or, *used to say*) *Do alms*,' thus erroneously creating a second precept. For these and other reasons I cannot feel sure that the saying 'I thirst,' about which we were just now conversing, may not be a paraphrase of the Lord's words about being 'forsaken.' John the son of Zebedee may have known that the latter words were misunderstood from the first by the soldiers, and also that they were misinterpreted by some Christians. Hence I think the aged apostle may have prayed for a revelation as to the true meaning of the words, and it may have been revealed to him, 'The Lord said—that is, He really said, His real meaning was—that He "*thirsted*".' This indeed would be a surprise or paradox compared with what the gospel says elsewhere. But the scriptures are full of such paradoxes."

" But how 'elsewhere'?" said I. " Do you mean that here Christ feels thirst whereas 'elsewhere' He quenches thirst? I do not remember that." " I forgot," replied Clemens, " that you had not read the new gospel. That gospel represents Christ as saying to a sinful woman, 'Give me to drink,' and afterwards, to the same woman, ' He that believeth on me shall never thirst,' and, after that, to the Jews, ' If any one be athirst, let him come unto me and drink.' This same gospel says that the 'food' of the Son is to do the will of the Father. This, then, may be described as His meat and drink. If, therefore, He 'thirsts,' He is athirst to do the Father's will, so that He hungers and thirsts for righteousness in the souls of sinful men and women, thirsting to free them from thirst by giving them the water of life. All through His life He has not thirsted because the living water has been passing freely from the Father to Him and from Him to others. But now, on the point of death, the Giver of the water of life is Himself caused to thirst for it! The Father, in His infinite love, causes the Son Himself to thirst for that love! Instead of helping others, the Son is constrained to ask as it were to be helped—in order that He may help others better. This is perhaps the deepest and most wonderful of all the Lord's deep sayings—'I thirst for the righteousness and love of God, that I and mine may be in the Father, and that the Father may be in me and mine.' In the end, this will be one of the Lord's words that 'will never pass away.' But what was its effect at the time? When Socrates uttered his last wishes, Crito was at hand to say, 'This shall be done.' But when Christ cried 'I thirst,' no friend was at hand to satisfy that thirst, and the cry was taken by the soldiers as meaning, 'I thirst for a little of your sour wine'!"

"It seems to me," said I, "that you regard this gospel, not exactly as history, but as history mingled with poetry or with vision?" "Not quite so," said Clemens. "I should prefer to say, 'as history *interpreted* through spiritual insight or poetic vision.' I take the historical fact to be that there came into the world, as man, a divine Being, endowed with a power of drawing man and God into one, by drawing the hearts of men towards Himself, and, through Himself, to the Father. Making men one with Himself, He also made them one with each other in Himself. This is the great historical fact, the fact of facts, foreordained before the foundation of the world. This, then, is the fact that needs to be brought out clearly in the history of Christ—not the facts (though they are facts) that the Pharisees often washed their hands and that the daughter of Herodias danced before John the Baptist was beheaded. Well, then, put yourself in the position of—whoever it was that wrote this fourth gospel, say, 'the Elder.' Imagine him returning fresh from an interview with the old man John, the son of Zebedee, who will not allow himself to be called a 'son of thunder'——."

"But why," said I, "should he not have allowed himself to be called John the son of Zebedee? And why should he object to be called one of the sons of thunder, if Jesus called him so?" "As to the latter name," replied Clemens, "I very much doubt whether Mark has translated the term correctly; I will tell you why, another time: but assuredly he was not a noisy 'son of thunder' as we should understand the phrase in the west.

"As to the former name, you will find in this gospel that

'Simon son of John' is thrice mentioned as Peter's name, in a passage where Peter is rebuked for having denied his Master. It is, so to speak, his name after the flesh, his unregenerate name. 'Peter,' or 'stone,' is his regenerate name. So, '*John son of Zebedee*' would be this disciple's unregenerate name. The fourth gospel never uses that name except once, in the phrase 'the sons of Zebedee,' on the same occasion on which Peter is rebuked as '*Simon son of John.*' For the most part John the son of Zebedee is described (in this gospel) as ' the other disciple '—that is, the one as yet unheard, the one whose testimony is still to be given. Or else, the name is connected with Christ's love—' the disciple that Jesus loved.' He feels that he owes all that he has, his very being, to the fact that Jesus *loved him*, that Jesus made him what he now is. Moreover Jesus gave him, by perpetual visions after His death, an insight into the meanings of His words uttered before death. Hence he might feel that Christ's words, once dark sayings, have now become clear. From being old, they have become quite new, so as to require an altogether new record."

"I am not sure," said I, "that I understand your meaning. Do you hold that the fourth gospel differs from the three because of the special character of John the son of Zebedee, or because of the special interpretation of ' the Elder '?" "Because of both," said Clemens. "Then," said I, "you think that John the son of Zebedee, far from being a ' son of thunder ' in the sense in which Pericles might be so called by Aristophanes, was a man of a retiring and vision-seeing nature, who merged himself in Christ; and that his namesake, the Elder, believed that the aged apostle was as it were a mirror, in whom, and in whose traditions, it was possible to discern more of Christ's real expression than in the ancient document of Mark."

"That comes near the truth, I think," replied Clemens. "And yet I should be very far from denying that Mark, and the other early gospels, are right in several features apparently omitted by John—for example, Christ's love of 'the little ones,' and His anxiety lest they should be caused to stumble, and His insistence on the necessity of receiving the Kingdom of God as little children. But it seems to me that some of these precepts about 'little ones' may have been misunderstood so that the brethren needed Paul's warning, 'Be *not little children* in your minds,' and again, 'In malice be babes, but *in understanding be men.*' The root of all these precepts was the divine feeling of 'littleness,' or 'childhood,' or 'sonship.' This is realised in the Son of God doing the will of the Father. In order to do that will on earth, He must be always keeping His eyes on the Father in heaven. The earlier gospels represent Christ with His eyes fixed on the 'little ones' on earth, the sick, the sorrowful, the ignorant, the sinful. That also is true. The new gospel appears to me to attempt to shew how the two truths are combined."

"But you surely do not mean to say," I exclaimed, "that Jesus, in the new gospel, never makes mention of the 'little ones' or the 'little children,' so frequently mentioned by the earlier evangelists!" "I do indeed," replied Clemens. "He does not make mention of either term once, except that, after the resurrection, seeing the disciples engaged in labour that has lasted through the night and effected nothing, He calls to them and says 'Little children!' But yet, although He does not elsewhere use the word 'children,' He has the thought constantly before Him. At the beginning of the gospel, He teaches that men must be '*born from above,*' that is, become little children in the eyes of God. Towards the end, He uses a mother's word to them ('*teknia*,' 'darlings'). He also says, 'I will not leave you *orphans,*' and declares that His disciples are to be in Himself, the Son. Now to be in the Son, means to be made 'a little child' in the perfect sense of Christ's meaning."

"Perhaps," said I, "this explains why Paul seldom mentions the word 'little children'." "'Seldom'," said Clemens, "is not the right word. Paul *never* mentions it, except in the warning I mentioned above. Moreover John, in his epistle, says, 'I have written unto you little children, *because ye have known the Father.*' That word '*known*' goes to the root of the matter. The essence of 'little childhood,' in Christ's sense, is *not ignorance, but knowledge*—'knowing the Father.' And 'knowing the Father' implies loving the Father, or desiring the Father.

There are cases where 'desire' may perhaps be well substituted for 'love,' so as to indicate that kind of love which leads one onwards to the object desired. This gospel seems to me to attempt to express—if I may so speak in accordance with the prophets of Israel—a desire of God for man, producing a desire of man for God. The work of the Son of God is to unite these two desires. This is a great mystery, a mystery past mere logic, that God, the Creator, should 'desire.' Yet I accept it— as it has been expressed by a certain holy woman of Athens, whom I verily believe to have been inspired by God, 'The Son of God chose to be lifted up upon the tree of the Cross that we might receive the food of angels. And what is this food of angels? It is the desire of God, which draws to itself the desire that is in the depths of the soul and they make one thing together'."

This saying was beyond me at the time. But I felt that it contained truth, and that I should grow into some apprehension of it. And what Clemens had said, though very strange at first, had been gradually growing to seem possible and even reasonable, if one may use the word concerning that which accords with the spiritual Logos—namely, that the Son of God, being human, was caused to feel forsaken by God, and to desire God, and to ask why this strange feeling of forsakenness, this unwonted, unsatisfied desire, was brought upon Him by the Father. Then, according to the saying of this holy woman of Athens, the answer of the Father was, "In receiving this forsakenness and this desire for my presence, thou art receiving from me my desire, which draws up to me thy desire, and they two make one together."

But to return to Clemens, whom I began to trust all the more because I felt that he was keeping back nothing from me. "What I am attempting," said he, "to express, but expressing very feebly, is this. I am trying to put myself in the position of the Elder, preaching the gospel for John the son of Zebedee in Ephesus, some time after the aged apostle returned from his martyrdom in Patmos, when he was quite decrepit and no longer able to be carried into the midst of the congregation, to utter even a few words. If I came into that old man's presence and heard from him traditions about the Master, whom he loved and who loved him, I might say, 'Here indeed is a revelation of Christ. Here I feel Christ Himself.' Nevertheless, on going out, I might find it very hard to make a chronological and consecutive history out of his utterances. Sometimes he might be describing past fact; sometimes he might be prophesying the future; sometimes he might speak of the past as if still present—as though he were even now with his Master in Cana or Jerusalem; sometimes he might be rapt in a present ecstasy; sometimes he might be describing ecstatic visions of the past; sometimes he might speak in poetic metaphor, sometimes in literal prose; but always he would be penetrated and imbued with the love of Christ. The result—for me, I confess it—would be that I should go out, thinking, 'This is not history in the common sense of the term. But it is something, I will not say better, but more needed by the church, than a mere history of facts such as a writer like Mark could have given with fuller information. It gives glimpses into a divine and human personality that includes in itself a real history—a history of a great invisible war of good against evil, a great invisible redemption, God coming down to earth to lift man up to heaven'."

"But," said I, "do not Matthew and Luke give these glimpses in their description of the incarnation?" "I should rather have said," replied Clemens, "that, instead of giving glimpses, they attempt to describe a spiritual fact in the language of material history. John, you will find, does not make this attempt. He simply says that 'the Logos became flesh.' Then he introduces disciples believing in their Master as Messiah, undeterred by their supposition that He is 'the son of Joseph' and 'from Nazareth.' John assumes all through his gospel that Jesus came down from heaven and is to go up thither again. He refuses to recognise that this coming down and this going up are impossible for the Son of God incarnate as the son of Joseph. All this appears to me true. And in many respects I admire this little book more than I can find time or words to express. Yet I must deal frankly with you and confess that this new gospel, like the rest, appears to me inadequate. What gospel would be otherwise? All the written records of Christ's words and acts seem to me to have, as their main use, the awakening in us of a want of something more, a sense of something insufficient and imperfect and unjust to the reality, so that we cry vehemently to God for the reality, the living truth, the spiritual light—such light as no words or books can give us. The Spirit alone can bestow it, crying within us Abba, Father. Some interpreters, however, seem in a special degree to have 'the mind of Christ.' Among the foremost of these seems to me to stand ' the disciple whom Jesus loved '."

"I understand," said I, "at least I think I do, a little. You mean that the written biographies must first make the reader feel that they are dead in comparison with the living person. Then the reader is to feel drawn towards his ideal of the living person, and more and more drawn, so that in the end——." "In the end," said Clemens, "assuredly the living Person will come to him, or draw him to Himself, if he will but be patient in waiting, walking according to the light he already has." On this he rose to depart. "One word more," said I. "You told me that John gives nearly a quarter of his gospel to the doctrine of the Lord on the night on which He was delivered over. Does he give much space to the period after the resurrection? And what does he say about that? Does he agree with Matthew and Luke?"

"No," said Clemens, "he differs greatly, and, as it appears to me, deliberately, intending to correct them. For example, Matthew represents certain women as taking hold of Christ's feet, before He sends them to carry word to His 'brethren.' John says that Jesus said to Mary Magdalene, 'Touch me not for I am not yet ascended to my Father,' and then sends her to His 'brethren.' Luke says that Christ said to all the disciples, 'Handle me,' to shew that He was not a bodiless spirit. John says that an offer of this nature was made to Thomas, but mentions no such offer to any other disciple. Luke says that the disciples gave Jesus food and He ate. John says that Jesus gave food to the disciples. In all these points John appears to me to be nearer than Matthew and Luke to the truth. And sometimes I think that the touching of Christ's body by the disciples in the Eucharist, that is to say, the touching of the bread and tasting of the wine in our sacred meal, has been taken by Luke (if not by Matthew) in a literal sense"—here Clemens agreed with Scaurus—" whereas John understood the meaning correctly. But at the same time I think that the Saviour may have been visibly present at the Eucharist, shewing the wounds in His body, though it was not a body that could be touched."

"Does it not seem to you," I asked, "that this agrees better with Paul's descriptions of the manifestations of Jesus after death?" "Yes," said Clemens, "and in other respects John seems to me to be nearer the truth. For he apparently represents Christ as having ascended to the Father before He could be 'touched,' that is to say, before His spiritual body and blood could be imparted to the disciples. Moreover, whereas Matthew places before the Resurrection a tradition relating how Christ imparts to the disciples authority to bind and to loose *i.e.* to forgive sins, John places it afterwards. And John also describes Peter as plunging into the water and coming to Jesus after the Resurrection,—which seems to me a symbol of Peter passing through the waters of temptation to the Saviour whom he had denied. But Matthew places it before the Resurrection and takes it literally, as though Peter tried to walk on literal water and was nearly drowned, but for the Lord's help."

"Then," said I, after a long pause—for I was not prepared to find Clemens so far in agreement with Scaurus, an unbeliever, concerning the facts of the Christian histories—"you are very far indeed from saying, 'I believe in every word of the gospels of Mark, Matthew, and Luke, as being historically accurate.' Nay, I can hardly think you would say that, even about the gospel of John?" "Assuredly," he replied, "I would not say that about any of the gospels. Indeed, dear friend, do you yourself think you would venture to say as much as that, even about the history of your favourite Thucydides? And does it not seem to you that, in any book that describes the life of a man, the greater the man, and the more living the life, the greater must be the failure of the book, and the deadness of the book, as compared with the inexpressible spirit, not to be expressed in any book, no, not in a universe of books?"

Then, rising, and pointing seaward, "Look!" he said, "the moon is up already! Now indeed I must stay with you no longer. I have done my best to deal fairly with you, even to the point perhaps of being not quite fair to this little book, which I now hold in my hand, and am about to place in yours, if you desire it. But are you sure that you do still desire it? If you do indeed, I shall most gladly lend it, and you can return it to me, this time to-morrow, at the house of Justus. But be honest with me as I have tried to be with you. Do not take it as yet if you are not prepared to read it as a book that comes from the east through a western medium; a book that mingles, so as not always to be clearly distinguished, words of the Lord with words of the evangelist, facts and visions, histories and prophecies, metaphors that may be misunderstood, and poems that may be taken as literal prose. It will make you feel perhaps irritated, certainly unsatisfied. Perhaps you may end in saying, 'I want much more, I want to see the person to whom this book points, but whom no book can make me feel.' Then it will have done you good. But perhaps you will put it aside and say, 'I want no more'."

He paused, and looked anxiously at me. "In that case," continued he, "I shall have done you harm. But what say you? After this warning, do you—a Roman with Greek training, a reader of Homer and Thucydides—do you still desire to see this little volume that is neither a true poem nor a true history, a biography that hardly professes to draw the life of Jesus as He was, but only to make us feel that it must be felt, if at all, through 'a disciple whom Jesus loved'?" I assured him that I greatly desired to read it and thanked him with all my heart for the loan, and for the frankness of his warning. "Farewell," said he, placing the book in my hand, "my friend, my brother —brother in the search after truth, farewell!" "Your help," said I, as he turned away from me, "has been more like that of a father." He stopped and looked round at me for a moment. "Would indeed," said he, "that it might prove so! Farewell!"

A.

CHAPTER XXXIII

SCAURUS ON THE FOURTH GOSPEL

THE sun had set, and the moon was well above the sea, when, after parting from Clemens, I turned towards Nicopolis, with the new gospel in my hand. Unrolling it, I found twilight enough to read the first few lines while I walked slowly for some two or three hundred paces. Then I stood still to read better in the fading light. When it had quite faded, I sat down repeating what I had read.

"In the beginning was the Logos." Never shall I forget the unexpectedness of those words. I had supposed that the Christians altogether rejected the Logos except as meaning "utterance" or "doctrine." "In the beginning" was, in some senses, familiar. I had read in Mark, "The *beginning* of the gospel of Jesus Christ." Luke, too, had spoken of "those who were from the *beginning* eyewitnesses and ministers of the Logos." But how different was Luke's "Logos" and Luke's "beginning" from this!

I read on: "In the beginning was the Logos and the Logos was with God." What did "with" mean? Was the Logos "at home with God"? Or "conversing with God"? Or "in union with God"? Or did "with" include all these meanings? And what was this Logos? The next words gave the answer: "The Logos was God."

These words alone, contrasted with Luke's preface, sufficed to indicate a difference between Luke and John, just such as Clemens had suggested. Luke began with a reference to many inadequate "attempts" to draw up a relation about what he called "the *facts*"—meaning "*facts*" as distinct from *fancies*—"consummated among us." Then, like a careful compiler, he distinguished his authorities, giving the first place to "*eyewitnesses*," the second to accessories, or "*ministers*." These were eyewitnesses, he said, "from the beginning"; and he declared that he had followed and traced their evidence from the fountain head. John, like a prophet, went back to a "beginning" of which there could be no "eyewitnesses." He did not say, as Luke did, "*it seemed good to me*" to write. He said—as though he had himself been with Him who was from the beginning—"*The Logos was God.*"

Glancing down the column before folding up the scroll, I could barely read in the fast expiring twilight the words, "And the Logos became flesh and tabernacled among us, and we beheld his glory, glory as of the only begotten from the Father." Clemens had prepared me for such words. As I understood them, the "glory" did not mean any splendour of material light or fire, such as is mentioned sometimes in the theophanies of Greek, Roman, and Hebrew writers, but the glory of God's constraining love. But I greatly desired to study the words in their context. Repeating them over and over again, as I rolled up the book, I hurried homeward. Star after star came out in the darkness; and with each new star a new suggestion of invisible "glory" shone on me more clearly. "This gospel," I said, "will grow on me like these visible glories. Night by night, and day by day, its words will become less strange and more wonderful."

On my arrival, I lit my lamp, and sat down at once, preparing to continue my reading, when my servant entered with a letter. Not recognising the superscription, I put it on one side. The boy waited about in the room, doing nothing that needed doing. I was on the point of dismissing him, when he said, "Sir, I think it is from Tusculum; but the superscription is not in my lord's handwriting." Looking again, I saw that it was in the handwriting of Marullus, Scaurus's secretary. Scaurus usually superscribed his letters to me with his own hand. In alarm about his health, I tore the letter open, and throwing the cover hastily aside, glanced at the beginning. This reassured me. It was from Scaurus, and in his handwriting.

My apprehensions were soon banished. He had been ill, he said, but had now recovered after a somewhat severe attack. Then the old war-horse passed on to his favourite battle-field—criticism of Christian gospels. I was in the act of putting the letter down—for I had had enough, for the present, of criticizing the old gospels, and was longing to study the new one—when I caught sight of the words "fourth gospel," and discovered that he had recently procured the very book I was beginning to read, and that his letter contained a discussion of it. This was not quite welcome—not, at least, at the moment. I wished to read the gospel first, for myself, before looking at Scaurus's criticism, which (I felt sure) would be destructive. "Yet," thought I, "I have heard Clemens on the one side; ought I not to hear Scaurus on the other? If Scaurus goes wrong, ought I not to be able to find it out?" Scaurus was always fair and honest, and had helped me hitherto, even when I had not agreed with him. These considerations made me finally decide to read the letter and the gospel together, comparing each criticism with the passage or subject criticized, as I went on.

"Let me begin," wrote Scaurus, "with the point that will most interest you. I have accused Epictetus of borrowing from the Christians. I now assert that this writer—Flaccus tells me that the Christians say it was John the son of Zebedee; I am sure they are wrong, but for convenience I will call him John—this man John deliberately contradicts Epictetus, using our friend's language but in a different or opposite sense, or with opposite conclusions.

"For example, Epictetus mocks at Agamemnon for calling himself a shepherd of the people. He dislikes the Homeric language and says 'Shepherd you are in truth; for you weep, *as the shepherds do, when a wolf snatches away one of their sheep.*' John makes Christ distinguish between the good shepherd and the hireling. It is only the hireling that *flees and lets the wolf snatch away the sheep.* In John, Christ says,

Chapter 33]   ON THE FOURTH GOSPEL   325

'I am the good shepherd,' and '*The good shepherd lays down his life for the sheep.*'

"Again, Epictetus declares that a good man never weeps. He blames Ulysses in particular for weeping at his separation from Penelope. John represents Christ as shedding tears in sympathy with a woman weeping for her dead brother.

"Epictetus constantly says that self-knowledge is everything—herein (I must admit) going with other philosophers. John represents Christ as saying, 'This is eternal life, to know thee, the only true God and Jesus Christ whom thou hast sent.' It is impossible that Christ could have uttered the last part of this sentence exactly as it stands. But that does not weaken my argument, which is, that John (alone of the evangelists) insists on other-knowledge, not on self-knowledge, as being the essential thing. And this he does throughout his gospel."

Then Scaurus came to that cardinal doctrine of Epictetus which had caused Glaucus and me so many searchings of heart. "You know," he said, "that Epictetus teaches that no good man is ever troubled. It is not John's custom to contradict what he deems errors in a formal and direct way. But if he had resorted for once to direct methods, he could hardly have contradicted this Epictetian doctrine more effectively than he does in his indirect dramatic fashion. He represents Christ as thrice 'troubled.' First—on the same occasion on which he lets fall tears in sympathy with the woman above mentioned—he is said to have 'troubled himself.' Secondly, on an occasion when he is (as I take it) preparing for some act of self-sacrifice, he says, 'Now is my soul troubled.' On a third occasion, when announcing that he is to be betrayed by one of the Twelve, he is said to have been 'troubled in spirit.' I cannot doubt that this description of threefold 'trouble' is intended to attack the Stoic doctrine that the wise and good man is to shrink from 'trouble'." This convinced me, and it convinces me still.

Scaurus proceeded to say, "Some innocent readers of this gospel might say, 'Well at all events John agrees with Epictetus in his use of the term Logos.' And (no doubt) the first three lines of the gospel might suggest this. But read on, and you will find the two are in absolute opposition. The Logos, in John, instead of being the philosophic Logos or reason, is really an unreasonable and hyperbolical sort of love, regarded by him as born from God, and as part of God's personality, and as constituting unity in God's nature. This Logos he regards as incarnate as a man for the purpose of uniting mankind to God! This doctrine Epictetus would absolutely reject.

"Later on, in this gospel, you will find Christ saying to the disciples, 'Ye are clean on account of the Logos that I have spoken to you.' Now Epictetus also connects cleanness with the Logos. 'It is impossible,' he says, 'that man's nature should be altogether clean, but the Logos being received into it, as far as possible attempts to make it cleanly.' Verbally, there is an appearance of agreement. Read the two contexts, however, and you will find that, whereas Epictetus makes 'cleanness' consist in right convictions, John makes it consist in a mystical doctrine of sacrifice, or service, typified by the Master's washing the feet of the disciples.

"I could give you other instances of the way in which John uses other language of philosophers in a non-philosophic sense. But his use of Logos suffices for my purpose. It gives the clue to the whole gospel. This writer adds one more to my list of Christian *retiarii*. The innocent reader, unrolling the book and reading its first words, prepares himself for a Platonic treatise in which he is to 'follow the Logos' in accordance with Socratic precept. Then, step by step, he is lured on into regions of non-logic and sentiment, till the net suddenly descends on him, and he finds himself repeating, 'the Logos became flesh'."

What Scaurus said interested me but did not convince me as to John's motive. Nor did Scaurus himself adhere to it. He did not always use the epithet "retiarian" in a bad sense. As I have said above, I had come to believe that right "feeling," rather than right "reason," may be regarded as revealing the nature of God. So I did not feel that John was beguiling his readers. But Scaurus's criticism helped me to recognise the extreme skill and tact—as well as the terseness, beauty, and solemnity—with which the evangelist introduces the doctrine of the incarnation. And I could not help agreeing with my friend's next remark, "The man that wrote the Apocalypse—though he, too, was a prophet and a poet in his line—could no more have written this prologue than Ennius could have written the Æneid."

After some more observations on the difference of style in the Apocalypse and the Gospel, he returned to the criticism of the latter. "Compare," he said, "the prologue and the conclusion with the rest of this book, and you will see that there is some mystery about its authorship. Under one style it conveys two currents of thought. Sometimes it repeats itself like an old man. Sometimes it is as brief and dark as an oracle. Moreover, some events—such as the expulsion of the tradespeople from the temple—which ought to come at the end—this writer places at the beginning. It has occurred to me that he must have started with the intention of describing nothing but Christ's acts in Judæa and then changed his mind. Or is it possible that documents arranged Hebrew-fashion—last, first—have been interpreted Greek-fashion and consequently reversed? Allegory is most strangely mixed with fact. There is a wedding in which water is changed into wine. This is allegory. The Bride is the Church. The water of the law is changed into the wine of the gospel. After that, comes a statement that Christ spoke about destroying the temple and building it in three days. This is, according to Mark and Matthew, history. Luke took it as not history and left it out. John took it as history and allegory and put it in. But how differently from Mark and Matthew! Look at the passages. John often does this. I mean, that where Luke differs from Mark, John (who prefers Mark) intervenes to support the latter."

This general remark (about John's "preferring Mark") agreed with what Clemens had said. As for the particular instance, I found that Scaurus was right. Mark and Matthew had mentioned a project to "destroy the temple" as having been imputed to Christ by false witnesses. Luke omitted it. John declared that Christ said to the Jews, "Destroy this temple!" and that Christ "spoke about the temple of his body."

"If I could believe," continued Scaurus, "that John the son of Zebedee, the author of the Apocalypse, had any part in the production of this gospel, I should be disposed to say that he must have contributed to it, not as a scribe, but as a prophet or seer. Take, for example, the description, recorded in this gospel alone, of a flow of blood and water from the side of Christ on the cross. I do not believe for a moment that this was invented, any more than Luke's description of the sweat of blood on the night before the crucifixion. But I should explain the two as resulting from two quite different causes, differing as the authors differ. Luke was not a seer, but a man of literature, a student of documents. He found some narrative based on the expression that it was 'a night of watching and sweat'—which you know very well means in Greek 'watching and anxious toil.' The narrator took this literally. This literal interpretation commended itself to Luke, who desired to connect the death of Christ with the Jewish sacrificial 'blood of sprinkling'." I had not noticed in Luke any tradition about "sweat." But on referring to my copy I found that, though not in the text, words of this kind were written in the margin.

Scaurus went on to shew in detail that John's tradition was quite different in origin. It was supported by an asseveration, "He that hath seen hath borne witness, and his witness is true; and *he knoweth* that he saith true that ye also may believe." As to this, Scaurus said, "Only a little child, a baby Gaius, would use such an asseveration as '*Gaius knows* that Gaius is telling the truth.' 'He knoweth' means 'HE knoweth,' *i.e.* 'The Lord knoweth.' HE is often thus used in the epistle that forms a sort of epilogue to this gospel. The prophet, or seer, is appealing to his Lord about the truth of the vision of blood and water, which the Lord has revealed to him. In the Bible 'he that seeth' is a common phrase for 'the seer,' a man habitually seeing visions. When John came back from Patmos and wrote the Apocalypse, he might naturally be called by preeminence, 'he that hath seen.' Or the phrase might apply to this special vision: 'The seer (he that hath seen) hath borne witness to the vision of the stream of blood and water, and HE (*i.e.* the Lord) knoweth that his witness is true.'

"I do not deny that the vision is a fulfilment of a prophecy—which you may have read in the book of Zechariah—concerning a certain 'fountain to cleanse sin and defilement.' But still I say that it is an honest, genuine, vision, not an invention. That it is not a fact could be proved, if needful. According to the other evangelists, some women were present near the cross, but no men are mentioned. It is extremely doubtful whether two streams of water and blood could issue from the side. If they had issued, and if John had been present, the soldiers would not have let him stand near enough to distinguish them. My copy of Matthew, in a marginal note, has a similar tradition, but *before the death*, and without any order from Pilate to kill the crucified criminals—as if a soldier would dare to do this at his own pleasure! A book called Acts of John (only recently circulated, Flaccus tells me) contains other visions of John, and, among them, some revealed during the crucifixion. The Acts is not written by the author of this new gospel, and it is very wild and fanciful; but it suggests that visions may have been falsely ascribed to John because he was known to have really seen visions (like laws falsely assigned to Numa because he was supposed to have really made laws). I take it that John the son of Zebedee may have had a vision of this kind about a 'fountain' of blood and water. This may have been current among the Christians for some time. My annotator in Matthew seems to have found it in a wildly improbable form. The new gospel gives it less improbably."

Scaurus then commented on the contrast between what he called the "soaring" thought of the book and its occasionally "pedestrian" or vernacular language, as when John preserves the old traditional "crib" for "bed"—a word abominated by Atticists and avoided by Luke. He also commented on his ambiguities, his subtle plays on words, his variations in the forms of words, and his veiled allusions—utterly unlike anything that might be expected from a fisherman of Galilee—declaring that the writer must have been conversant with the works of Philo as well as with the teaching of the Cynics.

Then he pointed out how Christ in this gospel never uses the word "cross" but always speaks of being "lifted up"—a phrase, he said, current among Jews as well as Roman slaves, to mean "hanged" or "crucified": and he gave it as an instance of the writer's irony—and of his recognition that things low in man's eyes are high in God's eyes—that a criminal's death is called by this writer "being exalted," or "being glorified." "Have you not"—he said—"heard your servants ever say that Geta has been 'lifted up,' or that Syrus has been a rich man and has 'fed multitudes'—meaning that the poor wretch has been crucified and has fed multitudes of crows with his flesh on the cross?" I had often heard it; and I was astonished that such a phrase could be used in this gospel. Scaurus continued, "He uses this vernacular talk, this unfeeling slavish jest, to represent the very highest truth of Christian doctrine, that the Redeemer is to be 'exalted' by suffering on the cross so as to give his flesh and blood to be the food of all the world!"

According to Scaurus, although the style was very different indeed from that of Philo, and although the writer knew (what Philo did not) that the Septuagint was often erroneous, yet there was a great likeness between John and Philo in respect of their symbolism. Of this he gave a great number of instances. And he also quoted allusions to Jewish proverbs or sayings, one of which I will set down here, because it has given rise to an error among some of the brethren at the present day.

John represents the Jews as saying to Jesus, "Thou art not yet fifty years old." Now, according to Scaurus, this referred to an enactment in the Law that the Levites must serve with laborious service "up to fifty years of age," after which they are exempt, so that the saying, "Thou art not yet fifty" meant, "Thou art but a junior Levite," used as a term of reproach. "This enactment," said Scaurus, "was applied by Philo to inferior spiritual attainment, and, I have no doubt, was used allusively by John. But it might easily give the impression that Christ was about fifty years old and that the Jews meant the saying literally."

I mention this because I have myself heard the young Irenæus maintain that Christ was actually about fifty years of age. And he not only quoted John in support of this assertion but declared that it was also the opinion of the elders conversant with John. When I heard him, I remembered what Scaurus had said. I have never had any doubt that Scaurus was right. At the same time it seems to me that a Jewish allusion of this kind was extremely liable to be misunderstood, and that the writer of this gospel would not perhaps have set it down if he had not received it from the originator, John the son of Zebedee. This, however, is only my conjecture. The error of Irenæus is a fact. And I could mention another of the brethren, who wrote a commentary on John, and actually altered "fifty" to "forty"—I suppose, to make sense! Both these errors arose from not understanding John's allusion.

Then Scaurus passed to the structure of the work which, he said, under appearance of great simplicity, and of an iteration that might sometimes seem almost garrulous or senile, conformed to certain Jewish rules of twofold and threefold attestation. He shewed how the book—describing a new creation of the world—begins and ends with six days. He also shewed how the author takes pleasure in refrains of words, and cycles or repetitions of events. For example, he describes Christ as being baptized at the beginning in one Bethany and anointed at the end in another Bethany. "I could give you," he said, "other instances of this sort of thing. The book is a poem, not a history."

About this I was not yet able to judge; but I felt that by "poem" he did not mean "mere fiction." For he had already admitted that the book contained historical as well as spiritual truth. And knowing his deep love of goodness, I was not altogether surprised at what came next: "O my dear Quintus, while reading this extraordinary book I have been more than once tempted to say, 'Along with a great deal that I do not want, this man almost gives me what I do want—what I have been long desiring.' I have told you how, years ago, I craved for a city of truth and justice. Well, I knew the Jews were a narrow, bigoted, and uncharitable race. No Jewish philosopher or prophet was likely to be my guide to such a city. But Isaiah was an exception. And somehow I fancied that this Jesus might be a developed Isaiah, and that his new city would have over its gates, 'Entrance free. Not even Roman patricians excluded.' But what did I find in some of the earliest gospels? In effect, this, 'None but the lost sheep of the House of Israel admitted here!'

"Now comes this latest of all the evangelists and says, 'We have changed all that. The old inscription is taken down. See the new inscription, ROOM FOR ALL! We welcome the universe. Read me, and see what I say about *other sheep*, and about *one flock, one shepherd*.' To all which I reply, 'Alas, my unknown but well-intentioned friend, I see, too clearly, that your friendliness exceeds your judgment. You honestly think that your gospel is so good that it must be true. You are not, I feel sure, decoying me—not consciously at least. You are the decoy bird. You have been decoyed yourself to decoy others. But Scaurus is too old a bird to be caught in such a manifest net. Whence this new doctrine? Why was it not in the earliest gospels?' I think John would find it hard to answer that question! If I had come to Jesus the Nazarene and said to him, 'What shall I do to inherit eternal life?' I doubt not that he would have replied to me, 'Marcus Æmilius Scaurus, you doubtless think yourself a great person, as much superior to the low born Pontius Pilate as Pilate thinks himself superior to me. Understand, then, that I have no message for you. You know what name I gave to the Syrophœnician woman. I give the same to you'."

This passage was written in very large irregular characters, especially towards the close, quite unlike my old friend's usual hand. Then followed these words, in his own neat regular writing—as though he had been interrupted and resumed his pen in a cooler mood—"Let me try to be honest. I may have said rather more than I meant. I meant this fifteen years ago. Perhaps I mean it still. But after reading this new gospel, I feel somewhat less certain. Still, I fear that the truth may be as I have said."

CHAPTER XXXIV

THE LAST WORDS OF SCAURUS

HAD I read to the end of Scaurus's letter I should not have been so startled by this sudden outburst. As it was, I had but a faint perception of the cause. I did not give weight enough to the indications—slight to others but they ought to have been clear to me—that the old man was writing under a great mental strain. Striving to be fair to the evangelists, he desired also to do justice to himself, half repenting that he had rejected the Saviour, half vindicating the rejection on the ground that truth constrained it. The whole tone of his letter—the handwriting itself, if I had only noted it more closely—should have made me perceive that he was passing rapidly through many transient phases, and that this outburst of passionate indignation—not with Christ but with what he supposed to be Mark's Christ—was but one of them. I did not notice these things. I was too much wrapped up in my own thoughts, and in imaginations of what I could have said, and how I could have pleaded with him for Christ.

It was now late, and I could read no more. I retired to rest—but not at first to peaceful rest. Thoughts and dreams, fancies and phantoms, passed indistinguishably before me: Scaurus and Clemens opposing one another, Hermas mediating, while Epictetus looked on; Troy, Rome, Jerusalem, and the City of Truth and Justice coming down from heaven; sunset and sunrise ushered by Hesper and Phosphor—with snatches of familiar utterances about "perceiving," "believing," and "deceiving," and mocking repetitions of "logos," "logos"—

a confused, shifting, and multitudinous medley that resolved itself at last into one vast and dizzying whirlpool, in which all existence seemed endlessly revolving round a central abyss, when suddenly I heard " In the beginning was the Logos." Then the whirlpool was drawn up to the sky as though it had been a painted curtain; and we were standing below, Scaurus and I, and Clemens, and Epictetus, and Hermas—all of us gazing upwards to an unspeakable glory ascending and descending between heaven and earth. Then I fell into a peaceful sleep.

Next morning I continued reading the letter. " About the marvels or miracles in this gospel," said Scaurus, " it is worth noting that the author mentions only seven, that is to say, seven before the resurrection. This, I believe, is the number assigned to Elijah, whereas Elisha has fourteen—having 'a double portion' of Elijah's spirit. This selection of seven is one among many indications that the work uses Jewish symbolism. I have shewn above that the Jewish genealogies are sometimes adapted in that way, as with Matthew's 'fourteen generations.' A more important fact is that this writer calls the miracles 'signs'—not ' mighty works,' which is the term in the three gospels. This is very interesting and I like him for it. He hates the words 'strong,' and 'mighty,' and 'mighty work.' For the matter of that, so does Epictetus. Both would agree that it is only slaves that obey 'the stronger.'

" He also dislikes arithmetical ' greatness' and discussions about ' who is the greatest?' He prefers to lay stress on unity. Christians, he thinks, are 'one with the Son,' or they are 'in' the Son, or the Son is 'in' them. They are also to be ' one,' as the Father and the Son are ' one.' When men are regarded in this way, arithmetical standards of greatness—based on one's income, or on the amount of one's alms, or the amount of one's prayers, or one's sufferings, or one's converts—become ridiculous. He is quite right.

" He makes no mention of 'repentance.' That, I think, is because he prefers such expressions as 'coming to God' or 'coming to the light,' rather than mere 'change of mind.' He never uses the noun 'faith' or 'belief.' Probably he found it in use as a technical term among some foolish Christians—speaking of 'faith that moves mountains'—who forgot to ask 'faith in *what*?' For the same reason, no doubt, he preferred the word 'signs' to 'mighty works,' because the former—at all events while it was a novel term—might make men ask 'signs of *what*?' The phrase 'mighty work' makes us ask nothing. Nor does a 'mighty' work prove anything, except that the doer is 'mighty'—perhaps a giant, perhaps a magician, perhaps a God. Who is to decide? Epictetus says that Ceres and Pluto are proved to be Gods because they produce 'bread.' So this John represents Christ as producing bread and wine and healing disease and raising the dead; and these are 'signs' that he is a Giver of divine gifts and a Healer, like Apollo.

"In the case of one miracle, omitted by Luke, John intervenes and gives the sign a different aspect—I mean the one in which Mark and Matthew represent Christ as walking over the water to the disciples in a storm and as coming into their boat. John represents Christ as standing on the edge of the sea and as drawing the disciples safely to himself as soon as they cry out to him. I have no doubt that the story is an allegory. But John seems to me to give it in the nobler, and perhaps the earlier, form.

"There were probably multitudes of exorcisms performed by Jesus, as I have said to you before. But John does not mention a single instance. Perhaps he thought that more than enough had been said about these things by the earlier evangelists. On the other hand, he describes the healing of a man born blind, and the raising of a man named Lazarus from the dead, after he had lain in the tomb three days.

"The nearest approach to this is a story in Luke about raising from the coffin a young man, the son of a widow. I was long ago inclined to think Luke's story allegorical, and a curious book, which recently came into my hands, confirms this view. It is assigned to Ezra, but was really written, at least in its present form, about five and twenty years ago. I think it mixes Jewish and Christian thought. Ezra sees a vision of a woman sorrowing for her only child. She has had no son till after 'thirty years' of wedlock. The son grew up and was to be married. When he 'entered into his wedding chamber, he fell down and died.' Presently it is explained, 'The woman is Sion.' For 'thirty years' there was 'no offering.' After 'thirty years,' Solomon 'builded the city and offered offerings.' Then Jerusalem was destroyed. But Ezra sees a new city builded, 'a large place.' It is a strange mixture. David, says the scripture, was a 'son of thirty years' when he began to reign, and he may be supposed to have died about the time when the Temple began to be built. On the other hand Christ also was a 'son of thirty years' when he began to preach the gospel, and Christ might be said to have died at the time when he entered the Temple to purify it (that is, as Jews might say, 'entered the wedding chamber').

"I don't profess to explain all this Ezra-allegory. The only point worth noting is that it describes events that befell *the City* and *the Temple* of the Jews as though they befell *persons* —a 'woman' and a deceased 'son.' Luke omits the charge brought against Christ that he threatened to destroy '*the temple*' and build another. But there can be no doubt that there was some basis of fact for the charge. John gives that basis, by saying that Christ had in view a '*body*,' meaning himself. This indicates that Luke was misled through not understanding Jewish metaphor. So here Luke may have been misled again. He found a tradition describing the 'raising up' of the 'widow's son,' and he took it literally." The explanation thus suggested by Scaurus seemed to me probable. It explained why Luke omitted "the raising up of the temple." It also explained why Mark and Matthew omitted "the raising up of the widow's son."

Scaurus proceeded to the account of the raising of Lazarus. "This narrative," he said, "is extremely beautiful and may perhaps have had some basis of historical fact. Luke speaks of a Lazarus, who dies, and is carried after death into Abraham's bosom. Some Christians might take this Lazarus for a historical character. But I do not think any confusion arising from that story can have had very much to do with the story in John. The latter seems to me to have been thrown into allegorical form, so that Lazarus may represent humanity, first, corrupt, mere '*flesh and blood*'; secondly, raised up by '*the help of God.*' 'My God helps' is the meaning of Eliezer or Lazarus. Philo sees in the name these two associations. Also a Christian writer named Barnabas has some curious traditions that may bear on this name; and so have the Jews. Possibly John may mean—over and above the man Lazarus—the human race, raised up to life by the Messiah at the intercession of two sisters, representing the Jewish and the Gentile Churches of the Christians. Similarly I am told that Christians describe the two sisters Leah and Rachel as representing the Synagogue and the Church.

"For my part, having spoken to many physicians, and having investigated some instances of revivification, I have come to the conclusion that Jesus possessed a remarkable power of healing the sick and even perhaps of restoring life to those from whom (to all appearance) life had recently departed. Nay, I am dreamer enough to go beyond anything that physicians would allow, and to suppose that Christ may have had a certain power of what I called above *teliatreia*, 'healing at a distance,' producing a corresponding *telepatheia*, or 'being healed at a distance.' But there is against this particular narrative the objection—not to be overcome except by very strong evidence indeed—that the other evangelists say nothing about this stupendous miracle. Having in view Christ's precept to the disciples, 'Raise the dead,' I see how easily honest Christians might be led to take metaphor for fact. It is much more easy to explain how the narratives of the widow's son and of Lazarus may have arisen from misunderstanding in the two latest gospels, than to explain how, though true, they were omitted in the two earliest."

Upon this, I read the story of the raising of Lazarus two or three times over. It appeared to me certain that the writer of the gospel must have taken the story as literally true. But I saw how easy it was to mistake metaphor for literal meaning in stories of this kind. I was also impressed by what Scaurus said concerning the precept, "Raise the dead," which is recorded by Matthew. No other writer mentions this; and I had assumed, at the time of which I am now speaking, that it was meant spiritually, and that Luke omitted it because he thought that it might be misunderstood as having a literal meaning. And here I may say, writing forty-five years afterwards, that I have lately spoken to several of the brethren about this precept. Some leave it out of their text of Matthew. Some refuse to say anything about it. But I have not as yet found a single brother ready to admit that Jesus must have used it, or even probably used it, metaphorically.

All this I did not know at the time when I was reading Scaurus's letter; but I recognised the force of his arguments and was constrained to sympathize with his disappointment when he proceeded as follows: "O, my dearest Quintus, what earthen vessels, what mere potsherds, these gospel writers are, even the best of them, in comparison with the man whom they fail to set before us! Yes, even this John, whom I regard as by far the greatest of them all, even he is a failure—but in his case, perhaps, from want of knowledge, not from want of insight. As for the others, why do they not trust to the greatness of their subject, the man Jesus Christ? Why can they not believe that the Logos might become incarnate as a man, that is to say, a real man—what Jesus himself calls 'son of man'? Why do they lay so much stress on mere 'mighty works,' some of which, even if they could be proved to have happened, would give us little insight into the real greatness of their Master, whom they wish us to worship?

"For my part, I take such stories as those of the destruction of the swine and the withering of the fig-tree, to be allegories misinterpreted as facts. But even if I were shown to be wrong, they would not prove to me that I was right in worshipping the doer of such wonders. If I can judge myself aright, I, Marcus Æmilius Scaurus, am quite prone enough already to worship the God of the Thunderbolts and the God of War. These Jews might have taught me better. They have, to some extent—especially this fourth writer. But how much more from the first might have been effected if, from the first, they had recognised the truth taught in the legend of Elijah—that the Lord is 'not in the earthquake' but 'in the still small voice'!"

At this point, Scaurus's handwriting became irregular and sometimes not easy to read. "I have been interrupted again," he said. "This time, it was Flaccus. Now I take up my pen positively for the last time, wondering why I take it up, and why I ramble on in this maundering fashion. I think it is because I feel as though you and I were dreaming together, and I am loth to leave off. There is no one else in the world with whom I can thus dream in partnership. This shall really be my last dreaming.

"Do not be vexed with me, Quintus, for charging Flaccus *not* to send you a copy of this little book. He told me that for some time past you had been interested in these subjects, and that, if he could find another copy, he intended to forward it to you. The rascal added something about 'mere literary interest.' I suspect him of Christian tendencies. Your recent letters have reassured me. But I cannot help feeling that there have been moments with you, as with me, when the 'interest' was more than 'merely literary.' I had half thought of sending you my copy. But I shall not. The subject is too fascinating—like chess; and, like chess, it leads to nothing. I was glad to hear—in your last letter, I think—that you were now giving your mind to practical affairs. If you decide on the army at once, there is likely to be work soon in Illyria.

"Things also look cloudy, not black yet but cloudy, in Syria. In spite of the thrashing they got from the late Emperor, these Jews have not yet learned their lesson. They are as stubborn and obstinate as Hannibal made us out to be:—

> '*Gens quae cremato fortis ab Ilio*
> *Jactata Tuscis aequoribus sacra*
> *Natosque maturosque patres*
> *Pertulit Ausonias ad urbes,*
> *Duris ut ilex tonsa bipennibus*
> *Nigrae feraci frondis in Algido*
> *Per damna, per caedes, ab ipso*
> *Ducit opes animumque ferro.*'

"How every word of this would suit the Jews! I mean in their past history. According to my news (from a friend of Rufus the new Governor) it may suit their future, too; and we may have to take Jerusalem again. Then—to quote Isaiah and Horace in one—there will be another 'lopping of the boughs' in the future. But I mean their past. I wonder whether you understand what I am dreaming of. Probably not, and it is not worth explaining. Nor indeed am I well enough to explain clearly and briefly. I have been going in too much for books of late, and feel at this moment (to quote an old friend) 'dead from the waist down.' However—as I am not going to write about these Jews again—I will scribble my last thoughts to the end.

"How strange it would have been, then, my dearest Quintus, if these Jews—I mean the Jewish Jews not the Christian Jews—how strange, I say, it would have been, looked at as a poem, if these fellows had fulfilled Hannibal's prophecy. They went some way towards it. Though their Ilium has been twice burned they are still alive, numerous, and active. Their 'ilex' has had 'pruning' enough, heaven knows, from the Roman axe of late, and from the Assyrian and Babylonian axes in days gone by. But they want pruning still. Witness a score of eastern cities, where they have lately been massacring myriads of Greeks—not, I own, without having seen myriads of their countrymen massacred first.

"Their disadvantage has been that they have never made a new start as Æneas did, so as to turn old Troy into new Rome. Æneas could take his gods with him. The Jews could not. The only place where they have done anything of the kind is Alexandria. There they have an imitation temple—not a rival temple of course, but an imitation—and there they are at their best. But elsewhere the stubborn creatures—from Gaul to Euphrates—recognise no home or sacred ground except in a little corner of Syria. Providence has done its best to detach them from this servitude by using Titus to destroy their temple a second time, and by leaving their sacred utensils no existence except upon Titus's arch. But still they are servants of the *genius loci*, so to speak. As they cannot serve the temple, they serve the ground on which it stands and the traditions that have collected round it.

"The Christian Jews have immense advantages. They are

like the Trojan Romans. The Christians have left their Troy (that is to say, carnal Jerusalem) in order to dwell in Rome (that is to say, heavenly Jerusalem) the city of truth, the city of justice, the city of freedom and universal brotherhood. Their sacred fire is the Holy Spirit. Their sacred vessels are human beings. Every great city in Asia contains their 'holy things.' To celebrate their feast on the body and blood of their Saviour, a table of pine wood, a platter, and a mug, supply them with all they need! A little bread, and wine mingled with water, have taken the place of Solomon's hecatombs! Surely this is the very perfection of religious simplicity—an ambassador in a plain Roman toga amid the courtiers of a Ptolemy!

"Again, when we Romans call on Jupiter, offering our costliest white oxen, who supposes that Jupiter descends? But when these Christians meet, without a denarius in their pockets, three in a room, they tell you that Christ is with them. What is more, many of them believe it! What is most, some of them act as though they believed it! I have called their city a city of dreams, and I repeat it. But, mark you, a city of dreams has one great advantage over a city of bricks or stone. You can smash the latter. But neither Nero, nor Trajan, has been able to smash the former; and I begin to doubt whether it could be smashed by Hadrian, if he tried. At the present rate, I should not be surprised if, in the next hundred years, the empire from the Euphrates to Britain were dotted with colonies of Christ.

"'Let arms of war give place to the gown of peace!' So sang the lawyer of Arpinum when he tried his hand at poetry. He was better advised, in his lawyer's gown, when he confessed 'Laws are silent among arms.' But there is a third power more powerful than either laws or arms. You won't believe me when I tell you its name. It is 'dreams.' Yes, 'Among dreams,' says Scaurus—and he knows, having been himself a dreamer, in his day, besides being a bit of a soldier and a good deal of a looker on—'Among dreams, arms are *vain.*' I don't say they are '*silent.*' That is their contemptible feature—they are *not* ' silent.' But they are impotent. Mars against dreams may make what fuss and bustle he pleases, clash, clang, thunder, like the brazen wheels of Salmoneus. But his thundering will effect nothing. Nor will his steel. '*Frustra diverberet umbras.*'

"When I say 'dreams,' do not take me to mean that the personality of a great prophet is a 'dream.' But the notion that an empire can be spun out of it, or built on it, seems to me a dream. Yet there is something attractive in it—I mean in the conception of a soul like a vast magnet, attracting and magnetizing a group of souls, of which each in turn becomes a new magnet, magnetizing a group of its own, and so on, and so on, till the whole empire (or family) of souls is bound together by this magnetic law. Yes, 'law' one may call it, not a magical incantation, but a natural law, the law of the spiritual magnet. It is all very strange. Yet, given the personality, it is possible.

"For it all comes to this, a personality—nothing more. There is nothing new in what the Christians call their Testament or Covenant—nothing new at all, from the Jewish point of view, except that the new Jews have cast aside a great deal of the Covenant of the old Jews. I sometimes think the Christian leader was really what Socrates calls himself, a 'cosmian' or 'cosmopolite,' going back, behind the law of Moses, to a beginning of things before unclean food was Levitically forbidden and before free divorce was Levitically sanctioned. His two fundamental rules are the same, both for Jews and for Christians, 'Love God,' 'Love man.'

"The difference is, that to the Christians (so they assert) Christ has introduced a new kind of love, a new power of love. He has not only breathed it into his disciples but also given them (they say) the power of breathing it into others. The question is, Have they this power? I am obliged to admit— from what I hear—that a good many of them appear to me to have it. This is the real miracle. This, if true, is sunlight. All the so-called miracles of their books, even if true, are the merest, palest moonlight compared with this.

"This dreamer seems to me to have planned an imperial peace throughout his cosmopolis, to be brought about, not by threats based on the power of inflicting death, not by edicts on stone backed by punishments with steel, but by means of a spirit that is to creep into our hearts, dethrone our intellects, drag us in triumph behind his chariot wheels, making us fanatically happy when we are in love with him—and with all the weak, the foolish, the suffering, and the oppressed—and making us unreasonably unhappy, foolishly sad and sick at heart, when we resist a blind affection for others and when we consult our own interests and our own pleasures, following the path of prudent wisdom.

"In one respect, this work of John's has proved me a false prophet. I prophesied that East and West could not unite in one religion. They *have* united—on paper, and in theory—in this little book. But I also said that, if they did unite, their offspring would be a portent. To that I adhere. If John's form of the Christian superstition were to overspread the world, do you seriously suppose that it would remain in his form? No, it is impossible but that the spiritual will be despiritualised. The superstition of pure spirit will probably become a superstition of unmixed matter. The life will be narrowed to the Body and the Blood. The Body and the Blood will be narrowed down still further to the Bread and the Wine. Then their hyperbolical self-sacrifice will give way to hyperbolical malignity. How these Christians will, in due time, hate one another! How they will wall in, and imprison, the Spirit that bloweth whither it listeth! How they will war against one another for their Prince of Peace! How they will philosophize and hair-split about the Father and the Son, tearing one another in pieces for the unity of the one God! And yet, and yet, even if all my prophecies of the worst come to pass, might not a Christian philosopher of those far-off days say that the 'worst is often the corruption of the best,' and that his Prophet had discovered a 'best,' buried for a time beneath all this rubbish and litter, but destined to emerge and grow into the tree of a great spiritual empire? It may be so. I do not deny that there may be such a 'best.' But it is not for me.

"I give it up. The problem of the Sphinx is too hard for my brains. Perhaps Destiny knows its own mind, and it may be a good mind—not my mind, but perhaps an infinitely better and wiser. Perhaps this Christian superstition is intended to found an empire after the Spirit, an empire of 'the Son of man,' like, but unlike, the empires of Egypt, Babylon, Greece, Rome. Daniel dreamed this for Jewish Jews. It may come true for Christian Jews. If it should come, what a tyranny it will be—for those, at least, who are tyrants at heart! The yoke of the Imperium Romanum will be nothing to the yoke of the Imperium Romanochristianum. We Romans despotize over bodies: the Roman Christians will despotize over souls. 'Debellare superbos' is only one of our arts. 'Pacis imponere mores' is a second. 'Parcere subjectis' is a third. These Roman Christians will know how to crush, but not how to spare. What saints it will create—for the spiritual! What devils—for the carnal! And which will win in the end, saint or devil? I incline, with oscillation, to the saint. But I am sick and tired of inclinations and oscillations; I want to *know*. I *know* that the sun shines. I want to *know*—just at this moment I feel very near knowing, nearer than I ever have been in my whole life—that the world has been made all of a piece, and is being shaped by the Maker to one end, and that, the best.

"O, my dear Silanus, I am weary of these books. I must go out into the fresh air and see the sun. Books, books, books! I agree with Epictetus, who thinks that Chrysippus wrote some two hundred too many. I agree with John, too, who says, in effect, that not all the pens and paper in the world could draw the portrait of his master—or rather his friend, for 'friend,' not 'servant,' is the title at the end of the book. That reminds me, by the way, of a beautiful thought in this gospel—I mean that the author is 'the disciple whom Jesus loved'! As much as to say, 'Do you want to know Jesus? Then get a *friend* of his—some one *whom Jesus loved*—to introduce you. There is no other way. Not an impartial biographer—he is of no use—but a *friend*.' And I think he means to hint, at the close of his little book, that there always will be, 'tarrying,' till Jesus comes again, a 'disciple whom Jesus loved,' to represent him to the world.

"That is most true. That is real insight, the insight of an artist and a prophet in one. I can forgive John almost all his faults—ambiguities, artificialities, statements of non-fact as fact, I can condone them all as orientalisms or Alexandrian Judaisms—for the sake of this one truth, that we cannot know the greatest of the departed great, save through a human being that has loved him and has been loved by him. This is the thought with which John ends and with which I will end. I wish to part friends with him. Indeed at this moment, for his sake, I could almost call myself an amateur Christian. But then I pull myself together and recognise that it only proves what I have said to you a score of times, and now repeat for the last time, that whereas we Romans are only coarse, clumsy, brutal Samnites, these Christians are the wiliest, kindest, and gentlest of retiarii.

"And that makes me think of old Hermas. You remember I told you of our last interview. It comes back to me while I am finishing this last dream. I always felt there was more in his face than I could understand. Now, after reading this gospel, I seem, just at this moment, to understand his face for the first time, quite well. The old man had in him the love of 'the disciple whom Jesus loved.' It had been breathed into his being. This it was that half fascinated me, shining out of his eyes as he silently left the room on that afternoon—to me unforgettable—when I dismissed him. What if I had not dismissed him? What if——."

These words were the last of a column. They were the last that Scaurus was ever to write. The next column was blank. At first I thought he had been again interrupted and had forgotten to finish the letter. But then I recollected with alarm that, quite contrary to custom, the cover had not been directed in his handwriting. I had thrown it hastily aside on the previous evening. Now I searched for it and my alarm was speedily justified. Inside was a short and hurried note from Marullus saying that my dear old friend had been struck suddenly with paralysis in the act of writing to me. A messenger (said Marullus) who happened to be at that moment waiting to carry Scaurus's letter, would carry at the same time Marullus's note. On the following day, whatever might happen, he would send a second letter by a special messenger.

It was now drawing towards evening. I hastened out to ascertain how soon a vessel, available for my purpose, would be leaving Nicopolis. Finding that I could start on the following day at noon, I determined not to wait for Marullus's second letter but to make preparations for an immediate return.

CHAPTER XXXV

CLEMENS ON THE SACRIFICE OF CHRIST

SCAURUS, and not the fourth gospel, nor any other book, person, or thing, was uppermost in my mind, when, late in the evening, I hurried to the house of Justus to keep my engagement with Clemens. Two or three hours ago, I had been longing for this interview. Now I would willingly have avoided it. I seemed to see my old friend speechless on his bed in Tusculum, saying to me with his eyes, "Do not desert me. Do not go over to the enemy." Not till later did I feel that Scaurus could not have called Clemens "enemy."

"I am tired of books"—so Scaurus had written. So was I, quite tired. I wanted to think, not talk; or, if to talk, to talk about Scaurus, not about gospels or books of any sort. "How glad should I be to exchange this interview for five minutes' chat with old Marullus!"—that was my thought when I found myself, more than an hour after sunset, sitting face to face with Clemens.

I returned him the book—so precious to me yesterday—with some words of formal thanks. What should I say next? About the one subject that filled all my thoughts I felt no desire to talk to a stranger—"yes" (I said to myself) "a stranger to Scaurus, though a friend, a real friend, to me." Yet something had to be said. I began by excusing myself, at an absurd length, for being late. Clemens acknowledged the excuse with a slight inclination of the head. His face was questioning me, and his eyes were reading me. But he left it to me to speak, and to open our interview if I desired one.

Then I blundered out some absurd stuff—in the way of humour!—about the possibility that he might suppose me to have forgotten my engagement.

Clemens did not seem in the least ruffled or even surprised. After a pause, in which the questioning look gave place to one of sympathy, he said, very slowly and gently, "No, my dear friend, I could not suppose that. Nor could you think that I could suppose that. Some trouble, I perceive, has befallen you. You felt bound to keep your engagement with me, and you have done so. You did right. But you will not do right if you stay longer, out of courtesy to me, when your conscience tells you that it would be better for you to be alone."

When I entered the room, I had distinctly preferred to be alone. Even now, I so far desired solitude that I murmured some words of thanks for his consideration, and rose to go. But something kept me standing irresolute. I do not know what it was at first. Certainly it was not any thought about the new gospel. Perhaps it was my new friend's directness, truthfulness and insight, in discerning and brushing aside my pretence, and his kind and courteous way of forgiving it, that made me suddenly feel, "This is a man that Scaurus would have liked to know. This is a man that Scaurus would like me to know. He tells me to go if I feel that it will be 'better' for me to be alone. But will it be 'better'?"

It may have been this that checked my going. I do not know for certain. But I do know what decided me to stay. I suddenly saw Scaurus. He was in the library at Tusculum, with his back to me, at his writing-table, but not writing, half risen from his seat, and looking towards the door, which was slowly closing. As it closed, he turned and looked round at me, with such a sadness as I had never seen on his face except once or twice, when I had gone wrong and he was striving to lead me right. I knew what he meant, as well as if he had said the words aloud, "Hermas is gone, and I shall repent it through my life. Do not let your Hermas go!" I resumed my seat and tried to collect my thoughts.

It seemed to me now only right and natural that I should

Chapter 35] ON THE SACRIFICE OF CHRIST 349

tell Clemens of Scaurus's illness and of my intention to leave Nicopolis on the morrow. He took my departure as a matter of course. Could he be of service, he asked, in making arrangements for my sailing? I assured him that everything had been done that was needful for that day. Then I told him how Scaurus had urged me to join Epictetus's classes, and that he wished me afterwards to join the army. Finding him interested and sympathetic, I gave him an account of my old friend's life, his affection for me, his love of research, his literary pursuits, and his study of Jewish as well as Greek literature, not omitting his early reading of the gospels, nor forgetting to tell him about old Hermas the Christian, his librarian. He listened with more and more attention. "I am not surprised," he said, "that you love so good a friend and so honest a man."

Presently I said, "I wonder whether it would be still possible and right for me to join the army, if——" and there I stopped. "Dear friend," said he, "if that unmentioned thing were to come to pass, trust me that nothing would be possible or right for you against which your conscience cried out, and nothing wrong that your conscience permitted. Some might condemn your decision—whether to join the army or not to join. But you would not be bound by their condemnation. Your conscience would receive guidance. Those who follow on that unmentioned path do not follow with an 'if.' Should that path be taken, it would be, not on conditions, but because of a friendly constraint. Let us not speak of that now. Tell me more about your friend." "I have his letter here," said I, "and would read it if you cared to hear it. But it deals freely, very freely, with the gospels. Once, at least, I think my old friend is unfair to them. It would perhaps pain you." "It would not pain but please me," said he. "I always like to hear honest, able, and educated men speak their minds freely about our Christian writings. The pity of it is, that we have hitherto had few such critics. If we had had them when the gospels were first written, perhaps they would have contained fewer things that may in after times cause some of the faithful to stumble."

So I began to read Scaurus's letter to him. At first I omitted portions here and there, either because they were personal, or because they might hurt the feelings of a Christian. Presently, halting in the middle of a bitter saying, I finished the sentence in my own way—somewhat awkwardly. Clemens smiled. "Pardon me," said he, "for interrupting you. I am not a master of styles. Yet, if I mistake not, those last words did not come from Æmilius Scaurus. If I am wrong, forgive me. But if I am right in thinking that you altered something to spare my feelings, then let me assure you again that it would trouble me that you should do this, even though the criticism came from the bitterest enemy of the Christians. As it is, I have learned already to esteem your friend as a genuine lover of truth, and one from whom I have even now learned some things and hope to learn more. The more you will allow me to learn (without giving pain to yourself) the better shall I be pleased." "Well then," said I, "we will talk about the letter afterwards. For the present, I will read on steadily without omitting a single word, unless you stop me." And so I did. Clemens listened intently, without stopping me, only he now and then, especially towards the end, expressed assent or interest, or sympathy, by a slight movement or inarticulate murmur; till we came to the last words, the uncompleted sentence, suggesting what might have happened on one memorable afternoon, if he had not dismissed a "disciple whom Jesus loved." This I did not read, but I placed the letter before him. "These," said I, "were his last words, the very last."

He read them, and turned away his face. I thought, and rightly, that he was feeling with me. But I am sure now that he was also praying for me, and for Scaurus too. For a time we sat in silence. I was the first to break it, expressing my sorrow that the story of the Syrophœnician woman should have led Scaurus to form what seemed to me a wrong conception of Christ. "But you see," replied Clemens, "he revolted from that wrong conception, or was ready to revolt from it, at the last moment of all. And I agree with you that, if he had approached that story with the preparation that Paul gave you, he would have regarded it as you did. I am sure Christ was never cruel to anyone. If He really uttered those seemingly cruel words

Chapter 35] ON THE SACRIFICE OF CHRIST 351

to that sorrowful woman, He was cruel in word, only that He might be the more kind and the more helpful in deed. He intended this gospel to be preached to all the world, though He waited for the Father to teach Him the time and the manner of the preaching to the Gentiles."

"Is there anything in John's gospel," said I, "that resembles this story?" "There is a dialogue," he replied, "between Christ and a Samaritan woman, who is described as living in sin, just as you have suggested concerning the Syrophœnician. And Christ chides her, but with great gentleness, and finally reveals Himself to her as Messiah. It has occurred to me that this is one of the many instances where John steps in to remove a misunderstanding liable to be caused by some passage in Mark, which Luke omits."

Then he added, "I will talk with you, if you please, about the letter or the gospel or anything else, if you really desire it. But if you would wish to be alone with your own thoughts (as you well might wish), do not, I beseech you, stay longer. You have laid me under a debt by introducing me to a genuine lover of truth on whom the Light of the World has dawned, even though it may not be given to him to see the full day. May he find peace!"

I was quite willing to stay now. "Do you agree with Scaurus," said I, "that John alludes in parts of his gospel to the teaching of Epictetus?" "I feel sure," replied Clemens, "that John alludes to the doctrine of the Stoics and Cynics. Now Epictetus has been, for some years past, most widely known among all classes, rich, poor—yes, and slaves, too—as the representative of the Cynic doctrine. So that your friend seems to me likely to be right." "Scaurus," said I, "mentions self-knowledge and God-knowledge as if the former were inculcated by Epictetus, the latter by John, in opposition. Is that so, in your opinion?" "Not quite," said he, "but nearly so. All the Stoics lay stress, as you know, on self-knowledge. Epictetus, perhaps more than most, teaches men to look for God within themselves. Luke also—alone of the evangelists—has one tradition of this kind, 'The kingdom of God is within you.' John, feeling that many were prevented thereby from looking for God out of themselves, laid stress on the latter. That is to say, John paraphrased Christ's teaching about 'the Father in heaven' in such a form that it should be more familiar to the Greeks, urging them to 'know God.' So Paul is said by Luke to have taken as his text on the Areopagus an inscription TO THE UNKNOWN GOD; and he tried to teach the philosophers that God could be 'known.' But neither Paul nor John would deny that self-knowledge, and the consciousness of our own sins, and the sense of our own burdens, are necessary if we are to have our burdens lightened, our sins forgiven, and our souls brought into the light of the glory of the knowledge of God."

"And as to the 'troubling' of Christ," said I, "mentioned thrice in the fourth gospel, do you agree with Scaurus that there, too, the author is alluding to Epictetus?" "I do indeed," said he. "I did so from the first moment when I read the new gospel. Man is born to trouble as the sparks fly upward. We are born to be lifted up to heaven by troubles. But trouble of soul does not mean confusion or turbidness of soul. Trouble is on the surface, peace is beneath, peace that is deeper than the deepest of depths. In the world, says the Saviour, we shall have tribulation, and tribulation brings trouble with it. But He bids us be of good cheer amidst and beneath all our trouble, because He has overcome the world. Perhaps, however, John emphasizes this doctrine of 'trouble,' not out of hostility to the Cynic philosophy, but rather out of a friendly feeling to it, as much as to say, 'This notion of yours, that you must avoid "trouble," is the weak point in your teaching. It tends to lower you to the level of the Epicureans. And it gives you a false and unworthy notion of God, who is our Father, and who bears the troubles of His children'."

From that we passed to other matters, most of which I shall omit—details about the fourth gospel, about its authorship and about Scaurus's view, that it blended history with allegory. On some of these he thought that Scaurus might be correct. But he was doubtful as to the possibility of explaining, as Scaurus had suggested, the different order in which the evangelists place the purification of the Temple. "For," said he, "it seems to me scarcely possible that, within the time from

Tiberius to Trajan, an evangelist should be led to change the order of such an event simply because of its order in some one book—because it was placed at what Gentiles might take to be the beginning (being really the end) of a Hebrew gospel." At the same time Clemens admitted that there was an astonishing difference of opinion among Christians as to the period of Christ's preaching, "and," said he, "instead of quoting statements or referring to historical facts, they often quote prophecies, or argue from the fitness of things. It is all very unsatisfactory."

Of this I afterwards had experience. For, after I had become a Christian, I found that some, even though they received the gospel of John, argued that Christ could only have preached for one year—because Isaiah contains the words, "to preach the acceptable year of the Lord"! On the other hand, the young Irenæus, bitterly attacking this view, maintained that Christ must have preached till His fortieth or fiftieth year! As I have said above, I have actually heard him supporting this extraordinary supposition by appealing to the authority of the elders that had seen John!

Clemens therefore admitted that he could not feel certain as to the order of events in John's gospel. It might be, he said, that two events, mentioned in different parts of the gospel as taking place at, or before, a feast, and apparently at, or before, different feasts, might really have taken place at, or before, the same feast. Among several details in which he agreed with Scaurus, one was the narrative of the Walking on the Water. Concerning this he said that, according to John, the walking was not really *on* the water, any more than a city is really "*on* a sea" when it is said to lie "*on* the Ægean" or "*on* the Hadriatic." He also agreed with Scaurus as to the story about Peter plunging into the water to come to Christ, which might (he thought) explain Matthew's story, according to which Christ first walked on the water, and then Peter attempted to walk on it towards the Lord, but failed. Both these, he thought, might be metaphorical.

As regards what Scaurus had said concerning the ambiguity of many words and phrases in the fourth gospel, Clemens admitted it. "But," said he, "my conviction is that the writer did not use them thus for the mere purpose of being ambiguous, like the oracle 'Aio te, Æacida.' I do not deny that he plays upon words, but so does Isaiah. He also repeats and varies phrases, but so do all the prophecies and the Psalms. Similarly he is often dark and obscure. But are there not obscurities also in Æschylus, and Pindar, and in the deepest thoughts of Plato? And whence do these arise? Not surely from a desire to be ambiguous, but from the lawful feeling of a great poet, prompted to use strange language, and sometimes dark language, that is put into his mind to express strange and dark thoughts. So it is with John, at least in my judgment. And as to other parts, which seem artificial—as, for example, when he repeats things twice or thrice in a kind of refrain—I should plead in the same way that a poet, even when most inspired, follows rules. Æschylus and Pindar do not break the laws of Greek metre. Well, Jewish tradition also has rules of its own, quite different from ours, and I believe John observes them."

Then he referred to John's use of the word "logos." Scaurus had described John as leading on his readers from *logos* to *pathos*. Clemens admitted that this was true if *pathos* meant the affections and included that one affection in particular which we call "love." And he justified John's course. "For," said he, "if the Logos is related to God as word is to thought, must we not say that 'word' should include every expression of thought, and that the perfect Logos must be the expression of the perfect thought? And what thought can be more perfect than that which Scaurus himself suggests, in his similitude of a magnet attracting all things to itself and causing each attracted object to attract others, so that the multitudinous world is made one harmony? And in the region of the affections, what is this but the highest kind of love, as your friend himself testifies, binding men together in families, cities, nations, and destined, in the end, to unite all as citizens of the city of the universe, or children in the family of God?"

Then Clemens added, without any questioning from me,

that he entirely concurred with Scaurus in his feeling that the miracles or signs of Christ, however far they might be literally true, would not be so convincing a proof of His greatness as the power of His Spirit to infuse peace and power, yes, and wisdom, and harmony of thought, into the minds of those who received Him. "I do not mean to assert," said he, "that all who receive Christ remain steadfast in Him. Many have fallen away through subtle temptations of the world and the flesh; some few, under persecution and the open cruelty of the devil. But as to these last I have noted this. Strong men have fallen while boasting 'We can endure every torture.' Weak women have stood fast confessing 'We can do nothing. Our strength is in the Lord. Our Saviour will stand fast for us.' Yes, that has been the great miracle, to see slaves changed to nobles, peasants and clowns to orators, fools become wise, and human beasts, not worthy to be called men—ape-like and wolf-like creatures—transmuted into citizens of the kingdom of God.

"And that reminds me of what I specially admired in your friend—the sagacity with which he penetrated to the root of the matter, declaring that our religion is, in reality, no religion at all (not at least what augurs or priests would call a religion) but only union with a personality, a Lord and Saviour and Friend, who is in us and in whom we are, 'a very present help in trouble.' We have no system of sacrifices. For He is our sacrifice offered up once visibly on the cross, and offering Himself up invisibly and continually in the hearts of His faithful disciples. We have no code of laws. For He is our law, uttered by Himself once to the ears of the disciples in the two commandments 'Love God' and 'Love thy neighbour,' when He shewed them how to make all men 'neighbours'; and now He utters the same law to our hearts, every moment of our lives, giving us a strong desire to do that which is best for our 'neighbours,' and helping us to see what is best, and, seeing it, to do it."

When Clemens said, "He is our sacrifice," I thought of Paul's words, "Christ our Passover is sacrificed for us," and of "the blood of sprinkling" about which Scaurus had written.

And this led me to ask concerning that other tradition which (Scaurus had told me) was written in the fourth gospel alone, about blood and water issuing from Christ's side.

"That," said Clemens, "was the only passage in your friend's letter where I was strongly moved to ask you to stop reading that we might talk of it at once. His view was new to me. Yet I confess I had always found it difficult to explain how the writer could call on himself to testify to what he himself had asserted. If Æmilius Scaurus should prove right, that difficulty of mine would be removed. Moreover I cannot but admit that John, or any other disciple, would probably have been prevented by the soldiers from approaching to the cross close enough to distinguish the water from the blood flowing from His side. Yet it came on me as a shock to believe that this particular narrative—to which I attach great importance—was based on a vision. Now the shock is somewhat softened. I have been thinking over your friend's arguments. He is quite right in saying that in John's epistle, which may be called an epilogue to his gospel, the words 'He knoweth,' as expressed in this particular emphatic phrase, would mean 'Jesus knoweth.' The meaning may be the same here. Nevertheless, even if it is so, and even if the narrative describes a vision, I should still feel as certain as ever that this vision expressed the real eternal truth."

"What do you mean," I said, "by eternal truth?" "I mean this," replied Clemens, "that the sacrifice of Christ on the cross appears to me foreordained from eternity and destined to last to eternity, as the symbol of the fundamental law of the universe, what Scaurus calls the Law of the Magnet. Call it a dream, if you please. Then such is my dream. But I act on it, or try to act on it, as a reality. The Father gives His life to men in giving His Son to them. The life, says the scripture, is the blood. Some of our brethren would not scruple to say 'God gives His blood to men.' I would rather say God has been giving of His life to men from the time when man was first created—not only as a Father and a Mother, but also as a Servant, serving His servants, nursing His children, 'washing their feet' (so to speak) as a nurse does, and as Christ did. There are two spiritual realities, or, if you like, two metaphors, to express this spiritual reality. One is, that life or blood is to be infused, like new blood, into our veins. The other is, that in this life, or life-blood, we are also to bathe ourselves, that we may be born again. I know that this will seem to you and to many others an exaggerated, or (as I have heard it called) an 'unsavoury and distasteful similitude.' But these protests are outweighed, in my mind, by the faith and feeling of multitudes of simple devout Christians of the deepest and purest insight. One of these, a woman—the most inspired of all women known to me with holy wisdom—continually speaks of bathing herself in the blood of Christ crucified; and so do some of our most inspired poets. You have spoken to me of 'the constraining love of Christ.' One of our poets—a man experienced in troubles and knowing only too well what it is to feel forsaken of God—describes it thus in the person of Christ:—

> *Mine is an unchanging love,*
> *Higher than the heights above,*
> *Deeper than the depths beneath,*
> *Free and faithful, strong as death.*

Do not these words seem to you to come from the heart? Are they not heart-realities? Yet they are metaphors. Well, this same poet speaks of 'seeing by faith' the 'stream' supplied by Christ's 'flowing wounds.' Are such visions, or metaphors, or heart-realities, lightly to be discarded? Speaking for myself, I cannot give up this heart-fact—if I may so call it—for fact it is to me, whether seen by the material or by the spiritual eye. Some may think it to be spiritually false. For them it must be (in efficacy) false, even if it were historically true. For me it is true."

He checked himself, and then continued, "Do not suppose, dear brother and fellow-seeker after truth, that I expect all others to see the truth in the same form in which I see it. Only I should hope to induce them to see the same truth in *some* form. See here these words"—and he took up a scroll and shewed them to me—"'Every wise man is a ransom for the bad.' Do they remind you of anything?" "Yes," said

I, "they are like the saying in Mark and Matthew, 'The Son of man came to give his soul a ransom for many.' Luke omits those words." "He does," said Clemens. "Luke has 'I am among you as one that serveth.' John combines the two views. For first he represents Jesus as girt with a napkin like a servant pouring forth water in a basin and washing the feet of the disciples; and then he represents Him as pouring forth His blood and water for their souls."

Then Clemens told me that the words " Every wise man is a ransom for the bad " were written by Philo of Alexandria, who, though a Jew, was also a philosopher, and he shewed me a similar passage in the same writer, to the effect that the good and worthy and wise are both the physicians and the ransoms of every community in which they exist. Then he took up Ezekiel and read to me the vision of the dry bones in the valley, and how they come together into living bodies, being quickened by the breath of the Lord. Next he turned to Greek literature, touching on the old allegory of Amphion, whose music was so sweet that the very stones were constrained by it to come together in unity building up the walls of a great city.

"Should we be wrong," said Clemens, " in saying that all these metaphors (to which others might be added) from various nations and literatures—about 'harmony,' and 'service,' and 'ransom,' and 'blood,' and 'breath'—point to one deep truth, not exaggerated by Philo, that the less are purified by the greater, and that the greater are intended to sacrifice their independence and to come together with the less, in order to create cities and nations, which are the larger families that lead men towards the Fatherhood of God ? No doubt, the greater are also purified by the less. Every community is built up and bound together by the self-sacrifice of all. And this binding together implies a purification of all, a cutting away of excessive protuberances, a purging away of selfish, isolating, schism-making qualities, so that each soul may take its place in the wall of the City of Concord. But still, as a rule, the less are purified by the greater; the most selfish by the least selfish ; families by the father and the mother ; peoples by their true princes, priests, and prophets. Prince, priest, prophet, each according to his several gift, washes the feet of his inferiors, and spends his life to increase and ennoble theirs. Looking back to our childhood, do we not recognise this, as a matter of our own experience? How then can we call God Father, and yet refuse to believe that He may be as loving as a human father, and that God's children may be purified by God Himself, giving His own blood in the blood of His Son as a ransom for the sinful souls of men?"

As he said these words, he stood up, extending his hand. "I have allowed myself," he said, "to keep you too long, when you have many things to do. Once or twice, intending to check myself, I have broken loose again. I will not a third time. Only this word, this one additional word. Believe me, Æmilius Scaurus was right, in saying 'The religion of the Christians is a person.' But your friend went on to say '*and nothing more.*' I should prefer to say the same thing differently. ' Our religion is a person—*and nothing less.*'"

CHAPTER XXXVI

SILANUS BECOMES A CHRISTIAN

IT was very late, but I was unwilling to say farewell. During the last two or three hours, Clemens had in some strange way so associated himself with my thoughts of Scaurus that I now began to feel as though, in parting from my new friend, I should be parting from the old one—whose living self I should perhaps not see again in Tusculum and whose likeness I was leaving in Nicopolis. But Clemens would not resume his seat. Quoting Scaurus's words with a kindly smile, "It takes a great deal," he said, "to make you 'tired of books'." "Perhaps my old friend would not have been tired," I replied, "if he had had you as his interpreter. I wish he could have been present with us to-night." "I shall always think of him as a friend," said Clemens, "for your sake, for his own sake, and for truth's sake."

Then he asked me at what hour I was to set sail, to-morrow, "or rather," said he, "to-day, for it is long past midnight." "About noon," I replied. "Long before noon," said he, "I must be at some distance from Nicopolis on a visit to some sick folk. But I expect to be returning, by way of the wood where we first conversed together, just in time to catch sight of your vessel before it disappears round the cape. So you must think of me then as wishing you over again from a distance the good things that I now wish you face to face." "When we last parted," said I, as we clasped hands at the open door, "you wished me peace. Wish it me again." "May peace," he said, "be multiplied to you!" Then, drawing me gently towards himself, after standing for a moment as though unable to speak, "that peace," he said, "which passes understanding!"

When I returned to my lodging I found a messenger awaiting me with a note from Marullus. Scaurus was still living, though unconscious. The doctors thought it possible, though not probable, that he might recover for a short time. "I fear," said Marullus, "that, by the time you receive these lines, my dear patron will be no more. If you wish to come, in the slight hope of seeing him, you will do well to come at once." I was prepared for this, so that it made no difference in my arrangements. These were nearly completed except for writing letters of farewell to friends in Nicopolis.

The sun was well above the horizon before I began the letter that I had reserved for the last—my farewell to Epictetus. To several acquaintances I had been scribbling away, fluently enough. Nor had I been at a loss for what to say to the one or two more intimate friends to whose kindness I was indebted. But, all the time, there had been in my mind an undercurrent of anxious questioning as to what I should say to the man to whom I owed most. Should I explain? Should I confess? Should I distinguish between what I had received from him for which I was his debtor, and what I had not been able to receive so that I could not call myself indebted? To what end? Whatever might happen in the future, I could never cease to be grateful to him for having raised me to a higher sense of a life above the level of the Beast, and for stimulating me to follow and revere the Man. What though a new ideal of the Man had been presented to me? Did that make me less Epictetus's debtor? Nay, did it not possibly increase my debt, because, but for him, I might not have taken—if ever I should be proved to have taken—the path that led towards a higher and nobler goal?

I wrote, tore up, re-wrote, corrected, re-corrected, and again re-wrote. There was a want of directness in all my attempts, and they all ended in tearing up. At last I said, "I will try to write as my Master himself would have written." That made my letter of the briefest. After explaining my sudden departure, and thanking him for his teaching, "I am your debtor," I wrote, "and always shall be." I was on the point of adding, "If ever I possess myself, I shall owe myself to you." But the words struck me as familiar. Then I remembered something like them in the Epistle to Philemon : "I say not unto thee how that thou owest to me even thine own self." Could I say with strict Epictetian truth that I owed to Epictetus as much as Philemon owed to Paul? I re-wrote it thus : "If ever I possess myself I shall in large measure owe myself to you." That had the disadvantage of being a little longer, but the advantage of being quite true. Sealing the letter that I might not be tempted to alter it again, I threw myself down for two or three hours of rest.

A little before noon my servant roused me. All was ready, and we went down at once to the quay. Besides the usual bustle—sailors, fishermen, merchants, passengers mostly in a hurry—there was some dispute (I know not what, but I think it was among the fishermen). This added to the confusion. Not many blows were interchanged, but there was no lack of threats, imprecations, scurrilous jests, and obscene abuse. As I was making my way through the crowd, some one touched me on the shoulder. It was my Epicurean friend, Apronius Rufus, whom I had last seen in the little village of Lycus, scattering nuts and figs to make the schoolboys scramble. I had caught sight of him, a minute or two before, lounging in a corner and looking on at the quarrelsome crowd ; but being in no mood for his jests I had turned aside in the vain hope that he would not see me. As soon as he overtook me, he began in his usual fashion, "What brings you here at this hour, most serious Cynic ? A truant humour, I fear. For it is lecture time, or at all events not much past : and Epictetus gives long lessons. Yet no. You are no truant. Truants don't look so serious. You have come here as a philosopher, to see life as it is, and to set up as a heretic. You come from books to things ; from ideals to facts. Good! Now begin to learn! Look at these bipeds! Look, and listen! Up above, in your school-room, they were 'sons of God,' were they not! Look, then, at that son of God hitting his brother son of God in the eye!

Listen to those two daughters of God and their harmonious antiphon!"

I was vexed, but let him talk on, as being the best means of getting myself free from him without explanation; and he, following close behind me, kept pouring his jests into my ear, till, I suppose, he got a clearer view of my face. For he suddenly checked himself, saying, "But, my dear Silanus, pardon me if something is really wrong. You would not, I am sure, let my idle talk pain you. Your servant is here with baggage. I fear some bad news is taking you from Nicopolis." Then I briefly explained.

He had some slight acquaintance with Scaurus and was instantly and sincerely apologetic. "I was a fool," said he, "not to have noticed that something was amiss. Really I am grieved. And Scaurus, too! That fine old soldier! Often have I heard my father speak of his splendid service in Moesia. Well, Silanus, there are humanities as well as philosophies. Believe me, I feel with you. Farewell! Forgive me as sincerely as I condemn myself." He pressed my hand, and I his. He was a good fellow at heart and died in Syria, a soldier's death— such as Scaurus would have approved and no Cynic could have censured.

In a few minutes, we were outside the port, seeing from a distance (without hearing) the bustle on the quay. It was not an unpleasing scene—now. A few minutes more, and the whole of the city stood out as a bright picture in a framework of fields. Presently Nicopolis was receding and lessening. Hills rose up behind. The frame was becoming the picture and Nicopolis a small part in it. I paced the deck, this way and that, turning in my mind all that had befallen me since I had gazed on these same scenes in reversed order, arriving from Italy. How few days ago in time! How many ages ago in thought and experience! "What strange things," I exclaimed, "what marvellous things have happened to me! Am I not a changed man?" Then a sense of unreality began to creep over me. "Am I not, after all, the same Silanus, recovering from a dream? Have these 'strange things' been real things? Have they not been mere pictures—pictures of the mind, phantasms, dreams, from which I, the old Silanus, am now awaking to find myself just what I was in old days when I was wasting my time in Rome?"

I looked back on Nicopolis and it was now little more than a hamlet, and the quay was a dot. But it still loomed large on my mind. I had spoken of "phantasms" and "dreams." But I could not think of the human scene in the harbour as a "dream." Only too life-like were those bipeds—noisy, scurrilous, vile, obscene! How unworthy of the bright and glorious sunlight in which all things were bathed at that moment of full noon—all things in heaven and earth! How glorious was everything except man! Yes, everything except man! Rufus spoke in jest, but did he not speak the truth? What were those "sons of God" on the quay? Surely, surely, they were "sons of clay," mere puppets to play with and break! To this day I cannot tell why just at this moment so strong a temptation should have so suddenly seized me. But seize me it did. I write it as it happened, that others may take heart if the same thing should happen to them. It was God's way of dealing with me, suffering me to be almost cast down by evil that He might lift me up for good.

Feeling the evil coming, I tried at first to strengthen myself with the sayings of my Master, Epictetus, "See then that thou do nothing as a beast. Else thou hast lost the Man. Thou hast not fulfilled the promise of the Man," and again, "Man is a being that has nothing more sovereign than his will. He has all other things in subjection to this." Then I thought of Man as the Psalmist describes him, saying to God, "Thou hast put all things under his feet…yea, and the beasts of the field," and how the Christians regarded this as meaning that Man was to triumph over sin.

But, against these hopeful thoughts, there rose up, first, the confessions of Epictetus that he had never succeeded in producing a Man of this kind, nor anything approaching to it; and then the words of the other Psalm, "Man being in honour hath no understanding, but is like unto the beasts that perish." I longed to believe the good Voices, but truth seemed to compel me to believe the bad Voices. Worst and strongest of all, there rose up recollections of my own evil deeds, words, and thoughts, from childhood upwards, and they strengthened the Voices of evil. I could not at that moment recall the brighter and better side of my own life. I could not remind myself how different a man in a crowd may be for a moment from the same man in his home and at his work during his daily life. It seemed to me that I ought to be on my guard against hoping contrary to facts. Was not Glaucus right in taunting me with "self-deceiving," which I called "believing"? Was it not the plain and manifest fact that the Beast was Lord over the Man?

Again and again this question put itself before me, as though from the mouth of the Beast, saying, "Am I not your Lord? Can you honestly deny it?" And at that instant I could not deny it. Never had I felt so weak, so forsaken—abandoned by all the hopes that had been lately gathering round me, more hopeless than if I had never entertained them.

But just when I seemed to be touching the bottom of the lowest depth, I received a sense of the nearness of help. If I could not trust in the Good, at least I could rebel against the Evil. What though the Beast be Lord of mankind? "At least," I exclaimed, "there are those who will not be his slaves—Epictetus, Scaurus, my father, others known to me, multitudes unknown. Rather than submit to the Beast, it is better to be on the conquered side—along with the good, and worthy and noble. It is better, yes much better, to be on the side of the Man crushed down, trampled on, destroyed!" Then a great longing fell on me that the Man thus crushed down and destroyed by the Beast might prove to be not destroyed in the end, for such a Man, if only He existed, seemed the only fit object of worship for mankind. Yes, victorious or defeated, He alone was to be worshipped. "Whom have I in heaven but thee? And there is none upon earth that I desire in comparison with thee, O thou FORSAKEN SON OF GOD!"

As I uttered these words I remembered where I had first uttered them—on the hills yonder, while I was thinking of

Glaucus's troubles just before I met my new friend Clemens. That made me think of him and of his promise to wait on the hill, and look on my vessel as it vanished, and "wish me well." I glanced back over the stern just in time to see our little coppice disappearing. "Clemens," I said, "is there. Clemens is praying for me." With that, there came back to me all he had said about the power of the FORSAKEN to help those who felt "forsaken"; and about the "cross," as the real throne whereon the Son of man reigns as the real king and subjects all things to Himself. In that moment I understood how both the Psalms were true: "Man being in honour—*as the world counts honour*—is like unto the beasts that perish." But "man being in honour—*as God counts honour*—is uplifted on the throne of suffering and reigns over those for whom He suffers and whom He redeems." A sudden conviction fell upon me that here at last I had the light that makes all things clear, and I cried from the deepest depth of my being, "Whom have I in heaven but thee, O thou forsaken one that art NOT FORSAKEN? And there is none upon earth that I desire in comparison with thee. Make no long tarrying, O my Helper and my Redeemer!"

All this, which takes time to describe, passed in the twinkling of an eye, and then something befell me that I cannot exactly describe. Only I know that it was no act of reason. Nor was it vision. It was more like feeling. The arm of the Lord seemed to lift me up and carry me to something that I felt to be the Cross. Then the thought of the Cross sent down upon me the thought of an overwhelming flood of the mighty love and pity of God, the Father of the fatherless and Servant of the meanest of His servants, descending on my soul from the side of the Saviour and bathing me in His purifying blood, creating me anew in the eternal Son. And thus, at last, after so many delays, refusals, and resistances, willingly led captive out of the dominion of darkness and fear and sin, I was carried as a little child into the joy of the family of God.

BECOMES A CHRISTIAN

When I reached Tusculum, Scaurus was in his grave. He had died on the day when I left Nicopolis, and about noon. I could not discover among his papers any last instructions, or indications of any wishes connected with the subject of his last letter. Only I found a paper with " For Hermas's tomb " on it. Below was written in large characters IN PEACE. I asked Marullus whether he understood this. He said that on the morning of the last day of his active and conscious life the old man had gone (with Marullus's aid, for he was very feeble) to see the tomb he had erected for Hermas in years gone by. After standing for some time silent he repeated aloud the last words of the inscription, "For memory's sake." "That," said he, " is not enough." Then, as they walked home, he said, " Hermas would have liked IN PEACE. There is room. See that those words are added." I saw that they were added. I also placed them on Scaurus's own tomb.

For the rest, in the years that followed—forty-five in number—nothing has befallen me that would greatly interest my readers. I became a soldier. Many of the brethren condemned me for it. But when the war broke out in Illyria I felt that, although a Christian, I had no right to cease to become a Roman, or to spare my blood, if need arose, in defence of the peace of the Empire. In doing this, I was glad to think that I had fulfilled Scaurus's last wish. Clemens also supported me.

From him I received several letters before I went to Illyria. Soon afterwards, he passed away in Corinth, but not before he had done for Glaucus the same service that he did for me. His first letter told me that he had seen my vessel at noontide from the hills above Nicopolis, and that he had kept his promise of "wishing me well." He always called me brother; and no brother could have been more brotherly. But assuredly he was more than that. Paul sowed the seed of the gospel in my heart, but it was the spirit of Clemens that helped to quicken and to foster it. He was my father in the faith.

Yet Scaurus, too, was a helper—helper in deed even when opposing in word—guiding me indirectly towards the City of Truth. I have read Apologies for the Christian faith written by worthy men—Justin for example and others. But they have not helped me towards Christ as Scaurus did. They have been special pleaders for their religion, and sometimes great manipulators of words and arguments. But what Scaurus said, even in dispraise of the gospels, was often so qualified by praise, admiration, yes, and love, of the character of the Saviour, that it had much more effect with me than the arguments of Justin afterwards had, when I came to know them. Moreover Scaurus was such a lover of truth, and so quick and keen to detect an untruth, that in meeting his attacks upon the gospels I felt I had met the worst. I doubt not that he has found peace in one of the "many mansions." If I may not call him my father in the faith, yet certainly he was the kindest of stepfathers, helping me to the living Truth by causing me to love all truth, and indirectly strengthening my feet in the path towards the Saviour by not suffering me to walk too soon.

And you, too, good Epictetus, truthloving, keen Epictetus— I will not say "kind Epictetus," not at least always kind in word, though always good at heart even when most bitter in word—always fervid against falsehood, always zealous with a fiery zeal for that strange cold aspect of a "Father of all" in which you placed your trust and strove to make us place ours : what shall I say of you and how thank you for the help you gave me! How often in Rome and Tusculum, how often on nightwatches in Illyria, Moesia, and the East, have I seen your face, dear Master, as I saw it for the last time in Nicopolis, leaving you without bidding you farewell, spying on you unfairly through the open door, and detecting you in the act of breaking the rules of your own philosophy by feeling trouble, real trouble, for a sorely troubled disciple! Epictetus in trouble, yes, Epictetus in trouble, that is how I shall remember you to my dying day, as seen in the moment when I trusted your teaching least and loved you most, when you dropped the veil of your philosophy to shew me your real human heart— my "tutor" to bring me to Christ.

THE END

www.ingramcontent.com/pod-product-compliance
Lightning Source LLC
Chambersburg PA
CBHW050330230426
43663CB00010B/1809